杭州统计年鉴 2016

HANGZHOU STATISTICAL YEARBOOK

杭州市统计局
国家统计局杭州调查队
杭州市社会经济调查局

中国统计出版社
China Statistics Press

图书在版编目（CIP）数据

杭州统计年鉴. 2016 / 杭州市统计局, 国家统计局杭州调查队, 杭州市社会经济调查局编. -- 北京：中国统计出版社, 2016.8
ISBN 978-7-5037-7926-8

Ⅰ. ①杭…
Ⅱ. ①杭… ②国… ③杭…
Ⅲ. ①统计资料－杭州－2016－年鉴
Ⅳ. ①C832.551-54

中国版本图书馆CIP数据核字(2016)第198752号

杭州统计年鉴 2016

作　　者/ 杭州市统计局　国家统计局杭州调查队
责任编辑/ 陈越月
装帧设计/ 张子杰
出版发行/ 中国统计出版社
地　　址/ 北京市丰台区西三环南路甲6号　邮政编码/100073
电　　话/ 邮购（010）63376909　书店（010）68783171
网　　址/ http://csp.stats.gov.cn
印　　刷/ 浙江新中商务印刷有限公司
经　　销/ 新华书店
开　　本/ 890mm×1240mm　1/16
字　　数/ 905千字
印　　张/ 26.25
版　　别/ 2016年8月 第1版
版　　次/ 2016年8月 第1次印刷

ISBN 978-7-5037-7926-8

定价：300.00元

如有印装差错，由本社发行部调换

HANGZHOU
STATISTICAL YEARBOOK
杭州统计年鉴
2016 编委会和编辑人员

HANGZHOU
STATISTICAL YEARBOOK
杭州统计年鉴

2016 Editorial Board and Staff

编者说明

一、《杭州统计年鉴—2016》是一部信息密集的资料性年刊。本年鉴系统收集了全市和各区、县（市）2015年经济和社会各方面的统计数据，以及多个重要历史年份和近年全市主要统计数据。

二、本年鉴分为13个篇章：综合；人口和就业人员；农业；工业、能源；建筑业；交通运输、邮电；固定资产投资；国内贸易；对外经济、旅游；财政、金融、保险；城市建设、环境保护；科技、教育、文化、卫生、体育；人民生活、物价、民政。为便于读者使用，各篇章附有简要说明和主要统计指标解释。

三、本年鉴辑中涉及到历史数据，均以最新出版的本年鉴数据为准；本年鉴中部分数据合计数或相对数由于单位取舍不同而产生的计算误差，均未做机械调整。

四、2001年起，萧山、余杭撤市建区，市区数据含萧山、余杭区；2014年起富阳撤市建区，市区数据包括富阳区在内。

五、本年鉴表中符号使用说明：“－”表示这一栏没有数字；“…”表示该数字不足本表最小计量单位；“#”表示其中的主要项；“空格”表示该项统计数据不详或无该项数据；“＊”表示表下有注解。

六、本年鉴所使用的度量衡单位均采用国际统一标准计量单位，金额除特别标明外，均以人民币计量。

七、与2015年版《杭州统计年鉴》相比较，本年鉴在篇章结构和内容上主要做了以下修订：在《国民经济和社会发展统计公报》中增加了“十二五”时期发展情况；第一篇增加了反映分区、县（市）主要年份地区生产总值、第一产业增加值、第二产业增加值、第三产业增加值、工业增加值5张数据表式；第二篇非农业人口调整为城镇人口；第三篇增加了2010－2015年农村基本情况；第四篇增加了分区、县（市）规上工业增加值、规上工业能源购进消费与库存统计表式；第五篇增加了2008－2015年全市具有资质等级建筑业企业主要生产经营指标统计表；第六篇增加了2010－2015年全市运输线路长度统计表；第七篇增加了2003－2015年分地区固定资产投资；第九篇增加了2000－2015年分地区外贸进出口总值统计表；第十篇增加了2010－2015年全市分税种支出科目财政支出情况；第十二篇增加了2007－2015年专利申请与授权情况、全市2000－2015文化事业单位数、医院诊疗次数和入院次数3张统计表。行业分类采用2011年版行业分类标准。根据最新统计报表制度对个别专业内容及相关统计指标进行了调整。

八、《杭州统计年鉴》公开出版以来，受到了社会各界的关心和支持，对此我们深表谢意。限于我们的水平，欢迎广大读者继续对年鉴的不足之处给予批评和指正，为帮助我们进一步提高统计年鉴的编辑工作，以期更好地为广大读者服务（网址：http://www.hzstats.gov.cn/）。

Editorial Note

Ⅰ. *Hangzhou Statistical Yearbook 2016* is an informative annuals that covers comprehensive data series of Hangzhou's social and economic development. Which contains very comprehensive statistics of Hangzhou's social and economic development in 2015. It covers Hangzhou's data in recent years and some historically important years.

Ⅱ. The Yearbook contains 13 chapters: 1. General Survey; 2. Population and Employment; 3. Agriculture; 4. Industry and Energy; 5. Construction; 6. Transportation, Post and Telecommunications; 7. Investment in Fixed Assets; 8. Domestic Trade; 9. Foreign Economic Cooperation and Tourism; 10. Finance, Banking and Insurance; 11. Urban Construction and Environmental Protection; 12. Science and Technology, Education, Culture, Public Health and Sports; 13. People's Livelihood, Price Indices and Civil Administration. To facilitate readers, each chaper provides brief introduction and explanatory notes on main statistical indicators.

Ⅲ. Please refer to the newly published version of the Yearbook for updated historical data. Statistical discrepancies on totals and relative figures due to rounding are not adjusted in the Yearbook.

Ⅳ. Because of the change of urban administrative division, the data of Xiaoshan District and Yuhang District have been included into the urban districts since 2001, and it is the same with Fuyang District since 2014.

Ⅴ. Notations used in this book:"—" indicates that the column has no figure;"…" indicates that the figure is not large enough to be measured with the smallest unit in the table;"blank space" indicates that the date are unknown, or are not available;"#" indicates the major items of the total;" * " indicates"see footnotes below".

Ⅵ. The international standard unit of measurement is applied in this book, all amounts are denominated in RMB, except those with special notes.

Ⅶ. In comparison with Hangzhou Statistical Yearbook 2015, following revisions have been made in this new version in terms of the statistical contents and editing: Contents of Statistical Communique of Hangzhou on the 2015 National Economic and Social Development are added reflecting the situation of 12th Five – Year Plan Period. The 1 chapter added five statistical tables, such as Gross Domestic Product by Region (Main Years), Value Added of Primary Industry by Region (Main Years), Value Added of Secondary Industry by Region (Main Years), Value Added of Tertiary Industry by Region (Main Years), Value Added of Industry by Region (Main Years) and so on . The 2 chapter of " Non – agriculture Population" is Changed with " Urban Population". The 3 chapter is added reflecting basic situations of rural areas (2010 – 2015). The 4 chapter is added reflecting added value of industrial enterprises above designated size by region and purchasing, consuming and stocking of energy in industrial enterprises above designated size. The 5 chapter is added reflecting major economic indicators of construction enterprises having class (2008 – 2015). The 6 chapter is added reflecting length of transportation routes. The 7 chapter is added reflecting investment in fixed assets by region (main years). The 9 chapter is added reflecting imports and exports by region. The 10 chapter is added reflecting local public financial budgetary expenditure by tax and expenditure account. The 12 chapter added three statistical tables, such as. Patent Application and Authorization (2007 – 2015), Number of Hospital Patients and so on. The 2011's edition of standard industrial classifications is applied in this Yearbook. According to the new statistical report system, a few contents and indicators are adjusted.

Ⅷ. Since published openly, Previous Editions of Hangzhou Statistics Yearbook have enjoyed wide concern and support; and we express heartfelt thanks. In order to get further improvement in the yearbook editing, we welcome all candid comments and criticism from our readers (website: http://www.hzstats.gov.cn/).

目　录
Contents

杭州市2015年暨“十二五”时期国民经济和社会发展统计公报 …… (1)
Statistical Communiqué on the National Economy and Social Development of Hangzhou in 2015 and during the “12th Five – Year Plan” Period

一、综合
Ⅰ. General Survey

1 – 01 行政区划(2015年末) …… (31)
Administrative Division(End of 2015)
1 – 02 土地面积和人口密度(2015年末) …… (32)
Land Area and Population Density(End of 2015)
1 – 03 平均每天主要社会经济活动(主要年份) …… (33)
Selected Indicators on Average Daily Social and Economic Activities(Main Years)
1 – 04 国民经济主要指标(主要年份) …… (34)
Major Indicators of National Economy(Main Years)
1 – 05 全市生产总值及发展指数(1978 – 2015年) …… (38)
Gross Domestic Product and its Indices(1978 – 2015)
1 – 06 市区生产总值及发展指数(1978 – 2015年) …… (39)
Gross Domestic Product and its Indices of Urban District (1978 – 2015)
1 – 07 全市生产总值指数(1978 – 2015年) …… (40)
Indices of Gross Domestic Product (1978 – 2015)
1 – 08 市区生产总值指数(1978 – 2015年) …… (41)
Indices of Gross Domestic Product of Urban District (1978 – 2015)
1 – 09 全市生产总值构成(2015年) …… (42)
Composition of Gross Domestic Product(2015)
1 – 10 地区生产总值(2015年) …… (44)
Gross Domestic Product (2015)
1 – 11 分地区生产总值(主要年份) …… (45)
Gross Domestic Product by Region (Main Years)
1 – 12 分地区第一产业增加值(主要年份) …… (46)
Value Added of Primary Industry by Region(Main Years)
1 – 13 分地区第二产业增加值(主要年份) …… (47)
Value Added of Secondary Industry by Region(Main Years)
1 – 14 分地区工业增加值(主要年份) …… (48)
Value Added of Industry by Region(Main Years)

1 - 15 分地区第三产业增加值(主要年份) …… (49)
Value Added of Tertiary Industry by Region(Main Years)
1 - 16 主要指标占全省比重(2015 年) …… (50)
Proportion of Main Indicators in Whole Province(2015)
1 - 17 国民经济主要指标人均水平(主要年份) …… (53)
Major Per Capita Indicators of National Economy(Main Years)
1 - 18 气象概况(2015 年) …… (54)
Meteorological Conditions by Region(2015)
1 - 19 市区分月气象概况(2015 年) …… (56)
Monthly Meteorological Conditions in Urban District(2015)
主要统计指标解释 …… (57)
Explanatory Notes on Main Statistical Indicators

二、人口和就业人员

Ⅱ. Population and Employment

2 - 01 历次普查常住人口情况 …… (61)
Long - term Residents in the Past Population Census
2 - 02 全市户籍人口和总户数(1978 - 2015 年) …… (62)
Registered Population and Households(1978 - 2015)
2 - 03 市区户籍人口和总户数(1978 - 2015 年) …… (63)
Registered Population and Households of Urban District(1978 - 2015)
2 - 04 分地区户籍人口和总户数(2015 年末) …… (64)
Registered Population and Households by Region(End of 2015)
2 - 05 分地区户籍人口年龄构成(2015 年末) …… (65)
Age Structure of Household Registered Population by Region(End of 2015)
2 - 06 全市户籍人口自然变动情况(1978 - 2015 年) …… (66)
Natural Changes of Registered Population(1978 - 2015)
2 - 07 市区户籍人口自然变动情况(1978 - 2015 年) …… (67)
Natural Changes of Registered Population of Urban District(1978 - 2015)
2 - 08 分地区户籍人口自然变动情况(2015 年) …… (68)
Natural Changes of Registered Population by Region(2015)
2 - 09 分地区户籍人口机械变动情况(2015 年) …… (69)
Mechanical Changes of Registered Population by Region(2015)
2 - 10 婚姻登记情况 …… (70)
Marriage Registration Situations
2 - 11 三次产业就业人员及构成(2010 - 2015 年) …… (71)
Number of Employed Persons by Three Industries(2010 - 2015)
2 - 12 全市含规上私营单位就业人员数(2015 年末) …… (72)
Number of Employed Persons of the Whole City Including Private Units Above Designated Size(End of 2015)

2 - 13 全市含规上私营单位平均人员数(2015 年) …… (74)
Everage Number of Employed Persons Including Private Units Above Designated Size(2015)

主要统计指标解释 …… (76)
Explanatory Notes on Main Statistical Indicators

三、农业
Ⅲ. Agriculture

3 - 01 农林牧渔业增加值(2015 年) …… (81)
Value - added of Agriculture, Forestry, Animal Husbandry and Fishery(2015)

3 - 02 农林牧渔业总产值(1978 - 2015 年) …… (82)
Gross Output Value of Agriculture, Forestry, Animal Husbandry and Fishery(1978 - 2015)

3 - 03 农林牧渔业总产值构成(1978 - 2015 年) …… (83)
Composition of Gross Output Value of Agriculture, Forestry, Animal Husbandry and Fishery(1978 - 2015)

3 - 04 农林牧渔业分项产值(主要年份) …… (84)
Gross Output Value of Agriculture, Forestry, Animal Husbandry and Fishery by Branch(Main Years)

3 - 05 农林牧渔业分项产值构成(主要年份) …… (85)
Composition of Gross Output Value of Agriculture, Forestry, Animal Husbandry and Fishery by Branch(Main Years)

3 - 06 分地区农林牧渔业总产值(2015 年) …… (86)
Gross Output Value of Agriculture, Forestry, Animal Husbandry and Fishery by Region(2015)

3 - 07 主要农作物播种面积及产量(2014 - 2015 年) …… (88)
Sown Areas and Yield of Major Farm Crops(2014 - 2015)

3 - 08 分地区粮食播种面积及产量(2015 年) …… (90)
Sown Areas and Yield of Grain Crops by Region(2015)

3 - 09 油、菜、茶、蚕、果生产情况(2015 年) …… (92)
Statistics on Rapeseeds, Vegetables, Tea, Silkworm Cocoons and Fruits Production(2015)

3 - 10 分地区畜牧业渔业生产(2015 年) …… (96)
Statistics on Animal Husbanday and Fishery by Region(2015)

3 - 11 分地区林业生产(2015 年) …… (100)
Statistics on Forestry by Region(2015)

3 - 12 分地区主要农机具年末拥有量(2015 年) …… (102)
Possession of Major Agricultural Machinery at the Year - end by Region(2015)

3 - 13 农业物资消耗情况(2015 年) …… (104)
Agricultural Material Consumption(2015)

3 - 14 乡(镇)基本情况(2015 年) …… (106)
Statistics on Towns and Townships(2015)

3 - 15 农村基本情况(2015 年末) …… (120)
Basic Situations of Rural Areas(End of 2015)

3 - 16 农村基本情况(2010 - 2015 年) …… (122)
Basic Situations of Rural Areas(2010 - 2015)

主要统计指标解释 ………………………………………………………………………………………………… (123)
Explanatory Notes on Main Statistical Indicators

四、工业、能源
Ⅳ. Industry and Energy

4 - 01　全市工业企业单位数(主要年份) ……………………………………………………………………… (127)
Number of Industrial Enterprises of the Whole City(Main Years)
4 - 02　市区工业企业单位数(主要年份) ……………………………………………………………………… (128)
Number of Industrial Enterprises in Urban District(Main Years)
4 - 03　全市工业总产值(主要年份) ……………………………………………………………………………… (129)
Gross Industrial Output Value of the Whole City(Main Years)
4 - 04　市区工业总产值(主要年份) ……………………………………………………………………………… (130)
Gross Industrial Output Value in Urban District(Main Years)
4 - 05　规模以上工业企业主要经济效益指标(1998 - 2015 年) ………………………………………………… (131)
Main Economic Indicators of Industrial Enterprises Above Designated Size(1998 - 2015)
4 - 06　分地区工业企业单位数(2015 年末) ……………………………………………………………………… (132)
Number of Industrial Enterprises by Region(End of 2015)
4 - 07　分地区工业总产值(2015 年) ……………………………………………………………………………… (134)
Gross Industrial Output Value by Region(2015)
4 - 08　分地区工业销售产值(2015 年) …………………………………………………………………………… (136)
Value of Industrial Products Sales by Region(2015)
4 - 09　全市规模以上工业企业主要经济指标(2015 年)(一) …………………………………………………… (138)
Main Economic Indicators of Industrial Enterprises Above Designated Size(2015)(Ⅰ)
4 - 10　全市规模以上工业企业主要经济指标(2015 年)(二) …………………………………………………… (144)
Main Economic Indicators of Industrial Enterprises Above Designated Size(2015)(Ⅱ)
4 - 11　全市规模以上工业企业主要经济指标(2015 年)(三) …………………………………………………… (150)
Main Economic Indicators of Industrial Enterprises Above Designated Size(2015)(Ⅲ)
4 - 12　市区规模以上工业企业主要经济指标(2015 年)(一) …………………………………………………… (156)
Main Economic Indicators of Industrial Enterprises Above Designated Size in Urban District(2015)(Ⅰ)
4 - 13　市区规模以上工业企业主要经济指标(2015 年)(二) …………………………………………………… (162)
Main Economic Indicators of Industrial Enterprises Above Designated Size in Urban District(2015)(Ⅱ)
4 - 14　市区规模以上工业企业主要经济指标(2015 年)(三) …………………………………………………… (168)
Main Economic Indicators of Industrial Enterprises Above Designated Size in Urban District(2015)(Ⅲ)
4 - 15　全市规模以上工业企业主要经济指标按登记注册类型分(2015 年) …………………………………… (174)
Main Economic Indicators of Industrial Enterprises Above Designated Size by Status of Registration(2015)
4 - 16　分地区规上工业增加值(2000 - 2015 年) ………………………………………………………………… (176)
Added Valve of Industrial Enterprises Above Designated Size by Region (2000 - 2015)
4 - 17　主要工业产品生产量(2015 年) …………………………………………………………………………… (178)
Output of Major Industrial Products(2015)

4 - 18 单位 GDP 能耗降低情况(2015 年) …… (181)
Increase or Decrease of Energy Consumption Per Unit of GDP(2015)
4 - 19 工业企业主要能源消费量按行业分(2015 年) …… (182)
Energy Consumption of Industrial Enterprises by Sector(2015)
4 - 20 全市规模以上工业能源购进消费与库存(2015 年) …… (186)
Purchasing, Consuming and Stocking of Energy in Industrial Enterprises Above Designated Size(2015)
4 - 21 电力消费量(2015 年) …… (187)
Electricity Consumption(2015)
4 - 22 水资源量和总用水量(2001 - 2015 年) …… (188)
Total Water Resources and Water Consumption(2001 - 2015)
主要统计指标解释 …… (189)
Explanatory Notes on Main Statistical Indicators

五、建筑业
Ⅴ. Construction

5 - 01 建筑业总产值(2015 年) …… (193)
Gross Output Value of Construction(2015)
5 - 02 建筑总专包企业财务指标(2015 年) …… (194)
Financial Indicators on Construction Enterprises of General Contractors and Specialist Contractors(2015)
5 - 03 建筑业企业生产情况(2010 - 2015 年) …… (198)
Statistics on Production of Construction Enterprises(2010 - 2015)
5 - 04 全市具有资质等级建筑业企业主要生产经营指标(2008 - 2015 年) …… (199)
Major Economic Indicators of Construction Enterprises Having Class(2008 - 2015)
主要统计指标解释 …… (200)
Explanatory Notes on Main Statistical Indicators

六、交通运输、邮电
Ⅵ. Transportation, Post and Telecommunications

6 - 01 全市客运量(1978 - 2015 年) …… (205)
Total Passenger Traffic (1978 - 2015)
6 - 02 全市货运量(1978 - 2015 年) …… (206)
Total Freight Traffic (1978 - 2015)
6 - 03 客货运输量(2010 - 2015 年) …… (207)
Total Passenger and Freight Traffic(2010 - 2015)
6 - 04 分地区交通运输情况(2015 年) …… (208)
Traffic and Transport Situation by Region(2015)
6 - 05 全市运输线路长度(2010 - 2015 年) …… (210)
Length of Transportation Routes(2010 - 2015)

6－06　民用机动车辆年末拥有量(2010－2015 年末) …… (211)
Total Number of Motor Vehicles End of the Year(End of 2010－2015)
6－07　邮政、电信主要指标(2010－2015 年) …… (212)
Main Indicators of Post and Telecommunications(2010－2015)
主要统计指标解释 …… (213)
Explanatory Notes on Main Statistical Indicators

七、固定资产投资
Ⅶ. Investment in Fixed Assets

7－01　全市固定资产投资总额(1978－2015 年) …… (217)
Investment in Fixed Assets (1978－2015)
7－02　市区固定资产投资总额(1990－2015 年) …… (218)
Investment in Fixed Assets of Urban District (1990－2015)
7－03　三次产业固定资产投资(1978－2015 年) …… (219)
Investment in Fixed Assets Grouped by Three Industries (1978－2015)
7－04　全市固定资产投资房屋建筑面积及造价(1978－2015 年) …… (220)
Floor Space of Buildings and Their Cost (1978－2015)
7－05　市区固定资产投资房屋建筑面积及造价(1978－2015 年) …… (221)
Urban District Floor Space of Buildings and Their Cost (1978－2015)
7－06　分地区固定资产投资(主要年份) …… (222)
Investment in Fixed Assets by Region(Main Years)
7－07　分地区固定资产投资(2015 年) …… (224)
Investment in Fixed Assets by Region(2015)
7－08　分地区工业投资(2015 年) …… (228)
Investment in Industrial Sector by Region(2015)
7－09　分地区房地产开发投资(2015 年) …… (232)
Investment in Real Estate Development by Region(2015)
7－10　房屋建筑面积及造价(2015 年) …… (234)
Floor Space of Buildings and Their Cost(2015)
7－11　分注册类型和资质等级房地产开发企业财务状况(2015 年) …… (236)
Financial Statistics of Enterprises for Real Estate Development Grouped by Registration Status and Qualification Grade(2015)
主要统计指标解释 …… (240)
Explanatory Notes on Main Statistical Indicators

八、国内贸易
Ⅷ. Domestic Trade

8－01　社会消费品零售总额(1978－2015 年) …… (245)
Total Retail Sale of Consumer Goods(1978－2015)

8－02　分地区社会消费品零售总额(1978－2015 年) …… (246)
Total Retail Sale of Consumer Goods by Region(1978－2015)

8－03　社会消费品零售总额(2015 年) …… (248)
Total Retail Sale of Consumer Goods(2015)

8－04　按登记注册类型分限额以上批发零售贸易企业商品销售总额(2015 年) …… (250)
Sales of Wholesale and Retail Trades Above Designated Size by Status of Registration(2015)

8－05　按国民经济行业分限额以上批发零售贸易企业商品销售总额(2015 年) …… (251)
Sales of Wholesale and Retail Trades Above Designated Size by Sector(2015)

8－06　按登记注册类型分限额以上批发零售贸易企业财务状况(2015 年) …… (525)
Main Financial Indicators of Enterprises Above Designated Size in Wholesale and Retail Trades by Status of Registration(2015)

8－07　按国民经济行业分限额以上批发零售贸易企业财务状况(2015 年) …… (256)
Main Financial Indicators of Enterprises Above Designated Size in Wholesale and Retail Trades by Sector(2015)

8－08　分地区限额以上批发零售业主要指标(2015 年) …… (260)
The Situation of Wholesale and Retail Trades by Region(2015)

8－09　按注册类型、行业分限额以上住宿业和餐饮业财务状况(2015 年) …… (262)
Main Financial Indicators of Hotels and Catering Services Enterprises Above Designated Size by Status of Registration and Sector(2015)

8－10　按登记注册类型和国民经济行业分限额以上住宿业和餐饮业经营情况(2015 年) …… (266)
Management Conditions of Hotels and Catering Services Enterprises Above Designated Size by Status of Registration and Sector (2015)

8－11　分地区限额以上住宿餐饮业主要指标(2015 年) …… (268)
The Situation of Lodging and Catering by Region(2015)

8－12　个体工商业登记注册情况(2015 年末) …… (270)
Statistics of Individual Owned Business(End of 2015)

8－13　私营企业登记注册情况(2015 年末) …… (273)
Statistics of Private Owned Business(End of 2015)

主要统计指标解释 …… (276)
Explanatory Notes on Main Statistical Indicators

九、对外经济、旅游

Ⅸ. Foreign Economic Cooperation and Tourism

9－01　外商直接投资情况(1978－2015 年) …… (281)
Foreign Direct Investment(1978－2015)

9－02　分行业外商直接投资情况(2015 年) …… (282)
Foreign Direct Investment by Sector(2015)

9－03　分国别(地区)外商直接投资情况(2015 年) …… (283)
Foreign Direct Investment by Region or Territory(2015)

9－04　分地区外商直接投资情况(2015 年) …… (284)
Foreign Direct Investment by Region(2015)

9－05 分地区国内招商引资情况(2014－2015 年) …… (285)
Domestic Investment by Region(2014－2015)
9－06 国家级开发区建设发展情况(2015 年) …… (286)
The Construction of National－Class Development Zones(2015)
9－07 省级产业集聚区建设发展情况 …… (288)
Development Statistics on Provincial－level Industry Cluster Districts
9－08 进出口情况(1989－2015 年) …… (289)
Imports and Exports (1989－2015)
9－09 分经济类型进出口情况(2014－2015 年) …… (290)
Imports and Exports by Status of Registration(2014－2015)
9－10 分地区外贸进出口情况(2015 年) …… (291)
Imports and Exports by Region(2015)
9－11 分地区外贸进出口总值(2004－2015 年) …… (292)
Imports and Exports by Region(2004－2015)
9－12 出口企业前 20 位排名(2015 年) …… (293)
The List of Top Twenty Export Enterprises(2015)
9－13 外贸出口分国别(地区)情况(2014－2015 年) …… (294)
Export of Foreign Trade by Main Countries or Regions(2014－2015)
9－14 旅游发展情况(1978－2015 年) …… (295)
Development of Tourism(1978－2015)
9－15 境外旅游者人数(1978－2015 年) …… (296)
Number of International Tourists (1978－2015)
9－16 接待境外游客及居民出境旅游情况(2014－2015 年) …… (297)
Number of International Tourists and Outbound Tourists(2014－2015)
9－17 接待境外游客分国别(地区)情况(2014－2015 年) …… (298)
Number of International Tourists by Country or Territory(2014－2015)
主要统计指标解释 …… (299)
Explanatory Notes on Main Statistical Indicators

十、财政、金融、保险

X. Finance, Banking and Insurance

10－01 财政收入及支出(1978－2015 年) …… (303)
Financial Revenue and Expenditure (1978－2015)
10－02 分地区财政总收入(2015 年) …… (304)
Local Financial Revenue by Region(2015)
10－03 分地区公共预算支出(2015 年) …… (306)
Local Public Financial Budgetary Expenditure by Region(2015)
10－04 全市分税种、支出科目财政收支情况(2010－2015 年) …… (308)
Local Public Financial Budgetary Expenditure by Tax and Expenditure Account(2010－2015)

10－05　全市金融机构存、贷款余额(1978－2015 年) …… (310)
Balance of Deposits and Loans of Financial Institutions (1978－2015)

10－06　市区金融机构存、贷款余额(1978－2015 年) …… (311)
Balance of Deposits and Loans of Financial Institutions of Urban District(1978－2015)

10－07　全市金融机构本外币存、贷款余额(2015 年末) …… (312)
Balance of Deposits and of Financial Institutions(End of 2015)

10－08　全市金融机构人民币存、贷款余额(2015 年末) …… (314)
Balance of RMB Deposits, RMB Loans of Financial Institutions(End of 2015)

10－09　住户存款余额(2015 年末) …… (316)
Balance of Savings Deposits of Rural and Urban Residents(End of 2015)

10－10　保险业务情况(2013－2015 年) …… (317)
Development of Insurance Business(2013－2015)

主要统计指标解释 …… (318)
Explanatory Notes on Main Statistical Indicators

十一、城市建设、环境保护

Ⅺ. Urban Construction and Environmental Protection

11－01　市区公共交通情况(主要年份) …… (323)
Urban Public Transportation in Urban Districts(Main Years)

11－02　市区城市供电、供水情况(主要年份) …… (324)
Urban Electricity and Water Supply in Urban Districts(Main Years)

11－03　市区市政建设情况(主要年份) …… (325)
Public Utilities in Urban Districts(Main Years)

11－04　市区园林绿化情况(主要年份) …… (326)
Urban Forestation(Main Years)

11－05　环境保护情况(2015 年) …… (327)
Environmental Protection Situation (2015)

主要统计指标解释 …… (328)
Explanatory Notes on Main Statistical Indicators

十二、科技、教育、文化、卫生、体育

Ⅻ. Science and Technology, Education, Culture, Public Health and Sports

12－01　全市科技活动情况(2012－2015 年) …… (333)
The Situation of the City's Scientific and Technological Activities(2012－2015)

12－02　分地区、行业含规上私营单位年末人才资源(2015 年) …… (334)
Trained Personnel Resource Including Private Units above Designated Size by Region(2015)

12-03 专利申请与授权情况(2015 年) …… (336)
Patent Application and Authorization(2015)
12-04 专利申请与授权情况(2000-2015 年) …… (337)
Patent Application and Authorization(2000-2015)
12-05 文化部门机构数(2015 年末) …… (338)
Number of Institutions for Culture(End of 2015)
12-06 全市文化事业单位数(2000-2015 年) …… (339)
Number of Institutions for Culture(2000-2015)
12-07 分地区艺术表演团体演出情况(2015 年) …… (340)
Basic Statistics on Performance of Art Troupes by Region(2015)
12-08 市区文化事业单位数(1978-2015 年) …… (341)
Cultural Institutions of Urban District (1978-2015)
12-09 幼儿园基本情况(1978-2015 年) …… (342)
Basic Statistics on Kindergartens(1978-2015)
12-10 小学基本情况(1978-2015 年) …… (343)
Basic Statistics on Primary Schools(1978-2015)
12-11 初中基本情况(1978-2015 年) …… (344)
Basic Statistics on Junior Middle Schools(1978-2015)
12-12 高中基本情况(1978-2015 年) …… (345)
Basic Statistics on Senior High Schools(1978-2015)
12-13 中等专业学校基本情况(1978-2015 年) …… (346)
Basic Statistics on Specialized Secondary Schools(1978-2015)
12-14 高等学校基本情况(1978-2015 年) …… (347)
Basic Statistics on Regular Institutions of Higher Education(1978-2015)
12-15 小学、幼儿园及特殊教育基本情况(2015 年) …… (348)
Basic Statistics on Primary Schools,Kindergartens and Special Education(2015)
12-16 普通中学、职业中学和技工学校基本情况(2015 年) …… (350)
Basic Statistics on Senior,Junior High Schools and Vacational,Technical Schools(2015)
12-17 高等学校基本情况(2015 年) …… (352)
Basic Statistics on Regular Institutions of Higher Education(2015)
12-18 各级成人教育基本情况(2015 年) …… (354)
Basic Statistics on Various Adult Education(2015)
12-19 医疗卫生机构数(1978-2015 年) …… (356)
Number of Health Institutions(1978-2015)
12-20 医疗病床数(1978-2015 年) …… (357)
Number of Beds in Health Institutions(1978-2015)
12-21 医疗卫生机构数(2015 年末) …… (358)
Number of Health Institutions(End of 2015)
12-22 医疗病床数(2015 年末) …… (360)
Number of Beds in Health Institutions(End of 2015)

12 - 23　医院诊疗次数和入院人数（2015 年）………………………………………… (362)
Number of Hospital Patients(2015)
12 - 24　卫生事业人员数(2015 年末) ………………………………………… (364)
Number of Medical Technical Personnel(End of 2015)
12 - 25　卫生技术人员(1978 - 2015 年) ………………………………………… (366)
Number of Medical Technical Personnel(1978 - 2015)
12 - 26　体育运动情况(2013 - 2015 年) ………………………………………… (367)
Basic Statistics on Sports Activities(2013 - 2015)
主要统计指标解释 ………………………………………… (368)
Explanatory Notes on Main Statistical Indicators

十三、人民生活、物价、民政
XIII. People's Livelihood, Price Indices and Civil Administration

13 - 01　居民家庭人均收入支出(2013 - 2015 年) ………………………………………… (373)
Per Capita Income and Expenditure of Households(2013 - 2015)
13 - 02　城镇住户调查情况(1978 - 2015 年) ………………………………………… (374)
Basic Conditions of Urban Households (1978 - 2015)
13 - 03　城镇居民家庭平均每百户耐用消费品拥有量(主要年份) ………………………………………… (375)
Number of Major Durable Consumer Goods Owned Per 100 Urban Households(Main Years)
13 - 04　全市农村住户调查情况(1978 - 2015 年) ………………………………………… (376)
Basic Conditions of Whole Municipality Rural Households(1978 - 2015)
13 - 05　农村居民家庭平均每百户耐用消费品拥有量(主要年份) ………………………………………… (377)
Number of Major Durable Consumer Goods Owned Per 100 Rural Households(Main Years)
13 - 06　全市就业人员工资总额(1978 - 2015 年) ………………………………………… (378)
Total Wages of Employed Persons(1978 - 2015)
13 - 07　全市就业人员年平均工资(1978 - 2015 年) ………………………………………… (379)
Average Annual Wages of Employed Persons(1978 - 2015)
13 - 08　全市含规上私营单位就业人员工资总额(2015 年) ………………………………………… (380)
Total Wages of Employed Persons Including Private Units Above Designated Size(2015)
13 - 09　全市含规上私营单位就业人员平均工资(2015 年) ………………………………………… (382)
Average Annual Wages of Employed Persons Including Private Units Above Designated Size(2015)
13 - 10　市区消费价格指数(1978 - 2015 年) ………………………………………… (384)
Consumer Price Indices in Urban District(1978 - 2015)
13 - 11　市区居民消费价格分类指数(2014 - 2015 年) ………………………………………… (385)
Consumer Price Indices by Category in Urban District(2014 - 2015)
13 - 12　市区零售价格分类指数(2014 - 2015 年) ………………………………………… (387)
Retail Price Indices by Category in Urban District(2014 - 2015)
13 - 13　工业生产者出厂价格指数(主要年份) ………………………………………… (389)
Producer Price Indices for Industrial Products by Category(Main Years)

13－14 工业生产者购进价格分类指数(主要年份) …… (391)
Purchasing Price Indices for Industrial Producers(Main Years)

13－15 住宅销售价格指数(2015年) …… (392)
Sales Price Indices of Houses(2015)

13－16 社会办福利院情况(2015年末) …… (393)
Basic Statistics on Welfare Homes(End of 2015)

13－17 优抚对象人员情况(2015年) …… (394)
Number of Persons Enjoying Public Subsidies(2015)

13－18 市、县级社会团体机构情况(2015年) …… (396)
Basic Statistics on Institutions and Organizations at County Level(2015)

13－19 社会保障情况(主要年份) …… (398)
Social Security(Main Years)

13－20 分地区社会保障情况(2015年末) …… (399)
Social Security by Region(End of 2015)

主要统计指标解释 …… (400)
Explanatory Notes on Main Statistical Indicators

杭州市2015年暨“十二五”时期国民经济和社会发展统计公报

杭 州 市 统 计 局
国家统计局杭州调查队
杭州市社会经济调查局
2016年2月

2015年是“十二五”规划的收官之年，也是杭州加快转型升级的关键一年，更是经济发展全面迈入新常态的重要一年。全市上下在市委、市政府的领导下，以加快“一号工程”推进为着力点，以集聚创新动能为支撑点，以深化改革增强体制活力为突破点，以发展和改善民生为落脚点，全力以赴推动经济行稳致远。全年经济总量实现历史性突破，成为全国第十个进入“万亿”方阵的城市，增速重回两位数增长。“十二五”时期杭州经济社会发展迈上了新台阶。

一、综　　合

（一）经济总量。

2015年，全市实现生产总值10050.21亿元，比上年增长10.2%。其中第一产业增加值287.95亿元，第二产业增加值3909.01亿元，第三产业增加值5853.25亿元，分别增长1.7%、5.5%和14.6%。人均生产总值112230元，增长9.1%。按国家公布的2015年平均汇率折算，为18019美元。

2010年－2015年全市生产总值及增幅

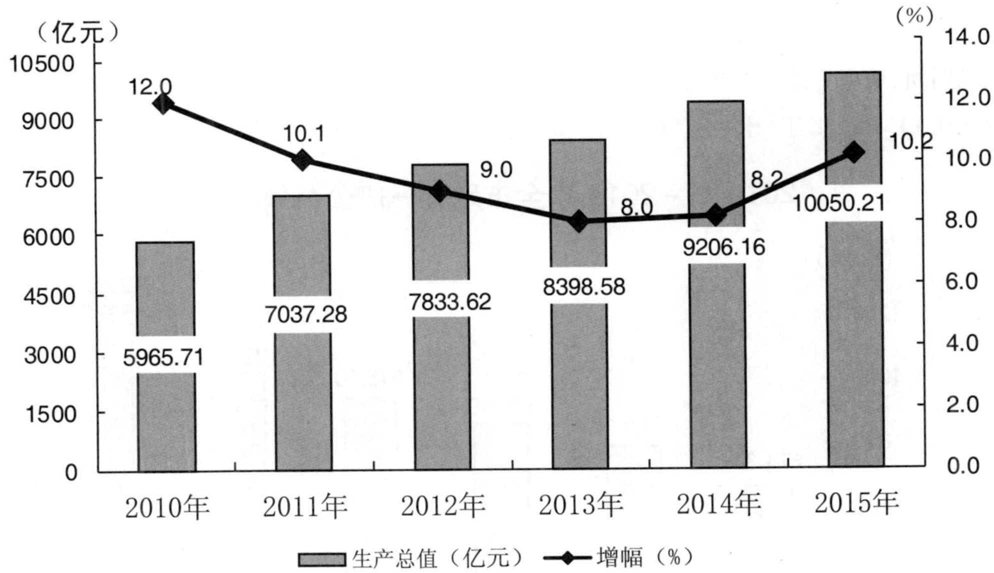

“十二五”期间，全市生产总值年均增长9.1%，低于“十一五”时期平均增速3.3个百分点。三次产业结构由2010年的3.5∶47.3∶49.2升级为2015年的2.9∶38.9∶58.2。

全市 GDP 三次产业比重(%)

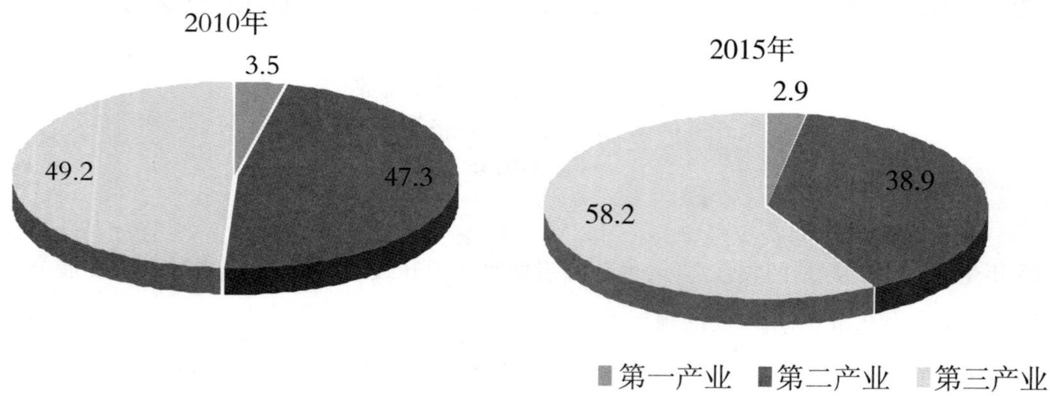

(二)民营经济。

全市民营经济实现增加值5951.72亿元,占全市的59.2%;实现财政收入912.56亿元,占全市财政总收入的40.8%。年末,全市私营企业33.47万户,比上年末增长21.3%;个体工商户38.61万户,增长11.8%。私营企业和个体工商户从业人员分别为258.74万人、79.45万人,增长16.1%和10.3%。

(三)信息经济。

全市信息经济实现增加值2313.85亿元,增长25.0%,占全市GDP的23%,同比提高4.9个百分点。其中电子商务、数字内容产业分别增长34.5%、35.5%,云计算与大数据、物联网、互联网金融和智慧物流分别增长29.6%、12.7%、33.5%和8.4%。

(四)财政收支。

全市财政总收入2238.75亿元,增长11.0%,其中地方一般公共预算收入1233.88亿元,增长9.8%。一般公共预算支出1205.48亿元,增长15.6%,其中用于民生支出921.92亿元,增长16.3%,增幅同比提高3.1个百分点;科学技术、住房保障等民生项目支出分别增长33.9%和31.3%。

"十二五"期间,地方一般公共预算收入和一般公共预算支出累计分别达到4851.54亿元和4556.18亿元,年均增长12.9%和14.3%,低于"十一五"时期平均增速8.9个和6.6个百分点。

2010年-2015年全市地方一般公共预算收入

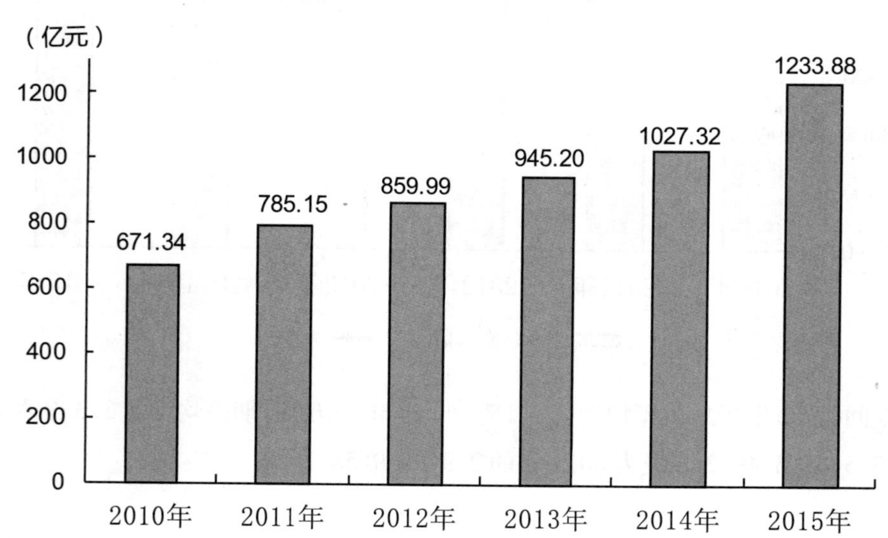

(五)市场价格。

市区居民消费价格比上年上涨1.8%,涨幅同比回落0.2个百分点。八大类商品和服务项目价格呈"七升一降"格局。

2015 年市区居民消费价格月度涨跌幅度

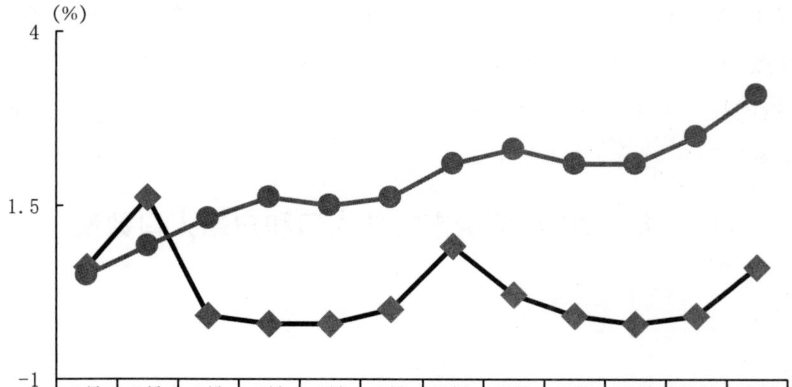

	1月	2月	3月	4月	5月	6月	7月	8月	9月	10月	11月	12月
环比	0.6	1.6	-0.1	-0.2	-0.2	0	0.9	0.2	-0.1	-0.2	-0.1	0.6
同比	0.5	0.9	1.3	1.6	1.5	1.6	2.1	2.3	2.1	2.1	2.5	3.1

市区居民消费价格比上年涨跌幅度

单位:%

项　　目	2014 年	2015 年
市区居民消费价格	2.0	1.8
1.食品	2.9	2.8
2.烟酒及用品	-0.1	3.9
3.衣着	1.7	1.1
4.家庭设备用品及维修服务	2.7	1.4
5.医疗保健和个人用品	1.4	2.4
6.交通和通信	-0.6	-3.4
7.娱乐教育文化用品及服务	1.8	1.0
8.居住	2.7	3.5

全市工业生产者出厂价格下降 3.5%,工业生产者购进价格下降 7.1%。

2015 年全市工业生产者价格月度同比涨跌幅度

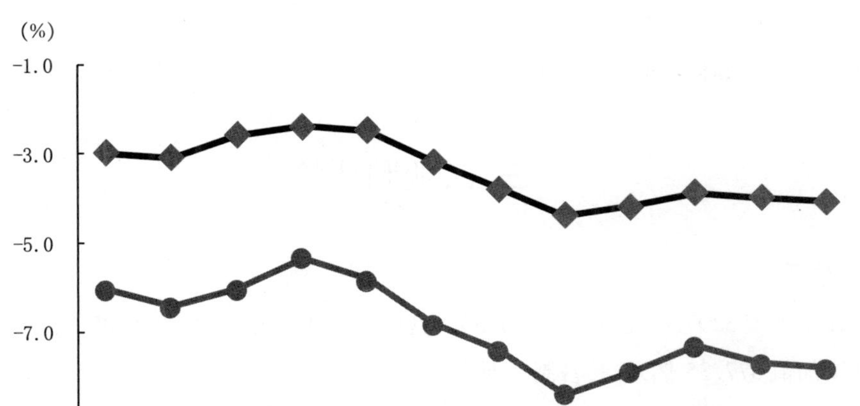

	1月	2月	3月	4月	5月	6月	7月	8月	9月	10月	11月	12月
出厂价格	-3.1	-3.2	-2.7	-2.5	-2.6	-3.3	-3.9	-4.5	-4.3	-4.0	-4.1	-4.2
购进价格	-6.2	-6.6	-6.2	-5.5	-6.0	-7.0	-7.6	-8.6	-8.1	-7.5	-7.9	-8.0

（六）人口就业。

至年末，全市常住人口901.8万人，比上年末增加12.6万人，其中城镇人口679.06万人，占比75.3%，比2014年提高0.2个百分点；人口出生率为10.6‰，人口自然增长率为5.4‰。全市户籍人口723.55万人，人口出生率为9.81‰，人口自然增长率为4.21‰。全市新增城镇就业人员28.79万人，安置失业人员再就业14.22万人。年末城镇登记失业率1.74%。

2010年－2015年全市常住人口和户籍人口数量

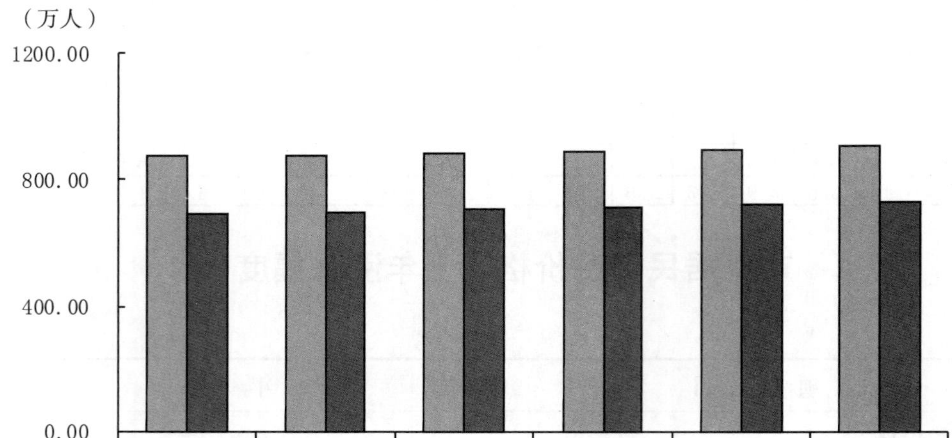

	2010年	2011年	2012年	2013年	2014年	2015年
常住人口	870.54	873.80	880.20	884.40	889.20	901.80
户籍人口	689.12	695.71	700.52	706.61	715.76	723.55

“十二五”期间，全市常住人口年均增长0.7%，比“十一五”时期低1.8个百分点；累计增加31.26万人，增量比“十一五”减少67.98万人。

二、农　　业

全市实现农林牧渔业增加值292.40亿元，增长1.8%。其中农业180.62亿元、林业39.33亿元、渔业28.45亿元，分别增长3.7%、4.5%和3.0%。牧业增加值39.55亿元，下降9.6%。农林牧渔服务业4.45亿元，增长7.1%。

全市粮食总产量63.38万吨，增长1.3%；水果产量78.96万吨，增长4.8%；水产品产量20.92万吨，增长0.1%；肉类产量27.84万吨，下降6.2%。新建省级现代农业园区18个，市级“菜篮子”基地42个，各级粮食生产功能区262个。

“十二五”期间，全市农林牧渔业增加值年均增长2.0%，低于“十一五”时期平均增速1.1个百分点。

三、工业和建筑业

（一）工业生产。

全市实现工业增加值3497.83亿元，增长5.5%，其中规上工业增加值2875.05亿元，增长5.4%。规上战略性新兴产业实现增加值877.35亿元，装备制造业实现增加值1086.12亿元，高新技术产业实现增加值1212.60亿元，分别增长9.4%、13.5%和9.8%。新产品产值率由上年31.2%提高到35.2%。工业产品产销率为98.50%。

“十二五”期间，全市工业增加值年均增长8.1%，规上工业增长9.2%，低于“十一五”时期平均增速2.8个和5个百分点。

(二)工业效益。

全市规模以上工业企业实现利税 1559.68 亿元,增长 4.4%,其中利润 891.12 亿元,增长 2.4%。企业亏损面 18.0%。

(三)建筑业。

全市实现建筑业增加值 412.54 亿元,增长 5.6%,全市有总承包和专业承包资格的建筑企业 1480 家,完成施工产值 4097.57 亿元,增长 3.2%;房屋建筑施工面积 28123.72 万平方米,下降 4.9%;房屋建筑竣工面积 10137.08 万平方米,增长 6.5%。

"十二五"期间,全市建筑业增加值年均增长 0.7%,低于"十一五"时期平均增速 7.1 个百分点。

四、固定资产投资和房地产业

(一)固定资产投资。

全市固定资产投资 5556.32 亿元,增长 12.2%。从产业投向看,第一产业 31.47 亿元,增长 65.0%;第二产业 931.78 亿元,增长 1.8%,其中工业 930.01 亿元,增长 1.8%;第三产业 4593.07 亿元,增长 14.3%。

"十二五"期间,全市固定资产投资 21595.66 亿元,年均增长 15.9%,高于"十一五"时期平均增速 0.2 个百分点。

2010 年 –2015 年全市固定资产投资及增幅

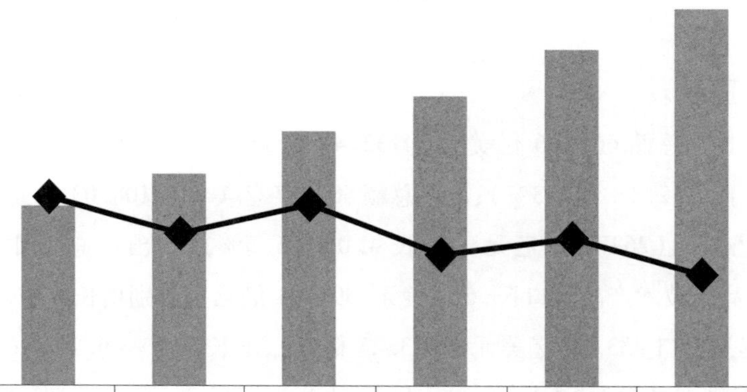

	2010年	2011年	2012年	2013年	2014年	2015年
投资（亿元）	2651.88	3100.02	3722.75	4263.87	4952.70	5556.32
增幅（%）	20.8	16.9	20.1	14.5	16.2	12.2

(二)房地产业。

全市房地产开发投资 2472.07 亿元,增长 7.4%。房屋施工面积 11142.68 万平方米,增长 6.1%;竣工面积 1665.23 万平方米,增长 10.9%。全年商品房销售面积 1481.45 万平方米,增长 32.1%,其中住宅销售 1291.64 万平方米,增长 35.9%。保障性安居工程项目开工 47394 套,竣工 57530 套。

"十二五"期间,全市房地产开发投资年均增长 20.9%,高于"十一五"时期平均增速 2.5 个百分点。

五、国内贸易

全市实现批发和零售业增加值 818.02 亿元,增长 2.3%。

全市社会消费品零售总额 4697.23 亿元,比上年增长 11.8%,扣除价格因素,实际增长 11.6%。其中商品零售额 4241.5 亿元,增长 12.3%,餐饮收入 455.73 亿元,增长 7.4%。城镇消费品零售额 4457.76 亿元,增长

11.7%；乡村消费品零售额239.47亿元，增长13.2%。

在限额以上批发零售贸易业零售额中，家具类、饮料类商品分别增长65.8%和46.6%，粮油食品类、服装鞋帽针纺织品类、烟酒类商品分别增长18.5%、15.5%、10.5%，金银珠宝类、汽车类商品分别增长12.6%、7.1%，石油及制品类下降7.4%。

全市网络零售额2679.83亿元，增长42.6%，全市居民网络消费额1119.1亿元，增长38.2%。

“十二五”期间，全市社会消费品零售额年均增长14.8%，低于“十一五”时期平均增速3.1个百分点。

2010年－2015年全市社会消费品零售总额及增幅

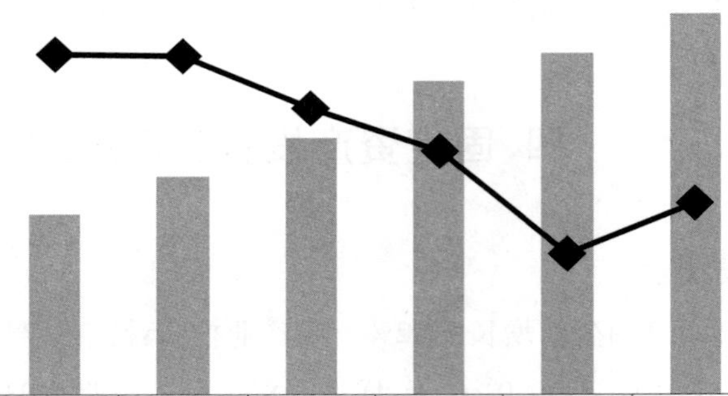

	2010年	2011年	2012年	2013年	2014年	2015年
零售总额（亿元）	2225.00	2690.22	3165.19	3864.84	4201.46	4697.23
增幅（%）	21.1	20.9	17.7	15.1	8.7	11.8

六、对外经济

（一）对外贸易。

全市货物进出口总额665.66亿美元(4132.43亿元)，下降2.1%(1.0%)。其中进口总额165亿美元(1024.40亿元)，下降12.3%(11.3%)；出口总额500.67亿美元(3108.03亿元)，增长1.8%(2.9%)。(不含省属出口444.65亿美元(2627.06亿元)，增长4.0%(5.5%))。出口总额中，机电产品出口201.92亿美元(1254.17亿元)，高新技术产品出口63.6亿美元(394.94亿元)，分别增长4.4%(5.5%)和6.2%(7.4%)。按贸易方式分，一般贸易出口433.78亿美元(2693.23亿元)，增长5.1%(6.2%)；进料加工贸易出口60.95亿美元(377.94亿元)，下降15%(14.2%)。出口市场中，大洋洲、北美洲、拉丁美洲、亚洲市场分别增长8.0%(9.2%)、6.3%(7.4%)、3.6%(4.6%)、3.4%(4.5%)；欧盟、欧洲市场分别下降1.6%(0.6%)和3.9%(2.9%)。全市服务贸易进出口190.33亿美元，增长25.4%。

“十二五”期间，全市货物进出口总额3252.91亿美元，其中出口2267.82亿美元，年均分别增长4.9%和7.2%，低于“十一五”时期平均增速7个和5.1个百分点。

2010年－2015年全市货物进出口额

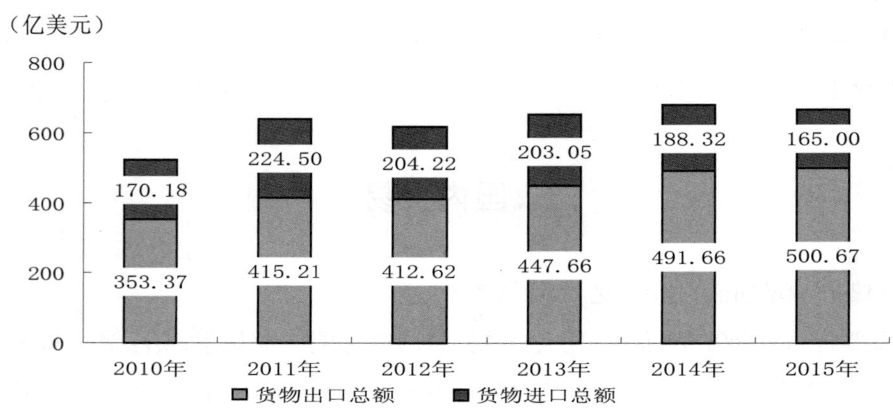

2015 年全市货物进出口总额及增幅

指　　标	总额(亿美元)	增长(%)
货物进出口总额	665.66	-2.1
货物出口额	500.67	1.8
一般贸易	433.78	5.1
进料加工贸易	60.95	-15.0
机电产品	201.92	4.4
高新技术产品	63.60	6.2
货物进口额	165.00	-12.3

(二)对外合作。

至年末,全市设立各类境外投资企业(机构)1341 个,其中非贸易企业 491 个。境外合同投资 26.49 亿美元,其中非贸易性投资 14.71 亿美元,增长 64.9%。对外承包工程和劳务合作营业额 17.69 亿美元,增长 69.8%。离岸服务外包合同执行额 51.94 亿美元,增长 26.7%。

(三)利用外资。

全市批准外商直接投资 475 项,实到外资 71.13 亿美元,增长 12.3%。新批总投资 3000 万美元以上项目 130 个,总投资 140.09 亿美元,占新批外商项目总投资的 84.9%。引进世界 500 强投资项目 10 个,至 2015 年末,有 112 家世界 500 强企业来杭投资 188 个项目。

"十二五"期间,全市累计实到外资 284.07 亿美元,年均增长 10.3%,低于"十一五"时期平均增速 10.2 个百分点。

(四)跨境电子商务。

全市跨境电商进出口总额 215.07 亿元(34.64 亿美元),占全市外贸进出口的 5.2%(5.2%)。其中,进口 73.94 亿元(11.91 亿美元),出口 141.13 亿元(22.73 亿美元)。

(五)浙商回归。

全市共引进内资项目 2376 个,到位资金 1249.27 亿元,增长 18.5%。其中浙商回归项目到位资金 660.58 亿元,增长 27.0%。

(六)开发区建设。

杭州经济技术开发区、杭州高新技术产业开发区、萧山经济技术开发区、杭州之江国家旅游度假区、余杭经济技术开发区、富阳经济技术开发区、临江国家高新区等 7 个国家级开发区全年实现规模以上企业主营业务收入 8974.60 亿元,企业利润 573.65 亿元,分别增长 6.6% 和 1.3%。

七、交通、邮电和旅游

(一)交通邮电。

全市实现交通运输、仓储和邮政业增加值 297.92 亿元,增长 8.2%。

全社会货物运输总量 2.94 亿吨,增长 1.7%。旅客运输量 2.39 亿人次,下降 0.5%。至年末,萧山国际机场已开通航线235条，其中国际航线32条，港澳台航线7条。内地航线进出港旅客2470.3万人次，增长10.1%；国际及地区航线进出港旅客365.1万人次，增长18.3%。境内公路总里程达到16210.02千米，其中高速公路615.08千米。

全市民用机动车拥有量达273.35万辆，其中私人汽车184.91万辆，比上年末分别增长1.4%和2.8%。

全市邮政企业和规模以上快递服务企业实现业务收入159.69亿元，增长35.7%。规模以上快递服务企业业务量12.57亿件，增长48.7%。建成并投入运营1824个便民"E邮站"。实现电信业务收入173.66亿元，增长3.3%。年末固定电话用户为293.44万户，下降5.7%，移动电话用户为1726.76万户，增长10.6%；宽带用户为294.96万户，增长5.8%。

（二）旅游业。

全市实现旅游产业增加值719.68亿元，增长12.8%。

旅游总收入达到2200.67亿元，增长16.7%，其中旅游外汇收入29.31亿美元，增长7.1%。接待入境旅游者341.56万人次，增长4.7%；接待国内游客1.20亿人次，增长13.5%。

至年末，全市各类旅行社达685家，增长4.1%；星级宾馆达到186家，其中五星级24家，四星级46家；A级景区54个，其中5A级景点3个，4A级景点34个。

"十二五"期间，全市旅游总收入年均增长16.5%，低于"十一五"时期平均增速0.6个百分点。

2010年－2015年全市国际国内旅游人数

年　份	入境旅游者(万人次)	国内旅游者(亿人次)
2010年	275.71	0.63
2011年	306.31	0.72
2012年	331.12	0.82
2013年	316.01	0.94
2014年	326.13	1.06
2015年	341.56	1.20

八、金　　融

全市实现金融业增加值941.47亿元，增长12.0%。

年末全市金融机构达到409家，当年新增35家；外资金融机构32家，当年减少17家。全市金融机构本外币存款余额29863.83亿元，增长13.9%；贷款余额23327.95亿元，增长9.3%，其中住户贷款5859.46亿元，增长19.1%，非金融企业及机关团体贷款17241.85亿元，增长6.1%。

"十二五"期间，全市本外币存款余额、贷款余额年均分别增长11.8%和9.1%，低于"十一五"时期平均增速8.6个和13个百分点。

2015 年全市金融机构本外币存贷款余额及增幅

指　　标	年末数(亿元)	比上年末增长(%)
各项存款余额	29863.83	13.9
其中:住户存款	7617.75	4.4
非金融企业存款	13120.73	10.3
各项贷款余额	23327.95	9.3
其中:住户贷款	5859.46	19.1
非金融企业及机关团体贷款	17241.85	6.1

全年新增上市公司 9 家,募集资金 255.98 亿元。至年末,全市上市公司累计 118 家,实现上市融资 3008.58 亿元。新三版挂牌企业 155 家。

全市保费收入 374.38 亿元,增长 16.8%,其中,财产险保费收入 156.91 亿元,增长 11.2%,人身险保费收入 217.47 亿元,增长 21.3%。支付各类保险赔款 139.68 亿元,增长 17.3%,其中财产险 93.72 亿元,增长 12.6%,人身险 45.95 亿元,增长 28.4%。

“十二五”期间,全市保费收入年均增长 13%。

九、教育和科技

(一)教育。

全市共有小学 443 所,在校学生 52.45 万人;初中 243 所,在校学生 21.13 万人;普通高中 75 所,在校学生 11.00 万人。学前三年幼儿入园率为 98.8%,初中毕业生升入各类高中比例为 99.7%。优质学前教育覆盖面由上年的 76.7% 提升到 78.6%;优质高中招生比例为 86.4%,提高 0.8 个百分点。普通高等院校 39 所,在校学生 47.56 万人,其中在校研究生 5.02 万人,比上年分别增长 0.2% 和 4.5%;毕业生 12.5 万人,比上年增长 1.4%。高等教育毛入学率由上年的 59.8% 提高到 60.4%。全市累计解决义务教育阶段外来务工人员子女入学 26.71 万人。

(二)科技。

全市发明专利申请量 17777 件,发明专利授权量 8296 件,增长 20.3% 和 49.4%。新认定国家重点扶持高新技术企业 311 家,累计达 1986 家。年内新增 14 个中国驰名商标,累计 146 个。年末培育认定研发中心 1438 家,其中省级研发中心 517 家。技术市场共吸纳科技成果 6243 项,实现交易额 77.42 亿元。科技企业孵化器 83 家、其中国家级 21 家,孵化总面积 239.36 万平方米,国家级孵化器总量连续 3 年居全国省会城市第一。纳入国家科技孵化器体系的众创空间达到 14 家,全市研究和试验发展(R&D)经费支出相当于地区生产总值的 3.01%。

“十二五”期间,全市发明专利授权量累计达到 2.88 万件,年均增长 20.7%,低于“十一五”时期平均增速 15.7 个百分点。

十、文化、卫生和体育

(一)文化。

全市实现文化创意产业增加值 2232.14 亿元,增长 20.4%。

全市有各类专业艺术表演团体 21 个、文化馆 15 个、公共图书馆 15 个,图书馆藏书 1785 万册。图书馆实现与全球 49 个国家和地区 1 万余家图书馆间的馆际互借和文献传递业务,“数字图书资源进学校”项目已成功覆盖 774 所城乡中小学校。全年拍摄电视剧 29 部,共 1221 集。生产原创动画片 14500 分钟。摄制完成 19 部电影。出版报纸22亿份，各类杂志1800万册，图书2.9亿册。全市拥有非物质文化遗产保护项目334个。

（二）卫生。

年末，全市拥有各类医疗卫生机构4428个，其中医院244个，比上年末分别增加230个和26个。拥有床位6.36万张，其中医院床位5.84万张，分别增长14.1%和15.0%。有各类专业卫生技术人员9.30万人，其中执业（助理）医师3.48万人，注册护士3.82万人，分别增长8.7%、8.9%和10.0%。全市医疗机构完成诊疗人数11733.03万人次，增长4.9%。全市婴儿死亡率和5岁以下儿童死亡率分别为2.32‰和3.0‰。每十万孕产妇死亡率为6.94人。

（三）体育。

全市共有3所国家级体育传统项目学校，1个国家级高水平体育后备人才基地，9所浙江省级体育后备人才基地。全市567所符合开放条件的公办中小学体育场地全部向社会开放。成功取得2022年亚运会举办权，成为第三个举办亚运会的中国城市。

十一、人民生活和社会保障

（一）人民生活。

全市居民人均可支配收入42642元，增长8.7%，扣除价格因素，实际增长6.8%。其中城镇居民人均可支配收入48316元，增长8.3%，农村居民人均可支配收入25719元，增长9.2%，扣除价格因素，实际分别增长6.4%和7.3%。城镇居民人均生活消费支出33818元，农村居民人均消费支出19334元，分别增长5.1%和8.5%。

2015年全市居民人均可支配收入

指标名称	城镇居民		农村居民	
	收入（元）	增幅（%）	收入（元）	增幅（%）
可支配收入	48316	8.3	25719	9.2
（一）工资性收入	28891	4.5	15860	7.1
（二）经营净收入	4502	3.1	6628	10.1
（三）财产净收入	6851	13.4	982	11.7
（四）转移净收入	8072	22.5	2249	21.8

2015年全市居民生活消费支出

指标名称	城镇居民		农村居民	
	支出（元）	增幅（%）	支出（元）	增幅（%）
人均生活消费支出	33818	5.1	19334	8.5
（一）食品烟酒	9171	5.6	5358	5.2
（二）衣着	2157	-1.6	1157	5.8
（三）居住	9111	6.4	4990	9.9
（四）生活用品及服务	1622	-3.6	1008	8.0
（五）交通通讯	5707	6.4	3904	18.3
（六）教育文化娱乐	3141	5.1	1507	1.5
（七）医疗保健	2002	17.2	1055	0.3
（八）其他用品和服务	907	-6.9	355	9.9

"十二五"期间,城镇居民人均可支配收入、农村居民人均可支配收入年均分别增长9.8%和11.7%。

年末,城镇居民人均现住房建筑面积35.5平方米,每百户居民家庭拥有家用汽车48.7辆、空调207.3台、家用电脑110.1台;农村居民人均现住房建筑面积68.8平方米,每百户农村居民家庭拥有家用汽车38.2辆、空调147.6台、家用电脑69.6台。

(二)社会保障。

年末全市参加基本养老保险人数达668.65万人,比上年末增加5.2万人;参加基本医疗保险870.71万人,增加30.5万人;参加职工失业、工伤、生育保险人数分别达349.42、418.17、326.65万人,比上年末净增17.59、11.52和17.42万人。城乡基本医疗保险参保率为98.96%。全年推出公共租赁住房配租房源10821套,新增廉租住房货币补贴保障家庭740户。市区城乡居民最低生活保障标准由每人每月660元调整为744元,各县(市)最低生活保障标准同步提高。全市城镇享受最低生活保障人数1.39万人,农村享受最低生活保障7.43万人。

(三)社会福利。

年末全市拥有城乡社区居家养老服务照料中心2329家,老年食堂1198家,分别比上年增加770家、106家。拥有各类福利院、敬老院316所,比上年增加8所,床位6.19万张,增长10.3%,收养人员2.3万人。开展第十五次"春风行动",共募集社会帮扶资金5057万元。

十二、城市建设

(一)城市基础设施建设。

全市完成基础设施投资1355.18亿元,增长34.8%。地铁4号线首通段、1号线下沙延伸段建成运营,轨道交通初步成网。秋石路三期四期、环城北路地下通道、吉鸿快速路等一批治堵重点工程建成通车,东湖路、文一路地下通道等建设快速推进。萧山机场公路改建工程西兴互通两对匝道正式开通。建成杭新景建德段等高速公路。

(二)公用事业。

全年杭州电网建设投入64.68亿元。新开工110千伏及以上输电工程42项,容量513万千伏安,线路403.94公里。全市用电量646.38亿千瓦时,增长1.0%,其中城乡居民生活用电90.26亿千瓦时,增长7.6%。

市区自来水日供水能力达到382万立方米。新辟公交线路14条,优化公交线路42条。

新增公交专用道133.2公里,新建停车泊位50156个。年末拥有公共交通运营线路716条。

全年地铁客运量达到2.23亿人次,增长53.9%。公交分担率有新提高。

十三、环境保护和安全生产

(一)环境保护。

市本级通过国家生态市技术评估,萧山、富阳通过国家生态区考核验收,桐庐、淳安入选首批国家生态保护与建设示范区,临安市获得"国家园林城市"称号,杭州经济开发区被评为国家生态工业示范区。市区完成截污纳管项目416个,新增截污量4.63万吨/日。完成84条137公里黑臭河整治。关停转迁落后产能企业426家。淘汰黄标车8.11万辆。城市污水集中处理率95.56%,比上年提高1.6个百分点;主要水系监测断面水质三类以上比例为85.1%。市区空气质量优良天数为242天,优良率66.3%,PM2.5年平均浓度为57$\mu g/m^3$,下降12.3%。至年末,市区建成区人均公园绿地面积达15.1平方米,建成区绿化覆盖率为40.5%。市区垃圾分类生活小区1836个,分类收集覆盖率80%,评为全国第一批生活垃圾分类示范城市。全年单位GDP综合能耗下降3.9%,规模以上工业单位增加值能耗下降1.2%。

（二）安全生产。

全年共发生各类事故2555起、死亡688人、受伤2616人，分别下降3.8%、0.6%、2.3%。亿元GDP安全生产事故死亡率由上年的0.077人降至0.0688人。

国民经济和社会发展困难与挑战：一是工业经济持续低位运行，投资形势依然不容乐观；二是消费外流现象日益突出，国内消费环境亟待改善；三是部分行业产能状况没有实质性改善，企业生产经营困难仍然较多；四是城市国际化程度还不够高，城乡区域发展还不够平衡，就业、养老、教育、医疗等民生保障与人民群众的期望仍有差距。

公报注释：

全市生产总值和各产业增加值绝对数按现行价格计算，增长速度按不变价格计算；三次产业划分执行国家统计局2012年制定的《三次产业划分规定》。

资料来源：

本公报中城镇新增就业、登记失业率、社会保障数据来自市人力社保局；财政数据来自市财政局；农业园区、粮食功能区数据来自市农业局；教育数据来自市教育局；货物进出口数据来自杭州海关；低保、社会服务和救助、福利彩票数据来自市民政局；货物运量、旅客运量数据来自市交通局；旅客进出港量、通航线路数据来自萧山机场；地铁客运量来自市地铁集团；春风行动捐款数据来自市总工会；垃圾分类小区数据来自市城管委；停车泊位、城市污水集中处理率、人均公园绿地面积数据来自市建委；生态建设、环境监测数据来自市环保局；各类事故发生起数、死亡人数、直接经济损失数据来自市安监局；网络零售额数据来自省商务厅；实到外资数据来自市商务委；旅游数据来自市旅委；货币金融数据来自人民银行杭州中心支行；保险业数据来自中国保监会浙江监管局；专利数据来自市科委；公共图书馆数据来自市文广新局；上市公司数据来自市金融办；卫生数据来自市卫生计生委；体育数据来自市体育局；价格数据来自国家统计局杭州调查队；其它数据均来自于市统计局。

Statistical Communiqué on the National Economy and Social Development of Hangzhou in 2015 and during the "12th Five - Year Plan" Period

Hangzhou Municipal Bureau of Statistics

Hangzhou Survey Office of National Bureau of Statistics

Hangzhou Socio - Economic Investigation Bureau

February, 2016

2015 is not only the year of the "12th Five - Year Plan" period, but also the crucial year of accelerating Hangzhou's transformation and upgrading. It's even futher an important year of the economic development entering the new normal. Under the leadership of the municipal Party committee, municipal government, the city went all out to promote the economic stability in the long run with the speeding up the "No. 1 project" as the focal point, gathering innovation momentum as the support point, deepening reform and enhancing the vitality of the system as a breakthrough point, developing and improving the livelihood of the people as the end result. Hangzhou achieved a historic breakthrough in the economic aggregate of the year, and has become the tenth of the country's "trillion" square, with the returning of two digit growth. The development of economic and social in Hangzhou stepped into to a new level during the period of the "12th Five - Year Plan" period.

I. General Outlook

Economic Aggregate

The gross domestic product (GDP) of the year was 1005.021 billion yuan, up by 10.2 percent over the previous year. Of this total, the value added of the primary industry was 28.795 billion yuan with an annual increase of 1.7%, that of the secondary industry was 390.901 billion yuan with an annual increase of 5.5%, and the tertiary industry was 585.325 billion yuan with an annual increase of 14.6%. The city's per capita GDP was 112,230 yuan, or 18019 U.S dollars using the average exchange rate in 2015 which published by the Central Bank, up by 9.1%.

Hangzhou GDP and Growth, 2010 - 2015

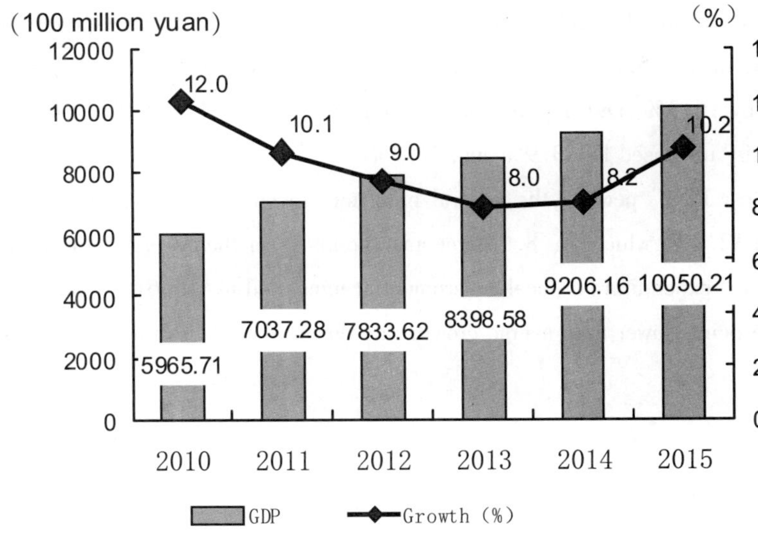

During the "12th Five - Year Plan" period, the GDP showed an annual increase of 9.1%, which was 3.3 percentage points lower than average growth rate during the "11th Five - Year Plan" period. The proportions of the three industries changed from 3.5∶47.3∶49.2 in 2010 to 2.9∶38.9∶58.2 in 2015.

Proportion of Hangzhou's Three Industries in 2010 and 2015

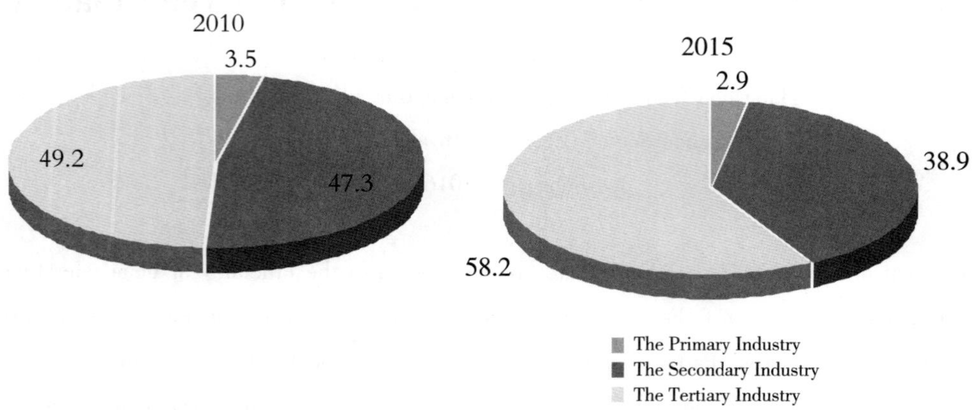

Non – State – Owned Economy

The value added of the non – state – owned economy was 595.172 billion yuan, accounting for 59.2% of Hangzhou's GDP. The fiscal revenue from the private economy reached 91.256 billion yuan, accounting for 40.8% of the total fiscal revenue. At the end of the year, there were 334.7 thousand private enterprises and 386.1 thousand individual businesses, up by 21.3% and 11.8% respectively. The employees of private enterprises reached 2,587.4 thousand with an annual increase of 16.1%, and that of individual businesses reached 794.5 thousand with an annual increase of 10.3%.

Information Economy

The value added of the information economy was 231.385 billion yuan, a 25.0% increase, and accounting for 23% of Hangzhou's GDP with an increase of 4.9 percentages over the previous year. E – commerce sectors, digital content grow respectively by 34.5%, 35.5%. Cloud computing and big data, things, internet finance, wisdom logistics grow respectively by 29.6%, 12.7%, 33.5% and 8.4%.

Fiscal Revenue and Expenditure

The general fiscal revenue of the city reached 223.875 billion yuan, up by 11.0%, of this total, the general budgetary revenue of the local government was 123.388 billion yuan, up by 9.8%. The fiscal expenditure of the local government was 120.548 billion yuan, up by 15.6%, of this total, the fiscal expenditure for promoting people's livelihood reached 92.192 billion yuan, up by 16.3%, and a year – on – year growth rate of 3.1%. The fiscal expenditure on science & technology, housing security increased by 33.9% and 31.3%.

During the "12th Five – Year Plan" period, the general budgetary revenue of local government accumulated to 485.154 billion yuan, an annual of 12.9%, which was 8.9 percentage points lower than averge growth rate during the "11th Five – Year Plan" period. The fiscal expenditure of local government accumulated to 455.618 billion yuan, an annual of 14.3%, which was 6.6 percentage points lower than averge growth rate during the "11th Five – Year Plan" period.

The General Budgetary Revenue of The Local Government from 2010 to 2015

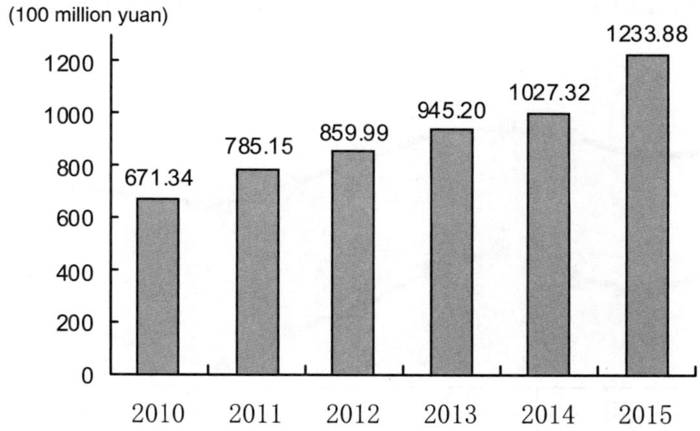

Commodity Price

The consumer prices in urban area went up by 1.8% over the previous year, down by 0.2 percentages compared with the previous year. The prices of 8 major kinds of commodity and service items presented the layout of '7 rising and 1 reducing'.

Monthly Changes in Urban Consumer Price in 2015

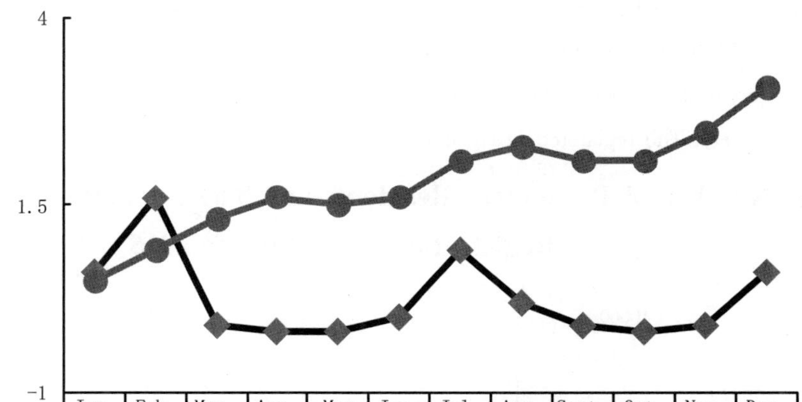

	Jan.	Feb.	Mar.	Apr.	May	Jun.	Jul.	Aug.	Sept.	Oct.	Nov.	Dec.
last month	0.6	1.6	-0.1	-0.2	-0.2	0	0.9	0.2	-0.1	-0.2	-0.1	0.6
previous month	0.5	0.9	1.3	1.6	1.5	1.6	2.1	2.3	2.1	2.1	2.5	3.1

Urban Consumer Price Index (previous year = 100)

Item	2014	2015
The general level of CPI in urban district	2.0	1.8
1. Food	2.9	2.8
2. Tobacco, Liquor and Articles	-0.1	3.9
3. Clothing	1.7	1.1
4. Household Facilities, Articles and Services	2.7	1.4
5. Health Care and Personal Articles	1.4	2.4
6. Transportation and Communication	-0.6	-3.4
7. Recreation, Education and Culture Articles	1.8	1.0
8. Residence	2.7	3.5

The producer prices for manufactured goods and the producer purchasing prices fell by 3.5% and 7.1% respectively.

Monthly Changes in producer prices in 2015

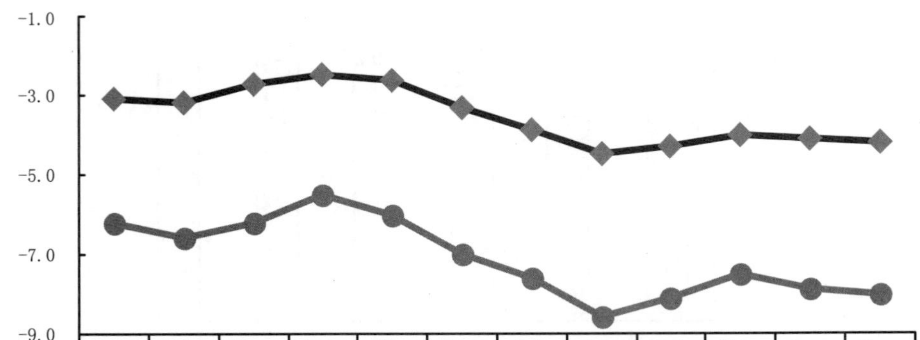

	Jan.	Feb.	Mar.	Apr.	May	Jun.	Jul.	Aug.	Sept.	Oct.	Nov.	Dec.
PPI	-3.1	-3.2	-2.7	-2.5	-2.6	-3.3	-3.9	-4.5	-4.3	-4.0	-4.1	-4.2
IPI	-6.2	-6.6	-6.2	-5.5	-6.0	-7.0	-7.6	-8.6	-8.1	-7.5	-7.9	-8.0

Population and Employment

By the end of the year, the total number of permanent residents in Hangzhou reached 9.018 million according to sample survey on population changing, an increase of 126 thousand over that at the end of the previous year. Of this total, urban population reached 6.7906 million, and the proportion increased to 75.3% from 75.1% of that at the end of the previous year; the crude birth rate was 10.6‰, and the natural growth rate of population was 5.4‰. The population of household registration reached 7.2355 million, the crude birth rate was 9.81‰, and the natural growth rate of population was 4.21‰. The newly increased employed people in urban areas numbered 287.9 thousand, and 142.2 thousand unemployed people were re – employed. The registered urban unemployment rate was 1.74% at the year end.

The Number of Permanent Residents and The Population of Household Registration from 2010 to 2015

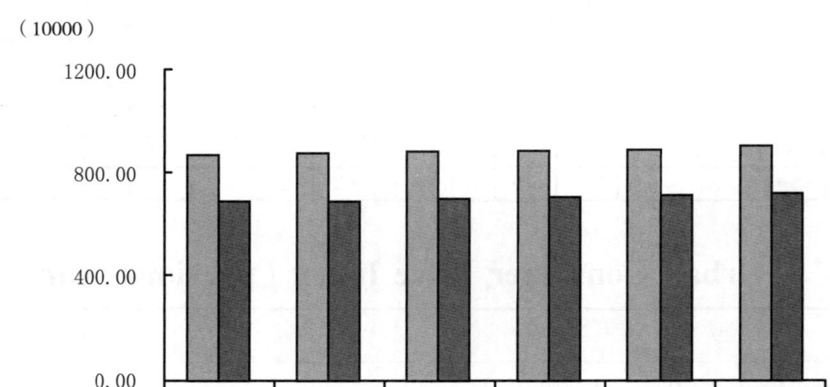

	2010	2011	2012	2013	2014	2015
permanent residents	870.54	873.80	880.20	884.40	889.20	901.80
household registration	689.12	695.71	700.52	706.61	715.76	723.55

During the "12th Five – Year Plan" period, the annual average growth rate of permanent residents was 0.7%, 1.8 percentage points lower than that during the "11th Five – Year Plan" period; accumulative increase was 312.6 thousand persons, reducing 679.8 thousand persons as compared with that during "11th Five – Year Plan".

II. Agriculture

The value added of agriculture, forestry, animal husbandry and fishery achieved 29.24 billion yuan, up by 1.8%. Of this total, the value added of agriculture, forestry and fishery was 18.062 billion yuan, 3.933 billion yuan and 2.845 billion yuan, up by 3.7% , 4.5% and 3.0% respectively. The value added of animal husbandry was 3.955 billion yuan, down by 9.6%. The value added of service industry for agriculture was 0.445 billion yuan, up by 7.1%.

The total output of grain was 0.6338 million tons, up by 1.3% ; the output of fruit was 0.7896 million tons, up by 4.8% ; the output of aquatic products was 0.2092 million tons, down by 0.1% ; and that of meat was 0.2784 million tons, down by 6.2%. In 2015, Hangzhou had newly built 18 provincial level modern agricultural parks, 42 municipal vegetable bases, and 262 grain production functional zones.

During the "12th Five - Year Plan" period , the annual average growth rate of value added of agriculture, forestry, animal husbandry and fishery was 2.0% ,1.8 percentage points lower than that during the "11th Five - Year Plan" period.

III. Industry and Construction

Industry Production

The value added of the industrial sector was 349.783 billion yuan, up by 5.5%. Of this total, the value added of industrial enterprises above the designated size was 287.505 billion yuan, up by 5.4%. The value added of strategic emerging industries, equipment manufacturing industries and high - tech industries reached 87.735 billion yuan, 108.612 billion yuan and 121.26 billion yuan respectively, up by 9.4% , 13.5% and 9.8%. The output value ratio of new products went up to 35.2% from 31.2% of the previous year. The sales - output ratio of industrial products reached 98.5%.

During the "12th Five - Year Plan" period, the value added of industrial sector of Hangzhou showed 8.1% of annual average growth,which was 2.8 percentage points lower than that during the "11th Five - Year Plan" period. The annual average growth rate of value added of industrial enterprises above the designated size was 9.2% ,5 percentage points lower than that during the "11th Five - Year Plan" period.

Industrial Efficiency

The profits & taxes of the industrial enterprises above designated size were 155.968 billion, up by 4.4% , of this total, the profits reached 89.112 billion yuan, up by 2.4%. The number of loss - making enterprises accounted for the entire enterprise was 18.0%.

Construction

The value added of construction enterprises was 41.254 billion yuan, up by 5.6% over the previous year. There were 1,480 construction enterprises with the qualification of general contract and special contract, and the construction output value amounted to 409.757 billion yuan, up by 3.2% ; the floor space of buildings under construction was 281.2372 million square meters, down by 4.9% , the floor space of buildings completed was 101.3708 million square meters, up by 6.5%.

During the "12th Five - Year Plan" period , the value added of construction enterprises of Hangzhou showed 0.7% of annual average growth,which was 7.1 percentage points lower than that during the "11th Five - Year Plan" period.

IV. Investment in Fixed Assets and Real Estate

Investment in Fixed Assets

The completed investment in fixed assets was 555.632 billion yuan, up by 12.2% over the previous year. Grouped by sectors, the investment in the primary industry was 3.147 billion yuan, up by 65.0% ; the investment in the secondary industry was 93.178 billion yuan, up by 1.8% , of which the industrial investment was 93.001 billion yuan, up by

1.8% ; the investment in the tertiary industry was 459.307 billion yuan, up by 14.3%.

During the "12th Five – Year Plan" period , the completed investment in fixed assets in Hangzhou had totaled 2,159.566 billion yuan. The annual average growth was 15.9% ,0.2 percentage points higher than that during the "11th Five – Year Plan" period.

Investment in Fixed Assets and the Growth Rates from 2010 to 2015

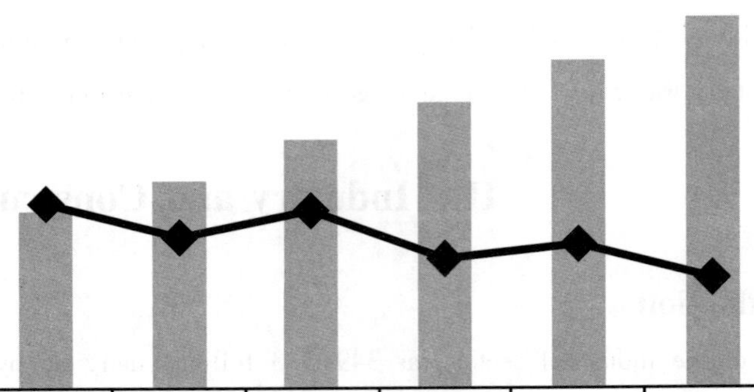

	2010	2011	2012	2013	2014	2015
Investment in fixed assets(100 million yuan)	2651.88	3100.02	3722.75	4263.87	4952.70	5556.32
Growth rate over the last year(%)	20.8	16.9	20.1	14.5	16.2	12.2

Investment in Real Estate

The completed investment in real estate development was 247.207 billion yuan, up by 7.4% over the previous year. The floor space under construction was 111.4268 million square meters, up by 6.1% ; the completed floor space was 16.6523 million square meters, up by 10.9%. The sold floor space of commercial buildings was 14.8145 million square meters, up by 1.6% , of this total, the sold floor space of commercial residential buildings was 12.9164 million square meters, up by 35.9%. A total of 47,394 sets of security housing were newly started to construct, and 57,530 units had been completed.

During the "12th Five – Year Plan" period, the annual average growth rate of completed investment in real estate development was 20.9% ,2.5 percentage points higher than that during the "11th Five – Year Plan" period.

V. Domestic Trade

The value added of wholesale and retail, hotel and food sectors was 81.802 billion yuan, up by 2.3% over the previous year.

The total retail sales of consumer goods reached 469.723 billion yuan, a growth of 11.8% over the previous year, or a real growth of 11.6% after deducting price factors.

Of this total, the retail sales was 445.776 billion yuan, up by 12.3% , the revenue of repast was 45.573 billion yuan, up by 7.4%. The retail sales of consumer goods in urban areas was 445.776 billion yuan, up by 11.7% ; and that in rural areas was 23.947 billion yuan, up by 13.2%.

Of the total retail sales of commodities by wholesale and retail enterprises above designated size, the year on year growth of sales for furniture 65.8% , for beverage 46.6% , for grain, oil and food 18.5% , for clothes, shoes, hats and textiles 10.8% , for tobacco and liquor 10.5% , for gold, silver and jewelry 12.6% , for motor vehicles 7.1% , and that for petroleum and petroleum products was down by 7.4%.

The online retail in Hangzhou reached 267.983 billion yuan, a growth of 42.6% over the previous year. The residents network spending reached 111.91 billion yuan, up by 38.2%.

During the "12th Five – Year Plan" period , the annual average growth rate of total retail sales of consumer goods was

14.8% ,3.1 percentage points higher than that during the "11th Five – Year Plan" period.

Total Retail Sales of Consumer Goods and Growth Rates from 2010 to 2015

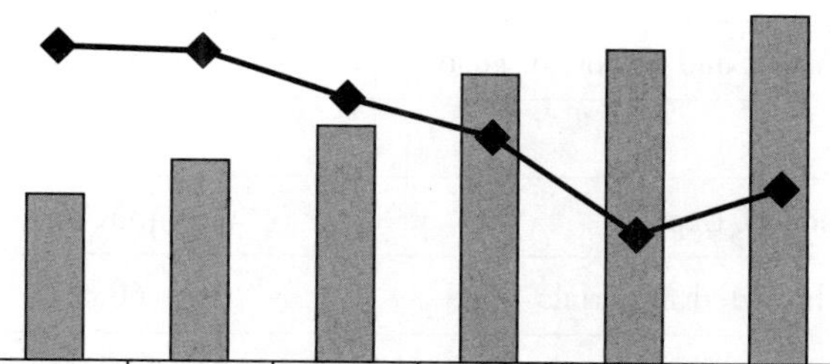

	2010	2011	2012	2013	2014	2015
Total retail sales of consumer goods(100 million yuan)	2225.00	2690.22	3165.19	3864.84	4201.46	4697.23
Growth rate over the last year(%)	21.1	20.9	17.7	15.1	8.7	11.8

VI. Foreign Economic Relations

International Trade

The total value of import and export of goods in 2015 was 66.566 billion US dollars(413.243 billion yuan), down by 2.1% (1.0%) over the previous year. Of this total, the value of goods imported was 16.5 billion SU dollars(102.44 billion yuan), down by 12.3% (11.3%); that of exported was 50.067 billion US dollars(310.803 billion yuan), up by 1.8% (2.9%) (the value of goods exported excluding the province – owned enterprises was 44.465 US dollars(262.706 billion yuan), up by 4.0% (5.5%)). Of the total value of export, the value of electromechanical products exported was 20.192 billion US dollars(125.417 billion yuan), and that of high – tech products exported was 6.36 billion US dollars (39.494 billion yuan), up by 4.4% (5.5%) and 6.2% (7.4%)respectively. Grouped by trading modes, the general trade of exports was 43.378 billion US dollars(269.323 billion yuan), up by 5.1% (6.2%); the processing trade of exports was 6.095 billion US dollars(37.794 billion yuan), down by 15.0% (14.2%). Grouped by exporting markets, the value of exports to Oceania, North America, Latin America and Asia increased by 8.0% (9.2%),6.3% (7.4%), 3.6% (4.6%) and 3.4% (4.5%); EU and Europe decreased by 1.6% (0.6%) and 3.9% (2.9%). The total value of import and export of service trade was 19.033 billion US dollars, up by 25.4% over the previous year.

During the "12th Five – Year Plan" period , the total value of import and export of goods in Hangzhou was 325.291 billion US dollars, the annual average growth was 4.9% ,7.0 percentage points lower than that during the "11th Five – Year Plan" period. Of which, the value of goods exported was 226.782 billion US dollars, the annual average growth was 7.2% , 5.1 percentage points lower than that during the "11th Five – Year Plan" period.

Value of Goods Exported and Value of Goods Imported from 2010 to 2015

The total value of import and export of goods in Hangzhou in 2015

Item	Total value (100 million US dollars)	Increase over the previous year (%)
Total Value of Import and Export of goods	665.66	-2.1
Export	500.67	1.8
General Trade of Exports	433.78	5.1
Processing Imported Materials	60.95	-15.0
Electromechanical Products exported	201.92	4.4
High - techPproducts Exported	63.60	6.2
Import	165.00	-12.3

International Cooperation

By the end of 2015, the total number of overseas enterprises (institutions) invested by Hangzhou investors was 1,1341, of which the non - trading enterprises was 491. The contracted overseas investment reached 2.649 billion US dollars, of which the non - trading investment was 1.471 billion US dollars, up by 64.9%. The accomplished business revenue through contracted overseas engineering projects and labor cooperation was 1.769 billion US dollars, up by 69.8%. The executed value of offshore service outsourcing was 5.194 billion US dollars, up by 26.7%.

Utilization of Foreign Capital

The year 2015 witnessed the authorizing of 475 projects with 7.113 billion US dollars of actually utilized foreign direct investment, up by 12.3% over the previous year. The investment of 130 newly authorized projects which of each over 30 million US dollars amounted 14.009 billion US dollars, accounting for 84.9% of the total newly approved foreign investment. There were 10 newly introduced investment projects which funded by companies of Fortune Global 500. By the end of 2015, 112 projects had been settled in Hangzhou that invested by 188 companies of Fortune Global 500.

During the "12th Five - Year Plan" period, actually utilized foreign direct investment in Hangzhou had totaled 28.407 billion US dollars. The annual average growth was 10.3%, 10.2 percentage points lower than that during the "11th Five - Year Plan" period.

Cross - border E - Commerce

The total value of import and export of Cross - border E - Commerce in Hangzhou was 21.507 billion yuan (3.464 billion US dollars), accounting for 84.9% of the total value of import and export of goods. Of this total, the value of Cross - border E - Commerce imported 7.394 billion yuan (1.191 billion US dollars), that of exported was 14.113 billion yuan (2.273 billion US dollars).

Return of Zhejiang Merchants

In 2015, 2376 projects of domestic investment were introduced with 124.927 billion yuan of actually utilized investment, up by 18.5%. Of this total, the return capital of Zhejiang Merchants reached 66.058 billion yuan, up by 27.0%.

Construction of Development Zones

There were 7 national - level development zones in Hangzhou including Hangzhou Economic and Technological

Development Zone, Hangzhou High – Tech Development Zone, Xiaoshan Economic & Technological Development Zone, Hangzhou Zhijiang National Holiday Resort Zone, Hangzhou Yuhang Economic and Technological Development Zone, Fuyang Economic, Technological Development Zone and. Linjiang National High – Tech Zone. The main business revenue of the enterprises above designated size was 813.019 billion yuan with an increase of 6.6% , and the total profits reached 58.63 billion yuan with an increase of 1.3%.

VII. Transportation, Post, Telecommunications and Tourism

Transportation and Post

The value added of transportation, storage and post achieved 29.792 billion yuan, up by 8.2%.

The annual total freight traffic was 0.239 billion tons, up by 1.7% over the previous year. The total passenger traffic was 0.239 billion persons, down by 0.5%. By the end of 2015, 235 air routes had been opened, including 32 international routes and 7 routes to Hongkong, Macao and Taiwan. 24.703 million passengers made arrivals and departure there in mainland routes ,up by 10.1%. 3.651 million passengers made arrivals and departure there in international and regional routes,up by 18.3%. The total length of highways within Hangzhou reached 16,210.02 km, including 615.08 km expressways.

The total possession of motor vehicles reached 2.7335 million of which private – owned cars numbered 1.8491 million, up by 1.4% and 2.8% over the previous year respectively.

The business income of postal enterprises and express delivery enterprises above designated size totaled 15.969 billion yuan, an annual increase of 35.7%. The express delivery enterprises above designated size reached 1.257 billion, up by 48.7%. There were 1824 'E – post stations' in the main urban areas. The business income of telecommunication services totaled 17.366 billion yuan, up by 3.3%. At the end of 2015, there were 2.9344 million fixed – line telephone subscribers and 17.2676 million mobile phone users, down by 5.7% and up by 10.6% respectively. The broadband subscribers amounted to 2.9496 million, up by 5.8%.

Tourism

The value added of tourism industry achieved 71.968 billion yuan, up by 12.8%.

The annual earnings from tourism reached 220.067 billion yuan, up by 16.7% over the previous year, of which the foreign exchange earnings from international tourism was 2.931 billion US dollars, up by 13.5%. The number of overseas visitor arrivals was 3.4156 million person – times, up by 4.7% ; that of domestic visitors was 0.12 billion person – times, up by 13.5%.

At the end of 2015, there were 685 travel agencies, up by 4.1% ; 186 star – rated hotels, including 24 5 – star hotels and 46 4 – star hotels; 54 A – rated scenic spots, including 3 AAAAA scenic spots and 34 AAAA scenic spots.

During the "12th Five – Year Plan" period, the annual average growth rate of accumulative income from domestic and forergn tourism was 16.5% ,0.6 percentage points lower than that during the "11th Five – Year Plan" period.

Overseas Visitor Arrivals and Domestic Visitors in Hangzhou from 2010 to 2015

year	Overseas visitor arrivals (million person – times)	Domestic visitors (billion person – times)
2010	2.7571	0.063
2011	3.0631	0.072
2012	3.3112	0.082
2013	3.1601	0.094
2014	3.2613	0.106
2015	3.4200	0.120

VIII. Financial Intermediation

The value added of financial intermediation achieved 94.147 billion yuan, up by 12.0%.

There were 409 financial institutions in Hangzhou at year – end, including 32 foreign financial institutions, 35 added and 17 decreased respectively. The saving deposits of RMB and foreign exchange from all of the financial institutions in Hangzhou was 2986.383 billion yuan, up by 13.9%; and the loans balance was 2332.795 billion yuan, up by 9.3%, of this total, the loan balance of household was 585.946 billion yuan, up by 19.1%; the loan balance of non – financial enterprise was 1724.185 billion yuan, up by 6.1%.

During the "12th Five – Year Plan" period, the annual average growth rate of saving deposits of RMB and foreign exchange from all of the financial institutions was 11.8%, 8.6 percentage points higher than that during the "11th Five – Year Plan" period. The annual average growth rate of the loans balance of RMB and foreign exchange from all of the financial institutions was 9.1%, 13 percentage points higher than that during the "11th Five – Year Plan" period.

Deposit and Loan Balance in RMB and Foreign Exchange from all of The Financial Institutions at the End of 2015

Item	Year – end Figure (100 million yuan)	Increase/Decrease of the Increased Amount
Total Deposit Balance	29863.83	13.9
Of which: Household Deposit	7617.75	4.4
Non – financial Enterprise Deposit	13120.73	10.3
Total Loan Balance	23327.95	9.3
Of which: Household Loans	5859.46	19.1
Non – financial Enterprise Loans	17241.85	6.1

In 2015, there were 9 newly authorized listed companies in Hangzhou, and raised a total of 25.598 billion yuan. By the end of the year, the number of listed companies in Hangzhou accumulated to 118, and funds raised through stock markets amounted to 300.858 billion yuan. 155 companies were listed on the New Third Board.

The premiums received by the insurance companies totaled 37.438 billion yuan with an annual increase of 16.8%, of this total, the premiums of property insurance was 15.691 billion yuan, up by 11.2%, that of life insurance was 21.747 billion yuan, up by 21.3%. The payments of insurance indemnity of various kinds totaled 13.968 billion yuan, up by 17.3%, of this total, the payments of property insurance was 9.372 billion yuan, up by 12.6%, that of life insurance was 4.595 billion yuan, up by 28.4%.

During the "12th Five - Year Plan" period, the annual average growth rate of premiums received by the insurance companies was 13%.

IX. Education, Science & Technology

Education

There were 443 primary schools with 524.5 thousand students, 243 junior secondary schools with 211.3 thousand students, and 75 regular senior secondary schools with 110 thousand students in Hangzhou. The ratio of enrollment to kindergartens of those who 3 years younger than the school age reached 98.8%, the enrollment rate to senior schools from junior secondary schools was 99.7%. The coverage ratio of high quality preschool education raised to 78.6% from 76.7% of the previous year, that of high quality senior secondary schools was 86.4%, an increase of 0.8 percentages. There were 39 regular institutions of higher education with 475.6 thousand students, of which 50.2 thousand were graduate students, up by 0.2% and 4.5%. 125 thousand were graduates, up by 1.4%. The gross enrollment rate to general colleges and universities rose to 60.4% from 59.8% of the previous year. 267.1 thousand children of migrant workers were enrolling in the stage of compulsory education.

Science & Technology

In 2015, 17,777 patents for invention were applied and 8,296 were authorized, up by 20.3% and 49.4% over the previous year respectively. There were accumulated 1,986 national - level supported high - tech enterprises, an annual increase of 311. There were 146 China's well - known trademarks, an annual increase of 14. At the year - end, there were 1438 foster recognized research and development center, 517 provincial level research and development center. A total of 6,243 scientific and technological achievements with 7.742 billion trading volume were received by technology market. A total of 83 high - tech business incubators with 2.3936 square meters were built, of which 21 were national - level. The quantity of national incubators ranked first among all of the provincial capitals in China. There were 14 maker spaces into the national science and technology incubator system. The expenditures on research and development activities (R&D) accounted for 3.01% of Hangzhou's GDP.

During the "12th Five - Year Plan" period, authorization related to invention patent had totaled 28,800. The annual average growth was 20.7%, 15.7 percentage points lower than that during the "11th Five - Year Plan" period.

X. Culture, Public Health and sports

Culture

The value added of culture creation industry achieved 223.214 billion yuan, up by 20.4%.

By the end of 2015, there were 21 professional arts performing organizations, 15 cultural centers, and 15 public libraries with 17.85 million books. The libraries of Hangzhou achieved interlibrary loan and literature transfere with 49 countries and regions, more than 10 thousand libraries. The project of digital library resources into the school had successfully covered 774 urban and rural primary and secondary schools. During the whole year, a total of 1,221 episodes in 29 TV dramas and 19 films were produced; also created and produced were 14,500 - minute - long animation film. The year saw the publication of 2.2 billion copies of newspaper, 18 million copies of magazines, and 290 million books . Hangzhou was listed with 334 intangible cultural heritage protection project.

Public Health

At the year – end, there were 4,428 medical and health institutions in Hangzhou, including 244 hospitals, increasing 230 and 26 over the previous year respectively. The number of beds was 63,600, of which 58,400 were hospital beds, up by 14.1% and 15.0% respectively. There were 93,00 professional medical personnel, of whom the licensed (assistant) doctors were 34,800 and registered nurses were 38,200, up by 8.7%, 8.9% and 10.0% respectively. A total of 117.3303 million patients receive diagnosis and treatment in medical institutions, up 4.9%. The infant mortality rate and mortality rate of children under five – year old were 2.32‰ and 3.0‰. The mortality per 100,000 pregnant women was 6.94 persons.

Sports

Hangzhou had 3 national traditional sports schools, 1 national high level sports reserve talent base, 1 Zhejiang provincial sports reserve talent base. 567 eligible public schools stadiums opened to the public. Hangzhou was awared the honor to host 19th Asian Games in 2022, as third Chinese cities hosting the Asian Games.

XI. Living Conditions and Social Security

Living Conditions

The annual per capita disposable income in Hangzhou was 42,642 yuan, an increase of 8.7% or a real increase of 6.8% after deducting price factors. In terms of resident areas, the annual per capita disposable income of urban households reached 48,316 yuan, up by 8.3% or a real increase of 6.4% after deducting price factors, and the annual per capita disposable income of rural households was 25,719 yuan, up by 9.2% or 7.3% after deducting price factor. The per capita consumption expenditure of urban households was 33,818 yuan, and that of rural households was 19,334 yuan, up by 5.1% and 8.5% respectively.

Per Capita Disposable Income in Hangzhou in 2015

Item	Urban Residents		Rural Residents	
	Income (yuan)	Increase over the previous year (%)	Income (yuan)	Increase over the previous year (%)
Disposable Income	48316	8.3	25719	9.2
(一) Income from Wages	28891	4.5	15860	7.1
(二) Income of Staff & workers in Other – owned Units	4502	3.1	6628	10.1
(三) Property Income	6851	13.4	982	11.7
(四) Transfer Income	8072	22.5	2249	21.8

Per Capita Consumption Expenditure of Urban Households and Rural Households in Hangzhou in 2015

Item	Urban Residents		Rural Residents	
	Consumption Expenditure (yuan)	Increase over the previous year (%)	Consumption Expenditure (yuan)	Increase over the previous year (%)
Expenditure	33818	5.1	19334	8.5
(一) Food alcohol and tobacco	9171	5.6	5358	5.2
(二) Clothing	2157	-1.6	1157	5.8
(三) Residence	9111	6.4	4990	9.9
(四) Daily necessities and services	1622	-3.6	1008	8.0
(五) Transportation and Communication	5707	6.4	3904	18.3
(六) Education, cultural and Recreation	3141	5.1	1507	1.5
(七) Medicine and Medical Service	2002	17.2	1055	0.3
(八) Other Supplies and Services	907	-6.9	355	9.9

During the "12th Five - Year Plan" period, per capita disposable income of urban households showed actual annual average growth of 9.8%; while that of rural households presented actual annual average growth of 11.7%.

By the end of the year, the per capita floor space of residential building in urban areas reached 35.5 square meters, and every 100 urban households had 48.7 family cars, 207.3 air conditioners, 110.1 home computers; the per capita floor space of residential building in rural areas reached 68.8 square meters, and every 100 rural households had 38.2 family cars, 147.6 air conditioners, 69.6 home computers.

Social Security

By the end of the year, a total of 6.6865 million people participated in the basic social pension insurance, a year - on - year increase of 0.52 million; a total of 8.7071 million people participated in the basic medical insurance program, an increase of 0.35 million; a total of 3.4942 million people participated in the unemployment insurance, 4.1817 million people participated in the work accident insurances, 3.2665 million people participated in the maternity insurance, a year - on - year increase of 0.1759 million, 0.1152 million and 0.1742 million respectively. The enrollment rates to basic medical insurance program reached 98.96%. 740 households were newly added as low - rent housing security families, and 2,865 units of public rental housing were available. 569 households were newly added as low - rent housing security families, and a total of 200,000 square meters of affordable housing and 2,865 units of public rental housing were available. The minimum subsistence guarantee for residents in urban areas increased to 744 yuan from 660 yuan, and that for residents in rural areas increased by the same percentage. 13,900 urban residents receive the basic cost of living allowance, and 74,300 rural residents receive the rural equivalent.

Social Welfare

There were 2,329 home – based care service stations and 1198 canteens for the aged, for the rural aged in Hangzhou, a year – on – year increase of 770 and 106 respectively. By the end of the year, there were all together 316 welfare institutions and nursing homes for the aged, an increase of 8 over the previous year, providing 61,900 beds, up by 10.3%, accommodating 23,000 inmates. A total of 50.57 million yuan of social funds was raised by the 15th 'Spring Breeze Action'.

XII. Urban Construction

Urban Infrastructure Construction

In 2015, the investment in infrastructure amounted to 135.518 billion yuan, up by 34.8%. The first section of Metro Line 4 and Xiasha extension of Metro Line 1 went into operation. Hangzhou had preliminarily framed a rail transit system. Some key projects of governance and blocking were opened to traffic such as 3th and 4th project of Qiushi Fast Road, underground passage of Huancheng Beilu Road, expressway of Jihong. Some major projects were being accelerated such as Donghu Road, underground passage of Wenyi Road. Two pairs of ramp of Xixing of Xiaoshan airport highway reconstruction project were opened officially. Hangzhou completed several highways such as the territory of Jiande of Hangxinjing speed.

Public Utilities

The annual investment in construction of power grids amounted to 6.468 billion yuan. A total of 42 transmission projects, each of which was above 110 KV, were newly under construction, the transmission capacity and the electrical wiring amounted to 5.13 million KVA and 403.94 km respectively. The electricity consumption of the whole city was 64.638 billion KWH, up by 1.0%, of this total, the consumption of residents in urban and rural areas was 9.026 billion KWH, up by 7.6%.

The daily capacity of water supply in urban areas reached 3.82 million cubic meters. 14 bus routes were newly added, and 42 routes were optimized.

133.2 km bus – only lanes were newly put into use. 50,156 parking spaces were newly completed. By the end of the year, Hangzhou had 716 public transport lines.

The annual passenger capacity of metro reached 2.23 billion, up by 53.9%. The public transit contribution rate was continuously improved.

XIII. Environment Protection and Work Safety

Environment Protection

Hangzhou Urban District passed without a hitch the National Ecological City acceptance technical assessment. Xiaoshan and Fuyang were honored with national eco – city. Tonglu and Chun'an were selected the first national demonstration zone of ecological protection and construction. Ling'an won the "national garden city" title. Hangzhou Economic Development Zone was named the national eco industrial demonstration zone. 416 sewage pipe projects were newly put into use with a newly increase of 46,300 tons of dairy treatment capacity of sewage. 84 black and smelly rivers with 137 km long were renovated. 426 backward production capacity enterprises were shut down or transferred. 95,000 heavy pollution vehicles were fallen into disuse. The centralized disposal rate of urban sewage reached 95.56%, up by 1.6 percentages compared with the previous year. The proportion of water quality above the third level in major river system was 85.1%. The number of days which the AQI reached Ⅱ – level or above amounted to 242, the excellent and good rate was 66.3%, the mean annual concentration of PM2.5 was 57μg/m^3, down by 12.3%. By the end of the year, the per capita green land of parks in urban areas reached 15.1 square meters, and the green coverage rate of built-up areas was 40.5%. There were 1836 communities in urban areas that carried out garbage classification, and the proportion reached to 80%. The proportion of communities in urban areas that carried out garbage classification reached to 97.2% from 94.3% of the previous year. Hangzhou was named the first batch of garbage classification model city. The comprehensive energy consumption per 10,000 yuan worth of GDP went down by 3.9% and that of the industrial enterprises above the designated size went down by 1.2%.

Work Safety

The number of accidents, the death doll, and the number of injure due to various work accidents were 2,555, 688, and 2616, down by 3.8%, 0.6% and 2.3% over the previous year respectively. The death toll due to work accidents for every 100 million yuan worth of GDP was decreased to 0.0688 people from 0.077 people of the previous year.

The major difficulties of economic and social development are as follows: firstly, the industrial economy is developing with a low speed continuously, and the prospect of investment in fixed assets is not cheerful; secondly, the phenomenon of consumption outflow becomes more and more prominent, and domestic consumption environment needs to be urgently improved; thirdly, there is no substantial improvement in the capacity of some industries, and till more difficulties in the production and operation of enterprises; fourthly, the degree of internationalization of the city is not high enough, the degree of internationalization of the city is not high enough, some public services, including employment, providing for the aged, education, and health care were still lagging behind the people's demands.

Notes:

GDP and absolute added value of various industries are calculated based on current price, whereas the growth rate is calculated based on constant price in 2010; the classification on primary, secondary and tertiary industries is subject to the Classification on Primary, Secondary and Tertiary Industries which is made by National Statistics Office in 2012.

Source of Statistics:

Statistics on newly increased employed people in urban areas, registered urban unemployment rate and social security are from Hangzhou Municipal Bureau of Human Resources and Social Security; fiscal statistics are from Hangzhou Bureau of Finance; statistics on agricultural park and grain production functional zone are from Hangzhou Agriculture Bureau; statistics on education are from Hangzhou Municipal Commission of Education; statistics on import and export are from Hangzhou Customs; statistics on subsistence allwance, social services and assistance, elfare lottery are from Hangzhou Municipal Bureau of Civil Affairs; statistics on highway mileage, freight traffic and passenger traffic are form Hangzhou Traffic Management Bureau; statistics on passengers made arrivals and departure, Route are form Xiaoshan International Airport; statistics on passenger capacity of metro are form Hangzhou Metro Group; statistics on 'Spring Breeze Action' are from Federation of trade Unions; statistics on garbage classification area are from Hangzhou Urban Management Committee; statistics on parking space, centralized disposal rate of urban sewage and per capita green land of parks are Hangzhou Municipal Commission of Housing and Urban-Rural Development; statistics on ecological construction and environmental monitoring are from Hangzhou Municipal Bureau of Environmental Protection; statistics on safety production are from Hangzhou Administration of Work Safety; statistics on online retail are from Zhejiang Provincial Department of Commerce; statistics on actually utilized foreign direct investment are from Hangzhou Municipal Commission of Commerce; statistics on tourism are from Hangzhou Municipal Commission of Tourism Development; statistics on money and finance People's Bank of Hangzhou Center Branch; statistics on insurance are from Zhejiang Bureau of China Insurance

Regulatory Commission; statistics on patent are from Hangzhou Municipal Science and Technology Commission; statistics on public library are from Hangzhou Municipal Administration of Press, Publication, Radio, Film and Telecision; statistics on newly authorized listed company are from Hangzhou Finance Office; statistics on healthcare are from Hangzhou Municipal Commission of Health and Family Planning; statistics on sports are from Hangzhou Municipal Bureau of Sports; statistics on price are from Hangzhou Survey Office of National Bureau of Statistics; other statistics are from Hangzhou Municipal Bureau of Statistics.

一、综合

GENERAL SURVEY

1

综　　合
General Survey

主要统计指标
Major Statistical Indicators

全市生产总值	Gross Domestic Product	10050.21	亿元	(100 million yuan)
为上年	As Compared with the Preceding Year	110.2	%	(%)
第一产业	Primary Industry	287.95	亿元	(100 million yuan)
为上年	As Compared with the Preceding Year	101.7	%	(%)
第二产业	Secondary Industry	3909.01	亿元	(100 million yuan)
为上年	As Compared with the Preceding Year	105.5	%	(%)
第三产业	Tertiary Industry	5853.25	亿元	(100 million yuan)
为上年	As Compared with the Preceding Year	114.6	%	(%)
常住居民人均生产总值	Per Capita GDP (Long-term Residents)	112230	元	(yuan)
为上年	As Compared with the Preceding Year	109.1	%	(%)
生产总值构成	Composition of Gross Domestic Product	100	%	(%)
第一产业	Primary Industry	2.9	%	(%)
第二产业	Secondary Industry	38.9	%	(%)
第三产业	Tertiary Industry	58.2	%	(%)

1-01 行政区划(2015年末)
Administrative Division(End of 2015)

单位:个 (unit)

地 区	Region	街 道 Subdistrict Offices	乡(镇) Towns and Townships	镇 Towns	村、社区 Villages and Communities	村 Villages
全 市	**Whole City**	**92**	**98**	**75**	**3101**	**2044**
市 区	Urban District	80	39	33	1904	920
上城区	Shangcheng	6	-	-	54	-
下城区	Xiacheng	8	-	-	74	-
江干区	Jianggan	10	-	-	179	4
拱墅区	Gongshu	10	-	-	106	-
西湖区	Xihu	10	2	2	202	45
高新(滨江)区	Hi-Tech(Binjiang)	3	-	-	57	-
萧山区	Xiaoshan	14	12	12	584	411
余杭区	Yuhang	14	6	6	344	184
富阳区	Fuyang	5	19	13	304	276
桐庐县	Tonglu	4	10	6	201	183
淳安县	Chun'an	-	23	11	437	425
建德市	Jiande	3	13	12	256	229
临安市	Lin'an	5	13	13	303	287

1-02 土地面积和人口密度(2015年末)
Land Area and Population Density(End of 2015)

地　区	Region	土地面积(平方千米) Land Area (sq. km)	年末总人口(万人) Population (10000 persons)	人口密度(人/平方千米) Population Density (person/sq. km)
全　市	**Whole City**	**16596**	**901.80**	**543**
市　区	Urban District	4876	721.30	1479
上城区	Shangcheng	18	35.30	19611
下城区	Xiacheng	31	53.50	17258
江干区	Jianggan	210	103.07	4908
拱墅区	Gongshu	88	57.10	6489
西湖区	Xihu	263	83.91	3190
高新(滨江)区	Hi-Tech(Binjiang)	73	33.08	4532
萧山区	Xiaoshan	1163	156.10	1342
余杭区	Yuhang	1222	125.89	1030
富阳区	Fuyang	1808	73.35	406
桐庐县	Tonglu	1780	42.20	237
淳安县	Chun'an	4452	34.91	78
建德市	Jiande	2364	44.65	189
临安市	Lin'an	3124	58.74	188

注:年末总人口和人口密度按常住人口计算。

The population and population density were calculated by long-term residents.

1-03 平均每天主要社会经济活动(主要年份)

Selected Indicators on Average Daily Social and Economic Activities(Main Years)

指标 Item	2000	2005	2010	2011	2012	2013	2014	2015
全市生产总值 (万元) Gross Domestic Product (10,000 yuan)	37878	80621	163444	192802	214620	230098	252224	275349
工业增加值 (万元) Value - Added of Industry (10,000 yuan)	16670	36427	67212	79181	84749	86477	93559	95831
规模以上工业企业利税总额 (万元) Total Pre - tax Profits of Industrial Enterprises above Designated Size (10,000 yuan)	4428	12347	33324	36452	36711	39748	42139	42731
农林牧渔业总产值 (万元) Gross Output Value of Farming,Forestry, Animal Husbandry and Fishery (10,000 yuan)	4182	6013	8667	9783	10530	10942	11468	12066
固定资产投资 (万元) Investment in Fixed Assets (10,000 yuan)	10319	35008	72654	84932	101993	116818	135690	152228
住宅竣工面积 (平方米) Floor Space of Residential Buildings Completed (sq. m)	11501	19327	21981	23038	18466	23154	25425	29323
社会消费品零售总额 (万元) Total Retail Sales of Consumer Goods (10,000 yuan)	14101	26724	60959	73705	86718	105886	115108	128691
住户存款新增额 (万元) The Increased Amount of Household Deposits (10,000 yuan)	1223	9767	19289	15247	14863	8729	9825	8739
财政总收入 (万元) Total Financial Revenue (10,000 yuan)	3914	14268	34121	40792	44600	47534	52606	61335

注:本表按当年价计算。2003 年起城乡居民储蓄新增额为本外币合并数据。

a) Figures in value terms in this table are calculated at current prices. The increased amount of residents´savings deposits include both RMB and foreign currencies since 2003.

1－04 国民经济
Major Indicators of

指　　标		Item	
年末常住人口	（万人）	Long－term Residents(End of 2014)	(10,000 persons)
年末户籍人口	（万人）	Honsehold Registration Population(End of 2014)	(10,000 persons)
#城镇人口	（万人）	Urban Population	(10,000 persons)
年末从业人员数	（万人）	Total Number of Employed Persons(End of 2014)	(10,000 persons)
全市生产总值	（亿元）	Gross Domestic Product	(100 million yuan)
第一产业	（亿元）	Primary Industry	(100 million yuan)
第二产业	（亿元）	Secondary Industry	(100 million yuan)
第三产业	（亿元）	Tertiary Industry	(100 million yuan)
人均生产总值(户籍)	（元）	Per Capita GDP(Household)	(yuan)
人均生产总值(常住)	（元）	Per Capita GDP(Long－term)	(yuan)
主要农产品产量		Output of Major Farm Products	
粮食	（万吨）	Grain	(10,000 tons)
棉花	（吨）	Cotton	(ton)
油菜籽	（吨）	Rapeseeds	(ton)
茶叶	（吨）	Tea	(ton)
蚕茧	（吨）	Silk－worm Cocoons	(ton)
生猪年末存栏	（万头）	Hogs in Stock at Year End	(10,000 heads)
肉类产量	（万吨）	Output of Meat	(10,000 tons)
淡水产品产量	（吨）	Freshwater Aquatic Products	(ton)
全部工业总产值	（亿元）	The Total Output Value of Industrial Enterprises	(100 million yuan)
规模以上工业总产值	（亿元）	The Output Valne of Industrial Enterprises Above Designated Size	(100 million yuan)
规模以上工业企业利税总额	（亿元）	Total Pre－tax Profits of Industrial Enterprises Above Designated Size	(100 million yuan)
客运量	（万人次）	Total Passenger Traffic	(10,000 person－times)
货运量	（万吨）	Total Freight Traffic	(10,000 tons)
固定资产投资	（亿元）	Investment in Fixed Assets	(100 million yuan)
社会消费品零售总额	（亿元）	Total Retail Sales of Consumer Goods	(100 million yuan)

注:1. 规模以上工业的计算口径,1997 年以前为乡及乡以上,1998 年－2010 年为主营业务收入 500 万元及以上,2011 年起为 2000 万元及以上。

2. 从 2014 年起,粮食数据以粮食生产统计监测抽样调查取得。

主要指标（主要年份）

National Economy(Main Years)

1980	1985	1990	1995	2000	2005	2010	2011	2012	2013	2014	2015
		583.21		701.7	771.3	870.54	873.8	880.2	884.4	889.2	901.80
515.53	543.05	574.78	597.96	621.58	660.45	689.12	695.71	700.52	706.61	715.76	723.55
128.88	153.46	169.00	191.43	226.99	297.54	365.24	376.03	384.09	393.88	404.27	495.38
293.98	330.37	363.49	422.55	408.11	481.1	626.33	637.77	644.43	650.51	654.92	663.03
40.65	90.49	189.62	762.01	1382.56	2943.84	5965.71	7037.28	7833.62	8398.58	9206.16	10050.21
8.15	15.97	30.94	69.25	103.96	148.21	208.41	236.77	255.11	261.60	274.35	287.95
25.36	52.08	96.17	410	709.32	1494.36	2819.81	3280.52	3500.13	3574.25	3845.58	3909.01
7.14	22.44	62.51	282.76	569.28	1301.27	2937.49	3519.99	4078.37	4562.73	5086.24	5853.25
791	1675	3310	12797	22342	44871	86932	101634	112211	119372	129448	139653
					38542	70024	80689	89323	95190	103813	112230
151.74	180	189.56	174.5	153.08	103.5	100.25	97.81	96.88	95.92	62.54	63.38
8007	6704	6693	8038	2112	1038	929	828	876	825	742	705
46621	51849	60683	61446	80436	70733	76676	79815	76589	79826	63580	66227
18880	22742	26429	19824	24810	25551	30500	31385	32283	28503	26548	28139
6165	7980	11085	13240	9308	16339	15637	16127	15514	14502	12294	10426
190.16	166.10	159.00	147.58	172.16	165.28	192.53	203.23	210.76	219.23	173.46	156.82
9.53	11.16	14.93	19.21	25.24	30.74	31.79	32.5	33.49	34.04	29.67	27.84
14080	30400	47588	63294	91626	147800	208945	212277	210527	197992	186026	178880
					6589.51	12810.52	14881.98	15595.28	15211.78	15851.40	15018.77
61.79	128.59	292.26	1020.03	1543.57	5441.13	11081.04	12352.92	12959.68	12418	12853.05	12415.68
13.6	24.81	31.54	63.05	161.61	450.68	1224.48	1330.48	1339.94	1450.55	1538.07	1559.68
3905	6724	8119	16620	18607	24124	33772	34778	35819	36409	24070	23942
2070	2488	6522	10347	11459	19909	25915	28831	30089	30734	29335	29384
4.58	14.19	22.92	156.63	376.65	1277.8	2651.88	3100.02	3722.75	4263.87	4952.70	5556.32
20.54	47.81	98.17	299.35	514.68	978.43	2225.00	2690.22	3165.19	3864.84	4201.46	4697.23

a) The standard for above designated size of industry, before 1997, it was above the sub - district level; 1998 - 2010, it was the annual sales income over 5 million yuan; since 2011, it was the annual sales income over 20 million yuan.

b) The data of grain was obtained from the sampling survey of grain production in 2014.

1-04 续表

指 标		Item	
境外旅游者人数	(万人次)	Number of Foreign Tourists	(10,000 person-times)
财政总收入	(亿元)	Total Financial Revenue	(100 million yuan)
一般公共财政预算支出	(亿元)	Financial Expenditure of Local Government	(100 million yuan)
金融机构存款余额	(亿元)	Deposits of Financial Institutions	(100 million yuan)
金融机构贷款余额	(亿元)	Loans of Financial Institutions	(100 million yuan)
住户存款余额	(亿元)	Household Deposits	(100 million yuan)
非私营单位就业人员工资总额	(亿元)	Total Wages of Employed Persons in Non-private Units	(100 million yuan)
非私营单位就业人员平均工资	(元)	Average Wage of Employed Persons in Non-private Units	(yuan)
市区居民消费价格指数	(以1978年为100)	Consumer Price Index in Urban District	(Year of 1978=100)
市区商品零售价格指数	(以1978年为100)	Retail Price Index in Urban District	(Year of 1978=100)
全体居民人均可支配收入	(元)	Per Capita Annual Disposable Income of Urban and Rural Residents	(yuan)
城镇居民人均可支配收入	(元)	Per Capita Annual Disposable Income of Urban Residents	(yuan)
农村居民人均可支配收入	(元)	Per Capita Annual Net Income of Rural Residents	(yuan)
高等学校在校学生数	(人)	Student Enrollment in Institutions of Higher Education	(person)
中等专业学校在校学生数	(人)	Student Enrollment in Secondary Specialized Schools	(person)
普通中学在校学生数	(人)	Student Enrollment in Secondary Schools	(person)
小学在校学生数	(人)	Student Enrollment in Primary Schools	(person)
卫生机构数	(个)	Number of Health Institutions	(unit)
#医院	(个)	Number of Hospitals	(unit)
卫生技术人员	(人)	Number of Medical Technical Personnel	(person)
#执业(助理)医师	(人)	Number of Certified Doctors(Include Assistant Doctors)	(person)
床位数	(张)	Number of Beds in Health Institutions	(unit)
#医院	(张)	Beds in Hospital	(unit)

continued

1980	1985	1990	1995	2000	2005	2010	2011	2012	2013	2014	2015
12.5	23.84	38.83	44.13	70.71	151.36	275.71	306.31	331.12	316.01	326.13	341.56
11.85	18.65	25.25	55.13	142.85	520.79	1245.43	1488.92	1627.89	1734.98	1920.11	2238.75
2.17	5.77	11.82	24.91	73.43	238.33	616.58	747.5	786.28	855.74	961.18	1205.48
18.1	48.5	133.77	707.97	2088.47	6748.72	17084.35	18396.57	20148.77	22174.71	24450.51	29863.83
17.34	58.01	162.27	567.2	1686.64	5545.3	15078.73	16573.74	18090.9	19350.46	21316.83	23327.95
4.04	15.96	69.75	342.34	788.56	2191.66	4990.97	5547.48	6089.98	6408.59	6767.2	7617.75
6.79	13.01	27.79	89.05	126.75	297.02	933.06	1122.28	1483.9	1758.23	1982.27	2152.40
777	1266	2382	7156	14257	31069	48772	54408	56417	63664	69209	76073
109.24	140.21	246.68	503.06	611.07	623.07	701.33	734.99	753.36	772.19	787.63	801.81
110.28	142.61	256.45	476.99	504.42	470.47	526.76	549.94	560.39	568.80	573.35	574.50
–	–	–	–	–	–	–	–	–	35763	39237	42642
521	1026	1985	6301	9668	16601	30035	34065	37511	40925	44632	48316
250	624	1171	3012	4894	7655	13186	15245	17017	21208	23555	25719
23545	36996	39866	63124	122386	351918	434811	446721	459181	471820	474652	475558
9453	16527	23564	42784	45238	20344	3999	4100	3909	3656	3974	3968
247734	244399	199940	257071	342533	362257	352997	340634	331353	327346	324414	321306
560244	414839	460514	513988	485679	458942	453897	465289	472613	483489	502688	524513
1381	1582	1738	1712	1599	2196	2819	2958	3017	4139	4198	4428
425	404	440	414	396	127	151	167	198	208	218	244
21110	25593	30990	34245	35487	42353	61117	65869	71618	78340	85614	93036
8311	11503	14483	16465	16317	17833	24345	25773	27369	29686	31977	34832
16317	19637	24121	26684	27166	33251	42828	45291	49471	52056	55779	63632
13478	15010	18879	21360	23303	25907	33611	39363	44019	46636	50805	58400

1－05　全市生产总值及发展指数(1978－2015年)

Gross Domestic Product and its Indices(1978－2015)

单位:万元　　(10000 yuan)

年份 Year	生产总值(当年价格) Gross Domestic Product (Current Price)	第一产业 Primary Industry	第二产业 Secondary Industry	第三产业 Tertiary Industry	人均生产总值(元)(按户籍) Per Capita GDP (Household Registered)	人均生产总值(元)(按常住) Per Capita GDP (Long-term Registered)	生产总值指数(%) Indices of Gross Domestic product(%) (1978=100)	第一产业 Primary Industry	第二产业 Secondary Industry	第三产业 Tertiary Industry
1978	284046	63372	169344	51330	565	－	100	100	100	100
1979	335285	83852	194132	57301	659	－	113.3	114.2	114.0	110.0
1980	406508	81524	253545	71439	791	－	135.7	105.6	151.1	130.7
1981	468206	90955	287632	89619	904	－	154.0	108.7	172.2	162.3
1982	501854	108769	294725	98360	957	－	165.1	129.8	177.7	176.3
1983	558947	101106	334413	123428	1054	－	183.6	115.6	203.1	219.9
1984	694690	126443	405535	162712	1298	－	225.3	140.1	245.4	283.7
1985	904897	159684	520853	224360	1675	－	268.9	139.9	300.8	352.8
1986	1053589	177589	601277	274723	1917	－	299.9	145.0	335.3	409.9
1987	1260162	204366	718892	336904	2276	－	338.4	148.7	382.2	471.6
1988	1525427	256838	855305	413284	2717	－	363.3	145.5	419.8	497.2
1989	1662945	282746	896736	483463	2928	－	352.1	145.1	396.5	509.0
1990	1896216	309404	961673	625139	3310	－	372.4	154.4	422.2	528.0
1991	2279545	334024	1131088	814433	3952	－	439.8	161.1	492.4	669.5
1992	2900690	349033	1487838	1063819	4996	－	540.5	161.6	637.5	814.8
1993	4247094	419364	2264440	1563290	7263	－	703.2	171.2	878.7	1004.7
1994	5855239	575131	3143430	2136678	9924	－	888.1	185.0	1161.6	1225.7
1995	7620055	692510	4100008	2827537	12797	－	1064.8	198.2	1434.6	1445.1
1996	9066133	839985	4776225	3449923	15095	－	1203.3	208.9	1644.0	1621.4
1997	10363299	913611	5415017	4034671	17113	－	1360.9	223.1	1852.8	1861.3
1998	11348899	960558	5879589	4508752	18611	－	1513.3	244.0	2071.4	2060.5
1999	12252795	975821	6307510	4969464	19961	－	1667.7	257.4	2280.6	2287.1
2000	13825616	1039641	7093233	5692742	22342	－	1867.8	272.1	2565.7	2563.9
2001	15680138	1114569	7935809	6629760	25074	－	2095.7	292.3	2891.6	2884.4
2002	17818302	1146388	9018225	7653689	28150	－	2372.3	304.2	3276.2	3308.4
2003	20997744	1265890	10757812	8974042	32819	－	2732.9	322.5	3885.6	3725.3
2004	25431796	1322341	13182254	10927201	39293	－	3142.8	338.9	4534.4	4258.0
2005	29438430	1482145	14943581	13012704	44871	－	3551.4	350.5	5037.8	4956.3
2006	34434972	1548594	17283905	15602473	51908	44128	4059.5	364.7	5672.8	5820.3
2007	41040117	1634719	20458811	18946588	61315	51416	4651.7	372.8	6483.5	6761.1
2008	47889748	1798300	23725807	22365641	70948	58862	5165.2	386.7	7062.8	7705.1
2009	51114007	1905093	23657646	25551268	75111	61821	5680.2	398.7	7486.6	8822.4
2010	59657106	2084144	28198060	29374902	86932	70024	6361.8	408.7	8332.6	9995.8
2011	70372782	2367708	32805209	35199865	101634	80689	7004.3	418.9	9057.5	11195.2
2012	78336168	2551127	35001330	40783711	112211	89323	7634.7	429.4	9709.6	12449.1
2013	83985753	2615974	35742503	45627276	119372	95190	8245.5	435.4	10389.3	13606.9
2014	92061634	2743492	38455759	50862382	129448	103813	8921.6	443.3	11220.4	14777.1
2015	100502079	2879492	39090099	58532488	139653	112230	9831.6	450.8	11837.6	16934.5

注:1. 根据经济普查资料对2009－2013年数据进行修订。

2. 从2013年起,三次产业划分执行国家统计局2012年制定的《三次产业划分规定》。

a) The data of 2009－2013 were vevised according to the result of economic sensus.

b) The indicators of Three Industry have been adjusted according to the national stadards since 2013.

1－06 市区生产总值及发展指数(1978－2015年)

Gross Domestic Product and its Indices of Urban District (1978－2015)

单位:万元 (10000 yuan)

年 份 Year	生产总值(当年价格) Gross Domestic Product (Current Price)	第一产业 Primary Industry	第二产业 Secondary Industry	第三产业 Tertiary Industry	人均生产总值(元)(按户籍) Per Capita GDP (Household Registered)	人均生产总值(元)(按常住) Per Capita GDP (Long－term Registered)	生产总值指数(%) Indices of Gross Domestic product(%) (1978＝100)	第一产业 Primary Industry	第二产业 Secondary Industry	第三产业 Tertiary Industry
1978	141995	5215	106663	30117	1389	－	100	100	100	100
1979	167206	6527	126517	34162	1555	－	116.4	109.4	118.1	111.6
1980	208220	5943	159161	43116	1863	－	145.3	94.0	150.9	133.9
1981	229243	6165	171946	51132	2005	－	159.9	90.3	163.9	157.2
1982	248297	7327	183284	57686	2125	－	173.7	107.3	176.0	175.6
1983	282171	5938	200334	75899	2369	－	197.9	83.1	193.8	229.5
1984	353781	8469	244445	100867	2919	－	245.4	114.9	235.5	298.4
1985	448574	11233	293579	143762	3633	－	289.9	120.7	270.1	382.2
1986	513639	12245	324585	176809	4042	－	317.3	122.6	287.7	445.1
1987	605234	15408	370668	219158	4724	－	353.2	137.1	313.8	517.4
1988	708474	19602	425319	263553	5441	－	370.8	136.0	332.7	534.0
1989	772208	23869	435847	312492	5848	－	347.0	146.7	296.7	545.2
1990	896496	23919	470844	401733	6722	－	366.5	147.6	314.6	573.6
1991	1096628	25767	547949	522912	8158	－	426.0	151.4	356.3	691.1
1992	1413278	27611	712697	672969	10420	－	535.3	153.1	447.4	877.8
1993	2086571	36208	1052187	998176	15196	－	687.6	157.7	583.7	1117.4
1994	2788314	48257	1395127	1344931	19945	－	870.9	172.3	779.6	1335.3
1995	3697794	57784	1866784	1773226	25969	－	1041.6	183.5	945.7	1574.3
1996	4727377	110881	2356408	2260088	28552	－	1194.9	194.7	1103.6	1769.5
1997	5414265	130062	2630349	2653853	32227	－	1354.9	214.2	1230.3	2052.6
1998	5905726	134320	2786159	2985247	34620	－	1482.5	230.7	1337.2	2266.1
1999	6317335	145242	2915614	3256479	36394	－	1599.3	254.5	1431.1	2467.8
2000	7111586	145715	3278310	3687561	40127	－	1785.5	255.5	1596.7	2763.9
2001	12260891	582492	6026353	5652046	32607	－	2017.2	275.7	1805.3	3126.0
2002	14042278	605433	6901224	6535621	36640	－	2300.8	290.0	2038.6	3607.4
2003	16647332	665083	8343138	7639111	42675	－	2664.8	302.2	2448.4	4058.3
2004	20362738	664676	10368453	9329609	51241	－	3077.4	313.1	2873.9	4630.5
2005	23495459	732463	11582930	11180067	57934	－	3461.2	318.2	3141.5	5406.6
2006	27483121	755663	13254773	13472684	66731	51073	3955.9	320.5	3493.9	6399.6
2007	32738842	773208	15546960	16418675	78541	58907	4525.3	322.7	3948.4	7455.8
2008	38139834	830741	17926048	19383045	90400	66808	5018.5	324.8	4266.5	8505.2
2009	41086525	874987	17987776	22223762	96251	70418	5539.5	334.6	4539.5	9704.4
2010	47768030	941591	21358545	25467894	110541	78665	6198.7	339.3	5029.8	10975.7
2011	56297165	1054368	24746674	30496123	128656	89967	6818.5	345.7	5437.2	12281.8
2012	62711287	1128362	26276722	35306203	141597	99616	7432.2	353.0	5796.0	13657.4
2013	67258795	1123778	26756092	39378925	150089	105497	8011.9	350.8	6196.0	14845.6
2014	79773702	1563084	32020016	46190602	153152	112322	8668.9	353.7	6697.8	16107.5
2015	87219983	1628558	32394494	53196931	164886	121681	9570.5	358.2	7052.8	18475.2

1-07 全市生产总值指数(1978-2015年)

Indices of Gross Domestic Product (1978-2015)

(上年=100) (Preceding Year=100)

年 份 Year	生产总值 Gross Domestic Product	第一产业 Primary Industry	第二产业 Secondary Industry	第三产业 Tertiary Industry	人均生产总值(按户籍) Per Capita GDP (Household Registered)	人均生产总值(按常住) Per Capita GDP (Long-term Registered)
1978	120.2	119.1	123.7	111.6	119.0	
1979	113.3	114.2	114.0	110.0	112.1	
1980	119.7	92.5	132.5	118.8	118.4	
1981	113.6	102.9	114.0	124.2	112.6	
1982	107.2	119.4	103.2	108.6	105.9	
1983	111.2	89.1	114.3	124.7	109.9	
1984	122.7	121.2	120.8	129.0	121.6	
1985	119.4	99.9	122.6	124.4	118.2	
1986	111.5	103.7	111.5	116.2	110.3	
1987	112.8	102.5	114.0	115.1	111.3	
1988	107.4	97.8	109.8	105.4	105.8	
1989	96.9	99.8	94.4	102.4	95.8	
1990	105.8	106.4	106.5	103.7	104.9	
1991	118.1	104.4	116.6	126.8	117.3	
1992	122.9	100.3	129.5	121.7	122.1	
1993	130.1	105.9	137.8	123.3	129.1	
1994	126.3	108.1	132.2	122.0	125.2	
1995	119.9	107.1	123.5	117.9	118.8	
1996	113.0	105.4	114.6	112.2	112.0	
1997	113.1	106.8	112.7	114.8	112.1	
1998	111.2	109.4	111.8	110.7	110.5	
1999	110.2	105.5	110.1	111.0	109.4	
2000	112.0	105.7	112.5	112.1	111.1	
2001	112.2	107.4	112.7	112.5	111.1	
2002	113.2	104.1	113.3	114.7	111.8	
2003	115.2	106.0	118.6	112.6	114.0	
2004	115.0	105.1	116.7	114.3	113.7	
2005	113.0	103.4	111.1	116.4	111.5	
2006	114.3	104.1	112.6	117.4	113.0	
2007	114.6	102.2	114.3	116.2	113.6	112.0
2008	111.0	103.7	108.9	114.0	110.1	108.9
2009	110.0	103.1	106.0	114.5	109.1	108.2
2010	112.0	102.5	111.3	113.3	111.0	108.7
2011	110.1	102.5	108.7	112.0	109.1	107.6
2012	109.0	102.5	107.2	111.2	108.2	108.4
2013	108.0	101.4	107.0	109.3	107.1	107.3
2014	108.2	101.8	108.0	108.6	107.0	107.6
2015	110.2	101.7	105.5	114.6	108.9	109.1

注:1.本表按可比价格计算。

a) The indices in this table are calculated at comparable prices.

1-08 市区生产总值指数(1978-2015年)

Indices of Gross Domestic Product of Urban District (1978-2015)

(上年=100) (Preceding Year=100)

年份 Year	生产总值 Gross Domestic Product	第一产业 Primary Industry	第二产业 Secondary Industry	第三产业 Tertiary Industry	人均生产总值 (按户籍) Per Capita GDP (Household Registered)	人均生产总值 (按常住) Per Capita GDP (Long-term Registered)
1978	120.1	118.8	122.3	113.6	118.0	
1979	116.4	109.4	118.1	111.6	111.4	
1980	124.8	85.9	127.8	120.0	119.7	
1981	110.1	96.1	108.6	117.4	107.6	
1982	108.6	118.8	107.4	111.7	106.3	
1983	113.9	77.5	110.1	130.7	111.7	
1984	124.0	138.2	121.5	130.0	121.8	
1985	118.2	105.0	114.7	128.1	116.0	
1986	109.4	101.6	106.5	116.7	107.4	
1987	111.3	111.8	109.1	116.0	109.4	
1988	105.0	99.2	106.0	103.2	103.3	
1989	93.6	107.9	89.2	102.1	92.2	
1990	105.6	100.6	106.0	105.2	104.6	
1991	116.2	102.6	113.3	120.5	115.3	
1992	125.7	101.1	125.6	127.3	124.5	
1993	128.5	103.0	130.5	127.3	126.9	
1994	126.6	109.3	133.6	119.5	124.4	
1995	119.6	106.5	121.3	117.9	117.4	
1996	114.7	106.1	116.7	112.4	105.3	
1997	113.4	110.0	111.5	116.0	104.7	
1998	109.4	107.7	108.7	110.4	107.8	
1999	107.9	110.3	107.0	108.9	106.0	
2000	111.6	100.4	111.6	112.0	109.3	
2001	113.0	107.9	113.1	113.1	111.2	
2002	114.1	105.2	112.9	115.4	111.9	
2003	115.8	104.2	120.1	112.5	113.8	
2004	115.5	103.6	117.4	114.1	113.4	
2005	112.5	101.6	109.3	116.8	110.2	
2006	114.3	100.7	111.2	118.4	112.5	
2007	114.4	100.7	113.0	116.5	113.0	110.8
2008	110.9	100.7	108.1	114.1	109.5	108.0
2009	110.4	103.0	106.4	114.1	109.1	108.0
2010	111.9	101.4	110.8	113.1	110.5	107.5
2011	110.0	101.9	108.1	111.9	108.6	106.7
2012	109.0	102.1	106.6	111.2	107.7	108.4
2013	107.8	99.4	106.9	108.7	106.8	106.7
2014	108.2	100.8	108.1	108.5	106.7	107.6
2015	110.4	101.3	105.3	114.7	108.7	109.3

1－09 全市生产

Composition of

单位:万元

行业	Sector	全 Whole 2015	为上年(%) As Compared with the Preceding Year(%)
全市生产总值	Gross Domestic Product	100502079	110.2
农、林、牧、渔业	Farming, Forestry, Animal Husbandry & Fishery	2924013	101.8
工业	Industry	34978318	105.5
建筑业	Construction	4125377	105.6
批发和零售业	Wholesale & Retail Trades	8180184	102.6
交通运输、仓储和邮政业	Transportation, Storage and Post	2979176	108.2
住宿和餐饮业	Hotels and Catering Services	1647371	107.5
信息传输、软件和信息技术服务业	Information Transmission, Software and Information Technology	12782542	131.9
金融业	Financial Intermediation	9414736	112.0
房地产业	Real Estate	6132346	112.4
租赁和商务服务业	Leasing and Busyness Service	3139755	124.8
科学研究、技术服务业	Scientific Research, Technical Service	2516342	108.1
水利环境和公共设施管理业	Management of Water Conservancy, Enviroment and Public Facilities	708549	105.1
居民服务、修理和其他服务业	Services to Households, Repair and other services	1266635	117.2
教育	Education	3079443	110.3
卫生和社会工作	Health Care and Social Work	2023950	117.9
文化、体育和娱乐业	Culture, Sports and Entertainment	1322511	137.4
公共管理、社会保障和社会组织	Public Management, Social Security and Social Organizations	3280831	113.0
第一产业	Primary Industry	2879492	101.7
第二产业	Secondary Industry	39090099	105.5
第三产业	Tertiary Industry	58532488	114.6

总值构成(2015 年)

Gross Domestic Product(2015)

(10000 yuan)

市 City		#市 区 Urban District			
比 重 (%) Proportion(%)		2015	为上年(%) As Compared with the Preceding Year(%)	比 重 (%) Proportion(%)	
2015	2014			2015	2014
100	100	87219983	110.4	100	100
2.9	3.0	1658676	101.4	1.9	2.0
34.8	37.1	28952807	105.4	33.2	35.6
4.1	4.7	3450168	104.4	4.0	4.6
8.1	8.5	7089513	101.6	8.1	8.6
3.0	3.0	2396221	106.9	2.7	2.8
1.6	1.6	1342780	105.4	1.5	1.6
12.7	10.4	12266616	131.9	14.1	11.5
9.4	9.6	8754371	111.7	10.0	10.3
6.1	6.1	5574277	113.1	6.4	6.4
3.1	2.7	2915391	124.5	3.3	2.9
2.5	2.5	2457581	108.1	2.8	2.8
0.7	0.7	629002	104.4	0.7	0.7
1.3	1.2	1047719	114.5	1.2	1.1
3.1	3.0	2735548	111.5	3.1	3.0
2.0	1.8	1847520	119.1	2.1	1.9
1.3	1.0	1254970	137.3	1.4	1.1
3.3	3.1	2846823	113.8	3.3	3.1
2.9	3.0	1628558	101.3	1.9	2.0
38.9	41.8	32394494	105.3	37.1	40.1
58.2	55.2	53196931	114.7	61.0	57.9

1－10 地区生产总值(2015 年)

Gross Domestic Product (2015)

单位:万元　　(10000 yuan)

地　区	Region	生产总值 Gross Domestic Product	第一产业 Primary Industry	第二产业 Secondary Industry	工　业 Industry	建筑业 Construction	第三产业 Tertiary Industry	户籍人口人均 GDP(元) Per Capita GDP (yuan) (Household Registered)	常住人口人均 GDP(元) Per Capita GDP (Long－term Registered)
全　市	**Whole City**	**100502079**	**2879492**	**39090099**	**34978318**	**4125377**	**58532488**	**139653**	**112230**
市　区	Urban District	87219983	1628558	32394494	28952807	3450168	53196931	164886	121681
#上城区	Shangcheng	8482025	－	3541784	3372607	169179	4940241	257960	240386
下城区	Xiacheng	7619880	－	424128	188912	235269	7195753	188535	142521
江干区	Jianggan	4938851	4869	1273302	618002	655481	3660680	124971	69852
拱墅区	Gongshu	4244220	－	868875	693832	175100	3375345	128575	74656
西湖区	Xihu	8878113	43005	1025825	630961	395130	7809284	136339	109952
高新(滨江)区	Hi－Tech (Binjiang)	7735050	14402	3973170	3812540	160722	3747479	390399	234431
萧山区	Xiaoshan	18127888	638480	9200966	8473528	730118	8288442	143946	116841
余杭区	Yuhang	12397057	469595	4611442	4196522	416980	7316020	132146	100357
富阳区	Fuyang	6451465	423572	3199297	2934656	267622	2828596	96726	88273
桐庐县	Tonglu	3344754	228557	1817277	1654178	164934	1298920	81801	80229
淳安县	Chun'an	2074215	320370	770033	608312	162471	983813	45169	59974
建德市	Jiande	3187469	304848	1660233	1510862	150648	1222388	62599	72049
临安市	Lin'an	4675658	397159	2448061	2252159	197156	1830438	88291	80345

1－11 分地区生产总值(主要年份)
Gross Domestic Product by Region (Main Years)

单位:万元　　(10000 yuan)

地　区	Region	2000	2005	2010	2011	2012	2013	2014	2015
全　市	**Whole City**	**13825616**	**29438430**	**59657106**	**70372782**	**78336168**	**83985753**	**92061634**	**100502079**
市　区	Urban District	7111586	23495459	47768030	56297165	62711287	67258795	79773702	87219983
#上城区	Shangcheng		2564579	5258963	6133492	6644749	7389318	8005940	8482025
下城区	Xiacheng		1981140	4515546	5319752	5873718	6400548	6898798	7619880
江干区	Jianggan		1155829	2970781	3478363	3957866	4289933	4566848	4938851
拱墅区	Gongshu		1607349	2942067	3467376	3894365	3764825	3939940	4244220
西湖区	Xihu		2084152	4758469	5677027	6372300	7008109	8020086	8878113
高新(滨江)区	Hi－Tech (Binjiang)		1376799	3439684	4246699	4880188	6073310	6930324	7735050
萧山区	Xiaoshan	2265882	5904071	12155961	14413914	16090498	16592205	17276336	18127888
余杭区	Yuhang	1370571	2883710	6562136	7689302	8718372	9800819	11012328	12397057
富阳区	Fuyang	998087	2006472	4121151	4878795	5377572	5668246	6014722	6451465
桐庐县	Tonglu	506572	1027441	1952611	2308431	2549395	2742048	3061292	3344754
淳安县	Chun'an	308140	584804	1178678	1407623	1603247	1736807	1920615	2074215
建德市	Jiande	589536	982458	1871486	2214747	2448213	2677482	2989338	3187469
临安市	Lin'an	675242	1341795	2765150	3266021	3646455	3902375	4316686	4675658

1－12 分地区第一产业增加值(主要年份)
Value Added of Primary Industry by Region(Main Years)

单位:万元 (10000 yuan)

地 区	Region	2000	2005	2010	2011	2012	2013	2014	2015
全 市	**Whole City**	**1039641**	**1482145**	**2084144**	**2367708**	**2551127**	**2615974**	**2743492**	**2879492**
市 区	Urban District	145715	732463	941591	1054368	1128362	1123778	1563084	1628558
#上城区	Shangcheng		－	－	－	－	－	－	－
下城区	Xiacheng		4902	－	－	－	－	－	－
江干区	Jianggan		25293	9556	8593	7327	6303	5573	4869
拱墅区	Gongshu		7019	2912	2004	614	－	－	－
西湖区	Xihu		40555	38686	42528	44853	43185	42407	43005
高新(滨江)区	Hi－Tech (Binjiang)		19785	16945	18236	18343	17320	17074	14402
萧山区	Xiaoshan	219040	335323	472211	528775	567823	584638	615991	638480
余杭区	Yuhang	175807	267280	384518	436754	471892	455379	455424	469595
富阳区	Fuyang	122071	182959	286661	331636	359913	379042	399288	423572
桐庐县	Tonglu	72156	107813	160028	183348	197441	206463	217828	228557
淳安县	Chun'an	87428	132422	218432	248773	270778	283787	301077	320370
建德市	Jiande	101328	157794	207552	238574	258136	270044	286495	304848
临安市	Lin'an	116096	168694	269880	311009	336497	352860	375008	397159

1－13　分地区第二产业增加值(主要年份)

Value Added of Secondary Industry by Region(Main Years)

单位:万元　　　　(10000 yuan)

地　区	Region	2000	2005	2010	2011	2012	2013	2014	2015
全　市	**Whole City**	**7093233**	**14943581**	**28198060**	**32805209**	**35001330**	**35742503**	**38455759**	**39090099**
市　区	Urban District	3278310	11582930	21358545	24746674	26276722	26756092	32020016	32394494
#上城区	Shangcheng		1383279	2328599	2748958	2920974	3323176	3555001	3541784
下城区	Xiacheng		457613	503515	528663	548891	519853	507846	424128
江干区	Jianggan		530387	1023232	1165033	1232278	1282251	1333886	1273302
拱墅区	Gongshu		1010185	1195898	1379983	1483426	1082440	989683	868875
西湖区	Xihu		597190	927948	1034458	1016631	1038356	1058316	1025825
高新(滨江)区	Hi－Tech (Binjiang)		816751	1633267	1961196	2188350	2990393	3680504	3973170
萧山区	Xiaoshan	1330688	3833572	7399022	8708660	9559330	9352948	9282655	9200966
余杭区	Yuhang	757169	1637762	3347711	3774134	4003780	4179815	4412453	4611442
富阳区	Fuyang	606480	1208899	2487569	2927977	3155766	3159057	3165902	3199297
桐庐县	Tonglu	283853	635743	1190528	1388187	1485433	1549978	1721284	1817277
淳安县	Chun'an	120712	220748	509526	612506	685730	711833	762658	770033
建德市	Jiande	344485	546726	1048611	1240160	1332896	1438668	1612988	1660233
临安市	Lin'an	371536	748535	1603281	1889706	2064784	2126875	2338814	2448061

1－14 分地区工业增加值(主要年份)

Value Added of Industry by Region(Main Years)

单位:万元 (10000 yuan)

地 区	Region	2000	2005	2010	2011	2012	2013	2014	2015
全 市	**Whole City**	**6084690**	**13263991**	**24532551**	**28900944**	**30933324**	**31564031**	**34148954**	**34978318**
市 区	Urban District	2627121	10221817	18363679	21599838	22997710	23420616	28375206	28952807
#上城区	Shangcheng		1251279	2138350	2567662	2723855	3135606	3369525	3372607
下城区	Xiacheng		352252	244306	264258	266569	257694	204456	188912
江干区	Jianggan		389088	461192	545880	563358	611014	636701	618002
拱墅区	Gongshu		923082	1059215	1232797	1326480	911180	806021	693832
西湖区	Xihu		366200	490551	563256	592165	599273	624695	630961
高新(滨江)区	Hi－Tech (Binjiang)		702955	1429247	1730844	1921883	2737768	3499731	3812540
萧山区	Xiaoshan	1220140	3578182	6821499	8076434	8889277	8685228	8526903	8473528
余杭区	Yuhang	668625	1445060	2995855	3397253	3595182	3754685	4008284	4196522
富阳区	Fuyang	581464	1121971	2298470	2711715	2931055	2921956	2917814	2934656
桐庐县	Tonglu	256912	584116	1057999	1244325	1336037	1388339	1556780	1654178
淳安县	Chun'an	91804	171216	388588	471183	534696	551863	582588	608312
建德市	Jiande	308654	485699	956561	1137197	1226161	1322121	1471828	1510862
临安市	Lin'an	329971	679171	1467252	1736687	1907666	1959136	2162550	2252159

1－15 分地区第三产业增加值(主要年份)

Value Added of Tertiary Industry by Region(Main Years)

单位:万元 (10000 yuan)

地 区	Region	2000	2005	2010	2011	2012	2013	2014	2015
全 市	**Whole City**	**5692742**	**13012704**	**29374902**	**35199865**	**40783711**	**45627276**	**50862382**	**58532488**
市 区	Urban District	3687561	11180067	25467894	30496123	35306203	39378925	46190602	53196931
#上城区	Shangcheng		1181299	2930364	3384534	3723775	4066142	4450938	4940241
下城区	Xiacheng		1518625	4012031	4791089	5324827	5880696	6390952	7195753
江干区	Jianggan		600150	1937993	2304736	2718262	3001379	3227389	3660680
拱墅区	Gongshu		590144	1743257	2085389	2410325	2682385	2950257	3375345
西湖区	Xihu		1446406	3791835	4600041	5310815	5926567	6919363	7809284
高新(滨江)区	Hi－Tech (Binjiang)		540263	1789472	2267267	2673495	3065597	3232746	3747479
萧山区	Xiaoshan	716154	1735176	4284727	5176479	5963345	6654619	7377691	8288442
余杭区	Yuhang	437595	978669	2829907	3478414	4242701	5165626	6144452	7316020
富阳区	Fuyang	269536	614613	1346921	1619182	1861893	2130147	2449532	2828596
桐庐县	Tonglu	150563	283885	602055	736897	866521	985608	1122181	1298920
淳安县	Chun'an	100000	231634	450720	546344	646739	741187	856881	983813
建德市	Jiande	143724	277938	615323	736013	857181	968770	1089854	1222388
临安市	Lin'an	187610	424566	891989	1065305	1245174	1422640	1602864	1830438

1－16　主要指标占全省比重(2015年)

Proportion of Main Indicators in Whole Province(2015)

指　标 Item		全　省 Zhejiang Province	杭州市 Hangzhou City	杭州市占全省(%) Proportion of Hangzhou in Zhejiang(%)
年末常住人口 Long－term Residents(End of 2013)	(万人) (10000 persons)	5539.00	901.80	16.3
年末户籍人口 Household Registration Population(End of 2013)	(万人) (10000 persons)	4873.34	723.55	14.8
#城镇人口 Urban Population	(万人) (10000 persons)	2501.97	495.38	19.8
年末就业人员数 Total Number of Employed Persons	(万人) (10000 persons)	3733.15	663.03	17.8
生产总值 Gross Domestic Product	(亿元) (100 million yuan)	42886.49	10050.21	23.4
第一产业 Primary Industry	(亿元) (100 million yuan)	1832.80	287.95	15.7
第二产业 Secondary Industry	(亿元) (100 million yuan)	19707.09	3909.01	19.8
第三产业 Tertiary Industry	(亿元) (100 million yuan)	21346.60	5853.25	27.4
常住人均生产总值 Per Capita GDP of Long－term Residents	(元) (yuan)	77644	112230	－
农林牧渔业总产值 Gross Output Value of Farming, Forestry, Animal Husbandry and Fishery	(亿元) (100 million yuan)	2933.44	440.41	15.0
主要农产品产量 Output of Major Farm Products				
#粮食 Grain	(万吨) (10000 tons)	752.20	63.38	8.4
蚕茧 Silk－worm Cocoons	(万吨) (10000 tons)	4.02	1.04	25.9
生猪年末存栏 Hogs in Stock at Year End	(万头) (10000 heads)	730.19	156.82	21.5
肉类产量 Output of Meat	(万吨) (10000 tons)	106.33	27.84	26.2
淡水产品总产量 Freshwater Aquatic products	(万吨) (10000 tons)	110.80	17.89	16.1

1-16 续表1 continued 1

指 标 Item		全 省 Zhejiang Province	杭州市 Hangzhou City	杭州市占全省(%) Proportion of Hangzhou in Zhejiang(%)
规模以上工业增加值 Value-added of Industrial Enterprises above Designated Size	(亿元) (100 million yuan)	13193.35	2875.05	21.8
规模以上工业企业利税总额 Total Pre-tax Profits of Industrial Enterprises above Designed Size	(亿元) (100 million yuan)	6575.72	1559.68	23.7
主要工业产品产量 Output of Major Industrial Products				
#发电量 Electricity	(亿千瓦时) (100 million kwh)	2905.26	189.21	6.5
氢氧化钠(烧碱)(折100%) Caustic Soda(100% discount)	(万吨) (10000 tons)	153.19	18.68	12.2
碳酸钠(纯碱) Soda Ash	(万吨) (10000 tons)	29.35	29.35	100.0
合成氨 Synthetic Ammonia	(万吨) (10000 tons)	75.07	20.44	27.2
水泥 Cement	(万吨) (10000 tons)	11286.51	1819.54	16.1
钢材 Steels	(万吨) (10000 tons)	4047.72	780.21	19.3
化学纤维 Chemical Fiber	(万吨) (10000 tons)	2186.42	669.64	30.6
纱 Yarn	(万吨) (10000 tons)	220.04	71.62	32.5
自行车 Bicycles	(万辆) (10000 units)	1028.82	262.56	25.5
彩色电视机 Colour TV Sets	(万台) (10000 units)	641.36	6.24	1.0
电冰箱 Household Refrigerator	(万台) (10000 units)	713.66	107.59	15.1
洗衣机 Washing Machine	(万台) (10000 units)	1526.56	311.76	20.4
客运量 Volume of Passenger Transport	(万人次) (10000 person-times)	113315	23942	21.1

1－16　续表2　continued 2

指　标 Item	全　省 Zhejiang Province	杭州市 Hangzhou City	杭州市占全省(%) Proportion of Hangzhou in Zhejiang(%)
货运量 (万吨) Volume of Goods Transport (10000 tons)	200710	29384	14.6
固定资产投资 (亿元) Investment in Fixed Assets (100 million yuan)	26664.72	5556.32	20.8
社会消费品零售总额 (亿元) Total Retail Sales of Consumer Goods (100 million yuan)	19784.74	4697.23	23.7
出口额 (亿美元) Total Exports (100 million USD)	2763.32	500.67	18.1
实际利用外资 (亿美元) Foreign Capital Actually Used (100 million USD)	169.60	71.13	41.9
境外旅游者人数 (万人次) Number of International Tourists (10000 person－times)	1012.04	341.56	33.8
财政总收入 (亿元) Total Financial Revenue (100 million yuan)	8549.05	2238.75	26.2
#地方一般公共预算收入 (亿元) Financial Revenue of Local Government (100 million yuan)	4809.53	1233.88	25.7
一般公共预算支出 (亿元) Financial Expenditure (100 million yuan)	6648.09	1205.48	18.1
金融机构存款余额(本外币) (亿元) Deposits of Financial Institutions (100 million yuan)	90301.61	29863.83	33.1
金融机构贷款余额(本外币) (亿元) Loans of Financial Institutions (100 million yuan)	76466.32	23327.95	30.5
住户存款余额 (亿元) Household Deposit (100 million yuan)	34787.31	7617.75	21.9
非私营单位就业人员平均工资 (元) Average Wage of Employed Persons of Non－private Units (yuan)	66668	76073	－
全体居民人均可支配收入 (元) Per Capita Annual Disposable Income of Urban and Rural Residents (yuan)	35537	42642	－
城镇居民人均可支配收入 (元) Per Capita Annual Disposable Income of Urban Residents (yuan)	43714	48316	－
农村居民人均可支配收入 (元) Per Capita Annual Disposable Income of Rural Residents (yuan)	21125	25719	－
高等学校在校学生数 (万人) Number of Institutions of Higher Education (10000 persons)	105.47	47.56	45.1
普通中学在校学生数 (万人) Number of Secondary Schools (10000 persons)	225.27	32.13	14.3
小学在校学生数 (万人) Number of Primary Schools (10000 persons)	356.99	52.45	14.7

1－17 国民经济主要指标人均水平(主要年份)

Major Per Capita Indicators of National Economy(Main Years)

指　标 Item	1995	2000	2005	2010	2011	2012	2013	2014	2015
全市生产总值 (元) Gross Domestic Product (yuan)	12797	22342	44871	70024	80689	89323	95190	103813	112230
规模以上工业总产值 (元) Gross Industrial Output Value above Designatted Size (yuan)	17131	24943	82936	130064	141634	147773	106639	144937	138645
农林牧渔业总产值 (元) Gross Output Value of Farming, Forestry, Animal Husbandry and Fishery (yuan)	1673	2467	3345	3713	4094	4382	4526	4720	4918
社会消费品零售总额 (元) Total Retail Sales of Consumer Goods (yuan)	5027	8317	14869	26117	30845	36091	43804	47378	52454
财政总收入 (元) Financial Revenue (yuan)	926	2308	7938	14618	17071	18562	19664	21652	25000
#地方一般公共预算收入 (元) General Public Budgetary Revenue of Local Government (yuan)	387	1118	3818	7880	9002	9806	10713	11585	13779
一般公共预算支出 (元) General Public Budgetary Expenditure (yuan)	418	1187	3633	7237	8571	8966	9699	10839	13462
全体居民可支配收入 (元) Annual Disposable Income of Urban and Rural Residents (yuan)	-	-	-	-	-	-	35763	39237	42642
全体居民消费性支出 (元) Annual Living Expendituer of Urban and Ruarual Residents (yuan)	-	-	-	-	-	-	26827	28492	30181
城镇居民可支配收入 (元) Annual Disposable Income of Urban Residents (yuan)	6301	9668	16601	30035	34065	37511	40925	44632	48316
城镇居民消费性支出 (元) Annual Living Expenditure of Urban Residents (yuan)	5559	7790	13438	20219	22642	22800	30659	32165	33818
农村居民可支配收入 (元) Annual Disposable Income of Rural Residents (yuan)	3012	4894	7655	13186	15245	17017	21208	23555	25719
农村居民消费性支出 (元) Annual Living Expenditure of Rural Residents (yuan)	2373	3393	6004	10267	12125	13612	16021	17816	19334

1-18 气　象
Meteorological

指　标		Item		市区 Urban District	萧山区 Xiaoshan
一、气　温		**The Atmospheric Temperature**			
全年平均气温	（度）	Annual Average Temperature	（℃）	17.5	17.6
极端最高气温	（度）	The Highest Temperature of the Year	（℃）	39.1	39.6
出现日期	（日/月）	Date	（d/m）	5/8	5/8
极端最低气温	（度）	The Lowest Temperature of the Year	（℃）	-2.2	-2.4
出现日期	（日/月）	Date	（d/m）	10/2	10/2
二、降　雨		**Rainfall**			
本年降雨日数	（日）	Total Rainy Days	（day）	169	171
全年降雨总量	（毫米）	Annual Rainfall	（millimeters）	2131.9	1927.4
最长连续降雨日数	（日）	Longest Consecutive Days of Rain	（day）	10	10
最长连续降雨总量	（毫米）	Rainfall	（millimeters）	201.1	187.3
最长连续降雨起止日期	（日/月）	Start/End	（d/m）	4-13/7	4-13/7
日最大降雨量	（毫米）	Maximum Daily Rainfall	（millimeters）	102.4	69.4
出现日期	（日/月）	Date	（d/m）	8/6	8/6
三、全年日照总时数	**（小时）**	**Total Sunshine Hours**	**（hours）**	**1315.8**	**1307.3**
四、降　霜		**Frost**			
全年降霜日数	（日）	Annual Frost Days	（day）	15	18
初霜日期	（日/月）	Start Date	（d/m）	14/11/2014	2/12/2014
终霜日期	（日/月）	End Date	（d/m）	2/3	11/3
五、降　雪		**Snow**			
全年降雪日数	（日）	Annual Frost Days	（day）	6	10
初雪日期	（日/月）	Start Date	（d/m）	28/1	6/1
终雪日期	（日/月）	End Date	（d/m）	5/3	5/3

概　　况(2015 年)
Conditions by Region(2015)

富阳区 Fuyang	桐庐县 Tonglu	淳安县 Chun'an	建德市 Jiande	临安市 Lin'an
17.4	17.4	17.7	17.4	16.5
38.0	38.8	38.1	38.8	37.9
5/8	4/8	4/8	6/8	4/8
-3.5	-4.2	-1.3	-3.8	-5.7
10/2	10/2	10/2	2/1	2/1、10/2
174	175	168	181	164
2022.6	1970.9	2015.1	2069.2	1992.8
10(两次)	9	9	15	8
226.8、111.8	143.2	164.8	153.0	171.3
4-13/7、16-25/11	20-28/2	20-28/2	20/2-6/3	4-11/7
84.1	66.6	81.1	84.3	99.8
8/6	8/6	8/11	8/11	8/6
1453.5	**1200.2**	**1503.9**	**1291.5**	**1437.4**
15	24	9	23	26
5/12/2014	4/12/2014	17/12/2014	5/12/2014	2/12/2014
10/2	13/2	11/2	2/3	11/3
7	10	5	4	12
28/1	7/1	1/2	7/1	6/1
5/3	5/3	5/3	4/3	5/3

1－19　市区分月气象概况(2015 年)

Monthly Meteorological Conditions in Urban District(2015)

月　份	Month	平均气温(度) Average Temperature(℃)	日照时数(小时) Sunshine Hours(hours)	降雨天数(天) Rainfall Days (day)	降水量(毫米) Precipitation(mm)
全　年	**Whole Year**	**17.5**	**1315.8**	**169**	**2131.9**
1　月	January	6.7	107.4	11	66.9
2　月	February	7.7	95.3	12	147.1
3　月	March	11.7	112.2	16	157.6
4　月	April	17.3	164.5	13	206.5
5　月	May	22.2	122.3	14	115.4
6　月	June	25.1	72.9	16	330.8
7　月	July	26.6	128.6	18	349.5
8　月	August	27.7	151.5	14	268.0
9　月	September	24.0	108.1	11	121.0
10　月	October	19.5	136.4	10	47.9
11　月	November	13.4	47.2	21	212.4
12　月	December	7.9	69.4	13	108.8

主要统计指标解释

地区生产总值(GDP) 指一个国家(或地区)所有常住单位在一定时期内生产活动的最终成果。地区生产总值有三种表现形态,即价值形态、收入形态和产品形态。从价值形态看,它是所有常住单位在一定时期内生产的全部货物和服务价值超过同期投入的全部非固定资产货物和服务价值的差额,即所有常住单位的增加值之和;从收入形态看,它是所有常住单位在一定时期内创造并分配给常住单位和非常住单位的初次收入分配之和;从产品形态看,它是所有常住单位在一定时期内最终使用的货物和服务价值与货物减去进出口货物和服务。在实际核算中,生产总值有三种计算方法,即生产法、收入法和支出法。三种方法分别从不同的方面反映生产总值及其构成。

三次产业 是根据社会生产活动历史发展的顺序对产业结构的划分,产品直接取自自然界的部门称为第一产业,对初级产品进行再加工的部门称为第二产业,为生产和消费提供各种服务的部门称为第三产业。它是世界上较为通用的产业结构分类,但各国的划分不尽一致。2012 年前的三次产业划分标准按照当年《统计年鉴》,从 2013 年起,三次产业划分调整为:

第一产业是指农、林、牧、渔业(不含农、林、牧、渔服务业)。

第二产业是指工业[采矿业(不含开采辅助活动),制造业(不含金属制品、机械和设备修理业),电力、热力、燃气及水生产和供应业]和建筑业。

第三产业即服务业,是指除第一产业、第二产业以外的其他行业。

降水量 从天空降落到地面的液态或固态(经融化后)降水,未经蒸发、渗透、流失而在水平面上积聚的深度。降水量以毫米为单位。

空气的温度(简称气温) 表示空气冷热程度的物理量。

日照时数 太阳在一地实际照射地面的时数。

Explanatory Notes on Main Statistical Indicators

Gross Domestic Product（GDP） refers to the final products of all resident units in a country (or a region) during a certain period of time. Gross domestic product is expressed in three different forms, i. e. value, income, and products respectively. The form of value refers to the total value of all products and services produced by all resident units during a certain period of time minus total value of intermediate input of materials and services of the nature of non – fixed assets or the summation of the value – added of all resident units; the form of income includes all the income created by all resident units and distributed primarily to all resident and non – resident units; the form of products refers to the value of all final goods and services for final use by all resident units minus imports of goods and services during a given period of time. In the practice of national accounting, gross domestic product is calculated with three approaches, i. e. production approach, income approach, and expenditure approach, which reflect gross domestic product and its composition from different aspects.

Three Industries Industry structure has been classified according to the historical sequence of development. Primary industry refers to extraction of natural resources; secondary industry involves processing of primary products; and tertiary industry provides services of various kinds for production and consumption. The above classification is universal although it varies to someextent from country to country. The explanatory notes on Three Industries were available on Hangzhou Statistical Yearbook of the year before 2012, and the indicators of Three lndustry have been revised according to the national standards since 2013.

Primary Industry refers to argriculture, forestry, animal husbandry and fishery industries (excluding their service activities).

Second Industry refers to industry [mining and quarrying (excluding its support activities), manufacturing (excluding the repair services of metal product, machine and equipment), production and supply of electricity, heat, water and gas] and construction.

Tertiary Industry is the service industry, refers to all other economic acitivities not included in the primary or secondary industries.

Precipitation refers to the depth of rainfall onto the ground (as well as liquefied from solid forms) from above the air prior to its vaporization, seepage, running off.

It is calculated in the unit of millimeter (mm).

Air Temperature refers to the physical quantity reflecting the extent of coldness and hotness of the air.

Duration of sunshine refers to the real time for the ground to receive sunshine at a certain place.

二、人口和就业人员

POPULATION AND EMPLOYMENT

2 人口和就业人员
Population and Employment

主要统计指标
Major Statistical Indicators

年末常住人口	Long-term Residents	901.80	万人	(10, 000 persons)
为上年	As Compared with the Preceding Year	101.4	%	(%)
年末户籍登记户数	Total Registration Households(year-end)	225.79	万户	(10, 000 Subscribers)
为上年	As Compared with the Preceding Year	101.5	%	(%)
年末户籍登记人口	Total Registration Population(year-end)	723.55	万人	(10, 000 persons)
为上年	As Compared with the Preceding Year	101.1	%	(%)
# 男性	Male	360.68	万人	(10, 000 persons)
为上年	As Compared with the Preceding Year	101.0	%	(%)
# 城镇人口	Urban Population	495.38	万人	(10, 000 persons)
人口自然增长率	Natural Growth Rate	4.21	‰	(‰)
年末就业人员	Number of Employed Persons(year-end)	663.03	万人	(10, 000 persons)
为上年	As Compared with the Preceding Year	101.2	%	(%)

2-01 历次普查常住人口情况

Long-term Residents in the Past Population Census

单位:万人　　(10000 person)

地区	Region	第一次人口普查 1953.7.1 the First Population Census (1953.7.1)	第二次人口普查 1964.7.1 the Second Population Census (1964.7.1)	第三次人口普查 1982.7.1 the Third Population Census (1982.7.1)	第四次人口普查 1990.7.1 the Fourth Population Census (1991.7.1)	第五次人口普查 2000.11.1 the Fifth Population Census (2000.11.1)	第六次人口普查 2010.11.1 the Sixth Population Census (2010.11.1)
杭州市	**Hangzhou**	**301.13**	**421.90**	**526.05**	**583.21**	**687.87**	**870.04**
市　区	Urban District	201.48	283.31	359.90	404.83	513.09	695.97
上城区	Shangcheng				21.10	33.51	34.46
下城区	Xiacheng				25.66	41.24	52.61
江干区	Jianggan				36.12	56.54	99.88
拱墅区	Gongshu				29.34	42.93	55.19
西湖区	Xihu				35.40	59.33	82.00
高新(滨江)区	Hi-Tech(Binjiang)					11.59	31.90
萧山区	Xiaoshan	56.32	82.34	106.11	113.06	123.33	151.13
余杭区	Yuhang	52.28	64.96	80.50	86.08	81.77	117.03
富阳区	Fuyang	29.22	39.66	54.13	58.07	62.86	71.77
桐庐县	Tonglu	19.73	26.20	34.83	37.66	37.81	40.64
淳安县	Chun'an	27.49	38.66	42.03	43.55	38.23	33.68
建德市	Jiande	26.42	38.15	43.64	47.63	47.31	43.08
临安市	Lin'an	26.01	35.57	45.65	49.55	51.42	56.67

注:历年普查市区口径均已按现行行政辖区调整。

a) The data of the past population censuses in urban district were adjusted according to the current administrative division.

2-02 全市户籍人口和总户数(1978-2015年)
Registered Population and Households(1978-2015)

年份 Year	总户数 (万户) Total Households (10000 households)	总人口数 (万人) Total Population (10000 persons)	城镇人口(万人) Urban Population (10000 persons)	按性别分 By Sex 男(万人) Male (10000 persons)	女(万人) Female (10000 persons)
1978	117.89	505.55	116.06	260.74	244.81
1979	116.61	511.83	124.60	263.97	247.86
1980	119.11	515.53	128.88	266.02	249.51
1981	125.96	520.73	134.56	268.69	252.04
1982	131.53	528.06	139.94	272.72	255.34
1983	135.55	533.06	143.34	275.64	257.41
1984	139.24	537.49	147.46	278.04	259.45
1985	145.23	543.05	153.46	281.11	261.94
1986	151.59	549.53	157.19	284.57	264.96
1987	157.66	557.63	161.12	288.70	268.93
1988	164.41	565.04	164.87	292.21	272.83
1989	169.09	570.98	167.28	295.15	275.83
1990	171.94	574.78	169.00	297.02	277.76
1991	174.78	578.73	171.25	298.85	279.88
1992	177.68	582.40	174.03	300.63	281.77
1993	179.17	587.10	179.11	303.03	284.07
1994	180.65	592.93	186.50	306.00	286.93
1995	182.55	597.96	191.43	308.25	289.71
1996	184.33	603.22	196.68	310.76	292.46
1997	186.28	607.96	204.39	313.02	294.94
1998	187.80	611.64	210.52	314.69	296.95
1999	191.60	616.05	219.05	316.63	299.42
2000	193.48	621.58	227.00	319.09	302.49
2001	195.56	629.14	237.77	322.78	306.36
2002	198.27	636.81	252.02	326.62	310.19
2003	201.12	642.78	263.67	329.04	313.74
2004	204.52	651.68	282.58	332.62	319.06
2005	207.42	660.45	297.54	336.12	324.33
2006	209.91	666.31	309.78	338.23	328.08
2007	211.99	672.35	323.75	340.50	331.85
2008	213.74	677.64	340.76	342.45	335.19
2009	215.28	683.38	354.48	344.51	338.87
2010	216.51	689.12	365.24	346.56	342.56
2011	218.26	695.71	376.03	349.09	346.62
2012	218.95	700.52	384.09	350.90	349.62
2013	220.66	706.61	393.88	353.32	353.29
2014	222.35	715.76	404.27	357.26	358.50
2015	225.79	723.55	495.38	360.68	362.87

注:1. 按公安户籍人口统计。
2. 城镇人口 2015 年前为非农业人口。
a) Figures in this table are based on the household registered statistics which published by Public Security Bureau.
b) Since 2015, the donotation of Non-agriculture Population has been adjusted to Urban Population.

2－03　市区户籍人口和总户数(1978－2015 年)
Registered Population and Households of Urban District(1978－2015)

年　份 Year	总户数 (万户) Total Households (10000 households)	总人口数 (万人) Total Population (10000 persons)	城镇人口(万人) Urban Population (10000 persons)	按性别分 By Sex 男(万人) Male (10000 persons)	女(万人) Female (10000 persons)
1978	25.52	104.53	78.73	53.95	50.58
1979	26.23	110.50	85.05	57.09	53.41
1980	27.23	113.08	87.93	58.56	54.52
1981	29.88	115.59	90.53	59.96	55.63
1982	31.24	118.05	92.72	61.28	56.77
1983	32.69	120.13	94.94	62.43	57.70
1984	34.07	122.29	97.34	63.63	58.66
1985	35.36	124.67	100.01	64.96	59.71
1986	37.02	127.07	102.59	66.29	60.78
1987	38.70	129.16	104.09	67.38	61.78
1988	40.05	131.26	107.30	68.46	62.80
1989	41.19	132.84	108.88	69.28	63.56
1990	42.26	133.89	109.97	69.75	64.14
1991	42.98	134.97	111.20	70.33	64.64
1992	43.63	136.30	112.70	71.08	65.22
1993	44.55	138.33	115.13	72.22	66.11
1994	45.04	141.27	118.48	73.82	67.45
1995	46.06	143.52	121.38	74.91	68.61
1996	52.39	166.73	128.76	87.15	79.58
1997	53.14	169.29	131.76	88.53	80.76
1998	53.92	171.89	134.62	89.86	82.03
1999	54.64	175.27	139.29	91.65	83.62
2000	55.34	179.18	143.69	93.64	85.54
2001	115.81	379.49	193.26	194.59	184.90
2002	117.11	387.01	205.98	198.47	188.54
2003	119.01	393.19	216.13	201.14	192.05
2004	120.56	401.59	233.08	204.43	197.16
2005	122.02	409.52	245.56	207.70	201.82
2006	123.31	414.18	256.42	209.45	204.73
2007	124.40	419.50	269.30	211.59	207.91
2008	125.56	424.30	285.11	213.54	210.76
2009	126.92	429.44	297.83	215.56	213.88
2010	128.43	434.82	307.52	217.65	217.16
2011	130.14	440.34	317.63	219.86	220.48
2012	131.48	445.43	325.50	221.99	223.43
2013	133.27	450.82	334.38	224.24	226.58
2014	157.11	525.07	358.56	261.17	263.90
2015	160.47	532.86	421.60	264.71	268.15

注:1. 市区数据从 2001 年起包括萧山区和余杭区,2014 年起含富阳区。
2. 城镇人口 2015 年前为非农业人口。
a) Figures in this table include Xiaoshan and Yuhang district since 2001, and include Fuyang district since 2014.
b) Since 2015, the donotation of Non－agriculture Population has been adjusted to Urban Population.

2－04 分地区户籍人口和总户数(2015 年末)

Registered Population and Households by Region(End of 2015)

地　区 Region	总户数 (户) Total Households (household)	总人口数 (人) Total Population (person)	城镇人口(人) Urban Population (person)	按性别分 By Sex 男(人) Male (person)	女(人) Female (person)
全　市 Whole City	**2257933**	**7235545**	**4953778**	**3606837**	**3628708**
市　区 Urban District	1604743	5328628	4215954	2647142	2681486
上城区 Shangcheng	114124	327924	327924	164109	163815
下城区 Xiacheng	129669	402526	402526	201524	201002
江干区 Jianggan	148812	501191	501191	249679	251512
拱墅区 Gongshu	115388	333592	333592	166843	166749
西湖区 Xihu	187034	676490	671500	341798	334692
高新(滨江)区 Hi－Tech(Binjiang)	57195	204864	204864	104127	100737
萧山区 Xiaoshan	374970	1263307	787785	619052	644255
余杭区 Yuhang	262526	950873	540803	464667	486206
富阳区 Fuyang	215025	667861	445769	335343	332518
桐庐县 Tonglu	147842	409381	218827	204362	205019
淳安县 Chun'an	146948	459416	100588	232980	226436
建德市 Jiande	171251	508673	174967	258874	249799
临安市 Lin'an	187149	529447	243442	263479	265968

注:城镇人口 2015 年前为非农业人口。

a)Since 2015,the donotation of Non－agriculture Population has been adjusted to Urban Population.

2-05 分地区户籍人口年龄构成(2015年末)

Age Structure of Household Registered Population by Region(End of 2015)

地区 Region	0-17岁 0~17 years old		18-34岁 18~34 years old		35-59岁 35~59 years old		60岁以上 over 60 years old	
	人数(人) Number of people (person)	占总人口% of the total population	人数(人) Number of people (person)	占总人口% of the total population	人数(人) Number of people (person)	占总人口% of the total population	人数(人) Number of people (person)	占总人口% of the total population
全市 Whole City	**1121160**	**15.5**	**1712915**	**23.7**	**2877203**	**39.8**	**1524267**	**21.0**
市区 Urban District	851801	16.0	1281278	24.0	2071762	38.9	1123787	21.1
上城区 Shangcheng	35759	10.9	75060	22.9	121871	37.2	95234	29.0
下城区 Xiacheng	50377	12.5	104221	25.9	147022	36.5	100906	25.1
江干区 Jianggan	91066	18.2	132681	26.5	183065	36.5	94379	18.8
拱墅区 Gongshu	47789	14.3	75689	22.8	127914	38.3	82200	24.6
西湖区 Xihu	115468	17.1	195216	28.8	249467	36.9	116339	17.2
高新(滨江)区 Hi-Tech(Binjiang)	42350	20.7	63190	30.8	71495	34.9	27829	13.6
萧山区 Xiaoshan	202344	16.0	270221	21.4	507543	40.2	283199	22.4
余杭区 Yuhang	162752	17.2	213434	22.4	382672	40.2	192015	20.2
富阳区 Fuyang	103896	15.6	151566	22.7	280713	42.0	131686	19.7
桐庐县 Tonglu	59758	14.6	93793	22.9	168152	41.1	87678	21.4
淳安县 Chun'an	67799	14.8	100428	21.9	200529	43.6	90660	19.7
建德市 Jiande	69335	13.6	119268	23.4	211000	41.5	109070	21.5
临安市 Lin'an	72467	13.7	118148	22.3	225760	42.6	113072	21.4

2-06 全市户籍人口自然变动情况(1978-2015年)

Natural Changes of Registered Population(1978-2015)

年份 Year	出生 Birth		死亡 Death		自然增长 Natural Growth	
	人数(人) Birth Population (person)	出生率(‰) Birth Rate(‰)	人数(人) Death Population (person)	死亡率(‰) Death Rate(‰)	人数(人) Natural Growth Population (person)	自然增长率(‰) Natural Growth Rate(‰)
1978	73550	14.63	29928	2.95	43622	8.68
1979	71442	14.04	29500	5.80	41942	8.24
1980	52145	10.15	30727	5.98	21418	4.17
1981	73015	14.09	31352	6.05	41663	8.04
1982	82910	15.81	30805	5.87	52105	9.94
1983	69940	13.18	33598	6.33	36342	6.85
1984	60091	11.23	33070	6.18	27021	5.05
1985	66757	12.36	33715	6.24	33042	6.12
1986	84702	15.50	33576	6.15	51126	9.35
1987	94127	17.00	33238	6.00	60889	11.00
1988	85472	15.23	35356	6.30	50116	8.93
1989	81048	14.27	34031	5.99	47017	8.28
1990	76579	13.37	34977	6.11	41602	7.26
1991	66144	11.47	33534	5.81	32610	5.66
1992	61708	10.63	34681	5.97	27027	4.66
1993	62465	10.68	34127	5.84	28338	4.84
1994	63580	10.78	35099	5.95	28481	4.83
1995	62586	10.51	36186	6.08	26400	4.43
1996	63680	10.60	25417	5.90	28263	4.70
1997	58471	9.65	34663	5.72	23808	3.93
1998	53951	8.85	38302	6.28	15649	2.57
1999	59085	9.63	36866	6.01	22219	3.62
2000	62300	10.07	40218	6.50	22082	3.57
2001	52088	8.33	33827	5.41	18261	2.92
2002	53064	8.38	35867	5.67	17197	2.72
2003	51420	8.04	36662	5.73	14758	2.31
2004	59940	9.26	34078	5.27	25862	3.99
2005	57233	8.72	35417	5.39	21816	3.33
2006	57790	8.71	38892	5.86	18898	2.85
2007	60296	9.01	37833	5.65	22463	3.36
2008	61332	9.09	42648	6.32	18684	2.77
2009	62441	9.18	39159	5.76	23282	3.42
2010	69606	10.14	46193	6.73	23413	3.41
2011	70337	10.16	38225	5.52	32112	4.64
2012	77349	11.08	49789	7.13	27560	3.95
2013	70850	10.07	37544	5.34	33306	4.73
2014	89743	12.62	40415	5.68	49328	6.94
2015	70617	9.81	40326	5.60	30291	4.21

注:本表按公安部门统计。

a) Figures in this table are based on the Public Security Bureau.

2-07 市区户籍人口自然变动情况(1978-2015年)
Natural Changes of Registered Population of Urban District(1978-2015)

年份 Year	出生 Birth		死亡 Death		自然增长 Natural Growth	
	人数(人) Birth Population (person)	出生率(‰) Birth Rate(‰)	人数(人) Death Population (person)	死亡率(‰) Death Rate(‰)	人数(人) Natural Growth Population (person)	自然增长率(‰) Natural Growth Rate(‰)
1978	11923	11.56	6449	6.25	5474	5.31
1979	13184	12.26	5808	5.40	7376	6.86
1980	9708	8.68	6511	5.82	3197	2.86
1981	14938	13.06	6599	5.77	8339	7.29
1982	18092	15.49	6494	5.56	11598	9.93
1983	17107	14.36	6949	5.84	10158	8.52
1984	16257	13.41	6892	5.69	9365	7.72
1985	15824	12.81	7403	6.84	8421	6.82
1986	17120	13.60	6865	5.45	10255	8.15
1987	18701	14.60	7070	5.52	11631	9.08
1988	18503	14.21	7503	5.76	11000	8.45
1989	15868	12.02	6985	5.29	8883	6.73
1990	14085	10.56	7490	5.62	6595	4.94
1991	10195	7.58	7025	5.22	3170	2.36
1992	9994	7.37	7259	5.35	2735	2.02
1993	10099	7.35	7196	5.24	2903	2.11
1994	9918	7.09	7082	5.06	2836	2.03
1995	9806	6.89	7367	5.17	2439	1.72
1996	12098	7.80	8221	5.30	3877	2.50
1997	12304	7.32	8630	5.13	3674	2.19
1998	11714	6.87	9060	5.31	2654	1.56
1999	13694	7.89	8148	4.69	5546	3.20
2000	15058	8.50	10996	6.20	4062	2.30
2001	30902	8.22	19439	5.17	11463	3.05
2002	33156	8.65	19922	5.20	13234	3.45
2003	29019	7.44	21176	5.43	7843	2.01
2004	34858	8.77	19445	4.89	15413	3.88
2005	34056	8.39	21310	5.25	12746	3.14
2006	33260	8.08	21156	5.14	12104	2.94
2007	37029	8.88	20051	4.81	16978	4.07
2008	38703	9.17	21428	5.08	17275	4.09
2009	40293	9.44	22178	5.20	18115	4.24
2010	47052	10.89	25404	5.88	21648	5.01
2011	47256	10.80	22140	5.06	25116	5.74
2012	51892	11.72	27271	6.16	24621	5.56
2013	48107	10.74	21332	4.76	26775	5.97
2014	69577	13.36	27249	5.23	42328	8.13
2015	55275	10.45	26492	5.01	28783	5.44

注:从2001年起市区数据包括萧山区和余杭区,2014年起含富阳区。

a) Figures in this table include Xiaoshan district and Yuhang district since 2001, and include Fuyang district since 2014.

2-08 分地区户籍人口自然变动情况(2015年)
Natural Changes of Registered Population by Region(2015)

地 区 Region	出 生 Birth		死 亡 Death		自然增长 Natural Growth	
	人数(人) Birth Population (person)	出生率(‰) Birth Rate(‰)	人数(人) Death Population (person)	死亡率(‰) Death Rate(‰)	人数(人) Natural Growth Population (person)	自然增长率(‰) Natural Growth Rate(‰)
全 市 Whole City	**70617**	**9.81**	**40326**	**5.60**	**30291**	**4.21**
市 区 Urban District	55275	10.45	26492	5.01	28783	5.44
上城区 Shangcheng	2484	7.56	1622	4.94	862	2.62
下城区 Xiacheng	3599	8.90	1576	3.89	2023	5.01
江干区 Jianggan	6392	12.98	2199	4.46	4193	8.52
拱墅区 Gongshu	3439	10.42	1597	4.84	1842	5.58
西湖区 Xihu	7342	10.94	2175	3.24	5167	7.70
高新(滨江)区 Hi-Tech(Binjiang)	3384	17.08	621	3.13	2763	13.95
萧山区 Xiaoshan	11667	9.26	7453	5.91	4214	3.35
余杭区 Yuhang	11057	11.79	5393	5.75	5664	6.04
富阳区 Fuyang	5911	8.86	3856	5.78	2055	3.08
桐庐县 Tonglu	3690	9.02	2766	6.76	924	2.26
淳安县 Chun'an	4017	8.75	3384	7.37	633	1.38
建德市 Jiande	3549	6.97	3661	7.19	-112	-0.22
临安市 Lin'an	4086	7.72	4023	7.60	63	0.12

2－09 分地区户籍人口机械变动情况(2015年)

Mechanical Changes of Registered Population by Region(2015)

单位:人 (person)

地 区 Region	本年迁入人数 Number of the Persons Moved in(person)		本年迁出人数 Number of the Persons Moved Out(person)		本年净迁入人数 Net Persons Moved in
	省 内 From Zhejiang Province	省 外 From Other Provinces	省 内 To Zhejiang Province	省 外 To Other Provinces	
全 市 Whole City	**32939**	**56253**	**17276**	**21120**	**50796**
市 区 Urban District	30040	50591	11062	18763	50806
上城区 Shangcheng	1786	2710	429	781	3286
下城区 Xiacheng	2482	3370	1251	1739	2862
江干区 Jianggan	6090	8478	2596	4710	7262
拱墅区 Gongshu	2705	2479	695	628	3861
西湖区 Xihu	6193	9977	3113	6339	6718
高新(滨江)区 Hi－Tech(Binjiang)	2870	3590	884	1028	4548
萧山区 Xiaoshan	1707	4113	634	1302	3884
余杭区 Yuhang	5517	14250	799	1297	17671
富阳区 Fuyang	690	1624	661	939	714
桐庐县 Tonglu	727	1321	1106	512	430
淳安县 Chun'an	666	1240	1573	458	－125
建德市 Jiande	682	1434	2135	650	－669
临安市 Lin'an	824	1667	1400	737	354

2－10 婚姻登记情况
Marriage Registration Situations

地　区 Region	2015			2014		
	准予登记结婚对数(对) Marriages Legally Registered(couples)	再婚人数(人) Re－married (person)	离婚对数(对) Divorces (couples)	准予登记结婚对数(对) Marriages Legally Registered(couples)	再婚人数(人) Re－married (person)	离婚对数(对) Divorces (couples)
全　市 Whole City	**67657**	**28037**	**19073**	**72846**	**28982**	**19293**
市　区 Urban District	51400	20647	13750	54780	21304	14091
#萧山区 Xiaoshan	9492	3219	2096	10411	3255	2296
余杭区 Yuhang	7629	3400	2374	7779	3389	2379
富阳区 Fuyang	5081	2205	1674	6355	2806	1749
桐庐县 Tonglu	3470	1581	1191	3903	1727	1231
淳安县 Chun'an	3895	1674	1168	4438	1736	1170
建德市 Jiande	4394	1833	1355	4814	1753	1317
临安市 Lin'an	4498	2302	1609	4911	2462	1484

2－11　三次产业就业人员及构成（2010－2015年）

Number of Employed Persons by Three Industries（2010－2015）

单位：万人　　　　（10000 persons）

指标名称	Item	2010	2011	2012	2013	2014	2015
全市总计	**Total**	**626.33**	**637.77**	**644.43**	**650.51**	**654.92**	**663.03**
第一产业	Primary Industry	75.70	72.21	70.39	70.07	66.39	67.01
第二产业	Secondary Industry	286.26	289.12	290.01	291.51	286.99	271.90
第三产业	Tertiary Industry	264.37	276.44	284.03	288.93	301.54	324.12
全市构成（以合计为100）	**Composition（Total＝100）**	**100**	**100**	**100**	**100**	**100**	**100**
第一产业	Primary Industry	12.1	11.3	10.9	10.8	10.1	10.1
第二产业	Secondary Industry	45.7	45.3	45.0	44.8	43.8	41.0
第三产业	Tertiary Industry	42.2	43.3	44.1	44.4	46.0	48.9

2－12 全市含规上私营单位

Number of Employed Persons of the Whole City

单位:人

地区、行业	Region, Sector	就业人员合计 Number of Employed Persons	非私营单位 Non－private
全市	**Total**	**4457316**	**2885605**
市区	Urban District	4054782	2676883
#上城区	Shangcheng District	253702	194444
下城区	Xiacheng District	266162	224082
江干区	Jianggan District	428923	210371
拱墅区	Gongshu District	347876	183973
西湖区	Xihu District	636618	526513
高新(滨江)区	Hi－Tech(Binjiang) District	289873	222709
萧山区	Xiaoshan District	896614	551979
余杭区	Yuhang District	471614	246327
富阳区	Fuyang District	240282	123239
桐庐县	Tonglu County	105278	42952
淳安县	Chun'an County	62705	36789
建德市	Jiande City	78651	43682
临安市	Lin'an City	155900	85299
按国民经济行业分组	**Grouped by Sector**		
农、林、牧、渔业	Farming, Forestry, Animal Husbandry & Fishery	1026	1004
采矿业	Mining	2875	1317
制造业	Manufacturing	1123018	680289
电力、热力、燃气及水生产和供应业	Production & Supply of Electricity, Heat, Gas & Water	20691	19159
建筑业	Construction	1627519	806765
批发和零售业	Wholesale & Retail Trades	283724	193475
交通运输、仓储和邮政业	Transportation, Storage and Posts	134780	109141
住宿和餐饮业	Hotels and Catering Services	98099	63751
信息传输、软件和信息技术服务业	Information Transmission, Software and Information Technology	144143	115793
金融业	Financial Intermediation	107110	106693
房地产业	Real Estate	126568	101681
租赁和商务服务业	Leasing and Business Services	142467	104589
科学研究、技术服务业	Scientific Research, Technical Services	111928	86886
水利、环境和公共设施管理业	Management of Water Conservancy, Environment and Public Facilities	42857	29531
居民服务、修理和其他服务业	Service to Households, Repair and Other Services	25794	13923
教育	Education	184178	178314
卫生和社会工业	Health Care and Social Work	116181	111965
文化、体育和娱乐业	Culture, Sports and Entertainment	26167	23138
公共管理、社会保障和社会组织	Public Management, Social Security and Social Organizations	138191	138191

就业人员数(2015 年末)

Including Private Units Above Designated Size(End of 2015)

(person)

女性 Female	非私营单位 Non - private	在岗职工 Staff and Workers	非私营单位 Non - private	其他就业人员 Other Employed Persons	非私营单位 Non - private
1358624	**936771**	**4126846**	**2709791**	**330470**	**175814**
1209508	855503	3747330	2512050	307452	164833
97465	81371	228730	179687	24972	14757
109150	92214	249089	210486	17073	13596
100419	65308	327138	187742	101785	22629
76497	52071	319414	162996	28462	20977
165411	138434	586430	490214	50188	36299
88368	71527	279709	214098	10164	8611
253763	148598	871237	537335	25377	14644
164151	94008	452593	235490	19021	10837
76622	41924	226810	115340	13472	7899
39244	19871	100051	40857	5227	2095
25932	13946	56223	34449	6482	2340
29619	16732	72566	41024	6085	2658
54321	30719	150676	81411	5224	3888
295	281	961	939	65	65
501	236	2736	1209	139	108
464612	263165	1108827	672174	14191	8115
5137	4766	20203	18686	488	473
137606	52598	1422801	739528	204718	67237
143712	95029	272100	183568	11624	9907
32257	24829	131987	107162	2793	1979
54501	34573	88531	55388	9568	8363
53323	44506	142824	114853	1319	940
62374	62138	88116	85806	20994	20887
46922	36846	120714	97099	5854	4582
52862	36572	131631	95601	10836	8988
33276	26772	105448	82197	6480	4689
15105	11457	40496	27903	2361	1628
14318	7708	24654	13252	1140	671
110683	108255	171626	165867	12552	12447
78254	75412	103232	99505	12949	12460
12174	10916	21334	18429	4833	4709
40712	40712	130625	130625	7566	7566

2－13 全市含规上私营单位

Everage Number of Employed Persons

单位:人

地区、行业	Region, Sector	就业人员年平均人数 Annual Average Number of Staff and Workers	非私营单位 Non－private
全市	**Total**	**4355111**	**2829392**
市区	Urban District	3954233	2618626
#上城区	Shangcheng District	256974	198271
下城区	Xiacheng District	261172	219828
江干区	Jianggan District	404224	209671
拱墅区	Gongshu District	330786	170770
西湖区	Xihu District	623143	512417
高新(滨江)区	Hi－Tech(Binjiang) District	284836	218100
萧山区	Xiaoshan District	867193	523317
余杭区	Yuhang District	461311	245622
富阳区	Fuyang District	234957	118718
桐庐县	Tonglu County	104013	42701
淳安县	Chun'an County	62367	37166
建德市	Jiande City	78228	43967
临安市	Lin'an City	156270	86932
按国民经济行业分组	**Grouped by Sector**		
农、林、牧、渔业	Farming, Forestry, Animal Husbandry & Fishery	1057	1035
采矿业	Mining	2809	1267
制造业	Manufacturing	1128267	687338
电力、热力、燃气及水生产和供应业	Production & Supply of Electricity, Heat, Gas & Water	21911	20376
建筑业	Construction	1534708	752075
批发和零售业	Wholesale & Retail Trades	287881	198448
交通运输、仓储和邮政业	Transportation, Storage and Posts	133126	109112
住宿和餐饮业	Hotels and Catering Services	99536	65569
信息传输、软件和信息技术服务业	Information Transmission, Software and Information Technology	141604	114206
金融业	Financial Intermediation	99877	99444
房地产业	Real Estate	123152	98791
租赁和商务服务业	Leasing and Business Services	139973	103797
科学研究、技术服务业	Scientific Research, Technical Services	112097	86197
水利、环境和公共设施管理业	Management of Water Conservancy, Environment and Public Facilities	42951	29697
居民服务、修理和其他服务业	Service to Households, Repair and Other Services	25198	13955
教育	Education	184988	179147
卫生和社会工作	Health Care and Social Work	112418	108396
文化、体育和娱乐业	Culture, Sports and Entertainment	26134	23118
公共管理、社会保障和社会组织	Public Management, Social Security and Social Organizations	137424	137424

平均人员数(2015 年)

Including Private Units Above Designated Size(2015)

(person)

在岗职工年平均人数 Staff and Workers	非私营单位 Non - private	其他就业人员年平均人数 Average Number of Other Employed Persons	非私营单位 Non - private
4039578	**2647516**	**315533**	**181876**
3360466	2447117	293767	171509
232160	183560	24814	14711
242079	206966	19093	12862
324964	186650	79260	23021
303092	150148	27694	20622
570490	474009	52653	38408
274679	209558	10157	8542
841445	507866	25748	15451
442876	235211	18435	10411
220933	110634	14024	8084
98781	40623	5232	2078
56237	34988	6130	2178
72946	41729	5282	2238
151148	83059	5122	3873
992	970	65	65
2690	1159	119	108
1113605	678723	14662	8615
21405	19884	506	492
1343073	677041	191635	75034
275645	188003	12236	10445
130057	106759	3069	2353
88964	56146	10572	9423
140112	113231	1492	975
84383	84116	15494	15328
117705	94551	5447	4240
129451	94956	10522	8841
105071	80974	7026	5223
40625	28115	2326	1582
23949	13182	1249	773
170413	164686	14575	14461
99987	96447	12431	11949
21237	18359	4897	4759
130214	130214	7210	7210

主要统计指标解释

人口数 指一定时点、一定地区范围内的有生命的个人的总和。

年度统计的年末人口数是指每年 12 月 31 日 24 时的人口数。

出生率(又称粗出生率) 指一定时期内(通常为一年)平均每千人所出生的人数的比率,一般用千分率表示。计算公式:

$$出生率 = \frac{年出生人数}{年平均人数} \times 1000‰$$

出生人数是指活产婴儿,即胎儿脱离母体时(不管怀孕月数),有过呼吸或其他生命现象。

年平均人数是年初、年底人口数的平均数,也可用年中人口数代替。

死亡率(又称粗死亡率) 指一定时期内(通常为一年)一定地区的死亡人数与同期平均人数(或期中人数)之比,一般用千分率表示。计算公式:

$$死亡率 = \frac{年死亡人数}{年平均人数} \times 1000‰$$

人口自然增长率 指一定时期内(通常为一年)人口自然增加数(出生人数减死亡人数)与该时期内平均人数(或期中人数)之比,一般用千分率表示。计算公式:

$$人口自然增长率 = \frac{本年出生人数 - 本年死亡人数}{年平均人数} \times 1000‰$$

人口自然增长率 = 人口出生率 - 人口死亡率

就业人员 指从事一定社会劳动并取得劳动报酬或经营收入人员,包括各级机关企事业单位就业人员、个体户主、个体就业人员、农村就业人员及其他未包括的就业人员(包括宗教职业者、现役军人等)。

单位就业人员 是指在各级国家机关、政党机关、社会团体及企业、事业单位中工作,并取得劳动报酬的全部人员。包括在岗职工、再就业的离退休人员、民办教师、在各单位中工作的外方人员和港、澳、台方人员以及聘用的外单位下岗职工、兼职人员、从事第二职业人员、使用的劳务派遣人员。各单位的就业人员反映了实际参加生产或工作的全部劳动力。

在岗职工 指在本单位工作并由单位支付劳动报酬的人员,以及在本单位有工作岗位,但由于学习、病伤产假等原因暂未工作,仍由单位支付劳动报酬的人,包括本单位临时性用工并支付劳动报酬的人员。2012 年开始在岗职工包含劳务派遣人员。

非私营单位 包括独立核算的机关、事业单位和国有、集体、股份制、港澳台投资及外商投资企业等。

含规上私营单位 包括独立核算的非私营单位、规模以上私营工业企业、限额以上私营批发零售住宿餐饮企业、私营房地产开发经营企业、具有资质的私营建筑企业、规模以上私营服务企业、100 人及以上的规模以下私营企业。

Explanatory Notes on Main Statistical Indicators

Total Population refers to the total number of people alive at a certain point of time within a given area.

The annual statistics on total population is taken at midnight, the 31st of December.

Birth Rate (or Crude Birth Rate) refers to the ratio of the number of births to the average population during a certain period of time (usually a year), which is often expressed in ‰. The following formula is used:

$$\text{Birth Rate} = \frac{\text{Number of Births}}{\text{Average Number of Population}} \times 1000‰$$

Number of births refers to live births, i. e. the births when babies had showed any vital phenomena regardless of the length of pregnancy.

Annual Average Number of Population is the average of the number of population at the beginning of the year and that at the end of the year. Sometimes it is substituted for with the mid – year population.

Death Rate (or Crude Death Rate) refers to the ratio of the number of deaths to the average population (or mid – year population) during a certain period of time (usually a year), which is often expressed in ‰. The following formula is used:

$$\text{Death Rate} = \frac{\text{Number of Deaths}}{\text{Annual Average Number of Population}} \times 1000‰$$

Natural Growth Rate of Population refers to the ratio of natural increase in population (number of births minus number of deaths) in a certain period of time (usually a year) to the average population (or mid – year population) of the same period, which is often expressed in ‰. The following formulas are applied:

$$\text{Natural Growth Rate of Population} = \frac{\text{Number of Births} - \text{Number of Deaths}}{\text{Average Number of Population}} \times 1000‰$$

Natural Growth Rate of Population = Birth Rate – Death Rate

Employed Persons refer to persons who are engaged in social labour and receive remuneration payment or earn business income, including all employees of government, enterprises and institutions, self – employed workers, employed persons in the rural areas and other employed workers (including religious professionals, servicemen, etc.).

Persons Employed in Various Units refer to all the persons who are working in government agencies of various levels, political and party organizations, social organizations, enterprises, institutions, and receiving wages or other forms of payment. Including fully employed staff and works, re – employed retirees, teachers in schools run by the local people, foreigners and Chinese compatriots from Hong Kong, Macao, and Taiwan working in various units, part – time employees, employees of other units working temporarily, employees holding the second job, dispatch personnels. Persons Employed in various units reflect the actual total labor force which are engaged in the production or work.

Fully Employed Staff and Workers refer to persons who work in, and receive wages from their working units, as well as persons who have their work posts, but are temporarily absent from work for reasons of study or on sick, injury or maternal leave and still receive wages from their working units. including persons who are engaged in temporary employment and receive remuneration payment. Since 2012, the number of fully employed staff included the labor dispatch personnel.

Non – private Units include independent accounting units of government organizations and institutions, state – owned enterprises, collective – owned enterprises, and enterprises with funds from Hongkong, Macao and Taiwan.

Including Units above Designated Size include independent accounting units of non – private, private industrial enterprises above designated size, private enterprises above designated size of wholesale & retail trades, hotels, catering serrices, private enterprises for real estate development, private construction enterprises with qualification grade, private enterprises of service industry above designated size, private enterprises below designated size with at least 100 employed persons.

三、农业

AGRICULTURE

3

农　　业
Agriculture

主要统计指标
Major Statistical Indicators

农村机械总动力	Total Power of Agricultural Machinery	299.47	万千瓦	(10, 000 kw)
为上年	As Compared with the Preceding Year	87.5	%	(%)
农村就业人员数	Total Employed Persons in Rural Areas	284.73	万人	(10, 000 persons)
为上年	As Compared with the Preceding Year	99.6	%	(%)
农林牧渔业增加值	Value-added of Farming,Forestry,Animal Husbandry and Fishery	292.40	亿元	(100 million yuan)
为上年	As Compared with the Preceding Year	101.8	%	(%)
粮食总产量	Total Output of Grain Crops	63.38	万吨	(10, 000 tons)
为上年	As Compared with the Preceding Year	101.3	%	(%)
肉类产量	Total Output of Meat	27.84	万吨	(10, 000 tons)
为上年	As Compared with the Preceding Year	93.8	%	(%)

3－01 农林牧渔业增加值(2015 年)

Value－added of Agriculture, Forestry, Animal Husbandry and Fishery(2015)

单位:万元 (10000 yuan)

地区 Region	农林牧渔业增加值合计 Total	农业 Agriculture	林业 Forestry	牧业 Animal Husbandry	渔业 Fishery	服务业 Service
全市 Whole City	**2924013**	**1806178**	**393332**	**395476**	**284506**	**44521**
市区 Urban District	1658676	1038216	142606	214903	232833	30118
#西湖区 Xihu	43338	18460	506	1798	22241	333
江干区 Jianggan	4906	3503	15	1177	174	37
高新(滨江)区 Hi－Tech(Binjiang)	14402	12225	2	1408	767	
萧山区 Xiaoshan	652920	442637	6859	106467	81517	14440
余杭区 Yuhang	483035	300875	54807	25069	88844	13440
富阳区 Fuyang	425440	250941	80378	74258	17995	1868
桐庐县 Tonglu	231439	140829	41642	31829	14257	2882
淳安县 Chun'an	323773	228537	44245	32123	15465	3403
建德市 Jiande	309482	205150	22491	60395	16812	4634
临安市 Lin'an	400643	193446	142348	56226	5139	3484

3-02 农林牧渔业总产值(1978-2015年)

Gross Output Value of Agriculture, Forestry, Animal Husbandry and Fishery(1978-2014)

单位:万元 (10000 yuan)

年份 Year	农林牧渔业总产值 Gross Output Value	#农业产值 Farming	种植业产值 Planting	林业产值 Forestry	牧业产值 Animal Husbandry	渔业产值 Fishery	服务业产值 Service
1978	85922	67365	64378	3430	14474	653	-
1979	115649	84727	81989	4629	25216	1077	-
1980	112377	79006	76059	7262	25015	1094	-
1981	120792	87354	81659	8309	23799	1330	-
1982	150606	107566	103346	8912	31801	2327	-
1983	148878	103685	96272	9800	32693	2700	-
1984	177029	122567	115286	14769	35922	3771	-
1985	212961	136893	126026	19095	50110	6863	-
1986	238285	150803	138254	19990	58197	9295	-
1987	281326	173080	155960	26427	70129	11690	-
1988	358500	208838	187648	31434	101013	17215	-
1989	386805	225969	201389	27857	113952	19027	-
1990	421045	260031	233055	26962	113424	20628	-
1991	463578	284275	254834	37763	117458	24082	-
1992	497915	300828	256833	35589	133867	27631	-
1993	600760	365124	300736	47476	154766	33394	-
1994	812473	496392	415366	58627	217217	40237	-
1995	996440	620057	526328	81321	244054	51008	-
1996	1173294	740202	617573	95740	271652	65700	-
1997	1287650	797812	665172	114510	294153	81175	-
1998	1367578	845106	701850	121197	289085	112190	-
1999	1414737	876685	737406	126000	293495	118557	-
2000	1526530	903322	754311	136848	331563	154797	-
2001	1649978	965005	816884	149264	362303	173406	-
2002	1685036	932995	886285	162227	391844	197970	-
2003	1890129	991556	949138	182595	417798	232599	65581
2004	1982683	1010947	972594	206787	457619	234080	73250
2005	2194799	1136559	1103981	233039	495900	270810	58491
2006	2253822	1224822	1191816	267748	490448	206082	64722
2007	2471427	1308047	1279758	294707	585536	222601	60536
2008	2737605	1408124	1374083	320212	636633	309270	63366
2009	2897371	1497362	1462791	362317	642892	325626	69174
2010	3163392	1698775	1673470	329278	705596	349011	80732
2011	3570744	1907895	1882876	348535	836532	389985	87797
2012	3843403	2077191	2041481	381802	868504	420006	95900
2013	3993712	2161055	2120540	408170	911324	407292	105871
2014	4185804	2333804	2291071	470164	828184	442023	111629
2015	4404121	2524163	2468981	498051	807001	452309	122597

注:本表按当年价格计算;从2003年起农林牧渔总产值包括农林牧渔业服务业产值(下同)。

a) Data in this table are calculated at current prices. From 2003, Gross Output Value includes the value of service for the agriculture, forestry, animal husbandry and fishery sector(the same below).

3－03　农林牧渔业总产值构成（1978－2015年）

Composition of Gross Output Value of Agriculture, Forestry, Animal Husbandry and Fishery(1978－2015)

单位:%　　　　(%)

年　份 Year	农林牧渔业总产值 Gross Output Value	#农业产值 Farming	种植业产值 Planting	林业产值 Forestry	牧业产值 Animal Husbandry	渔业产值 Fishery	服务业产值 Service
1978	100	78.4	74.9	4.0	16.8	0.8	–
1979	100	73.3	70.9	4.0	21.8	0.9	–
1980	100	70.3	67.7	6.5	22.2	1.0	–
1981	100	72.3	67.6	6.9	19.7	1.1	–
1982	100	71.4	68.6	5.9	21.1	1.6	–
1983	100	69.6	64.7	6.6	22.0	1.8	–
1984	100	69.2	65.1	8.3	20.3	2.2	–
1985	100	64.3	59.2	9.0	23.5	3.2	–
1986	100	63.3	58.0	8.4	24.4	3.9	–
1987	100	61.5	55.4	9.4	24.9	4.2	–
1988	100	58.2	52.3	8.8	28.2	4.8	–
1989	100	58.4	52.1	7.2	29.5	4.9	–
1990	100	61.8	55.4	6.4	26.9	4.9	–
1991	100	61.3	55.0	8.2	25.3	5.2	–
1992	100	60.4	51.6	7.2	26.9	5.5	–
1993	100	60.8	50.1	7.9	25.8	5.5	–
1994	100	61.1	51.1	7.2	26.7	5.0	–
1995	100	62.2	52.8	8.2	24.5	5.1	–
1996	100	63.1	52.6	8.2	23.1	5.6	–
1997	100	62.0	51.7	8.9	22.8	6.3	–
1998	100	61.8	51.3	8.9	21.1	8.2	–
1999	100	62.0	52.1	8.9	20.7	8.4	–
2000	100	59.2	49.4	9.0	21.7	10.1	–
2001	100	58.5	52.2	9.0	22.0	10.5	–
2002	100	55.4	52.6	9.6	23.3	11.7	–
2003	100	52.5	50.2	9.7	22.1	12.3	3.4
2004	100	51.0	49.1	10.4	23.1	11.8	3.7
2005	100	51.8	50.3	10.6	22.6	12.3	2.7
2006	100	54.3	52.9	11.9	21.8	9.1	2.9
2007	100	52.9	51.8	11.9	23.7	9.0	2.5
2008	100	51.4	50.2	11.7	23.3	11.3	2.3
2009	100	51.7	50.5	12.5	22.2	11.2	2.4
2010	100	53.7	52.9	10.4	22.3	11.0	2.6
2011	100	53.4	52.7	9.8	23.4	10.9	2.5
2012	100	54.0	53.1	9.9	22.6	10.9	2.6
2013	100	54.1	53.1	10.2	22.8	10.2	2.7
2014	100	55.8	54.7	11.2	19.8	10.6	2.6
2015	100	57.3	56.1	11.3	18.3	10.3	2.8

3-04 农林牧渔业分项产值(主要年份)

Gross Output Value of Agriculture, Forestry, Animal Husbandry and Fishery by Branch (Main Years)

单位:万元 (10000 yuan)

指 标	Item	1995	2000	2005	2010	2011	2012	2013	2014	2015
农林牧渔业总产值(现价)	**Gross Output Value (Current Price)**	**996440**	**1526530**	**2194799**	**3163392**	**3570744**	**3843403**	**3993712**	**4185804**	**4404121**
一、农业产值	**Farming**	**620057**	**903322**	**1136559**	**1698775**	**1907895**	**2077191**	**2161055**	**2333804**	**2524163**
1. 种植业产值	Planting	526328	754311	1103981	1673470	1882876	2041481	2120540	2291071	2468981
粮食	Grain	262321	208546	178981	215990	230246	241471	248550	224164	228341
油料	Oil-bearing Crops	19675	19583	21608	31137	35245	35482	37649	37530	48373
棉花	Cotton	11829	2205	1146	1255	1155	1424	1571	1152	1094
麻类	Fiber Crops	3863	384	176	42	21	16	25	8	6
甘蔗	Sugarcane	14274	23815	19075	18756	20067	18417	18496	17347	16322
烟叶	Tobacco	1	5	7	1	2	2	1	1	1
药材类	Crude Drugs	1725	6005	15800	42927	50530	60454	67623	75180	86538
蔬菜	Vegetables	151614	303583	357734	535623	607469	664937	665429	686995	748644
茶、桑、果、坚果	Tea, Mulberry & Fruits	48599	106727	254379	484261	565641	605200	630899	749516	802647
其他	Others	12427	83458	255075	343478	372500	414078	450297	499178	537015
2. 其他农业产值	Other Farming	93729	149011	32578	25305	25019	35710	40515	42733	55182
二、林业产值	**Forestry**	**81321**	**136848**	**233039**	**329278**	**348535**	**381802**	**408170**	**470164**	**498051**
人造林木生长	Artificial Forestry	11286	18226	23140	27964	23828	32802	33734	31640	32574
林产品	Forest Products	45123	89914	168348	184740	197815	214198	227962	267839	294806
竹木采伐	Lumbering	24912	28708	41551	82063	90806	93552	103425	130794	127670
采集野生植物	Wild Plant collected				34511	36086	41250	43049	39891	43001
三、牧业产值	**Animal Husbandry**	**244054**	**331563**	**495900**	**705596**	**836532**	**868504**	**911324**	**828184**	**807001**
牲畜	Livestock Raising	143879	175732	292025	430193	534840	556742	589952	522674	522001
家禽饲养	Poultry Raising	35302	65548	68631	70201	69653	82132	77869	72333	72394
活的畜禽产品	Livestock Products	37197	44098	68143	109625	124024	125886	132151	127075	112964
捕猎野兽野禽	Hunting Wild Beast and Wild Fowl	491	2102	2856	4455	4698	5454	5126	6260	5256
其他动物饲养	Other Animals Raising	27185	44083	64245	91122	103317	98290	106226	99842	94386
四、渔业产值	**Fishery**	**51008**	**154797**	**270810**	**349011**	**389985**	**420006**	**407292**	**442023**	**452309**
五、服务业产值	**Service**	**-**	**-**	**58491**	**80732**	**87797**	**95900**	**105871**	**111629**	**122597**

3-05 农林牧渔业分项产值构成(主要年份)

Composition of Gross Output Value of Agriculture, Forestry, Animal Husbandry and Fishery by Branch (Main Years)

单位:% (%)

指标	Item	1995	2000	2005	2010	2011	2012	2013	2014	2015
农林牧渔业总产值(现价)	**Gross Output Value (Current Price)**	**100**	**100**	**100**	**100**	**100**	**100**	**100**	**100**	**100**
一、农业产值	**Farming**	**62.2**	**59.2**	**51.8**	**53.7**	**53.4**	**54.0**	**54.1**	**55.8**	**57.3**
1.种植业产值	Planting	52.8	49.4	50.3	52.9	52.7	53.1	53.1	54.7	56.1
粮食	Grain	26.3	13.7	8.2	6.8	6.4	6.3	6.2	5.4	5.2
油料	Oil Plants	2.0	1.3	1.0	1.0	1.0	0.9	0.9	0.9	1.1
棉花	Cotton	1.2	0.1	0.1	-	-	-	-	-	-
麻类	Fiber Crops	0.4	-	-	-	-	-	-	-	-
甘蔗	Sugarcane	1.4	1.6	0.9	0.6	0.6	0.6	0.5	0.4	0.4
烟叶	Tobacco	-	-	-	-	-	-	-	-	-
药材类	Crude Drugs	0.2	0.4	0.7	1.4	1.4	1.6	1.7	1.8	2.0
蔬菜	Vegetables	15.2	19.9	16.3	16.9	17.0	17.3	16.7	16.4	16.9
茶、桑、果、坚果	Tea, Mulberry & Fruits	4.9	7.0	11.6	15.3	15.8	15.7	15.8	17.9	18.2
其他	Others	1.2	5.4	11.5	10.9	10.5	10.7	11.3	11.9	12.2
2.其他农业产值	Other Farming	9.4	9.8	1.5	0.8	0.7	0.9	1.0	1.0	1.3
二、林业产值	**Forestry**	**8.2**	**9.0**	**10.6**	**10.4**	**9.8**	**9.9**	**10.2**	**11.2**	**11.3**
人造林木生长	Artificial Forestry	1.2	1.2	1.1	0.9	0.7	0.8	0.8	0.8	0.7
林产品	Forest Products	4.5	5.9	7.6	5.8	5.5	5.6	5.7	6.4	6.7
竹木采伐	Lumbering	2.5	1.9	1.9	2.6	2.5	2.4	2.6	3.1	2.9
采集野生植物	Wild Plant collected				1.1	1.1	1.1	1.1	0.9	1.0
三、牧业产值	**Animal Husbandry**	**24.5**	**21.7**	**22.6**	**22.3**	**23.4**	**22.6**	**22.8**	**19.8**	**18.3**
牲畜	Livestock Raising	14.4	11.5	13.3	13.6	15.0	14.5	14.8	12.5	11.9
家禽饲养	Poultry Raising	3.6	4.3	3.1	2.2	2.0	2.1	1.9	1.7	1.6
活的畜禽产品	Livestock Products	3.7	2.9	3.2	3.5	3.5	3.3	3.3	3.0	2.6
捕猎野兽野禽	Hunting Wild Beast and Wild Fowl	-	0.1	0.1	0.1	0.1	0.1	0.1	0.1	0.1
其他动物饲养	Other Animals Raising	2.8	2.9	2.9	2.9	2.8	2.6	2.7	2.4	2.1
四、渔业产值	**Fishery**	**5.1**	**10.1**	**12.3**	**11.0**	**10.9**	**10.9**	**10.2**	**10.6**	**10.3**
五、服务业产值	**Service**	**-**	**-**	**2.7**	**3.4**	**2.5**	**2.6**	**2.7**	**2.6**	**2.8**

3-06 分地区农林牧

Gross Output Value of Agriculture, Forestry,

单位:万元

指 标	Item	全 市 Whole City	市 区 Urban District	江干区 Jianggan	西湖区 Xihu
合 计	**Gross Output Value**	**4404121**	**2542748**	**7925**	**64678**
一、农业产值	**Farming**	**2524163**	**1447535**	**6310**	**26743**
(一)种植业产值	Planting	2468981	1430092	6310	26519
#副产品产值	By - products	12346	6650	-	65
1. 粮食作物	Grain	228341	126122	0	851
谷 物	Cereal	173699	103398	0	811
豆 类	Beans	21541	14587	-	23
薯 类	Tubers	33101	8137	-	17
2. 油 料	Oil Plants	48373	20602	-	13
3. 棉 花	Cotton	1094	563	-	-
4. 麻 类	Fiber Crops	6	3	-	-
5. 甘 蔗	Sugarcane	16322	12680	-	213
6. 烟 叶	Tobacco	1	-	-	-
7. 药 材 类	Crude Drugs	86538	17609	-	46
8. 蔬 菜	Vegetables	748644	531447	4229	11388
9. 茶、桑、果、坚果	Tea, Mulberry & Fruits	802647	288203	130	6377
10. 其 他	Others	537015	432863	1951	7631
(二)其他农业产值	Other Farming	55182	17443	-	224
二、林业产值	**Forestry**	**498051**	**179475**	**17**	**586**
1. 人造林木生长	Artificial Forestry	32574	17917	17	576
2. 林产品	Forest Products	294806	101895	-	-
3. 村及村以下竹木采伐	Lumbering	127670	44009	-	10
4. 采集野生植物	Wild Plant collected	43001	15654	-	-
三、牧业产值	**Animal Husbandry**	**807001**	**451120**	**1315**	**3330**
1. 牲畜	Livestock	522001	340800	1315	2613
2. 家禽饲养	Poultry Raising	72394	45990	-	286
3. 活的畜禽产品	Livestock Products	112964	30477	-	81
4. 捕猎野兽野禽	Hunting Wild Beast and Wild Fowl	5256	2730	-	-
5. 其他动物饲养	Other Animals Raising	94386	31123	-	350
四、渔业产值	**Fishery**	**452309**	**377298**	**202**	**32960**
五、服务业产值	**Service**	**122597**	**87320**	**81**	**1059**

渔业总产值(2015 年)
Animal Husbandry and Fishery by Region(2015)

(10000 yuan)

高新(滨江)区 Hi - Tech(Binjiang)	萧山区 Xiaoshan	余杭区 Yuhang	富阳区 Fuyang	桐庐县 Tonglu	淳安县 Chun'an	建德市 Jiande	临安市 Lin'an
22441	**1044227**	**742162**	**598319**	**340002**	**455568**	**488081**	**577722**
18304	**619282**	**421772**	**340464**	**201528**	**303690**	**297000**	**274410**
18304	619253	417662	327393	196275	302685	272171	267758
17	2607	1757	2189	1133	1880	1718	965
390	44534	40667	39368	20444	28137	30172	23466
388	33661	36096	32143	16677	13996	25580	14048
–	9265	2816	2478	1403	3267	1774	510
–	1608	1755	4747	2364	10874	2818	8908
–	7874	1992	10719	8889	8808	7054	3020
–	408	155	–	–	314	215	2
–	2	1	–	–	3	–	–
11	9241	1826	1389	1959	416	1230	37
–	–	–	–	–	1	–	–
–	5049	5408	7106	7975	26492	26304	8158
5247	273263	152390	82130	51480	56374	56390	52953
471	43439	112666	113585	78793	160352	135342	139957
12185	235443	102557	73096	26735	21788	15464	40165
–	29	4110	13071	5253	1005	24829	6652
3	**13600**	**74900**	**90302**	**49781**	**60167**	**27808**	**180820**
3	4953	11644	657	3275	7122	1760	2500
–	6848	42947	52100	32775	32187	13297	114652
–	1672	17361	24966	6821	13721	9241	53878
–	127	2948	12579	6910	7137	3510	9790
2227	**238370**	**57491**	**139079**	**59251**	**61776**	**129113**	**105741**
2204	210775	31146	88855	28464	35032	43320	74385
23	13199	14704	17771	3049	2029	17548	3778
–	7184	9039	8764	5651	5491	61962	9383
–	365	504	1861	929	127	567	903
–	6847	2098	21828	21158	19097	5716	17292
1907	**133615**	**145999**	**23654**	**21780**	**23463**	**22108**	**7660**
–	**39360**	**42000**	**4820**	**7662**	**6472**	**12052**	**9091**

3-07 主要农作物播种面积及产量(2014-2015年)
Sown Areas and Yield of Major Farm Crops(2014-2015)

指标	Item	2015			2014		
		播种面积(千公顷) Sown Area (1000 hectares)	总产量(吨) Total Output (ton)	公顷产量(公斤) Yield per Hectare (kg/hectare)	播种面积(千公顷) Sown Area (1000 hectares)	总产量(吨) Total Output (ton)	公顷产量(公斤) Yield per Hectare (kg/hectare)
农作物总计	**Total Farm Crops**	**297.69**	**-**	**-**	**294.97**	**-**	**-**
一、粮食	**Grain Crops**	**106.02**	**633820**	**5978**	**107.26**	**625429**	**5831**
#春粮	#Spring Grain	14.73	58863	3996	15.83	61836	3906
秋粮	Autumn Grain	60.49	430125	7111	61.65	430376	6981
(一)谷物	Cereals	76.64	517941	6758	76.19	509587	6689
1.稻谷	Rice	46.78	376011	8039	47.09	373402	7930
①早稻及早中稻	Early Rice & Semi-late Rice	2.26	14906	6598	2.26	14283	6331
②晚稻及迟中稻	Late Rice & Semi-late Rice	44.52	361106	8112	44.83	359119	8010
#单季稻	#Single-crop Rice	43.27	352011	8135	43.53	349266	8024
2.小麦	Wheat	10.40	42473	4082	11.03	43795	3971
3.大麦	Barley	0.54	2147	4006	0.45	1690	3789
4.玉米	Corn	18.11	93546	5166	17.30	89230	5158
5.其他谷物	Other Cereals	0.82	3764	4607	0.32	1470	4551
(二)豆类	Beans	18.16	57830	3184	21.02	64466	3066
1.大豆	Soybeans	16.22	52196	3217	18.84	57962	3077
2.蚕(豌)豆	Broad Beans	1.58	4494	2852	1.61	4618	2867
3.杂豆	Other Beans	0.36	1139	3138	0.57	1886	3286
(三)薯类	Tubers	11.22	58050	5176	10.05	51376	5114

3-07 续表 continued

指 标	Item	2015			2014		
		播种面积(千公顷) Sown Area (1000 hectares)	总产量(吨) Total Output (ton)	公顷产量(公斤) Yield per Hectare (kg/hectare)	播种面积(千公顷) Sown Area (1000 hectares)	总产量(吨) Total Output (ton)	公顷产量(公斤) Yield per Hectare (kg/hectare)
二、油料	**Oil Plants**	**32.42**	**78264**	**2414**	**30.06**	**67171**	**2234**
1.油菜籽	Rapeseeds	28.5	66227	2324	28.58	63580	2225
2.花生	Peanuts	2.6	9656	3718	0.79	2540	3199
3.芝麻	Sesame	1.26	2232	1766	0.69	1051	1517
4.其他	Others	0.06	150	2727			
三、棉花(皮棉)	**Cotton**	**0.45**	**705**	**1563**	**0.5**	**742**	**1480**
四、麻类	**Fiber Cropers**	**0.006**	**21**	**3500**	**0.01**	**25**	**3571**
五、糖类	**Sugar Crops**	**1.65**	**97999**	**59465**	**1.81**	**110179**	**60872**
六、烟叶	**Tobacco**	**-**	**1**	**-**	**-**	**1**	**-**
七、药材	**Crude Drugs**	**4.92**	**30256**	**6148**	**4.68**	**27534**	**5878**
八、蔬菜	**Vegetables**	**94.17**	**3188439**	**33859**	**92.24**	**2969929**	**32199**
九、果用瓜	**Melon as Fruit**	**11.3**	**361735**	**32000**	**10.71**	**341068**	**31861**
#西瓜	Watermelon	8.19	280909	34291	7.72	260239	33701
草莓	Strawberry	1.21	37812	31327	1.01	33816	33548
十、花卉苗木	**Flower Gardening**	**34.97**	**-**	**-**	**35.61**	**-**	**-**
十一、其他作物	**Others**	**11.79**	**-**	**-**	**12.09**	**-**	**-**
#绿肥	Green Manure	1.54	-	-	1.7	-	-

3－08 分地区粮食

Sown Areas and Yield of

指　标		Item		全市 Whole City	市区 Urban District	江干区 Jianggan	西湖区 Xihu	高新(滨江)区 Hi－Tech (Binjiang)
一、播种面积总计	**（公顷）**	**Sown Area of Grain Crops**	**（hectare）**	**106021**	**57530**	**－**	**570**	**194**
春粮	（公顷）	Spring Grain	（hectare）	14732	9444	－	13	94
早稻	（公顷）	Early Rice	（hectare）	2259	1427	－	－	－
晚稻	（公顷）	Late Rice	（hectare）	44516	28995	－	503	100
薯类	（公顷）	Tubers	（hectare）	11216	2620	－	11	－
玉米	（公顷）	Corn	（hectare）	18109	5624	－	23	－
大豆	（公顷）	Soybeans	（hectare）	16224	9509	－	19	－
杂豆	（公顷）	Other Beans	（hectare）	363	222	－	1	－
其他谷物	（公顷）	Other Cereals	（hectare）	817	549	－	－	－
二、总产量	**（吨）**	**Yield of Grain Crops**	**（ton）**	**633820**	**366039**	**－**	**4445**	**1152**
春粮	（吨）	Spring Grain	（ton）	58863	39875	－	46	327
早稻	（吨）	Early Rice	（ton）	14906	9724	－	－	－
晚稻	（吨）	Late Rice	（ton）	361106	237682	－	4150	825
薯类	（吨）	Tubers	（ton）	58050	14959	－	77	－
玉米	（吨）	Corn	（ton）	93546	29694	－	111	－
大豆	（吨）	Soybeans	（ton）	52196	35311	－	58	－
杂豆	（吨）	Other Beans	（ton）	1139	802	－	2	－
其他谷物	（吨）	Other Cereals	（ton）	3764	2468	－	－	－
三、公顷产量	**（公斤）**	**Yield per Hectare**	**（kg）**	**5978**	**6363**	**－**	**7798**	**5938**
春粮	（公斤）	Spring Grain	（kg）	3996	4222	－	3538	3479
早稻	（公斤）	Early Rice	（kg）	6599	6814	－	－	－
晚稻	（公斤）	Late Rice	（kg）	8112	8197	－	8251	8250
薯类	（公斤）	Tubers	（kg）	5176	5710	－	7000	－
玉米	（公斤）	Corn	（kg）	5166	5280	－	4826	－
大豆	（公斤）	Soybeans	（kg）	3217	3713	－	3053	－

播种面积及产量(2015 年)
Grain Crops by Region(2015)

萧山区 Xiaoshan	余杭区 Yuhang	富阳区 Fuyang	桐庐县 Tonglu	淳安县 Chun'an	建德市 Jiande	临安市 Lin'an
22910	**15645**	**18024**	**9017**	**16986**	**13856**	**8632**
3966	1747	3544	916	1009	1693	1670
840	438	82	82	–	750	–
8112	9949	10326	4267	1619	5956	3679
509	555	1540	896	4879	1113	1708
2598	1067	1908	1830	6167	2900	1588
6741	1688	1059	971	3832	1561	351
79	51	92	25	41	59	16
139	327	83	112	58	41	57
131049	**109939**	**118526**	**54503**	**74729**	**86032**	**52517**
19492	6159	13572	3418	3516	6061	5993
5796	2989	504	513	–	4669	–
65095	84258	83327	32822	12121	49123	29358
3284	3332	8241	4999	22701	5706	9685
13563	5781	10086	9229	30562	16237	7824
23757	6719	4768	3108	8305	4378	1094
247	188	365	67	77	141	52
740	1284	444	658	131	162	345
5720	**7027**	**6576**	**6045**	**4399**	**6209**	**6084**
4915	3525	3830	3731	3485	3580	3589
6900	6824	6146	6256	–	6225	–
8025	8469	8069	7692	7487	8248	7980
6452	6004	5351	5579	4653	5127	5670
5221	5418	5286	5043	4956	5599	4927
3524	3981	4502	3201	2167	2805	3117

3-09 油、菜、茶、

Statistics on Rapeseeds, Vegetables, Tea,

指标	Item	全市 Whole City	市区 Urban District	江干区 Jianggan	西湖区 Xihu	高新(滨江)区 Hi-Tech (Binjiang)
一、油料	**Oil Plants**					
播种面积 (公顷)	Sown Area (hectare)	32415	13192	-	36	-
每公顷产量 (公斤)	Yield per Hectare (kg)	2414	2708	-	1694	-
总产量 (吨)	Total Output (ton)	78264	35728	-	61	-
二、蔬菜	**Vegetables**					
播种面积 (公顷)	Sown Area (hectare)	94167	63683	1235	2252	611
总产量 (吨)	Total Output (ton)	3188439	2297742	31794	43284	27618
三、茶叶	**Tea**					
(一)茶园面积 (公顷)	Tea Garden Area (hectare)	34413	10346	23	1124	49
(二)总产量 (吨)	Output of Tea (ton)	28139	15928	8	407	9
春　茶 (吨)	Spring Tea (ton)	19881	10909	8	264	9
夏　茶 (吨)	Summer Tea (ton)	5362	3544	-	33	-
秋　茶 (吨)	Autumn Tea (ton)	2896	1475	-	110	-
四、桑蚕	**Silkworm Cocoons & Mulberry**					
(一)桑园总面积 (公顷)	Mulberry Garden Area (hectare)	12568	1996	-	-	-
(二)蚕茧总产量 (吨)	Output of Silkworm Cocoons (ton)	10426	2127	-	-	-
春　茧 (吨)	Spring Silkworm Cocoons (ton)	5032	1053	-	-	-
夏　茧 (吨)	Summer Silkworm Cocoons (ton)	766	253	-	-	-
秋　茧 (吨)	Autumn Silkworm Cocoons (ton)	4628	821	-	-	-

蚕、果生产情况(2015 年)
Silkworm Cocoons and Fruits Production(2015)

			桐庐县 Tonglu	淳安县 Chun'an	建德市 Jiande	临安市 Lin'an
萧山区 Xiaoshan	余杭区 Yuhang	富阳区 Fuyang				
4699	1604	6850	4490	7740	5038	1955
2922	2139	2700	2258	1960	2412	2595
13732	3431	18498	10140	15171	12152	5073
26080	22369	10363	6447	9018	7783	7236
1160899	662566	357088	214054	249187	245173	182283
1237	3649	3903	3855	12620	4107	3485
573	7952	6827	2750	4523	2398	2540
457	5129	4943	1559	3590	1824	1999
32	1594	1874	538	453	447	380
84	1229	10	653	480	127	161
55	954	987	1169	6528	1367	1508
–	166	1961	1627	3718	925	2029
–	147	910	845	1674	354	1106
–	7	245	4	481	14	14
–	16	806	778	1563	557	909

3－09 续表

指标	Item	全市 Whole City	市区 Urban District	江干区 Jianggan	西湖区 Xihu	高新(滨江)区 Hi－Tech (Binjiang)
五、水果生产	**Fruits**					
(一)果园面积合计 (公顷)	Area of Orchards (hectare)	30042	9119		60	85
柑桔园 (公顷)	Citrus (hectare)	9307	365		9	5
梨　园 (公顷)	Pears (hectare)	4159	1671		13	30
桃　园 (公顷)	Peaches (hectare)	3863	1443		6	－
杨梅园 (公顷)	Red Bayberry (hectare)	3074	1353		1	47
枇杷园 (公顷)	Loquat (hectare)	2438	938		－	－
柿子园 (公顷)	Persimmons (hectare)	875	217		1	－
葡萄园 (公顷)	Grapes (hectare)	1381	944		29	3
其他果园 (公顷)	Others (hectare)	4945	2188		1	－
(二)水果总产量 (吨)	Yield of Fruits (ton)	789563	306666		2460	1030
柑　桔 (吨)	Citrus (ton)	197791	4083		188	13
梨　头 (吨)	Pears (ton)	60751	27364		467	293
桃　子 (吨)	Peaches (ton)	70037	38814		118	－
杨　梅 (吨)	Red Bayberry (ton)	11459	5093		20	18
枇　杷 (吨)	Loquat (ton)	13111	5781		－	－
柿　子 (吨)	Persimmons (ton)	7440	2254		9	－
葡　萄 (吨)	Grapes (ton)	22799	14957		739	18
果用瓜 (吨)	Melon as Fruit (ton)	361735	198361		885	688
其他水果 (吨)	Others (ton)	44440	9959		34	－

continued

萧山区 Xiaoshan	余杭区 Yuhang	富阳区 Fuyang	桐庐县 Tonglu	淳安县 Chun'an	建德市 Jiande	临安市 Lin'an
2690	3449	2836	3814	8491	6688	1930
35	52	266	264	4662	3896	120
217	851	559	1350	552	307	279
192	483	763	809	965	341	305
667	240	398	539	425	563	194
2	870	67	131	854	502	13
82	29	106	47	444	137	30
212	367	332	143	83	62	149
1283	557	345	531	506	880	840
110594	83482	107669	87833	122904	218820	53340
420	650	2812	3328	69673	119591	1116
1206	13462	11935	18640	5280	6163	3304
1562	8372	28763	9009	9132	7677	5405
2075	1210	1770	1808	1452	1689	1417
31	5636	113	405	4548	2252	125
814	658	773	414	3417	1029	326
4707	5488	4006	1695	843	2424	2880
96055	44335	54967	48692	22839	66176	25667
3724	3671	2530	3842	5720	11819	13100

3－10 分地区畜牧业

Statistics on Animal

指 标	Item	全市 Whole City	市区 Urban District	江干区 Jianggan	西湖区 Xihu
一、生猪	**Hogs**				
生猪年末存栏 （万头）	Being Raised at Year－end （10000 heads）	156.82	104.18		
#能繁殖的母猪 （万头）	#Reproducible （10000 heads）	12.55	9.23		
年内肥猪出栏 （万头）	Slaughtered Hogs of the Year （10000 heads）	300.58	198.61		1.89
全年饲养量 （万头）	Number of Hogs Raised in the year （10000 heads）	457.4	302.79		1.89
二、牛	**Cattle & Buffaloes**				
牛年末存栏 （头）	Being Raised at Year－end （head）	16628	8281		
#良种及改良种乳牛 （头）	#Improved Milk Cows （head）	7542	5086		
牛年内出栏 （头）	Slaughtered Cattle & Buffaloes of the Year （head）	15454	9650		2
三、羊	**Sheep & Goats**				
羊年末存栏 （万只）	Being Raised at Year－end （10000 heads）	24	16.07	2.95	
羊年内出栏 （万只）	Slaughtered Sheep & Goats of the Year （10000 heads）	30.88	23.7	2.95	0.11
四、兔	**Rabbits**				
兔年末存栏 （万只）	Being Raised at Year－end （10000 heads）	21.66	6.54		
兔年内出栏 （万只）	Slaughtered Rabbits of the Year （10000 heads）	86.76	17.82		
五、家禽	**Poultry**				
家禽年末存栏 （万只）	Being Raised at Year－end （10000 heads）	1143.64	526.48		3.02
家禽内出栏 （万只）	Slaughtered Poultry of the Year （10000 heads）	2829.1	1802.35		19.48
六、年末养蜂箱数 （箱）	**Beehives （case）**	**183070**	**55588**		
七、畜禽产品产量	**Output of Livestock Products**				
1. 肉类产量 （吨）	Output of Meat （ton）	278409	179734	801	1699
#猪 肉 （吨）	Pork （ton）	223743	144565		1418

渔业生产(2015 年)
Husbanday and Fishery by Region(2015)

高新(滨江)区 Hi-Tech(Binjiang)	萧山区 Xiaoshan	余杭区 Yuhang	富阳区 Fuyang	桐庐县 Tonglu	淳安县 Chun'an	建德市 Jiande	临安市 Lin'an
	82.86	5.18	15.77	8.86	14.7	10.56	18.52
	7.67	0.53	1.01	0.45	0.58	0.98	1.31
1.67	127.56	11.21	55.79	16.74	21.74	22.17	41.32
1.67	210.43	16.4	71.56	25.6	36.44	32.73	59.84
	2848	515	2431	1703	1543	1802	3299
	2592	7				476	1980
	600	473	4689	1514	781	828	2681
	4.92	5.63	2.54	1.34	0.41	2.03	4.15
0.3	7.2	6.13	7.31	1.74	0.39	0.92	4.13
	0.8	4.43	1.3	2.95	0.14	0.93	11.1
	2.14	4.75	10.93	6.92	0.2	4.24	57.58
0.06	210.16	125.18	187.95	60.39	56.26	440.41	60.1
0.91	516.97	474.14	790.52	115.98	78.99	695.59	136.19
	20142	**3135**	**32311**	**67015**	**29130**	**18000**	**13337**
1360	99842	18167	57120	14280	18067	29708	36620
1296	90621	8328	42572	11672	16676	18843	31987

3－10 续表

指 标		Item		全市 Whole City	市区 Urban District	江干区 Jianggan	西湖区 Xihu
牛 肉	（吨）	Beef	（ton）	2373	1439		
羊 肉	（吨）	Mutton	（ton）	6312	4869	801	19
兔 肉	（吨）	Rabbit Meat	（ton）	1502	303		
禽 肉	（吨）	Poultry Meat	（ton）	44045	28510		261
2.禽蛋产量	（吨）	Poultry Eggs	（ton）	113996	18466		159
3.蜂蜜产量	（吨）	Honey	（ton）	29327	16151		
4.蜂皇浆产量	（公斤）	Honey Tonic	（kg）	546545	137632		
5.牛奶产量	（吨）	Milk	（ton）	34176	24556		
6.兔毛产量	（吨）	Rabbit Wool	（ton）	41	12		
八、渔业生产		**Fishery**					
（一）淡水产品产量总计	（吨）	Total Output of Freshwater Aquatic Products	（ton）	178880	141115	347	20517
其中：养殖产量	（吨）	Artificially Cultured	（ton）	168983	137638	267	19791
1.鱼 类	（吨）	Fish	（ton）	116190	84470	287	15289
#鲫 鱼	（吨）	#Crucians	（ton）	13558	8891	40	2674
鳊 鱼	（吨）	Breams	（ton）	7004	3520	5	856
黑 鱼	（吨）	Snake Heads	（ton）	14770	14761	－	1236
2.虾蟹类	（吨）	Shrimps，Prawns & Crabs	（ton）	29592	28973	－	836
3.贝 类	（吨）	Shellfish	（ton）	2734	1479	－	51
4.其 他	（吨）	Others	（ton）	30364	26193	60	4341
#甲 鱼	（吨）	Turtles	（ton）	27708	24427	－	4333
（二）淡水养殖面积合计	（公顷）	Freshwater Aquiculture Area	（hectare）	59227	12135	40	1947

continued

高新(滨江)区 Hi-Tech(Binjiang)	萧山区 Xiaoshan	余杭区 Yuhang	富阳区 Fuyang	桐庐县 Tonglu	淳安县 Chun'an	建德市 Jiande	临安市 Lin'an
	127	105	802	281	115	133	405
60	1315	1515	1156	328	56	184	875
	32	107	165	138	4	68	989
3	7748	8112	12377	1796	1216	10434	2089
	2038	7499	8763	5138	5573	78546	6273
	1263	387	14502	7871	3169	1150	986
	53833	25537	58262	300540	40194	13622	54557
	9915					2973	6647
		12				1	28
1050	36710	59748	12355	8591	12986	11290	4898
650	35989	59068	11661	8283	10262	8524	4276
698	12407	41701	10923	5138	12491	9959	4132
183	-	2722	3150	1113	1555	1104	895
30	-	1692	927	95	1250	1763	376
1	2854	10373	52	9	-	-	-
177	19948	912	677	188	148	213	70
-	-	1225	203	-	195	888	172
175	4355	15910	552	3265	152	230	524
175	4113	14604	402	2723	152	59	347
60	2911	4342	1503	1420	41041	1916	2715

3-11 分地区林业
Statistics on Forestry

指 标	Item	全市 Whole City	市区 Urban District
一、营林情况	**Afforestation**		
1. 当年造林面积 (公顷)	Afforested Areas (hectare)	2644	695
2. 迹地更新面积 (公顷)	Area of Forest Updating (hectare)	3395	226
3. 封山育林面积 (公顷)	Area of Afforestation in Enclosed Mountain (hectare)	92439	37534
4. 零星(四旁)植树 (万株)	Planting Trees (10000 plant)	397	204
5. 中、幼龄林抚育面积(公顷)	Area of Grown Forest Cultivated (hectare)	32565	8458
二、林产品产量	**Output of Forest Products**		
1. 油茶籽 (吨)	Camellia Seeds (ton)	11225	5
2. 竹笋干 (吨)	Dried Bamboo Shoots (ton)	61105	21776
3. 核 桃 (吨)	Walnuts (ton)	17537	221
4. 板 栗 (吨)	Chestnuts (ton)	12046	1767
三、竹木采伐量	**Lumbering**		
1. 木 材 (万立方米)	Timber Cut (10000 cu. m)	25.77	3.15
2. 竹 材 (万支)	Bamboo Cut (10000 pieces)	3614	2128

生产(2015 年)

by Region(2015)

萧山区 Xiaoshan	余杭区 Yuhang	富阳区 Fuyang	桐庐县 Tonglu	淳安县 Chun'an	建德市 Jiande	临安市 Lin'an
280	122	240	467	466	453	563
–	26	200	470	767	987	945
13339	–	23133	40846	7387	3339	3333
30	144.275	30	20	70.829	33	69.1
837	403	6667	5573	1333	6333	10868
–	–	5	1520	7800	1800	100
1850	9892	10034	7421	6440	2068	23400
–	21	200	1400	5857	84	9975
425	142	1200	1600	4893	2860	926
0.01	0.66	2.45	2.70	5.61	5.78	8.53
136	787	1203	267	522	237	460

3－12 分地区主要农
Possession of Major Agricultural

指 标		Item		全市 Whole City	市区 Urban District
一、农业机械总动力	**（千瓦）**	**Total Power of Agricultural Machinery**	**（kw）**	**2994664**	**1813684**
耕作机械动力	（千瓦）	Cultivation Machinery	（kw）	213117	136719
收获机械动力	（千瓦）	Harvest Machinery	（kw）	44970	32559
植保机械动力	（千瓦）	Plant Protection Machinery	（kw）	49888	11246
排灌机械动力	（千瓦）	Drainage & Irrigation Machinery	（kw）	413650	248258
农副产品加工机械动力	（千瓦）	Processing Machinery of Agricultural Products	（kw）	173185	63091
运输机械动力	（千瓦）	Transport Machinery	（kw）	520220	317162
渔业机械动力	（千瓦）	Fishery Machinery	（kw）	117134	101381
其他机械动力	（千瓦）	Other Machinery	（kw）	1462500	903268
二、主要农机具		**Agricultural Machinery and Machinery For Processing Farm Products**			
大中型拖拉机	（台）	Large & Medium Tractors	（unit）	1182	1030
机引农具	（台）	Mechanized Farm Implement	（unit）	2461	2268
农用小型拖拉机	（台）	Mini－tractors	（unit）	11987	7170
联合收获机	（台）	Combine Harvesters	（unit）	918	738
机动割晒机	（台）	Motorized Harvesters	（unit）	7	6
机动脱粒机	（台）	Motorized Thresher	（unit）	102106	73570
谷物烘干机	（台）	Cereal Dryer	（unit）	418	238
机动喷雾（粉）器	（架）	Motorized Sprayer	（unit）	30958	7076
农用水泵	（台）	Water Pump for Agricultural Use	（unit）	142901	54614
节水喷灌机械	（套）	Saving Water and Sprinkling Machinery	（set）	4188	623
粮食加工机械	（台）	Grain Processing Machinery	（unit）	19841	3723
棉花加工机械	（台）	Cotton Processing Machinery	（unit）	231	126
油料加工机械	（台）	Oil Processing Machinery	（unit）	1670	296
农用运输机械	（台）	Vehicles for Agricultural Use	（unit）	23805	15349

机具年末拥有量(2015 年)
Machinery at the Year - end by Region(2015)

萧山区 Xiaoshan	余杭区 Yuhang	富阳区 Fuyang	桐庐县 Tonglu	淳安县 Chun'an	建德市 Jiande	临安市 Lin'an
631464	**448517**	**439836**	**182577**	**305520**	**288969**	**403914**
57637	42756	34153	11402	12991	25051	26954
11122	7779	12559	5243	1066	4664	1438
4381	3000	3543	1516	2851	4584	29691
86895	82758	56134	33470	22009	48577	61336
30918	15320	13032	11658	48352	23048	27036
142447	78859	86739	30021	51325	50618	71094
77712	9170	2114	1299	12160	2147	147
220352	208875	231562	87968	154766	130280	186218
506	251	172	71	13	41	27
1593	501	173	77	18	65	33
1756	2691	2523	806	1246	2217	548
374	114	231	63	23	65	29
–	4	2	–	1	–	–
13266	31847	28317	14133	2474	11331	598
123	62	53	52	23	76	29
3064	1596	1644	736	2203	2042	18901
16844	18052	16390	14286	5126	24574	44301
193	405	9	47	527	2933	58
1406	1063	1148	1417	7113	2078	5510
65	9	52	21	62	16	6
155	45	85	254	606	316	198
6844	3593	4377	1843	1953	2284	2376

3－13 农业物资
Agricultural Material

指　标		Item		全市 Whole City	市区 Urban District
一、农村用电量	**（万千瓦时）**	**Electricity Consumed in Rural Area**	**（10000 kwh）**	**1081720**	**879162**
二、农业化肥施用量		**Consumption of Chemical Fertilizer**			
（一）按实物量计算	（吨）	Physical Quantity Consumption	（ton）	485774	273910
1. 氮　肥	（吨）	Nitrogenous Fertilizer	（ton）	210550	121259
2. 磷　肥	（吨）	Phosphate Fertilizer	（ton）	71139	43598
3. 钾　肥	（吨）	Potash Fertilizer	（ton）	37196	15696
4. 复合肥	（吨）	Compound Fertilizer	（ton）	166889	93356
（二）按折纯法计算	（吨）	Pure Consumption	（ton）	97222	48054
1. 氮　肥	（吨）	Nitrogenous Fertilizer	（ton）	45646	22853
2. 磷　肥	（吨）	Phosphate Fertilizer	（ton）	10751	5288
3. 钾　肥	（吨）	Potash Fertilizer	（ton）	7432	2734
4. 复合肥	（吨）	Compound Fertilizer	（ton）	33393	17180
三、农用塑料薄膜使用量	**（吨）**	**Use of Plastic Film**	**（ton）**	**11028**	**3319**
四、农用柴油使用量	**（吨）**	**Consumption of Diesel Oil**	**（ton）**	**25756**	**9551**
五、农药使用量	**（吨）**	**Consumption of Pesticide**	**（ton）**	**6904**	**3496**

消耗情况(2015 年)
Consumption(2015)

萧山区 Xiaoshan	余杭区 Yuhang	富阳区 Fuyang	桐庐县 Tonglu	淳安县 Chun'an	建德市 Jiande	临安市 Lin'an
176373	**226878**	**389449**	**50536**	**13168**	**21394**	**117460**
189217	53815	23443	36649	57683	49870	67662
79169	27035	11958	17183	30813	22934	18361
32108	7939	2525	7607	6656	6953	6325
9279	5344	567	3981	6259	4841	6419
68661	13497	8393	7878	13955	15143	36557
22582	13013	9906	10849	7238	17026	14055
11113	5678	5020	4289	2976	9632	5896
2898	1166	909	1590	768	2016	1089
1118	1175	284	1217	394	1743	1344
7453	4994	3693	3753	3100	3634	5726
2041	**370**	**257**	**730**	**4122**	**1711**	**1146**
6507	**2394**	**410**	**4891**	**1833**	**3357**	**6124**
1585	**974**	**779**	**699**	**638**	**1007**	**1064**

3－14 乡(镇)
Statistics on Towns

乡镇名称 Town		社区(居民委员会) Number of communities (residents committees)	村民委员会(个) Number of Villagers' Committees (unit)	乡镇常住户数(户) Resident Households in Towns (household)
江干区	**Jianggan District**	**81**	**4**	**57829**
丁兰街道	Dinglan Subdistrict	22	2	15267
笕桥街道	Jianqiao Subdistrict	20	–	13798
彭埠街道	Pengbu Subdistrict	18	–	12686
九堡街道	Jiubao Subdistrict	21	2	16078
西湖区	**Xihu District**	**83**	**36**	**101543**
留下街道	Liuxia Subdistrict	11	1	7245
转塘街道	Zhuantang Subdistrict	34	8	21267
双浦镇	Shuangpu	7	23	15037
三墩镇	Sandun	31	4	57994
高新(滨江)区	**Hi－Tech(Bingjiang) District**	**51**	**–**	**121352**
浦沿街道	Puyan Subdistrict	18	–	77154
长河街道	Changhe Subdistrict	20	–	29155
西兴街道	Xixing Subdistrict	13	–	15043
西湖风景名胜区	**The West Lake Scenic Zone**	**6**	**9**	**3854**
西湖街道	West Lake Subdistrict	6	9	3854
萧山区	**Xiaoshan District**	**121**	**416**	**442095**
楼塔镇	Louta	1	12	8502
河上镇	Heshang	1	15	8464
戴村镇	Daicun	1	22	10838
浦阳镇	Puyang	–	18	12989
进化镇	Jinhua	1	25	15906
临浦镇	Linpu	5	20	16996

基本情况(2015 年)
and Townships(2015)

乡镇常住人口数(人) Resident Population in Towns (person)	乡镇就业人员数(人) Employed Persons in Towns (person)	乡镇常用耕地面积(亩) Commonly used cultivated area of township (mu)	公共财政总收入(万元) Public Finance Income (10000 yuan)	公共财政支出(万元) Public Finance Expenditure (10000 yuan)
242200	**139828**	**8921**	**217542**	**81900**
77332	29400	285	79225	9514
56695	37509	3931	14562	16700
52995	41787	1965	89302	18006
55178	31132	2740	34453	37680
418005	**195424**	**55294**	**341357**	**243240**
74700	27990	326	9600	9612
99769	33063	17340	223829	125359
59880	31648	22665	7864	7655
183656	102723	14963	100064	100614
401847	**115975**	**8049**	**150991**	**83201**
191301	45447	3105	57951	14478
110783	25997	2595	56203	45416
99763	44531	2349	36837	23307
7426	**4272**	**-**	**11149**	**10304**
7426	4272	-	11149	10304
1557588	**868516**	**563138**	**1146687**	**816362**
33224	19914	12605	17830	17689
28730	15098	13050	20156	18869
37624	23462	17775	24861	24901
44777	31993	17055	23600	17100
52632	30419	18165	19435	26955
75227	46801	16200	62900	33600

3－14 续表1

乡 镇 名 称 Town		社区(居民委员会) Number of Communities (residents committees)	村民委员会(个) Number of Villagers' Committees (unit)	乡镇常住户数(户) Resident Households in Towns (household)
义桥镇	Yiqiao	2	21	14451
所前镇	Suoqian	1	19	12353
衙前镇	Yaqian	2	11	7103
闻堰镇(街道)	Wenyan(Subdistrict)	4	6	9260
宁围镇(街道)	Ningwei(Subdistrict)	2	20	18304
新街镇(街道)	Xinjie(Subdistrict)	4	15	17083
瓜沥镇	Guali	11	63	69697
益农镇	Yinong	1	19	14491
靖江街道	Jingjiang Subdistrict	3	10	13294
南阳街道	Nanyang Subdistrict	2	13	10783
义蓬街道	Yipeng Subdistrict	4	22	26258
河庄街道	Hezhuang Subdistrict	1	20	13158
党湾镇	Dangwan	1	17	12258
新湾街道	Xinwan Subdistrict	1	12	10222
城厢街道	Chengxiang Subdistrict	33	－	49171
北干街道	Beigan Subdistrict	16	6	22219
蜀山街道	Shushan Subdistrict	18	8	15087
新塘街道	Xintang Subdistrict	5	17	24880
前进街道	Qianjin Subdistrict	－	3	4239
临江街道	Linjiang Subdistrict	1	2	4089
余杭区	**Yuhang District**	**129**	**188**	**346391**
运河街道	Yunhe Subdistrict	5	14	10895
乔司街道	Qiaosi Subdistrict	4	11	20112
塘栖镇	Tangqi	9	27	26889

continued 1

乡镇常住人口数（人）Resident Population in Towns (person)	乡镇就业人员数（人）Employed Persons in Towns (person)	乡镇常用耕地面积（亩）Commonly used cultivated area of township (mu)	公共财政总收入（万元）Public Finance Income (10000 yuan)	公共财政支出（万元）Public Finance Expenditure (10000 yuan)
49152	29307	20640	55300	23000
45035	21903	13391	15635	15567
27901	15571	7875	67582	67571
30596	26189	3885	23363	22842
61912	40746	24689	97934	24247
55982	31748	29385	78312	26007
231450	124186	93645	204693	111700
48312	27613	42390	19148	18949
53026	24016	21210	14094	14038
57253	22707	19935	51625	14691
87743	54614	48660	28860	27332
50662	29317	37771	13719	12830
43680	38394	34485	16470	16375
33877	16095	19229	13842	7659
147298	69933	1365	71395	71390
65924	29611	2960	162380	162380
62061	33360	13440	17930	15047
92834	48960	10215	14013	14013
21371	14105	8805	3200	3200
19305	2454	14313	8410	8410
1454294	**886604**	**387623**	**895735**	**472467**
53998	32393	10275	18565	18107
81026	49437	13294	57603	36149
135607	82978	30840	74177	53797

3 - 14　续表 2

乡 镇 名 称	Town	社区(居民委员会) Number of Communities (residents committees)	村民委员会(个) Number of Villagers´ Committees (unit)	乡镇常住户数(户) Resident Households in Towns (household)
仁和街道	Renhe Subdistrict	1	18	18136
崇贤街道	Chongxian Subdistrict	2	11	12147
余杭街道	Yuhang Subdistrict	7	14	45121
闲林街道	Xianlin Subdistrict	5	8	28571
仓前街道	Cangqian Subdistrict	1	9	9218
中泰街道	Zhongtai Subdistrict	4	10	9246
良渚街道	Liangzhu Subdistrict	12	23	34219
瓶窑镇	Pingyao	6	13	20687
径山镇	Jingshan	2	13	12165
黄湖镇	Huanghu	1	5	5101
鸬鸟镇	Luniao	1	6	3670
百丈镇	Baizhang	1	6	3121
临平街道	Linping Subdistrict	20		31382
南苑街道	Nanyuan Subdistrict	22		38816
星桥街道	Xingqiao Subdistrict	15		10322
五常街道	Wuchang Subdistrict	11		6573
富阳区	**Fuyang District**	**28**	**276**	**274305**
万市镇	Wanshi	1	15	7181
洞桥镇	Dongqiao		11	6088
胥口镇	Xukou		13	5637
永昌镇	Yongchang		5	3650
渌渚镇	Luzhu		13	5402
新登镇	Xindeng	4	28	38640
上官乡	Shangguan		5	2706

continued 2

乡镇常住人口数（人）Resident Population in Towns (person)	乡镇就业人员数（人）Employed Persons in Towns (person)	乡镇常用耕地面积(亩) Commonly used cultivated area of township (mu)	公共财政总收入（万元）Public Finance Income (10000 yuan)	公共财政支出（万元）Public Finance Expenditure (10000 yuan)
71483	42420	36226	19316	14263
67892	43110	15150	32149	15648
120048	66304	48750	61579	22735
85831	35986	11469	75021	68839
75467	48528	24540	77807	18462
35621	20052	18597	18949	8966
221087	139274	44940	153804	104788
70859	41807	40920	55754	34083
39252	21646	47625	25106	25528
18928	11996	14370	5433	5336
12807	5311	11670	872	3500
9519	6933	2318	5619	3194
90131	63967	2340	24982	11410
113526	80666	8531	56272	8038
43173	26577	3746	4276	5952
108039	67219	2022	128451	13672
859616	**459992**	**293690**	**279291**	**199224**
22790	13901	19245	7494	7494
17831	11907	16234	6553	6530
13909	10408	12252	13853	13830
10835	6067	8460	12058	12047
16655	10783	11355	14882	14837
108016	69346	37317	23668	23609
8206	4789	2388	3551	3531

3 - 14 续表3

乡镇名称	Town	社区(居民委员会) Number of Communities (residents committees)	村民委员会(个) Number of Villagers' Committees (unit)	乡镇常住户数(户) Resident Households in Towns (household)
常绿镇	Changlu		8	5226
大源镇	Dayuan		15	11509
灵桥镇	Lingqiao		13	7301
里山镇	Lishan		5	3250
渔山乡	Yushan		4	3840
场口镇	Changkou	1	24	13641
龙门镇	Longmen		4	2541
环山乡	Huanshan		7	3781
常安镇	Chang'an		16	7472
湖源乡	Huyuan		10	3297
春建乡	Chunjian		6	3013
新桐乡	Xintong		7	3725
鹿山街道	Lushan Subdistrict		9	7884
富春街道	Fuchun Subdistrict	22	12	89907
春江街道	Chunjiang Subdistrict		9	11816
东洲街道	Dongzhou Subdistrict		15	12005
银湖街道	Yinghu Subdistrict		22	14793
桐庐县	**Tonglu County**	**15**	**183**	**155413**
桐君街道	Tongjun Subdistrict	8	6	20058
旧县街道	Jiuxian Subdistrict		5	3065
富春江镇	Fuchunjiang	2	15	10371
江南镇	Jiangnan	1	20	14233
凤川街道	Fengchuan Subdistrict		8	5955
新合乡	Xinghe		5	1662

continued 3

乡镇常住人口数（人）Resident Population in Towns (person)	乡镇就业人员数（人）Employed Persons in Towns (person)	乡镇常用耕地面积（亩）Commonly used cultivated area of township (mu)	公共财政总收入（万元）Public Finance Income (10000 yuan)	公共财政支出（万元）Public Finance Expenditure (10000 yuan)
15559	8688	3160	4036	4055
37081	28513	9015	13063	12951
24279	15965	7564	6279	6344
10150	6280	3825	3616	2290
13317	8807	8910	3335	3321
42103	25664	21855	10456	10427
5857	4603	4355	2311	2315
12580	7611	5790	4328	3983
25415	18199	15435	6372	6372
10695	9492	9015	3680	3664
9284	6129	7545	3490	3472
11630	7874	8970	3562	3560
23316	12768	11415	5811	5774
284416	85360	18525	102647	27375
40646	29592	6705	6957	6956
44936	27235	19875	10938	10937
50110	30011	24480	6351	3550
452697	**259596**	**217548**	**128272**	**63149**
56516	30937	5175	9151	3007
8852	5768	6420	3086	729
26299	14014	12960	30144	30144
45487	31205	25440	23841	3891
17570	12638	9300	4023	3373
4940	3337	4125	732	779

3－14　续表4

乡镇名称 Town		社区(居民委员会) Number of Communities (residents committees)	村民委员会(个) Number of Villagers' Committees (unit)	乡镇常住户数(户) Resident Households in Towns (household)
横村镇	Hengcun		24	14573
莪山畲族乡	Eshan		7	2973
钟山乡	Zhongshan		11	5736
分水镇	Fenshui		26	25658
瑶琳镇	Yaolin		16	10916
百江镇	Baijiang		15	5053
合村乡	Hecun		6	2808
城南街道	Chengnan Subdistrict	4	19	32352
淳安县	**Chun'an County**	**12**	**425**	**139328**
千岛湖镇	Qiandaohu	9	22	28392
文昌镇	Wenchang		16	4004
石林镇	Shilin		8	1393
临歧镇	Linqi		17	5990
威坪镇	Weiping	1	44	14989
姜家镇	Jiangjia	1	28	6993
梓桐镇	Zitong		19	5936
汾口镇	Fenkou	1	51	16489
中洲镇	Zhongzhou		19	5715
大墅镇	Dashu		17	4320
枫树岭镇	Fengshuling		28	5823
里商乡	Lishang		16	3250
金峰乡	Jinfeng		11	1683
富文乡	Fuwen		10	2035
左口乡	Zuokou		11	3311

continued 4

乡镇常住人口数（人）Resident Population in Towns (person)	乡镇就业人员数（人）Employed Persons in Towns (person)	乡镇常用耕地面积（亩）Commonly used cultivated area of township (mu)	公共财政总收入（万元）Public Finance Income (10000 yuan)	公共财政支出（万元）Public Finance Expenditure (10000 yuan)
43147	24036	41130	8321	2165
9144	5403	6699	1219	2221
15968	9989	17730	1220	1134
71842	38205	28995	18235	9201
32206	20154	26979	5828	2269
15063	9255	13470	1766	1239
9126	6046	8205	574	999
96537	48609	10920	20132	1998
429090	**292034**	**181261**	**20203**	**151795**
83171	63750	8012	6229	11445
12471	8562	6424	470	5579
4590	2983	2599	111	2241
19906	12918	13028	425	11523
44280	37642	15606	979	16435
22713	16328	12449	803	12970
18130	12879	10965	136	6454
53112	24004	23131	1548	19473
18533	12280	9039	104	7199
13714	9564	9426	4548	4035
17811	13066	13526	304	7276
10448	7000	3384	313	4696
5006	3484	3885	212	2514
6310	4317	4350	105	2697
10662	6723	5685	106	3664

3－14 续表5

乡镇名称 Town		社区(居民委员会) Number of Communities (residents committees)	村民委员会(个) Number of Villagers´ Committees (unit)	乡镇常住户数 (户) Resident Households in Towns (household)
屏门乡	Pingmen		15	3195
瑶山乡	Yaoshan		11	2808
王阜乡	Wangfu		18	5988
宋村乡	Songcun		8	2016
鸠坑乡	Jiukeng		9	2599
浪川乡	Langchuan		19	6132
界首乡	Jieshou		13	2757
安阳乡	Anyang		15	3510
建德市	**Jiande City**	**38**	**229**	**175789**
新安江街道	Xin´anjiang Subdistrict	11	4	38239
洋溪街道	Yangxi Subdistrict	4	2	4910
更楼街道	Genglou Subdistrict	2	14	7375
莲花镇	Lianhua	1	6	3087
乾潭镇	Qiantan	1	24	13860
钦堂乡	Qintang	1	7	2556
梅城镇	Meicheng	5	13	18456
杨村桥镇	Yangcunqiao	1	13	5957
下涯镇	Xiaya	1	11	7704
大洋镇	Dayang	3	19	9988
三都镇	Sandu	1	19	8919
寿昌镇	Shouchang	1	23	16132

continued 5

乡镇常住人口数（人）Resident Population in Towns (person)	乡镇就业人员数（人）Employed Persons in Towns (person)	乡镇常用耕地面积（亩）Commonly used cultivated area of township (mu)	公共财政总收入（万元）Public Finance Income (10000 yuan)	公共财政支出（万元）Public Finance Expenditure (10000 yuan)
10544	5110	4590	2852	2852
9369	6064	3960	122	3953
17684	11202	3750	100	6312
5750	3929	1860	40	3232
7281	4955	1688	56	2996
18234	11871	11394	258	6350
8256	5653	4800	128	3311
11115	7750	7710	254	4588
522054	**316873**	**236469**	**189183**	**72939**
99803	55770	2820	77258	5332
16208	8780	2486	24429	4294
23109	13306	9870	3144	2028
10732	7383	5655	2400	2201
46890	29317	23100	18563	5236
8208	5224	6900	6828	1909
44000	34583	15378	18216	13811
19682	10705	13620	1600	1600
25878	19389	15615	3939	3939
33396	21139	20846	2476	2476
26957	14453	17775	3065	2647
51566	23776	18975	8188	9859

3－14　续表6

乡镇名称 Town		社区(居民委员会) Number of Communities (residents committees)	村民委员会(个) Number of Villagers´ Committees (unit)	乡镇常住户数(户) Resident Households in Towns (household)
航头镇	Hangtou	1	18	9595
大慈岩镇	Daciyan	1	12	6494
大同镇	Datong	3	34	16562
李家镇	Lijia	1	10	5955
临安市	**Lin'an City**	**25**	**287**	**220779**
玲珑街道	Linlong Subdistrict		16	9360
锦南街道	Jinnan Subdistrict		9	7233
锦城街道	Jincheng Subdistrict	17	5	51557
锦北街道	Jinbei Subdistrict	5	12	20340
青山湖街道	Qingshanghu Subdistrict	1	19	14347
高虹镇	Gaohong		9	5367
太湖源镇	Taihuyuan		20	11614
於潜镇	Yuqian	1	30	19978
太阳镇	Taiyang		18	8833
潜川镇	Qianchuan		16	8405
昌化镇	Changhua	1	14	8405
河桥镇	Heqiao		11	5100
湍口镇	Tuankou		13	3771
清凉峰镇	Qingliangfeng		17	9649
岛石镇	Daoshi		16	8937
板桥镇	Banqiao		15	8549
天目山镇	Tianmushan		23	12340
龙岗镇	Longgang		24	6994

continued 6

乡镇常住人口数（人）Resident Population in Towns (person)	乡镇就业人员数（人）Employed Persons in Towns (person)	乡镇常用耕地面积（亩）Commonly used cultivated area of township (mu)	公共财政总收入（万元）Public Finance Income (10000 yuan)	公共财政支出（万元）Public Finance Expenditure (10000 yuan)
30558	19554	23715	3050	3033
11678	10778	15600	3507	2032
53685	31586	33315	9346	9100
19704	11130	10799	3174	3442
1831803	**377827**	**245325**	**150275**	**86638**
26224	16715	9345	14452	4184
17996	8286	5058	9822	2454
1330106	80624	5142	21333	5959
51902	25210	4950	14222	3683
54310	26297	11790	49351	22925
23983	16927	8700	5825	3450
33724	22539	27945	13076	7248
57383	33873	30465	4454	5200
23945	16837	17672	1223	2484
21037	16010	9765	1861	3160
25270	10659	12683	3093	6359
15100	10700	13155	539	1622
11748	9542	7142	644	1578
27473	17873	16004	1896	2796
26273	16435	8967	199	2575
27085	14080	12390	3677	3130
35583	20247	27555	1667	3643
22661	14973	16597	2941	4188

3-15 农村基本

Basic Situations

指标	Item	全市 Whole City	市区 Urban District	江干区 Jianggan	西湖区 Xihu
一、农村人口与从业人员	**Rural Population and Employed Persons**				
农村户数 （万户）	Rural Household (10000 households)	132.15	80.93	1.71	4.24
农村人口 （万人）	Rural Population (10000 persons)	482.63	325.62	7.59	16.37
男	Male	243.47	164.18	3.70	8.00
女	Female	239.16	161.44	3.89	8.37
农村劳动力资源数 （万人）	Rural Laboar Resources (10000 persons)	313.79	209.49	4.49	10.00
男	Male	163.94	109.45	2.35	5.17
女	Female	149.85	100.04	2.14	4.83
农村从业人员 （万人）	Jobholders in Rural Areas (10000 persons)	284.73	189.71	3.76	9.13
男	Male	151.21	100.72	1.94	4.75
#从事农业人员	Persons Involved in Agriculture	37.58	18.97	0.22	0.98
女	Female	133.52	88.99	1.82	4.38
#从事农业人员	Persons Involved in Agriculture	30.22	14.72	0.15	0.86
二、农村基础设施	**Public Facilities in Rural Areas**				
自来水受益村数	Number of Villages with Access to Tap Water	2054	927	4	36
通有线电视村数	Number of Villages Connecting to Cable TV	2054	927	4	36
通宽带村数	Number of Villages Connecting to Prroadband	2054	927	4	36

情况(2015 年末)
of Rural Areas(End of 2015)

高新(滨江)区 Hi-Tech(Binjiang)	萧山区 Xiaoshan	余杭区 Yuhang	富阳区 Fuyan	桐庐县 Tonglu	淳安县 Chun'an	建德市 Jiande	临安市 Lin'an
2.90	35.25	19.28	16.98	11.13	11.48	12.51	16.10
10.98	125.01	108.74	55.92	33.66	35.70	40.06	47.59
5.32	61.67	56.25	28.76	17.16	18.03	20.49	23.61
5.66	63.34	52.49	27.16	16.50	17.67	19.57	23.98
6.98	78.20	72.93	36.26	22.06	24.31	25.69	32.24
3.52	40.10	38.94	19.03	11.43	12.56	13.84	16.66
3.46	38.10	33.99	17.23	10.63	11.75	11.85	15.58
6.51	69.93	66.36	33.41	20.55	23.31	22.16	29.00
3.31	36.32	36.18	17.90	10.68	12.83	11.84	15.14
0.08	6.21	4.56	6.78	2.86	5.93	5.58	4.24
3.20	33.61	30.18	15.51	9.87	10.48	10.32	13.86
0.04	5.03	3.06	5.44	2.37	5.15	4.41	3.57
–	411	188	279	183	425	232	287
–	411	188	279	183	425	232	287
–	411	188	279	183	425	232	287

3－16 农村基本情况(2010－2015年)

Basic Situations of Rural Areas(2010－2015)

指标 Item	2010	2011	2012	2013	2014	2015
一、农村人口与从业人员 Rural Population and Employed Persons						
农村户数 (万户) Rural Household (10000 households)	131.82	132.94	129.29	132.18	131.96	132.15
农村人口 (万人) Rural Population (10000 persons)	431.34	434.23	425.49	469.90	480.04	482.63
男 Male		218.03	213.81	236.03	241.82	243.47
女 Female		216.2	211.68	233.87	238.22	239.16
农村劳动力资源数 (万人) Rural Laboar Resources (10000 persons)	280.05	281.16	276.62	304.14	314.45	313.79
男 Male		146.23	143.66	157.27	163.98	163.94
女 Female		134.93	132.96	146.87	150.47	149.85
农村从业人员 (万人) Jobholders in Rural Areas (10000 persons)	261.77	262.10	257.30	279.91	286.01	284.73
男 Male	138.18	137.33	134.85	145.70	151.05	151.21
#从事农业人员 Persons Involved in Agriculture					36.50	37.58
女 Female	123.59	124.77	122.45	134.21	134.96	133.52
#从事农业人员 Persons Involved in Agriculture					29.75	30.22
二、农村基础设施 Public Facilities in Rural Areas						
自来水受益村数 Number of Villages with Access to Tap Water	2097	2081	2078	2058	2054	2054
通有线电视村数 Number of Villages Connecting to Cable TV	2098	2081	2078	2058	2054	2054
通宽带村数 Number of Villages Connecting to Prroadband			2078	2058	2054	2054
三、农林牧渔业增加值 Value－added of Agriculture, Forestry, Animal Husbandry and Fishery	**2084144**	**2367708**	**2551127**	**2654059**	**2783252**	**2924013**
农业 Farming	1219343	1386520	1510382	1571300	1685668	1806178
林业 Forestry	260287	277061	302796	324240	371932	393332
牧业 Animal	351494	421453	435191	458201	405348	395476
渔业 Fishery	226096	253456	270629	262233	280544	284506
服务业 Service	26924	29218	32129	38085	39760	44521

主要统计指标解释

农林牧渔业总产值　是以货币表现的农、林、牧、渔业全部产品的总量和对农林牧渔生产活动进行的各种支持性服务活动的价值。他反映一定时期内农林牧渔业生产的总规模和总成果。

农林牧渔业的统计范围是:

(1)农业　包括农作物种植业和其他农业。

农作物种植业　包括谷类、豆类、薯类、棉花、麻类、烟叶、蔬菜、药材、瓜类和其他农作物的种植以及茶园、桑园、果园的生产经营。

其他农业　包括采集野生植物的果实、纤维、树脂、油料以及柴草、野生药材、菌类等。

(2)林业　包括林木的栽培(不包括茶园、桑园和果园的栽培、管理和收获等活动)、林产品的采集、村及村以下合作经济组织和农户的竹木砍伐。

(3)牧业　包括除渔业养殖以外的一切动物饲养和放牧以及野生动物的捕猎和饲养。

(4)渔业　包括水生动物和海藻类植物的养殖和捕捞。

(5)农林牧渔服务业　包括对农林牧渔生产活动进行的各种支持性服务活动。

粮食产量　指全社会的产量,包括国营农场等全民所有制经营、集体统一经营和农民家庭经营的产量,还包括工矿企业家属办的农场和其他生产单位的产量。粮食除包括稻谷、小麦、大麦、玉米、高粱、谷子及其他杂粮外,还包括薯类和豆类。其产量计算方法,豆类按去豆荚后的干豆计算,薯类按5公斤鲜薯折1公斤粮食计算,其他粮食一律按脱粒后的原粮计算。

猪、牛、羊肉产量　指当年出栏并已屠宰的猪、牛、羊的肉产量,即屠宰后除去头蹄下水后带骨的(即胴体重)重量。

水产品产量　指人工养殖的水产品和天然生长的水产品的捕捞量。包括海水的鱼类、虾蟹类、贝类和藻类以及内陆水域的鱼类、虾蟹类和贝类,不包括淡水生植物。

有效灌溉面积　指具有一定水源,地块比较平整、灌溉工程或设备已经配套,在一般年景下当年能够进行正常灌溉的耕地面积。

农业机械总动力　指主要用于农、林、牧、渔业的各种动力机械的动力总和。包括耕作机械、排灌机械、收获机械、农用运输机械、植物保护机械、牧业机械、林业机械和其他农业机械[内燃机按引擎马力折成瓦(特)计算,电动机按功率折成瓦(特)计算]。不包括专门用于乡、镇、村、组办工业、基本建设、非农业运输、科学试验和教学等非农业方面的动力机械与作业机械。

农村用电量　指本年度内扣除在农村中的全民所有制工业、交通、基建单位的用电量以后的农村生产上和生活上的全年用电总度数(全年累计数),包括国家电网的供电量,也包括农村自办电站的供电量。

农用化肥施用量　指本年内实际用于农业生产的化肥数量。包括氮肥、磷肥、钾肥及复合肥。化肥施用量要求按折纯量计算数量。折纯量是指氮肥、磷肥、钾肥分别按含氮、含五氧化二磷、含氧化钾的百分之一百成份进行折算后的数量。复合肥按其所含主要成份折算。

Explanatory Notes on Main Statistical Indicators

Gross Output Value of Farming, Forestry, Animal Husbandry and Fishery refers to the total volume of products of farming, forestry, animal husbandry and fishery in value terms and output value of all kinds of service activities that support farming, forestry, animal husbandry and fishery production. It reflects the total scale and total result of agricultural production during a given period of time.

The statistical scopes for Farming, Forestry, Animal Husbandry and Fishery are:

(1) **Farming** include crop cultivation and other farming crop cultivation, include planting of grain, beans, tubers, cotton, oil-bearing crops, sugar crops, fiber crops, tobacco, vegetables, medicinal materials, melons and others, as well as tea, mulberry and fruit plantation.

Other farming include gathering of wild plant fruits, fiber, gum, oil, firewood, wild medicinal materials, fungi and commodity industry run by rural household.

(2) **Forestry** include planting of trees (not including planting, management & harvest of tea, mulberry and fruit plantation), collection of forest products, cutting and felling of bamboo and trees by villages and other cooperative organizations under villages.

(3) **Animal Husbandry** include raising and grazing of any kind of animal and hunting and raising of wild animal, excluding fish breeding.

(4) **Fishery** include cultivation and catches of aquatic animals and seaweed.

(5) **Service Industry for Farming, Forestry, Animal Husbandry and Fishery** refers to all kinds of service activities that support farming, forestry, animal husbandry and fishery production.

Grain Yield refers to the total yield including grains produced by state farms, collective units, industrial enterprises and mines. Grain includes rice, wheat, corn, sorghum, millet and other miscellaneous grains as well as tubers and beans. Output of beans refers to dry beans without pods. The output of tubers was converted into that of grain at the ratio 5:1. Output of all other grains refers to husked grain.

Output of Pork, Beef, and Mutton refers to the meat of slaughtered hogs, cattle, sheep and goats with head, feet and offal taken away.

Output of Aquatic Products refers to catches of both artificially cultured and naturally grown aquatic products, including fish, shrimps, crabs and shellfish in sea and inland water as well as seaweed. Freshwater plants are not included.

Irrigated Area refers to areas that are effectively irrigated, i. e. level land which has water source and complete sets of irrigation facilities to lift and move adequate water for irrigation purpose under normal conditions.

Total Power of Farm Machinery refers to total mechanical power of machinery used in farming, forestry, animal husbandry, and fishery, including ploughing, irrigation and drainage, harvesting, transport, plant protection, stock breeding, forestry and fishery. The power of internal combustion engines is required to convert horsepower into watts and the power of electric motors is required to be converted into watts. Machinery employed for non-agricultural purposes, such as the machines used in township-run and village-run industry, construction, non-agricultural transport, scientific experiments and teaching, is excluded.

Electricity Consumption in Rural Areas refers to the total degree of electricity consumption in rural production and living (annual aggregate) after discounting the ownership by the whole people in the rural areas of industrial, transport and infrastructure unit of electricity consumption, including the national grid power supply, and also including the power supply in rural areas on their own power station.

Consumption of Chemical Fertilizers in Agriculture refers to the quantity of chemical fertilizers applied in agriculture in the year, including nitrogenous fertilizer, phosphate fertilizer, potash fertilizer, and compound fertilizer. The consumption of chemical fertilizers is required in calculation to convert the gross weight into weight into weight containing 100% effective component (e. g. 100% nitrogen content in nitrogenous fertilizer, 100% phosphorous pentoxide contents in phosphate fertilizer, 100% potassium oxide contents in potash fertilizer). Compound fertilizer is converted with its major component.

四、工业、能源

INDUSTRY AND ENERGY

4

工 业 、 能 源
Industry and Energy

主 要 统 计 指 标
Major Statistical Indicators

规模以上工业企业单位数	Number of Industrial Enterprises above Designated Size	6073	个	(unit)
为上年	As Compared with the Preceding Year	98.5	%	(%)
规模以上工业增加值	Value-added of Industrial Enterprises above Designated Size	2875.05	亿元	(100 million yuan)
为上年	As Compared with the Preceding Year	105.4	%	(%)
规模以上工业总产值	Gross Output Value of Industrial Enterprises above Designated Size	12415.68	亿元	(100 million yuan)
为上年	As Compared with the Preceding Year	100.6	%	(%)
轻工业	Light Industry	4820.80	亿元	(100 million yuan)
为上年	As Compared with the Preceding Year	99.7	%	(%)
重工业	Heavy Industry	7594.88	亿元	(100 million yuan)
为上年	As Compared with the Preceding Year	101.2	%	(%)

4-01 全市工业企业单位数(主要年份)

Number of Industrial Enterprises of the Whole City (Main Years)

单位:个 (unit)

年份 Year	合计 Total	国有经济 State - owned Enterprises	集体经济 Collective - owned Enterprises	其他各种经济类型 Enterprises of Other Types of Ownership
1978	2868	680	2188	-
1980	3519	691	-	-
1985	5800	823	-	-
1990	6183	921	4966	11
1991	6234	933	5219	82
1992	6235	941	5162	132
1995	6744	1086	4722	936
1996	6148	1011	4268	869
1997	4980	760	3250	970
1998	2559	464	815	1280
1999	2474	396	689	1389
2000	2715	282	598	1835
2001	3580	237	252	3091
2002	4015	172	232	3611
2003	4689	144	219	4326
2004	7738	185	192	7361
2005	7359	124	169	7066
2006	7826	110	162	7554
2007	8674	71	131	8472
2008	9907	73	101	9733
2009	10032	71	84	9877
2010	10370	74	68	10228
2011	5868	52	25	5791
2012	5927	56	20	5851
2013	6284	25	11	6248
2014	6169	22	9	6138
2015	6073	17	5	6051

注:1997 年及以前为乡及以上工业;1998 -2010 年为主营业务收入 500 万及以上;2011 年为主营业务收入 2000 万及以上(后同)。

a) Data after 2011 refer to all the industrial enterprises with annual Sales income of over 20 million yuan, data in 1998 - 2010 refer to all the industrial enterprises with annual sales income of over 5 million yuan, data in 1997and before refer to enterprises at township and above level.

4-02 市区工业企业单位数(主要年份)

Number of Industrial Enterprises in Urban District(Main Years)

单位:个 (unit)

年份 Year	合计 Total	国有经济 State - owned Enterprises	集体经济 Collective - owned Enterprises	其他各种经济类型 Enterprises of Other Types of Ownership
1978	787	313	414	–
1980	894	315	579	–
1985	1250	345	859	7
1990	1360	361	971	28
1991	1411	382	990	39
1992	1490	395	1024	71
1995	1998	440	1102	456
1996	2043	458	1109	476
1997	1733	372	951	410
1998	1019	315	315	389
1999	959	255	284	420
2000	1005	182	253	570
2001	2645	195	200	2250
2002	2838	140	178	2520
2003	3230	115	158	2957
2004	5527	156	122	5249
2005	4995	98	104	4793
2006	5195	85	91	5019
2007	5726	54	77	5595
2008	6530	55	64	6411
2009	6477	52	49	6376
2010	6478	51	37	6390
2011	3867	36	10	3821
2012	3862	37	7	3818
2013	4145	18	5	4122
2014	4716	17	5	4694
2015	4584	12	3	4569

注:2001 年起市区数据含萧山、余杭区,2014 年起含富阳区。

a) The data in this table include Xiaoshan District and Yuhang District since 2001, and include Fuyang District since 2014.

4-03 全市工业总产值(主要年份)

Gross Industrial Output Value of the Whole City(Main Years)

单位:万元 (10000 yuan)

年 份 Year	规模以上工业 Industry above Designated Size	轻 工 业 Light Industry	重 工 业 Heavy Industry	国有经济 State-owned	集体经济 Collective-owned	其他经济 Other Types of Ownership
1978	429624	-	-	334799	94825	-
1980	617910	-	-	451349	166561	-
1985	1285888	793766	492122	726172	546642	13074
1990	2922600	1848911	1073689	1532900	1300900	88800
1991	3524900	2201757	1323143	1779400	1601400	144200
1992	4527400	2735168	1792232	2141000	2084000	302400
1995	10200259	5600664	4599595	3585284	3999638	2615337
1996	8831167	4606720	4224447	2905614	3320757	2604796
1997	9114651	4871887	4242764	3185886	2971634	2957131
1998	11099357	5726407	5372950	3422316	2824793	4852248
1999	12000796	6129963	5870833	3164602	2543981	6292213
2000	15435682	7623300	7812382	1860336	2698406	10876940
2001	19195133	9957027	9238106	1788783	1911315	15495035
2002	24002972	12435498	11567474	2147066	2151485	19704421
2003	32025226	15652463	16372763	2484171	2444002	27097053
2004	44865779	19761946	25103833	3419970	558890	40886919
2005	54411271	24059690	30351581	6054280	603438	47753553
2006	69754590	29093450	40661140	6776754	667615	62310221
2007	83514029	35878400	47635629	7688908	517878	75307243
2008	93795792	38735329	55060463	7440679	386111	85969002
2009	93907334	40115956	53791378	7576482	354714	85976138
2010	110810397	45764739	65045658	9050510	300262	101459625
2011	123529249	48660810	74868439	10220511	171901	113136837
2012	129596777	51377588	78219189	11507163	167343	117922271
2013	124180035	48663751	75516284	7140899	39776	116999360
2014	128530518	49979222	78551296	6922198	32246	121576073
2015	124156803	48207987	75948816	2309361	14146	121833295

4-04 市区工业总产值(主要年份)

Gross Industrial Output Value in Urban District(Main Years)

单位:万元 (10000 yuan)

年 份 Year	规模以上工业 Industry above Designated Size	轻 工 业 Light Industry	重 工 业 Heavy Industry	国有经济 State - owned	集体经济 Collective - owned	其他经济 Other Types of Ownership
1978	304242	-	-	248534	55708	-
1980	433623	-	-	335789	97834	-
1985	812246	512767	301998	536498	267613	8135
1990	1533000	1026764	599899	1067400	416500	49100
1991	1814600	1140394	674072	1237600	496800	80200
1992	2291300	1379154	917085	1497400	601200	192700
1995	4760900	2507752	2753196	2252300	908900	1599700
1996	4599778	2460319	2139459	2018768	951432	1629578
1997	4997257	2889406	2609217	2537740	819984	1639533
1998	6110192	3068600	3041592	2989467	1123013	1997712
1999	6280838	3178286	3102552	2668519	979070	2633249
2000	7804302	3635578	4168724	1498595	968509	5337198
2001	16156245	8377563	7778681	1695132	1792228	12668885
2002	20252484	10431428	9821056	2036097	2045450	16170937
2003	26945006	13080771	13864235	2390424	2305431	22249151
2004	37564968	16361706	21203262	3097656	419720	34047592
2005	44775260	19601053	25174207	5592419	390555	38792286
2006	57255453	23722868	33532585	6305071	347788	50602594
2007	67565456	29452269	38113187	7123810	323842	60117804
2008	74564803	31236743	43328060	6812616	219140	67533047
2009	74059755	32178951	41880805	6880470	148937	67030348
2010	86653885	36440816	50213069	8155395	156026	78342464
2011	97800625	39467105	58333520	9253445	70299	88476881
2012	101396009	41428864	59967145	10452692	72743	90870574
2013	94197123	38407906	55789218	6332681	22398	87842044
2014	110230328	42840596	67389732	6463681	22354	103744292
2015	105641721	40775608	64866113	1841145	8633	103791944

4-05 规模以上工业企业主要经济效益指标(1998-2015年)

Main Economic Indicators of Industrial Enterprises Above Designated Size(1998-2015)

单位:亿元 (100 million yuan)

年份 Year	规模以上工业总产值 Output Value of Industrial Enterprises Above Designated Size	规模以上工业增加值 Added Value of Industrial Enterprises Above Designated Size	资产总计 Total Assets	流动资产合计 Total Current Assets	主营业务收入 Revenne from Principal Business	利润总额 Total Profits	利税总额 Total Profits and Tax
1998	1109.94	274.70	1486.02	732.72	1036.09	38.44	101.36
1999	1200.07	298.90	1620.93	800.60	1132.80	54.47	127.89
2000	1543.57	360.97	1828.35	946.32	1465.49	76.20	161.61
2001	1919.51	444.91	2148.96	1122.07	1828.28	107.56	208.54
2002	2400.30	597.01	2514.19	1313.92	2288.21	145.48	274.98
2003	3202.52	783.51	3258.93	1783.50	3117.46	194.16	359.54
2004	4486.58	1019.47	4118.31	2300.84	4363.27	226.74	427.23
2005	5441.13	1126.54	4781.34	2692.73	5282.80	234.99	450.68
2006	6975.46	1363.17	5564.68	3215.19	6807.64	314.49	576.51
2007	8351.40	1717.65	6573.12	3880.23	8057.03	414.55	730.50
2008	9379.58	1743.20	7506.26	4437.50	8976.46	453.92	802.13
2009	9390.73	1792.00	8405.62	4968.21	9026.32	510.97	882.62
2010	11081.04	2153.83	9937.41	6011.68	10843.24	764.47	1224.48
2011	12352.92	2369.00	10968.69	6709.76	12022.57	795.53	1330.48
2012	12959.68	2492.00	11983.52	7215.40	12525.39	771.68	1339.94
2013	12418.00	2664.13	12680.28	7609.51	12424.15	853.60	1450.55
2014	12853.05	2813.51	13376.72	7938.51	12833.70	904.60	1538.07
2015	12415.68	2875.05	14015.54	8306.78	12237.39	891.12	1559.68

4-05 续表 continued

年份 Year	资产负债率 (%) Ratio of Debts to Assets(%)	流动资产周转次数 (次) Turnover of Current Assets(times)	成本费用利润率 (%) Ratio of Profits to Costs(%)	全员劳动生产率 (元/人) Overall Labor Productivity (Yuan/Person)	产品销售率(%) Rate of Production Sold (%)
1998	57.02	1.47	3.86	37976	95.91
1999	55.69	1.46	5.06	44307	98.07
2000	58.59	1.62	5.49	52713	97.19
2001	57.20	1.70	6.26	59518	97.40
2002	56.82	1.82	6.84	76402	97.76
2003	58.70	1.87	6.69	91284	97.68
2004	59.80	2.00	5.50	98809	98.10
2005	60.12	2.06	4.69	105786	98.25
2006	59.83	2.23	4.87	120289	98.36
2007	60.43	2.21	5.44	138016	98.17
2008	60.42	2.10	5.34	152070	98.14
2009	59.07	1.86	5.86	151002	98.63
2010	58.34	1.96	7.60	166516	98.83
2011	59.12	1.91	6.96	190110	98.61
2012	49.57	1.74	6.60	232587	98.63
2013	58.09	1.63	7.39	222570	99.18
2014	56.83	1.62	7.61	245726	98.48
2015	55.69	1.54	7.91	257020	98.50

4-06 分地区工业
Number of Industrial Enterprises

单位:个

项目	Item	全市 Whole City	市区 Urban District	上城区 Shangcheng	下城区 Xiacheng	江干区 Jianggan
规模以上工业合计	**Industrial above Designated Size**	**6073**	**4584**	**50**	**28**	**80**
一、按轻重工业分	**Grouped by Light & Heavy Industry**					
轻工业	Light Industry	2933	2190	20	9	37
重工业	Heavy Industry	3140	2394	30	19	43
二、按所有制分	**Grouped by Ownership**					
国有企业	State - owned Enterprises	17	12	1	-	-
集体企业	Collective - owned Enterprises	5	3	-	-	2
股份合作企业	Cooperative Enterprises	8	8	-	-	-
联营企业	Joint Ownership Enterprises	1	1	-	1	-
有限责任公司	Limited Liability Corporations	978	749	15	13	13
股份有限公司	Share - holding Corporations Ltd.	194	144	6	3	4
私营企业	Private Enterprises	3811	2735	16	6	46
外商及港澳台投资企业	Enterprises with Investment from Foreign、Hong Kong、Macao and Taiwan	1054	928	12	5	15
其他企业	Other Enterprises	5	4	-	-	-
合计中:国有控股企业	Of the Total:Controlling Share Hold Enterprises	219	170	7	7	2
三、按企业规模分	**Grouped by Size of Enterprises**					
大型企业	Large	123	113	1	1	1
中型企业	Medium - sized	659	570	9	3	14
小微企业	Small	5291	3901	40	24	65

企业单位数(2015 年末)
by Region(End of 2015)

(unit)

拱墅区 Gongshu	西湖区 Xihu	高新(滨江)区 Hi - Tech (Binjiang)	萧山区 Xiaoshan	余杭区 Yuhang	富阳区 Fuyang	桐庐县 Tonglu	淳安县 Chun'an	建德市 Jiande	临安市 Lin'an
95	**148**	**210**	**1742**	**1267**	**665**	**400**	**126**	**356**	**607**
37	53	54	994	606	258	235	74	161	273
58	95	156	748	661	407	165	52	195	334
–	1	2	1	2	1	1	1	1	2
–	–	–	1	–	–	1	–	1	–
2	–	–	1	3	2	–	–	–	–
24	53	50	242	166	110	30	23	52	124
6	5	29	27	46	13	8	4	12	26
49	66	73	1123	860	455	294	89	277	416
14	23	56	346	188	84	66	9	13	38
–	–	–	1	2	–	–	–	–	1
7	9	19	35	35	20	9	5	14	21
1	4	18	42	14	5	2	–	2	6
9	17	31	211	136	64	20	14	16	39
85	127	161	1489	1117	596	378	112	338	562

4－07 分地区工业
Gross Industrial

单位:万元

项 目	Item	全 市 Whole City	市区 Urban District	上城区 Shangcheng	下城区 Xiacheng	江干区 Jianggan
规模以上工业合计	**Industrial above Designated Size**	**124156803**	**105641721**	**7264098**	**516631**	**1749015**
一、按轻重工业分	**Grouped by Light & Heavy Industry**					
轻工业	Light Industry	48207987	40775608	3562304	73734	326549
重工业	Heavy Industry	75948816	64866113	3701794	442897	1422466
二、按所有制分	**Grouped by Ownership**					
国有企业	State－owned Enterprises	2309361	1841145	1061	－	－
集体企业	Collective－owned Enterprises	14146	8633	－	－	6551
股份合作企业	Cooperative Enterprises	52391	52391	－	－	－
联营企业	Joint Ownership Enterprises	4338	4338	－	4338	－
有限责任公司	Limited Liability Corporations	38448270	34825737	6753028	227520	152690
股份有限公司	Share－holding Corporations Ltd.	11299925	8546359	325652	221470	37328
私营企业	Private Enterprises	37160734	27448756	73355	22226	321110
外商及港澳台投资企业	Enterprises with Investment from Foreign、Hong Kong、Macao and Taiwan	34186209	32235082	111001	41076	1231338
其他企业	Other Enterprises	681428	679280	－	－	－
合计中:国有控股企业	Of the Total:Controlling Share Hold Enterprises	22773691	21407163	6595774	289188	55968
三、按企业规模分	**Grouped by Size of Enterprises**					
大型企业	Large	32389809	29999968	159699	211525	816913
中型企业	Medium－sized	36127126	31187369	299023	72874	475908
小微企业	Small	55639867	44454385	6805376	232232	456195

总产值（2015 年）
Output Value by Region (2015)

（10000 yuan）

拱墅区 Gongshu	西湖区 Xihu	高新（滨江）区 Hi-Tech (Binjiang)	萧山区 Xiaoshan	余杭区 Yuhang	富阳区 Fuyang	桐庐县 Tonglu	淳安县 Chun'an	建德市 Jiande	临安市 Lin'an
1816628	**2088648**	**11857763**	**37912714**	**14763489**	**12718175**	**4996692**	**2507630**	**4183598**	**6827161**
757659	789244	1249242	18445514	5583354	3219540	2141251	1755991	1304390	2230747
1058969	1299403	10608521	19467200	9180135	9498634	2855441	751639	2879208	4596414
–	8600	32735	896377	480526	386692	92745	64836	119641	190996
–	–	–	2082	–	–	2031	–	3482	–
5175	–	–	15129	16047	16040	–	–	–	–
–	–	–	–	–	–	–	–	–	–
1055986	604105	4357123	11385800	3492492	4570027	329615	407146	1235877	1649895
119686	45003	2459075	2553224	2151109	558594	127172	107152	640156	1879086
334115	611160	665204	13167441	5813529	5508334	3374102	1710817	1915053	2712006
301667	819780	4343627	9890212	2770766	1678489	1071027	217680	269389	393031
–	–	–	2450	39020	–	–	–	–	2148
885573	318754	4333178	4986601	1408782	1942647	201138	87840	453831	623719
493318	544659	6934043	1034389	2071134	1137608	159868		808367	1421607
684168	727947	2098249	12710951	5246380	4248723	1242316	895675	954663	1847103
639141	816042	2825471	14857884	7445975	7331844	3594508	1611955	2420568	3558452

4-08 分地区工业

Value of Industrial

单位:万元

项 目	Item	全 市 Whole City	市区 Urban District	上城区 Shangcheng	下城区 Xiacheng	江干区 Jianggan
规模以上工业合计	**Industrial above Designated Size**	**122300173**	**103962353**	**7062427**	**515180**	**1732393**
一、按轻重工业分	**Grouped by Light & Heavy Industry**					
轻工业	Light Industry	47299494	39925365	3365084	76661	327949
重工业	Heavy Industry	75000679	64036988	3697343	438519	1404444
二、按所有制分	**Grouped by Ownership**					
国有企业	State - owned Enterprises	2258048	1789818	1153	-	-
集体企业	Collective - owned Enterprises	13796	8333	-	-	6251
股份合作企业	Cooperative Enterprises	40804	40804	-	-	-
联营企业	Joint Ownership Enterprises	4338	4338	-	4338	-
有限责任公司	Limited Liability Corporations	37449955	33859623	6551270	227101	152059
股份有限公司	Share - holding Corporations Ltd.	11443431	8679562	324449	215613	37221
私营企业	Private Enterprises	36523224	26928095	73080	23329	319689
外商及港澳台投资企业	Enterprises with Investment from Foreign、Hong Kong、Macao and Taiwan	33959824	32047051	112475	44799	1217173
其他企业	Other Enterprises	606753	604729	-	-	-
合计中:国有控股企业	Of the Total:Controlling Share Hold Enterprises	22046950	20686075	6393537	284761	46554
三、按企业规模分	**Grouped by Size of Enterprises**					
大型企业	Large	32089615	29677738	156632	205677	816913
中型企业	Medium - sized	35690704	30797272	301004	72972	469121
小微企业	Small	54519854	43487344	6604792	236531	446360

销售产值(2015 年)
Products Sales by Region(2015)

(10000 yuan)

拱墅区 Gongshu	西湖区 Xihu	高新(滨江)区 Hi - Tech (Binjiang)	萧山区 Xiaoshan	余杭区 Yuhang	富阳区 Fuyang	桐庐县 Tonglu	淳安县 Chun'an	建德市 Jiande	临安市 Lin'an
1779128	**2066456**	**11873955**	**36958514**	**14512894**	**12578274**	**4935221**	**2498822**	**4129059**	**6774717**
714420	784643	1308249	17976368	5462986	3180793	2116591	1752261	1281862	2223415
1064708	1281812	10565706	18982146	9049908	9397480	2818631	746561	2847197	4551302
–	8887	32665	896377	480652	334254	92745	64856	119641	190990
–	–	–	2082	–	–	2004	–	3459	–
5182	–	–	15039	15497	5085	–	–	–	–
–	–	–	–	–	–	–	–	–	–
1025388	611487	4194788	10961396	3420461	4528305	331663	404681	1226589	1627399
117753	41283	2633641	2570584	2127102	546931	124400	104393	631481	1903596
330589	599624	660064	12778202	5697982	5491519	3341203	1708219	1885158	2660549
300215	805174	4352797	9732456	2732459	1672180	1043208	216674	262732	390159
–	–	–	2378	38740	–	–	–	–	2024
863954	322212	4185240	4731268	1391886	1873363	203390	88195	449594	619696
457067	550442	6945877	10108094	2061715	1119738	159295		806217	1446364
693872	709837	2115937	12411715	5134403	4187179	1217787	893319	945808	1836519
628189	806177	2812141	14435705	7316775	7271357	3558140	1605503	2377034	3491834

4－09　全市规模以上工业

Main Economic Indicators of Industrial

单位：万元

项　目	Item	企业单位数（个）Number of Enterprises (unit)	亏损企业（个）Loss Making Enterprises (unit)	工业总产值（当年价格）Gross Industrial Output Value (current price)	新产品产值 Output of New Products
总　　计	**Total**	**6073**	**976**	**124156803**	**43289990**
按隶属关系分	**Grouped by Subordination**				
中　央　属	Central	37	10	7180007	1129093
省　　属	Provincial	49	4	7271258	464073
市　　属	Municipal	79	19	6456135	2247810
县（市）属	County and below	60	12	4894492	1862325
按所有制分	**Grouped by Ownership**				
国有企业	State－owned Enterprises	17	1	2309361	13790
集体企业	Collective－owned Enterprises	5	－	14146	－
股份合作企业	Cooperative Enterprises	8	1	52391	8794
联营企业	Joint Ownership Enterprises	1	－	4338	－
有限责任公司	Limited Liability Corporations	978	164	38448270	14376929
股份有限公司	Share－holding Corporations Ltd.	194	21	11299925	5454813
私营企业	Private Enterprises	3811	542	37160734	10473300
外商及港澳台投资企业	Enterprises with Investment from Foreign、Hong Kong、Macao and Taiwan	1054	247	34186209	12938672
其他企业	Other Enterprises	5	－	681428	23693
按企业规模分	**Grouped by Size of Enterprises**				
大型企业	Large	123	14	32389809	16842176
中型企业	Medium－sized	659	74	36127126	15026175
小微企业	Small	5291	888	55639867	11421639
按轻重工业分	**Grouped by Light & Heavy Industry**				
轻工业	Light Industry	2933	440	48207987	12730415
重工业	Heavy Industry	3140	536	75948816	30559575

企业主要经济指标(2015年)(一)
Enterprises Above Designated Size(2015)(Ⅰ)

(10000 yuan)

工业销售产值 Value of Industrial Products Sales	出口交货值 Export delivery value	实收资本 Total Capital Hold	国家资本 State Capital	个人资本 Personal Capital	港澳台资本 Hongkong, Macau and TaiWan Capital	外商资本 Foreign Capital	就业人员年平均人数(人) Annual Average Number of Staff and Workers (person)
122300173	**17176261**	**25991467**	**2047029**	**6651204**	**2590380**	**3746375**	**1118602**
6825770	9231	694887	265558	14615	139082	14495	12880
7245339	134758	1008692	452316	92685	106204	189276	24605
6372436	1028227	1393435	417263	115289	92874	142921	53438
4695391	195988	589344	141293	27558	47418	23746	22204
2258048	1968	126656	117721	–	–	–	5127
13796	–	1456	–	589	–	–	214
40804	30	9569	–	9442	–	–	1036
4338	–	100	–	–	–	–	65
37449955	2964363	6073703	866126	1045446	1655	13029	245655
11443431	1458553	4055308	538663	1319722	15352	74081	96050
36523224	5140839	6320697	2189	3879308	1667	4164	429371
33959824	7603421	9324365	522330	394524	2571706	3655102	338085
606753	7088	79614	–	2174	–	–	2999
32089615	5244360	6037261	677205	971469	716997	921879	256192
35690704	5376262	7867968	585358	1613307	777442	1158468	332735
54519854	6555639	12086238	784466	4066428	1095940	1666027	529675
47299494	7946648	9592157	663040	2771114	1034123	1630624	534307
75000679	9229613	16399310	1383989	3880090	1556257	2115751	584295

项　目	Item	企业单位数(个) Number of Enterprises (unit)	亏损企业(个) Loss Making Enterprises (unit)	工业总产值(当年价格) Gross Industrial Output Value (current price)	新产品产值 Output of New Products
按市、县分	**Grouped by County**				
市　区	Urban District	4584	782	105641721	37395721
#萧山区	Xiaoshan	1742	255	37912714	13233786
余杭区	Yuhang	1267	248	14763489	5714828
富阳区	Fuyang	665	115	12718175	4192560
桐庐县	Tonglu	400	30	4996692	1715137
淳安县	Chun′an	126	8	2507630	368946
建德市	Jiande	356	29	4183598	1303416
临安市	Lin′an	607	127	6827161	2506771
按国民经济行业分	**Grouped by Economic Sector**				
采掘业	Mining and Quarrying	38	6	282776	65117
煤炭开采和洗选业	Coal Mining and Dressing	1	–	2147	–
黑色金属矿采选业	Ferrous Metals Mining and Dressing	1	1	–	–
有色金属矿采选业	Nonferrous Metals Mining and Dressing	6	1	51544	100
非金属矿采选业	Nonmetal Minerals Mining and Dressing	30	4	229085	65016
制造业	Manufacturing Industry	5951	956	114717062	43147584
农副食品加工业	Agricultural Products Processing	133	14	1336006	235702
食品制造业	Food Manufacturing	110	15	1894091	305388
酒、饮料和精制茶制造业	Wine, Beverage and Tea Manufacturing	54	6	2128085	319544
烟草制品业	Tobacco Processing	2	–	3235754	51765
纺织业	Textile Industry	765	100	9227470	1927482
纺织服装、服饰业	Textile Products and Costune Indnstry	347	66	2906323	690301
皮革、毛皮、羽毛及其制品和制鞋业	Leather. Furs. Downand Related and Shoes Products	159	23	1592872	326448
木材加工和木、竹、藤、棕、草制品业	Timber Processing, Bamboo, Cane, Palm Fiber and Straw Products	41	6	262804	52080
家具制造业	Furniture Manufacturing	87	13	1523089	731766

continued 1 (10000 yuan)

工业销售产值 Value of Industrial Products Sales	出口交货值 Export delivery value	实收资本 Total Capital Hold	国家资本 State Capital	个人资本 Personal Capital	港澳台资本 Hongkong, Macau and TaiWan Capital	外商资本 Foreign Capital	就业人员年平均人数(人) Annual Average Number of Staff and Workers (person)
103962353	13801135	22664409	1790352	5584537	2412893	3573363	940029
36958514	4410028	8937161	392850	2080144	1197562	1217931	338092
14512894	2456998	3212347	162432	1119061	343555	316427	201141
12578274	756724	2556973	254451	933042	63790	198745	98446
4935221	1308374	859682	43559	308313	52679	78357	43726
2498822	157011	292370	23485	119802	17563	3440	18029
4129059	676390	671950	102194	213096	18286	37615	38491
6774717	1233352	1503058	87439	425456	88959	53600	78327
286259	2339	105383	36799	29779	–	15	2578
2063	–	98	–	98	–	–	15
3280	–	500	–	–	–	–	9
52619	–	38080	24719	12861	–	–	756
228297	2339	66705	12080	16820	–	15	1798
112915994	17173922	24271139	1072162	6585459	2506572	3661459	1094122
1358717	72157	185032	670	68163	27767	21418	9940
1915529	136090	636742	28944	121894	80126	204220	24564
2090547	25426	437288	18769	43614	69003	156852	16806
3033448	8207	69040	–	3630	1400	–	2822
9082120	1637786	1693873	7951	739072	188578	202224	123853
2865400	1541592	646831	3641	137450	287530	97412	68430
1570986	958625	226534	–	55384	39635	29419	26335
254560	37700	48615	–	22924	1632	98	4042
1486598	499455	279102	–	75282	29001	84143	28140

项 目	Item	企业单位数(个) Number of Enterprises (unit)	亏损企业(个) Loss Making Enterprises (unit)	工业总产值(当年价格) Gross Industrial Output Value (current price)	新产品产值 Output of New Products
造纸和纸制品业	Paper Making and Paper Products	271	40	3540973	855147
印刷和记录媒介复制业	Printing and Record Media	84	16	600127	105791
文教、工美、体育和娱乐用品制造业	Cultural, Educational. Industrial Arts. Sports and Entertainment Goods	138	20	1618578	449623
石油加工、炼焦和核燃料加工业	Petroleum Processing, Coking and Nuclear Fuel Processing	12	2	92287	14216
化学原料和化学制品制造业	Raw Chemical Materials and Chemical Products	335	45	9793711	3451094
医药制造业	Medical and Pharmaceutical Products	88	11	3615456	957649
化学纤维制造业	Chemical Fiber	118	21	5830611	2083931
橡胶和塑料制品业	Rubber and Plastic Products	302	35	6263939	1870260
非金属矿物制品业	Nonmetal Minerals Products	340	54	4590913	980535
黑色金属冶炼和压延加工业	Smelting and Processing of Ferrous Metals	110	28	2013981	517136
有色金属冶炼和压延加工业	Smelting and Processing of Nonferrous Metals	73	16	4337132	846789
金属制品业	Metals Products	358	67	4204381	1591870
通用设备制造业	Ordinary Machinery	510	77	8788330	4391771
专用设备制造业	For Special Purpose Equipment Manufacturing	237	52	1798287	651690
汽车制造业	Automobile Manufacturing	212	39	6702968	3990919
铁路、船舶、航空航天和其他运输设备制造业	Railway. watercraft. Avigation spaceflight and other Equipment Manufacturing	60	11	457194	118944
电气机械和器材制造业	Electric Equipment and Machinery	515	102	11196097	5515802
计算机、通信和其他电子设备制造业	Computers. Telecommunications and Other Electronic Equipment Manufacturing	295	50	11578056	8403504
仪器仪表制造业	Instruments and Meters Manufacturing	147	24	2220434	1128818
其他制造业	Other Manufacturing	23	–	239003	113122
废弃资源综合利用业	Multiple Utilization of Waste Resouces	24	3	1124011	468499
金属制品、机械和设备修理业	Metal Products, Machinery and Equipment Repair	1	–	4100	–
电力、燃气及水的生产和供应业	Produotion and supply of electricity, gas & water	84	14	9156965	77289
电力、热力生产和供应业	Production and Supply of Electric Power and Hot Water	51	5	6784987	70200
燃气生产和供应业	Production and Supply of Gas	14	3	2099774	–
水的生产和供应业	Production and Supply of Tap Water	19	6	272204	7088

continued 2 (10000 yuan)

工业销售产值 Value of Industrial Products Sales	出口交货值 Export delivery value	实收资本 Total Capital Hold	国家资本 State Capital	个人资本 Personal Capital	港澳台资本 Hongkong, Macau and TaiWan Capital	外商资本 Foreign Capital	就业人员年平均人数(人) Annual Average Number of Staff and Workers (person)
3518594	220088	717636	2235	361831	23423	24096	38918
589539	13951	201642	21598	57916	37378	2689	9408
1569496	430337	260098	396	62184	34089	84102	20230
91295	1088	13220		10208	334		541
9639965	888589	2091969	39891	294524	60468	242364	52208
3469420	288891	914451	184492	71314	20482	271850	35099
5616231	353183	1181380		537478	94750	91448	28215
6225258	876655	932448	63546	280271	35183	232917	54507
4571455	178770	911757	45234	320720	94298	85599	39172
1968207	43229	307307	6780	135195	22912	13172	11274
4358529	227742	346625	8375	85270	4215	23958	8613
4126325	684099	862296	38714	399453	133984	54462	46897
8685015	1306101	2116956	63985	567652	167553	318947	97169
1773076	367083	688912	38176	216286	89962	176346	32746
6589566	451218	1946356	160979	263619	345117	281710	51766
452127	173286	153108	30020	36092	–	9389	7778
10990433	2009094	2848010	60470	529861	228897	397980	100391
11482641	3348834	2848859	243561	809241	324597	457833	114008
2154978	373973	609733	3735	224771	58839	86850	34024
254490	20674	27242	–	15281	5421	4138	3921
1126376	–	67080	–	38880	–	5525	2204
5075	–	1000	–	–	–	300	101
9097920	–	1614946	938068	35966	83808	84901	21902
6726615	–	753938	287343	16855	50000	9819	14240
2103200	–	394702	286363	11111	31308	52582	2281
268105	–	466306	364362	8000	2500	22500	5381

4－10 全市规模以上工业

Main Economic Indicators of Industrial

单位:万元

项 目	Item	资产合计 Total Assets	流动资产合计 Total Circulating Funds	应收账款 Receivables	存货 Stock
总 计	**Total**	**140155445**	**83067772**	**25342659**	**16878426**
按隶属关系分	**Grouped by Subordination**				
中央属	Central	6524571	3833202	706572	1880922
省属	Provincial	5421854	1572649	356786	295647
市属	Municipal	8952588	4590098	1119484	1344068
县(市)属	County and below	5036991	2862137	1123534	485315
按所有制分	**Grouped by Ownership**				
国有企业	State－owned Enterprises	1198053	162036	22033	24823
集体企业	Collective－owned Enterprises	16281	13835	3382	576
股份合作企业	Cooperative Enterprises	84911	75473	19503	6484
联营企业	Joint Ownership Enterprises	1813	1730	1048	660
有限责任公司	Limited Liability Corporations	44000295	24006295	7946407	5233932
股份有限公司	Share－holding Corporations Ltd.	22445441	11982516	3610067	2311907
私营企业	Private Enterprises	34670849	22551568	6793578	4829593
外商及港澳台投资企业	Enterprises with Investment from Foreign、Hong Kong、Macao and Taiwan	37223633	23847650	6786900	4401874
其他企业	Other Enterprises	514171	426668	159741	68576
按企业规模分	**Grouped by Size of Enterprises**				
大型企业	Large	39177502	23082081	7888055	3692020
中型企业	Medium－sized	40152868	23711373	6979522	4609135
小微企业	Small	60825076	36274319	10475081	8577270
按轻重工业分	**Grouped by Light & Heavy Industry**				
轻工业	Light Industry	53049599	31410331	7121411	7715362
重工业	Heavy Industry	87105847	51657441	18221248	9163063

企业主要经济指标(2015 年)(二)
Enterprises Above Designated Size(2015)(Ⅱ)

(10000 yuan)

产成品 Finished Products	固定资产合计 Fixed Assets	累计折旧 Accumulated Depreciation	本年折旧 Depreciation of the year	负债合计 Total Liabilities	流动负债合计 Total Current Liabilities	非流动负债合计 Total Non - current Liabilities	所有者权益合计 Creditors´Equity
7002947	**33174295**	**22347292**	**3329913**	**78057657**	**67545500**	**9658419**	**62065173**
385451	2199797	1429667	188782	3436057	2909282	526775	3088513
142102	4421472	3088251	353702	3084434	1559307	1501512	2337420
747317	2439161	1528149	217658	5028416	3905300	1110638	3924169
200439	1611490	820377	149525	3402986	2921538	471589	1632006
9862	1007641	831254	126354	354649	284374	69723	843403
380	1446	4360	265	4651	4636	–	11630
4009	7045	7999	972	51843	50783	60	33068
130	83	162	20	1455	1455	–	358
1820647	12681121	7966745	1102734	28465651	22451403	5825377	15518547
949229	3020485	2215644	298278	9315742	7729607	1546273	13129698
2183704	7515382	5141641	896722	21420838	20085012	924036	13231344
2001159	8860689	6150622	896633	18113410	16608813	1292950	19112372
33828	80404	28865	7933	329418	329418	–	184753
1677568	8018590	4447999	763046	20772415	17898236	2791436	18405086
1846356	9398086	7237307	1050345	21642775	18810891	2578330	18510085
3479022	15757619	10661986	1516522	35642466	30836374	4288652	25150003
3143289	12805521	8980593	1210956	28297539	25293252	2651476	24728982
3859658	20368774	13366699	2118957	49760118	42252248	7006942	37336191

项 目	Item	资产合计 Total Assets	流动资产合计 Total Circulating Funds	应收账款 Receivables	存货 Stock
按市、县分	**Grouped by County**				
市 区	Urban District	122753597	73295347	22180740	15084440
#萧山区	Xiaoshan	48298661	25963552	6549511	5228503
余杭区	Yuhang	16402515	10107225	3378875	2146348
富阳区	Fuyang	14863491	9159023	2492724	1489395
桐庐县	Tonglu	4080063	2372137	625302	513261
淳安县	Chun'an	1511712	800697	224954	161294
建德市	Jiande	3939606	1886289	492087	298342
临安市	Lin'an	7870468	4713303	1819576	821089
按国民经济行业分	**Grouped by Economic Sector**				
采掘业	Mining and Quarrying	368810	174431	40725	15263
煤炭开采和洗选业	Coal Mining and Dressing	1509	508	340	74
黑色金属矿采选业	Ferrous Metals Mining and Dressing	2521	2436	－399	2519
有色金属矿采选业	Nonferrous Metals Mining and Dressing	113769	40866	4404	3365
非金属矿采选业	Nonmetal Minerals Mining and Dressing	251011	130621	36380	9305
制造业	Manufacturing Industry	126783236	80328635	25086071	16791749
农副食品加工业	Agricultural Products Processing	930113	540790	167982	148061
食品制造业	Food Manufacturing	2466854	1419739	694594	210529
酒、饮料和精制茶制造业	Wine, Beverage and Tea Manufacturing	1858572	924304	212697	185491
烟草制品业	Tobacco Processing	2980427	2155302	326400	1599787
纺织业	Textile Industry	9215733	5586698	1078400	1273963
纺织服装、服饰业	Textile Products and Costune Indnstry	2630145	1748218	389439	414905
皮革、毛皮、羽毛及其制品和制鞋业	Leather. Furs. Downand Related and Shoes Products	1366880	1041994	297733	263896
木材加工和木、竹、藤、棕、草制品业	Timber Processing, Bamboo, Cane, Palm Fiber and Straw Products	217598	130731	35959	32601
家具制造业	Furniture Manufacturing	1233520	866967	190413	147174

continued 1 (10000 yuan)

产成品 Finished Products	固定资产合计 Fixed Assets	累计折旧 Accumulated Depreciation	本年折旧 Depreciation of the year	负债合计 Total Liabilities	流动负债合计 Total Current Liabilities	非流动负债合计 Total Non - current Liabilities	所有者权益合计 Creditors´Equity
6295973	29050646	19520937	2880077	68724688	59494879	8545035	54008267
2257937	11318583	7336300	1152535	28521879	25233310	2986754	19765326
906299	3804047	2398932	397355	9435729	8611809	749495	6967606
686481	3158267	1790323	330999	9401825	7936109	1274659	5456005
198266	1026056	673806	117541	2440439	2100805	271632	1639620
55969	441255	342602	54846	661171	548012	103652	850540
128333	1274248	880073	128579	2087930	1732206	333246	1850380
324405	1382091	929873	148870	4143429	3669599	404853	3716367
9173	99118	39640	10616	190524	169531	19906	178286
74	840	142	66	553	553		956
2384	86	713	25	2935	2935		-414
2411	39142	5731	1387	39838	29831	8920	73931
4304	59050	33054	9138	147197	136211	10986	103814
6975971	26024917	17164506	2745726	69845445	63091071	5933742	56905176
65317	238059	104831	20751	561343	531709	25447	368768
106461	625964	359497	56288	951130	929852	10548	1506176
42875	700620	713422	80331	917353	859781	55401	939787
283196	824012	350678	35401	747346	747064	282	2233081
653864	2254368	2063838	288399	5566914	5166890	291501	3642471
184807	599915	392218	57210	1430893	1315800	62229	1196921
50229	177317	103446	17737	1000210	968036	18054	366668
15482	43544	30840	4713	158059	153880	4120	59538
54003	245083	126010	18964	748873	716626	30522	484647

项　目	Item	资产合计 Total Assets	流动资产合　计 Total Circulating Funds	应收账款 Receivables	存　货 Stock
造纸和纸制品业	Paper Making and Paper Products	4499894	2954646	785280	452968
印刷和记录媒介复制业	Printing and Record Media	820205	447345	152479	81384
文教、工美、体育和娱乐用品制造业	Cultural, Educational. Industrial Arts. Sports and Entertainment Goods	938841	597677	127062	207208
石油加工、炼焦和核燃料加工业	Petroleum Processing, Coking and Nuclear Fuel Processing	62067	46517	21330	10497
化学原料和化学制品制造业	Raw Chemical Materials and Chemical Products	10356765	5347504	1276628	905582
医药制造业	Medical and Pharmaceutical Products	4421213	2275496	676195	567426
化学纤维制造业	Chemical Fiber	8155278	3924136	364430	764790
橡胶和塑料制品业	Rubber and Plastic Products	5301103	2922242	857841	724752
非金属矿物制品业	Nonmetal Minerals Products	5609055	3785538	1840421	408768
黑色金属冶炼和压延加工业	Smelting and Processing of Ferrous Metals	1695676	1135948	203111	312259
有色金属冶炼和压延加工业	Smelting and Processing of Nonferrous Metals	2685804	1960919	244228	363779
金属制品业	Metals Products	4027705	2689983	926127	739932
通用设备制造业	Ordinary Machinery	11509353	7424004	2435205	1585301
专用设备制造业	For Special Purpose Equipment Manufacturing	2626130	1758655	624530	434836
汽车制造业	Automobile Manufacturing	9003798	5234677	2199558	770708
铁路、船舶、航空航天和其他运输设备制造业	Railway. watercraft. Avigation spaceflight and other Equipment Manufacturing	501700	294916	99106	67545
电气机械和器材制造业	Electric Equipment and Machinery	12695147	8426255	3254439	1683843
计算机、通信和其他电子设备制造业	Computers. Telecommunications and Other Electronic Equipment Manufacturing	14907973	11699633	4692223	1885888
仪器仪表制造业	Instruments and Meters Manufacturing	3103883	2245908	832495	432029
其他制造业	Other Manufacturing	196777	145679	19305	34552
废弃资源综合利用业	Multiple Utilization of Waste Resouces	760871	592490	59262	80417
金属制品、机械和设备修理业	Metal Products, Machinery and Equipment Repair	4155	3727	1203	877
电力、燃气及水的生产和供应业	Produotion and supply of electricity, gas & water	13003399	2564706	215863	71414
电力、热力生产和供应业	Production and Supply of Electric Power and Hot Water	8833219	1288308	144703	32329
燃气生产和供应业	Production and Supply of Gas	1345208	225132	49448	11757
水的生产和供应业	Production and Supply of Tap Water	2824973	1051266	21712	27328

continued 2 (10000 yuan)

产成品 Finished Products	固定资产合计 Fixed Assets	累计折旧 Accumulated Depreciation	本年折旧 Depreciation of the year	负债合计 Total Liabilities	流动负债合计 Total Current Liabilities	非流动负债合计 Total Non - current Liabilities	所有者权益合计 Creditors´Equity
214956	1002628	763120	119803	2985509	2788617	111316	1514381
40200	288749	273278	31820	475616	412270	61931	344588
63379	249229	207995	26865	510898	494252	14712	427942
3181	11131	10648	1486	39772	39772	-	22294
449327	2786401	1550475	286557	5187477	4391797	747333	5167531
230708	1057911	444290	83365	1985277	1541514	437228	2433937
440209	1892938	1085263	133644	4587089	4140907	433206	3568188
474095	1625119	1252890	210013	2972718	2757324	195816	2327997
205264	1236983	988457	139588	3712594	3438746	210917	1894411
160140	357579	317219	51526	1008306	909657	63579	684307
106084	450595	172842	39408	2053303	1915142	138159	632500
246905	816893	508153	85500	2441276	2326228	55971	1588112
571126	1832297	1135173	200129	5924599	5419437	366389	5580490
133112	575905	391538	58681	1340352	1192327	146223	1285774
373113	2146183	956546	231369	6274684	5438000	814039	2729152
21456	137359	73158	12906	277049	266669	8979	224373
786092	2085052	1368371	215319	6725855	5776208	887022	5970481
828649	1256480	1057490	173693	7299748	6702774	572003	7606180
142393	387903	293739	41386	1272966	1190141	82236	1830916
8615	37278	24319	3226	77925	77925	-	118852
20699	81283	44671	19627	607047	478463	88578	153824
37	141	93	22	3265	3265	-	890
17802	7050260	5143146	573571	8021688	4284899	3704771	4981711
3998	5287325	4016690	454352	5697085	3069483	2606102	3136133
8245	768210	270271	54275	857473	553700	303773	487735
5559	994726	856185	64944	1467130	661716	794897	1357843

4－11 全市规模以上工业

Main Economic Indicators of Industrial

单位:万元

项　目	Item	主营业务收　入 Revenues in Main Business	主营业务成　本 Costs in Main Business	主营业务税金及附加 Sales Taxes and Extra Charges in Main Business
总　计	**Total**	**122373886**	**98935693**	**2547936**
按隶属关系分	**Grouped by Subordination**			
中　央　属	Central	6835596	4237478	1847135
省　　属	Provincial	7320264	6716774	25648
市　　属	Municipal	6352694	4938431	42682
县(市)属	County and Below	4287131	3573920	114288
按所有制分	**Grouped by Ownership**			
国有企业	State－owned Enterprises	2295951	2145669	9506
集体企业	Collective－owned Enterprises	13829	12399	45
股份合作企业	Cooperative Enterprises	50245	40103	331
联营企业	Joint Ownership Enterprises	4338	4112	14
有限责任公司	Limited Liability Corporations	37428212	30506269	2028423
股份有限公司	Share－holding Corporations Ltd.	12247937	9548750	68858
私营企业	Private Enterprises	36125477	31007204	194984
外商及港澳台投资企业	Enterprises with Investment from Foreign、Hong Kong、Macao and Taiwan	33601125	25393574	240714
其他企业	Other Enterprises	606772	277613	5062
按企业规模分	**Grouped by Size of Enterprises**			
大型企业	Large	32069356	24686955	313547
中型企业	Medium－sized	36014842	29594029	165566
小微企业	Small	54289687	44654709	2068823
按轻重工业分	**Grouped by Light & Heavy Industry**			
轻工业	Light Industry	47038306	35655136	2054188
重工业	Heavy Industry	75335581	63280557	493748

企业主要经济指标(2015 年)(三)
Enterprises Above Designated Size(2015)(Ⅲ)

(10000 yuan)

销售费用 Sales Expenses	管理费用 Management Expenses	财务费用 Financial Expenses	利息支出 Interest Expenditure	营业利润 Business Profits	利润总额 Total Profits	利税总额 Total Pre - tax Profits	本年应交增值税 Value Added Tax Payable
5339762	**7037074**	**1412003**	**1799078**	**8012005**	**8911224**	**15596768**	**4045860**
134699	204133	60870	73221	274834	292836	2704635	483466
69785	241072	11181	27890	186013	292736	503320	183863
669866	421991	87834	77987	240665	358622	624276	219395
51160	210014	53930	53319	308276	327420	533122	91239
3871	89697	9676	10259	40542	43124	136576	83518
308	701	79	89	298	365	683	273
853	4929	2124	1867	1919	2084	4437	2022
36	160	–	–	16	16	104	74
1061775	1721123	433626	533407	1836591	2114823	5481010	1254809
664179	969585	91909	173969	1164293	1324645	1790342	393608
930710	1786603	622030	682086	1744624	1862186	3078951	1018399
2451596	2428608	244723	381290	3169309	3504966	5000701	1253270
226435	35668	7837	16111	54414	59015	103964	39886
2163357	2086685	218208	321221	2985412	3375568	4773378	1083947
1597635	2172075	413209	559131	2345451	2535747	3834829	1131328
1578769	2778315	780587	918726	2681143	2999909	6988562	1830585
3122892	2606380	590395	799407	3315545	3544939	7638993	1953189
2216870	4430695	821609	999671	4696461	5366285	7957775	2092671

单位:万元 4－11 续表1

项 目	Item	主营业务收入 Revenues in Main Business	主营业务成本 Costs in Main Business	主营业务税金及附加 Sales Taxes and Extra Charges in Main Business
按市、县分	**Grouped by County**			
市 区	Urban District	104591641	83918987	2452114
#萧山区	Xiaoshan	26751725	23452920	134783
余杭区	Yuhang	14434941	11830521	79626
富阳区	Fuyang	12436145	10910579	48760
桐庐县	Tonglu	4763052	4096848	21557
淳安县	Chun'an	2433078	2064398	15167
建德市	Jiande	4000464	3390778	26319
临安市	Lin'an	6585652	5464683	32780
按国民经济行业分	**Grouped by Economic Sector**			
采掘业	Mining and Quarrying	283049	192551	10060
煤炭开采和洗选业	Coal Mining and Dressing	2063	1573	124
黑色金属矿采选业	Ferrous Metals Mining and Dressing	2428	2467	1
有色金属矿采选业	Nonferrous Metals Mining and Dressing	54146	39112	712
非金属矿采选业	Nonmetal Minerals Mining and Dressing	224413	149399	9224
制造业	Manufacturing Industry	112938860	90243229	2504226
农副食品加工业	Agricultural Products Processing	1360947	1201337	3987
食品制造业	Food Manufacturing	2231536	1680351	8563
酒、饮料和精制茶制造业	Wine, Beverage and Tea Manufacturing	1975536	1357134	36643
烟草制品业	Tobacco Processing	2952188	604359	1795481
纺织业	Textile Industry	8935688	7821887	42446
纺织服装、服饰业	Textile Products and Costune Indnstry	2858081	2419338	18096
皮革、毛皮、羽毛及其制品和制鞋业	Leather. Furs. Downand Related and Shoes Products	1552964	1383233	7486
木材加工和木、竹、藤、棕、草制品业	Timber Processing, Bamboo, Cane, Palm Fiber and Straw Products	252240	216736	1694
家具制造业	Furniture Manufacturing	1460963	1097488	7913

continued 1 (10000 yuan)

销售费用 Sales Expenses	管理费用 Management Expenses	财务费用 Financial Expenses	利息支出 Interest Expenditure	营业利润 Business Profits	利润总额 Total Profits	利税总额 Total Pre - tax Profits	本年应交增值税 Value Added Tax Payable
4752085	6107534	1232948	1586763	6928630	7757643	13745302	3446033
476195	1177008	409632	519066	1417254	1478183	2259190	645083
698118	1040265	143103	207659	766577	869603	1456043	506053
200392	493269	341255	371171	545716	591542	946220	305497
115532	195697	48273	51126	301423	305055	502485	175704
76831	79261	18346	19208	187173	200310	294912	79344
140984	198361	43765	56055	240961	262242	417102	127503
254330	456221	68672	85926	353819	385975	636967	217276
9417	22061	9166	9074	39992	39657	64183	14437
74	78	-	-	215	227	444	93
-	37	137	128	-215	-214	-214	-
1166	7940	1598	1610	3648	3650	8254	3861
8177	14008	7431	7336	36343	35993	55700	10483
5301236	6814401	1308955	1679970	7596974	8367416	14754174	3792297
42912	43493	20981	20426	50348	54912	86303	27380
245665	127350	3188	14438	205032	213480	299198	77155
384395	66266	14645	18090	154144	173105	300503	90646
86266	121565	-357	3392	260841	249903	2509968	383702
129211	360948	161827	200506	464600	479575	759595	236811
84899	199341	28365	42922	114242	127443	267853	122190
39682	57972	15398	30338	51248	52484	110689	50607
6309	12813	3225	3830	9060	10071	20210	8381
94396	94195	14686	19332	234189	231608	282906	43346

单位:万元　　　　　　　　　　　　　　　　　　4－11　续表2

项　目	Item	主营业务收　入 Revenues in Main Business	主营业务成　本 Costs in Main Business	主营业务税金及附加 Sales Taxes and Extra Charges in Main Business
造纸和纸制品业	Paper Making and Paper Products	3407378	2912513	17473
印刷和记录媒介复制业	Printing and Record Media	625397	530724	3609
文教、工美、体育和娱乐用品制造业	Cultural,Educational. Industrial Arts. Sports and Entertainment Goods	1564823	1416945	6750
石油加工、炼焦和核燃料加工业	Petroleum Processing, Coking and Nuclear Fuel Processing	89928	77077	643
化学原料和化学制品制造业	Raw Chemical Materials and Chemical Products	9730053	7616584	32023
医药制造业	Medical and Pharmaceutical Products	3401991	1528760	35973
化学纤维制造业	Chemical Fiber	5357185	4896712	12269
橡胶和塑料制品业	Rubber and Plastic Products	5900276	5066931	33267
非金属矿物制品业	Nonmetal Minerals Products	4446519	3812278	21057
黑色金属冶炼和压延加工业	Smelting and Processing of Ferrous Metals	1953285	1809995	5780
有色金属冶炼和压延加工业	Smelting and Processing of Nonferrous Metals	4371921	4139994	6201
金属制品业	Metals Products	4121889	3602963	22134
通用设备制造业	Ordinary Machinery	8797617	7094786	46616
专用设备制造业	For Special Purpose Equipment Manufacturing	1766727	1351249	12649
汽车制造业	Automobile Manufacturing	6522360	5424530	172878
铁路、船舶、航空航天和其他运输设备制造业	Railway. watercraft. Avigation spaceflight and other Equipment Manufacturing	459549	380920	3899
电气机械和器材制造业	Electric Equipment and Machinery	10987776	8979642	47793
计算机、通信和其他电子设备制造业	Computers. Telecommunications and Other Electronic Equipment Manufacturing	12272593	9007405	80309
仪器仪表制造业	Instruments and Meters Manufacturing	2157447	1514195	16086
其他制造业	Other Manufacturing	338670	303000	1465
废弃资源综合利用业	Multiple Utilization of Waste Resouces	1080329	990247	2996
金属制品、机械和设备修理业	Metal Products,Machinery and Equipment Repair	5006	3914	49
电力、燃气及水的生产和供应业	Produotion and supply of electricity, gas & water	9151977	8499913	33651
电力、热力生产和供应业	Production and Supply of Electric Power and Hot Water	6728118	6261252	24546
燃气生产和供应业	Production and Supply of Gas	2110678	1973522	7057
水的生产和供应业	Production and Supply of Tap Water	313182	265138	2047

continued 2 (10000 yuan)

销售费用 Sales Expenses	管理费用 Management Expenses	财务费用 Financial Expenses	利息支出 Interest Expenditure	营业利润 Business Profits	利润总额 Total Profits	利税总额 Total Pre - tax Profits	本年应交增值税 Value Added Tax Payable
69878	164272	125467	136433	146415	154610	265281	93006
13798	42830	9411	10773	35309	37712	64400	22884
26833	57269	14559	19683	44723	43208	80480	30377
3056	4243	995	1093	4214	4037	6487	1796
611020	697984	144432	156589	732523	786517	1139229	320614
1027902	345801	18319	39165	466813	505562	828834	287226
24455	123642	114388	142519	222449	231746	308383	64330
208095	227411	99131	80068	281811	309982	493925	150610
150058	190072	98427	111981	198405	201893	349534	126321
15184	45881	31006	38502	58582	60540	95156	28678
17885	55083	55989	77936	109964	121584	202533	74747
83012	217231	62820	68183	157465	168365	290392	99678
288190	678413	68841	98729	699190	736653	1104512	319678
92188	219292	21274	26552	92903	107515	176885	56521
134902	436943	84660	79028	335968	419857	696280	103093
14264	48074	2944	6447	11079	18261	38611	16352
580084	724520	113573	153642	629238	665776	997886	283325
659576	1162880	-29465	55219	1516924	1828093	2396079	484686
158518	267916	1833	15370	218207	270233	386260	99683
4621	11652	630	1941	17567	20096	31367	9683
3170	8124	7588	6687	72690	81579	163132	78556
812	927	177	160	831	1018	1306	240
29108	200612	93882	110034	375040	504151	778411	239126
1996	133741	68662	68750	280234	379654	598327	193272
16531	34742	15243	15687	83059	84780	128666	36829
10581	32129	9977	25597	11746	39717	51418	9025

4－12　市区规模以上工业

Main Economic Indicators of Industrial Enterprises

单位:万元

项　目	Item	企业单位数（个）Number of Enterprises (unit)	亏损企业(个) Loss Making Enterprises (unit)	工业总产值（当年价格）Gross Industrial Output Value (current price)	新产品产值 Output of New Products
总　　计	**Total**	**4584**	**782**	**105641721**	**37395721**
按隶属关系分	**Grouped by Subordination**				
中　央　属	Central	27	7	6938719	1079975
省　　属	Provincial	41	4	6853811	454521
市　　属	Municipal	67	18	5671656	1835265
按所有制分	**Grouped by Ownership**				
国有企业	State－owned Enterprises	12	1	1841145	13790
集体企业	Collective－owned Enterprises	3	－	8633	－
股份合作企业	Cooperative Enterprises	8	1	52391	8794
联营企业	Joint Ownership Enterprises	1	－	4338	－
有限责任公司	Limited Liability Corporations	749	130	34825737	13195637
股份有限公司	Share－holding Corporations Ltd.	144	14	8546359	3932215
私营企业	Private Enterprises	2735	415	27448756	7856800
外商及港澳台投资企业	Enterprises with Investment from Foreign、Hong Kong、Macao and Taiwan	928	221	32235082	12364794
其他企业	Other Enterprises	4	－	679280	23693
按企业规模分	**Grouped by Size of Enterprises**				
大型企业	Large	113	14	29999968	15670447
中型企业	Medium－sized	570	67	31187369	12742524
小微企业	Small	3901	701	44454385	8982750
按轻重工业分	**Grouped by Light & Heavy Industry**				
轻工业	Light Industry	2190	364	40775608	10918975
重工业	Heavy Industry	2394	418	64866113	26476746

企业主要经济指标(2015 年)(一)

Above Designated Size in Urban District(2015)(Ⅰ)

(10000 yuan)

工业销售产值 Value of Industrial Products Sales	出口交货值 Export delivery value	实收资本 Total Capital Hold	国家资本 State Capital	个人资本 Personal Capital	港澳台资本 Hongkong, Macau and TaiWan Capital	外商资本 Foreign Capital	就业人员年平均人数(人) Annual Average Number of Staff and Workers (person)
103962353	**13801135**	**22664409**	**1790352**	**5584537**	**2412893**	**3573363**	**940029**
6593609	9231	653559	235959	13115	137500	14495	10937
6827728	131684	969724	429333	91703	106204	189276	22563
5582485	922678	1206117	394760	66767	92874	141897	49195
1789818	1968	107001	106541	–	–	–	3275
8333	–	1225	–	589	–	–	151
40804	30	9569	–	9442	–	–	1036
4338	–	100	–	–	–	–	65
33859623	2552395	5263161	661173	907750	1655	12842	206714
8679562	885666	3328844	503059	1095931	14449	74081	77223
26928095	3485302	5079997	1654	3204962	1265	4164	331926
32047051	6869770	8795197	517926	363779	2395523	3482277	316687
604729	6005	79314	–	2084	–	–	2952
29677738	4867840	5576090	638197	917623	716997	899404	235772
30797272	4477055	6893212	509349	1315368	704092	1097995	288692
43487344	4456240	10195107	642806	3351546	991803	1575964	415565
39925365	5829018	8448061	599955	2305575	970791	1522257	449659
64036988	7972117	14216347	1190397	3278961	1442102	2051106	490370

项　目	Item	企业单位数（个）Number of Enterprises (unit)	亏损企业(个) Loss Making Enterprises (unit)	工业总产值（当年价格）Gross Industrial Output Value (current price)	新产品产值 Output of New Products
按国民经济行业分	**Grouped by Economic Sector**				
采掘业	Mining and Quarrying	16	5	130855	60795
黑色金属矿采选业	Ferrous Metals Mining and Dressing	1	1	–	–
有色金属矿采选业	Nonferrous Minerals Mining and Dressing	3	1	20137	100
非金属矿采选业	Nonmetal Minerals Mining and Dressing	12	3	110719	60695
制造业	Manufacturing Industry	4508	767	97000953	37257637
农副食品加工业	Agricultural Products Processing	65	13	773038	179542
食品制造业	Food Manufacturing	83	12	1678813	257927
酒、饮料和精制茶制造业	Wine, Beverage and Tea Manufacturing	31	3	1434985	144638
烟草制品业	Tobacco Processing	2	–	3235754	51765
纺织业	Textile Industry	607	91	7628879	1687222
纺织服装、服饰业	Textile Products and Costume Industry	245	59	2006105	491783
皮革、毛皮、羽毛及其制品和制鞋业	Leather. Furs. Downand Related and Shoes Products	127	20	1246363	256820
木材加工和木、竹、藤、棕、草制品业	Timber Processing, Bamboo, Cane, Palm Fiber and Straw Products	21	4	134098	33638
家具制造业	Furniture Manufacturing	63	12	1289197	693717
造纸和纸制品业	Paper Making and Paper Products	211	29	2956789	653403
印刷和记录媒介复制业	Printing and Record Media	74	14	551788	100261
文教、工美、体育和娱乐用品制造业	Cultural, Educational. Industrial Arts. Sports and Entertainment Goods	93	18	1383016	358379
石油加工、炼焦和核燃料加工业	Petroleum Processing, Coking and Nuclear Fuel Processing	9	2	73588	6168
化学原料和化学制品制造业	Raw Chemical Materials and Chemical Products	247	31	8188623	2875576

continued 1 (10000 yuan)

工业销售产值 Value of Industrial Products Sales	出口交货值 Export delivery value	实收资本 Total Capital Hold	国家资本 State Capital	个人资本 Personal Capital	港澳台资本 Hongkong, Macau and TaiWan Capital	外商资本 Foreign Capital	就业人员年平均人数(人) Annual Average Number of Staff and Workers (person)
135688	–	53010	12080	18130	–	–	1109
3280	–	500	–	–	–	–	9
21037	–	9480	–	8980	–	–	387
111372	–	43030	12080	9150	–	–	713
95372226	13801135	21151202	939543	5531401	2331713	3488463	920641
803195	57637	144290	670	44340	26898	21385	6663
1704095	80432	584233	23815	99978	66565	204220	21445
1398001	13159	317060	369	6470	68173	152495	12385
3033448	8207	69040	–	3630	1400	–	2822
7489846	1263921	1594823	7951	678770	175874	202224	108985
1977647	954811	566996	3641	102077	282321	90467	59223
1226733	693722	200012	–	48871	39211	27320	20356
129368	17168	34720	–	14348	1231	–	2544
1254368	434363	220033	–	53663	27696	61668	24444
2944084	63999	567642	2235	288743	12642	12104	31547
542657	11725	193661	21598	50435	37378	2689	8710
1338166	337277	240952	396	51991	30759	83612	16770
72890	1009	9808	–	8208	–	–	352
8054195	585367	1745512	24422	213751	41122	202333	41396

单位:万元

4-12 续表2

项　目	Item	企业单位数(个) Number of Enterprises (unit)	亏损企业(个) Loss Making Enterprises (unit)	工业总产值(当年价格) Gross Industrial Output Value (current price)	新产品产值 Output of New Products
医药制造业	Medical and Pharmaceutical Products	74	10	3280421	749474
化学纤维制造业	Chemical Fiber	115	21	5789346	2083581
橡胶和塑料制品业	Rubber and Plastic Products	237	31	5115438	1444189
非金属矿物制品业	Nonmetal Mineral Products	232	33	3370923	719654
黑色金属冶炼和压延加工业	Smelting and Processing of Ferrous Metals	95	24	1883001	491309
有色金属冶炼和压延加工业	Smelting and Processing of Nonferrous Metals	52	14	4089104	836158
金属制品业	Metal Products	267	51	3614981	1484224
通用设备制造业	Ordinary Machinery	404	63	7007455	3499064
专用设备制造业	For Special Purpose Equipment Manufacturing	203	45	1604166	596198
汽车制造业	Automobile Manufacturing	193	37	6511835	3919138
铁路、船舶、航空航天和其他运输设备制造业	Railway. watercraft. Avigation spaceflight and other Equipment Manufacturing	49	10	384305	96867
电气机械和器材制造业	Electric Equipment and Machinery	302	54	8572791	4394913
计算机、通信和其他电子设备制造业	Computers. Telecommunications and Other Electronic Equipment Manufacturing	237	42	10643383	7876830
仪器仪表制造业	Instruments and Meters Manufacturing	143	24	2185666	1127319
其他制造业	Other Manufacturing	21	-	224578	103003
废弃资源综合利用业	Multiple Utilization of Waste Resouces	5	-	138426	44878
金属制品、机械和设备修理业	Metal Products, Machinery and Equipment Repair	1	-	4100	-
电力、燃气及水的生产和供应业	Produotion and supply of electricity, gas & water	60	10	8509913	77289
电力、热力生产和供应业	Production and Supply of Electric Power and Hot Water	36	4	6173706	70200
燃气生产和供应业	Production and Supply of Gas	9	1	2079836	-
水的生产和供应业	Production and Supply of Tap Water	15	5	256372	7088

continued 2 (10000 yuan)

工业销售产值 Value of Industrial Products Sales	出口交货值 Export delivery value	实收资本 Total Capital Hold	国家资本 State Capital	个人资本 Personal Capital	港澳台资本 Hongkong, Macau and TaiWan Capital	外商资本 Foreign Capital	就业人员年平均人数(人) Annual Average Number of Staff and Workers (person)
3141772	224282	786367	184492	37151	17682	231370	30138
5576629	351396	1176180	–	537378	94750	91448	27826
5090521	808258	820329	24823	248440	22997	230797	42348
3359122	160069	623179	11919	257546	31332	84958	29169
1835079	37512	286726	6780	122990	22912	13172	10047
4113212	221920	326365	6875	72324	4215	23958	7550
3552366	535037	758869	32714	347886	129736	54362	38302
6910684	1082192	1632825	58483	418413	151972	309913	81154
1586988	350826	631323	31176	184998	87827	173541	29212
6402575	442010	1860514	160979	257353	345117	281710	49400
381109	168989	145593	30000	32067	–	9139	6534
8395559	1380619	2287057	58910	350096	227479	379417	72456
10557279	3125254	2696469	243561	759633	320166	452874	100281
2117680	373973	598933	3735	222771	58839	86850	33837
240259	16000	26342	–	14381	5421	4138	3790
137627	–	4350	–	2700	–	–	854
5075	–	1000	–	–	–	300	101
8454439	–	1460197	838729	35006	81180	84901	18279
6117286	–	652397	228625	16855	50000	9819	11371
2084227	–	379074	283323	10151	28680	52582	2103
252926	–	428725	326781	8000	2500	22500	4805

4－13 市区规模以上工业

Main Economic Indicators of Industrial

单位:万元

项 目	Item	资产合计 Total Assets	流动资产合计 Total Circulating Funds	应收账款 Receivables	存货 Stock
总 计	**Total**	**122753597**	**73295347**	**22180740**	**15084440**
按隶属关系分	**Grouped by Subordination**				
中央属	Central	6318682	3734381	667446	1862509
省属	Provincial	5069149	1533036	353865	290188
市属	Municipal	7736832	3952768	869801	1213315
按所有制分	**Grouped by Ownership**				
国有企业	State－owned Enterprises	860964	138220	21974	23044
集体企业	Collective－owned Enterprises	11796	9800	2444	287
股份合作企业	Cooperative Enterprises	84911	75473	19503	6484
联营企业	Joint Ownership Enterprises	1813	1730	1048	660
有限责任公司	Limited Liability Corporations	40034736	21862781	7319932	4919606
股份有限公司	Share－holding Corporations Ltd.	17822331	9640716	2771153	1976905
私营企业	Private Enterprises	27993587	18277559	5384536	3904592
外商及港澳台投资企业	Enterprises with Investment from Foreign、Hong Kong、Macao and Taiwan	35431177	22863088	6500511	4184654
其他企业	Other Enterprises	512282	425980	159639	68207
按企业规模分	**Grouped by Size of Enterprises**				
大型企业	Large	36247007	21683897	7278477	3492368
中型企业	Medium－sized	34549285	20635089	6232836	4010910
小微企业	Small	51957305	30976361	8669428	7581162
按轻重工业分	**Grouped by Light & Heavy Industry**				
轻工业	Light Industry	46704851	27763438	5982776	7039635
重工业	Heavy Industry	76048745	45531909	16197964	8044805

企业主要经济指标(2015 年)(二)

Enterprises Above Designated Size in Urban District(2015)(Ⅱ)

(10000 yuan)

产成品 Finished Products	固定资产合计 Fixed Assets	累计折旧 Accumulated Depreciation	本年折旧 Depreciation of the year	负债合计 Total Liabilities	流动负债合计 Total Current Liabilities	非流动负债合计 Total Non - current Liabilities	所有者权益合计 Creditors´Equity
6295973	**29050646**	**19520937**	**2880077**	**68724688**	**59494879**	**8545035**	**54008267**
375062	2106350	1222314	177686	3278729	2770028	508701	3039953
139898	4117359	2865675	320891	2931187	1447980	1459592	2137962
700302	2307689	1463178	206031	4444299	3437945	993875	3292531
9373	703443	582754	94066	227798	193017	34229	633166
274	1104	3217	151	3805	3805	–	7991
4009	7045	7999	972	51843	50783	60	33068
130	83	162	20	1455	1455	–	358
1692122	11570781	7076898	992034	26069559	20573772	5341912	13959376
807792	2397906	1864741	237999	7480971	6168098	1289074	10341358
1861839	5851922	4133691	696172	17319217	16367138	656103	10657382
1886819	8438432	5822989	850808	17242162	15808934	1223658	18191165
33616	79930	28485	7855	327879	327879	–	184403
1594117	7528343	4153810	714560	19463623	16775363	2621501	16783384
1645183	8127411	6213748	900613	18908679	16395855	2266266	15640598
3056673	13394892	9153380	1264903	30352385	26323661	3657268	21584286
2881204	11359451	8041566	1051087	24922844	22401529	2228181	21769766
3414770	17691195	11479371	1828989	43801843	37093350	6316854	32238501

单位:万元　　　　4－13　续表1

项　目	Item	资产合计 Total Assets	流动资产合　计 Total Circulating Funds	应收账款 Receivables	存　货 Stock
按国民经济行业分	**Grouped by Economic Sector**				
采掘业	Mining and Quarrying	207672	112998	23947	8849
黑色金属矿采选业	Ferrous Metals Mining and Dressing	2521	2436	－399	2519
有色金属矿采选业	Nonferrous Minerals Mining and Dressing	24026	13199	1162	2074
非金属矿采选业	Nonmetal Minerals Mining and Dressing	181125	97364	23184	4255
制造业	Manufacturing Industry	110575724	70947566	21956367	15014523
农副食品加工业	Agricultural Products Processing	652040	360507	97058	104208
食品制造业	Food Manufacturing	2257087	1307053	670068	178915
酒、饮料和精制茶制造业	Wine, Beverage and Tea Manufacturing	1288560	680340	158185	108616
烟草制品业	Tobacco Processing	2980427	2155302	326400	1599787
纺织业	Textile Industry	8565379	5158426	964535	1176762
纺织服装、服饰业	Textile Products and Costume Industry	2208598	1500299	307903	362767
皮革、毛皮、羽毛及其制品和制鞋业	Leather. Furs. Downand Related and Shoes Products	1177726	936596	246421	237084
木材加工和木、竹、藤、棕、草制品业	Timber Processing, Bamboo, Cane, Palm Fiber and Straw Products	152777	91753	19934	23852
家具制造业	Furniture Manufacturing	1087225	767768	166380	127731
造纸和纸制品业	Paper Making and Paper Products	3793915	2580383	677706	368734
印刷和记录媒介复制业	Printing and Record Media	776438	422939	146429	77707
文教、工美、体育和娱乐用品制造业	Cultural, Educational. Industrial Arts. Sports and Entertainment Goods	825079	524291	100573	193746
石油加工、炼焦和核燃料加工业	Petroleum Processing, Coking and Nuclear Fuel Processing	46455	34979	17179	6691
化学原料和化学制品制造业	Raw Chemical Materials and Chemical Products	8376100	4406338	1006593	764468

continued 1 (10000 yuan)

产成品 Finished Products	固定资产合计 Fixed Assets	累计折旧 Accumulated Depreciation	本年折旧 Depreciation of the year	负债合计 Total Liabilities	流动负债合计 Total Current Liabilities	非流动负债合计 Total Non - current Liabilities	所有者权益合计 Creditors´Equity
5987	48958	17986	5642	123742	112405	10319	83930
2384	86	713	25	2935	2935	–	-414
1658	4736	3386	456	13046	11128	900	10980
1944	44136	13886	5161	107761	98342	9419	73364
6278018	22573896	14936375	2357259	61160545	55392980	5115780	49394538
49030	164707	80720	14825	393945	365752	25071	258093
93616	570706	331428	51369	860506	852855	7542	1396580
29793	437452	522663	49501	642148	630787	9230	644980
283196	824012	350678	35401	747346	747064	282	2233081
615210	2091818	1922330	263059	5220531	4861366	270483	3338663
168449	490650	322926	42835	1185939	1082773	57076	1020328
41175	146882	82259	14285	896694	873761	10194	281029
11266	28297	23459	3185	109654	107194	2456	43123
48434	209459	105153	15827	683014	653850	28359	404211
174569	805156	651694	98954	2568781	2416384	67945	1225130
38633	274229	259064	30023	449498	389103	58981	326939
56955	218437	186493	23627	443767	428906	14236	381312
1711	7669	8195	1127	34004	34004	–	12452
373462	2358232	1257567	242441	4262807	3564613	653556	4111538

单位:万元　　　　4-13　续表2

项　目	Item	资产合计 Total Assets	流动资产合　计 Total Circulating Funds	应收账款 Receivables	存　货 Stock
医药制造业	Medical and Pharmaceutical Products	3890792	2111060	618013	529999
化学纤维制造业	Chemical Fiber	8137754	3916505	362423	762062
橡胶和塑料制品业	Rubber and Plastic Products	4659853	2637916	758239	675682
非金属矿物制品业	Nonmetal Mineral Products	4371190	3156745	1606231	328755
黑色金属冶炼和压延加工业	Smelting and Processing of Ferrous Metals	1612881	1089840	189988	302231
有色金属冶炼和压延加工业	Smelting and Processing of Nonferrous Metals	2581913	1889558	221010	346144
金属制品业	Metal Products	3538576	2382570	811260	662056
通用设备制造业	Ordinary Machinery	9155894	5995549	1934503	1231957
专用设备制造业	For Special Purpose Equipment Manufacturing	2395468	1607081	577713	394145
汽车制造业	Automobile Manufacturing	8478452	4948393	2149514	751691
铁路、船舶、航空航天和其他运输设备制造业	Railway. watercraft. Avigation spaceflight and other Equipment Manufacturing	455405	265779	89585	55810
电气机械和器材制造业	Electric Equipment and Machinery	9607207	6343363	2335256	1373831
计算机、通信和其他电子设备制造业	Computers. Telecommunications and Other Electronic Equipment Manufacturing	14154417	11243524	4527676	1801562
仪器仪表制造业	Instruments and Meters Manufacturing	3077710	2225838	825333	425164
其他制造业	Other Manufacturing	183532	139566	17774	33531
废弃资源综合利用业	Multiple Utilization of Waste Resouces	82721	63580	25286	7963
金属制品、机械和设备修理业	Metal Products, Machinery and Equipment Repair	4155	3727	1203	877
电力、燃气及水的生产和供应业	Produotion and supply of electricity, gas & water	11970200	2234783	200425	61068
电力、热力生产和供应业	Production and Supply of Electric Power and Hot Water	8215699	1218576	133842	30130
燃气生产和供应业	Production and Supply of Gas	1316585	218668	48254	11588
水的生产和供应业	Production and Supply of Tap Water	2437916	797540	18330	19350

continued 2 (10000 yuan)

产成品 Finished Products	固定资产合计 Fixed Assets	累计折旧 Accumulated Depreciation	本年折旧 Depreciation of the year	负债合计 Total Liabilities	流动负债合计 Total Current Liabilities	非流动负债合计 Total Non－current Liabilities	所有者权益合计 Creditors′Equity
215181	995404	396447	75848	1829116	1411504	411085	2059677
438230	1889837	1077400	132769	4573526	4127343	433206	3564227
450128	1341080	1086685	178924	2598597	2404106	184091	2061254
168320	844868	672995	94583	2981646	2818795	115861	1388242
154932	336325	297482	49041	955466	864634	56896	654353
101497	428898	162108	37709	2000889	1862774	138112	581024
211916	678253	411144	69667	2112125	2015329	50603	1428135
460198	1484210	957472	165781	4709484	4328077	244084	4442148
114965	523348	363460	53396	1226969	1083183	142512	1168496
365457	2106435	937289	227363	5938331	5220619	695226	2540158
18951	123416	63756	11324	245097	235576	8121	210030
648554	1685528	1107509	171406	5295912	4491778	778105	4313606
795754	1081591	977386	157739	6807467	6215977	570642	7344905
137669	385596	291658	41054	1262087	1179673	81825	1815621
8102	31020	23403	3011	70567	70567	–	112965
2631	10245	5460	1166	51371	51371	–	31350
37	141	93	22	3265	3265	–	890
–	6427793	4566576	517176	7440400	3989493	3418937	4529800
3735	4763025	3481788	404038	5387362	2861321	2504541	2828337
8235	755270	265795	53225	842011	545767	296243	474575
–	909497	818993	59913	1211027	582406	618152	1226889

4－14 市区规模以上工业

Main Economic Indicators of Industrial

单位:万元

项 目	Item	主营业务收入 Revenues in Main Business	主营业务成本 Costs in Main Business	主营业务税金及附加 Sales Taxes and Extra Charges in Main Business
总　计	**Total**	**104591641**	**83918987**	**2452114**
按隶属关系分	**Grouped by Subordination**			
中 央 属	Central	6598844	4045250	1845848
省　　属	Provincial	6902594	6379718	22173
市　　属	Municipal	5576860	4287080	39662
按所有制分	**Grouped by Ownership**			
国有企业	State－owned Enterprises	1831044	1750596	6464
集体企业	Collective－owned Enterprises	8367	7465	28
股份合作企业	Cooperative Enterprises	50245	40103	331
联营企业	Joint Ownership Enterprises	4338	4112	14
有限责任公司	Limited Liability Corporations	33995562	27576342	2009362
股份有限公司	Share－holding Corporations Ltd.	9512137	7306850	56780
私营企业	Private Enterprises	26846877	23125147	146749
外商及港澳台投资企业	Enterprises with Investment from Foreign、Hong Kong、Macao and Taiwan	31738482	23832522	227338
其他企业	Other Enterprises	604590	275850	5048
按企业规模分	**Grouped by Size of Enterprises**			
大型企业	Large	29696443	22615817	305370
中型企业	Medium－sized	31281114	25793496	136025
小微企业	Small	43614084	35509674	2010719
按轻重工业分	**Grouped by Light & Heavy Industry**			
轻工业	Light Industry	39855363	29660352	2009007
重工业	Heavy Industry	64736278	54258635	443107

企业主要经济指标(2015 年)(三)
Enterprises Above Designated Size in Urban District(2015)(Ⅲ)

(10000 yuan)

销售费用 Sales Expenses	管理费用 Management Expenses	财务费用 Financial Expenses	利息支出 Interest Expenditure	营业利润 Business Profits	利润总额 Total Profits	利税总额 Total Pre－tax Profits	本年应交增值税 Value Added Tax Payable
4752085	**6107534**	**1232948**	**1586763**	**6928630**	**7757643**	**13745302**	**3446033**
126479	197489	58078	70385	248345	266839	2661778	467922
68334	184897	5032	21668	172529	277833	457586	156836
648709	359096	81131	70121	188006	302969	544174	198140
3748	36846	4927	5429	31253	33071	99056	59215
227	531	37	36	79	117	333	188
853	4929	2124	1867	1919	2084	4437	2022
36	160	－		16	16	104	74
973819	1534244	397091	489424	1645951	1893567	5123024	1137587
555785	770456	65258	130451	949680	1092382	1469994	317652
630069	1401134	524890	584909	1167088	1259701	2105380	697064
2361202	2323851	230860	358610	－	3417739	4839140	1192410
226346	35382	7762	16036	3132645	58965	103835	39821
2064039	1947784	206076	299183	2896069	3279652	4607815	1022478
1383246	1860301	379316	508932	1957862	2117447	3208505	952956
1304799	2299449	647556	778648	2074699	2360544	5928982	1470599
2811846	2302168	519825	713315	2827691	3015261	6813511	1703104
1940239	3805365	713123	873449	4100939	4742382	6931791	1742929

项 目	Item	主营业务收入 Revenues in Main Business	主营业务成本 Costs in Main Business	主营业务税金及附加 Sales Taxes and Extra Charges in Main Business
按国民经济行业分	**Grouped by Economic Sector**			
采掘业	Mining and Quarrying	132599	76189	6440
黑色金属矿采选业	Ferrous Metals Mining and Dressing	2428	2467	1
有色金属矿采选业	Nonferrous Minerals Mining and Dressing	20537	14321	353
非金属矿采选业	Nonmetal Minerals Mining and Dressing	109634	59401	6087
制造业	Manufacturing Industry	95942508	75849103	2416683
农副食品加工业	Agricultural Products Processing	808846	710520	1846
食品制造业	Food Manufacturing	2012247	1499437	7504
酒、饮料和精制茶制造业	Wine, Beverage and Tea Manufacturing	1330037	914954	25174
烟草制品业	Tobacco Processing	2952188	604359	1795481
纺织业	Textile Industry	7380896	6442716	36096
纺织服装、服饰业	Textile Products and Costume Industry	1988797	1655025	13435
皮革、毛皮、羽毛及其制品和制鞋业	Leather. Furs. Downand Related and Shoes Products	1218443	1098373	5841
木材加工和木、竹、藤、棕、草制品业	Timber Processing, Bamboo, Cane, Palm Fiber and Straw Products	131392	109424	1129
家具制造业	Furniture Manufacturing	1231722	901407	6845
造纸和纸制品业	Paper Making and Paper Products	2868994	2472867	14889
印刷和记录媒介复制业	Printing and Record Media	579838	493011	3246
文教、工美、体育和娱乐用品制造业	Cultural, Educational. Industrial Arts. Sports and Entertainment Goods	1335493	1223324	4674
石油加工、炼焦和核燃料加工业	Petroleum Processing, Coking and Nuclear Fuel Processing	70825	63242	280
化学原料和化学制品制造业	Raw Chemical Materials and Chemical Products	8179870	6293912	25895

continued 1 (10000 yuan)

销售费用 Sales Expenses	管理费用 Management Expenses	财务费用 Financial Expenses	利息支出 Interest Expenditure	营业利润 Business Profits	利润总额 Total Profits	利税总额 Total Pre - tax Profits	本年应交增值税 Value Added Tax Payable
5788	9470	6278	6289	28565	28257	41368	6671
–	37	137	128	-215	-214	-214	–
1033	1980	747	747	2103	2094	4259	1813
4755	7453	5394	5415	26676	26378	37323	4859
4719545	5960699	1143871	1481471	6576983	7284192	13029148	3239697
34007	32652	14174	14079	17618	21560	39662	16241
236886	117577	-18	11181	187327	194377	272464	70582
289154	46556	11653	11291	72111	77813	158010	54913
86266	121565	-357	3392	260841	249903	2509968	383702
110828	328929	147132	184733	360297	373922	610336	199735
75317	174328	20719	34595	58099	71208	174452	89685
29026	47031	13881	28487	26018	26703	71893	39237
4413	8800	2475	3084	2735	3451	9414	4770
84259	84189	13399	18220	223217	220231	262368	35253
46241	121820	118540	126157	118425	126291	218771	77407
12842	39202	8333	9684	33353	35248	59267	20577
19750	49075	12341	17404	28649	27349	53997	21926
1576	2003	644	735	3395	3232	4523	1003
555730	585168	127409	133971	658779	714592	1025083	284585

项　目	Item	主营业务收　入 Revenues in Main Business	主营业务成　本 Costs in Main Business	主营业务税金及附加 Sales Taxes and Extra Charges in Main Business
医药制造业	Medical and Pharmaceutical Products	3093846	1352116	33190
化学纤维制造业	Chemical Fiber	5321493	4864091	12166
橡胶和塑料制品业	Rubber and Plastic Products	4771444	4053411	29721
非金属矿物制品业	Nonmetal Mineral Products	3353984	2912283	13889
黑色金属冶炼和压延加工业	Smelting and Processing of Ferrous Metals	1820853	1688162	5176
有色金属冶炼和压延加工业	Smelting and Processing of Nonferrous Metals	4136789	3925909	4866
金属制品业	Metal Products	3574032	3127528	18815.5
通用设备制造业	Ordinary Machinery	7049422	5611349	39049
专用设备制造业	For Special Purpose Equipment Manufacturing	1583976	1217127	11414
汽车制造业	Automobile Manufacturing	6352648	5283105	171924
铁路、船舶、航空航天和其他运输设备制造业	Railway. watercraft. Avigation spaceflight and other Equipment Manufacturing	390590	322706	3521
电气机械和器材制造业	Electric Equipment and Machinery	8426444	6842491	36333
计算机、通信和其他电子设备制造业	Computers. Telecommunications and Other Electronic Equipment Manufacturing	11384793	8270419	76781
仪器仪表制造业	Instruments and Meters Manufacturing	2120557	1483258	15327
其他制造业	Other Manufacturing	324463	291018	1403
废弃资源综合利用业	Multiple Utilization of Waste Resouces	142580	117646	727
金属制品、机械和设备修理业	Metal Products, Machinery and Equipment Repair	5006	3914	49
电力、燃气及水的生产和供应业	Produotion and supply of electricity, gas & water	8516534	7993696	28991
电力、热力生产和供应业	Production and Supply of Electric Power and Hot Water	6127807	5783579	20533
燃气生产和供应业	Production and Supply of Gas	2090907	1957040	6916
水的生产和供应业	Production and Supply of Tap Water	297820	253076	1542

continued 2 (10000 yuan)

销售费用 Sales Expenses	管理费用 Management Expenses	财务费用 Financial Expenses	利息支出 Interest Expenditure	营业利润 Business Profits	利润总额 Total Profits	利税总额 Total Pre - tax Profits	本年应交增值税 Value Added Tax Payable
965649	306905	16891	36162	433211	468951	766253	264050
23841	122402	113740	142407	221982	231237	307011	63569
189566	184649	92250	72739	236418	262923	417945	125234
106039	141102	79459	88754	121276	123681	228046	90231
13646	42161	29964	37492	54580	56239	88408	26834
16646	51570	54400	76397	96515	107576	177885	65444
71508	186408	51564	57688	140376	150032	255383	86423
239469	551290	51161	77553	615767	648364	960815	272913
83890	198916	17936	22958	77173	90139	150760	49006
130912	425191	83124	77454	330615	407587	677483	97519
13086	42480	2244	5749	8105	15268	33450	14563
483303	560193	87306	120625	489702	508649	750711	204816
632387	1106267	-31859	48856	1447267	1751559	2291661	460339
157959	266357	1653	15052	215012	267042	381863	99236
4265	11213	211	1510	16618	19138	30222	9559
269	3776	3325	2902	20672	28908	39741	10106
812	927	177	160	831	1018	1306	240
26751	137365	82798	99004	323082	445194	674786	199665
1870	74963	57782	57953	229524	329007	504585	154565
15188	33460	15206	15633	82574	84295	127843	36632
9693	28942	9811	25418	10984	31892	42358	8469

4－15 全市规模以上工业企业

Main Economic Indicators of Industrial Enterprises

单位：万元

项 目	Item	企业单位数（个）Number of Enterprises (unit)	亏损企业（个）Loss Making Enterprises (unit)	工业总产值（当年价格）Gross Industrial Output Value (current price)	新产品产值 Output of New Products
按登记注册类型分组	**Grouped by Status of Registration**				
内资企业	Domestic－funded Enterprises	5019	729	89970594	30351318
国有企业	State－owned Enterprises	17	1	2309361	13790
中央企业	Central Enterprises	4	1	1291663	－
地方企业	Local Enterprises	13	－	1017698	13790
集体企业	Collective－owned Enterprises	5	－	14146	－
股份合作企业	Cooperative Enterprises	8	1	52391	8794
联营企业	Joint Ownership Enterprises	1	－	4338	－
集体联营企业	Collective Joint Ownership Enterprises	1	－	4338	－
有限责任公司	Limited Liability Corporations	978	164	38448270	14376929
国有独资公司	State－funded Corporations	31	6	7176011	222438
其他有限责任公司	Other Limited Liability Corporations	947	158	31272259	14154491
股份有限公司	Share－holding Corporations Ltd.	194	21	11299925	5454813
私营企业	Private Enterprises	3811	542	37160734	10473300
私营独资企业	Private－funded Enterprises	165	18	855805	103681
私营合伙企业	Private Partnership Enterprises	19	2	94868	2883
私营有限责任公司	Private Limited Liability Corporations	3557	514	34754546	9654117
私营股份有限公司	Private Share－holding Corporations Ltd.	70	8	1455515	712619
港、澳、台商投资公司	Enterprises with Investment from Hong Kong, Macao and Taiwan	470	124	15604779	7085178
内地与港澳台合资经营企业	Joint－venture Enterprises with funds from Hong Kong, Macao and Taiwan	282	68	10534009	4071744
内地与港澳台合作经营企业	Cooperative Enterprises with funds from Hong Kong, Macao and Taiwan	2	－	77111	49544
港澳台商独资经营企业	Enterprises with Sole Investment from Hong Kong, Macao and Taiwan	174	52	3672242	1811816
港澳台商投资股份有限公司	Share－holding Corporations Ltd. with Investment from Hong Kong, Macao and Taiwan	8	2	1280311	1134905
其他港澳台商投资	Other Enterprises with Investment from Hong Kong, Macao and Taiwan	4	2	41107	17169
外商投资企业公司	Enterprises with Foreign Investment	584	123	18581429	5853494
中外合资经营企业	Joint－venture Enterprises	295	55	9155145	3579511
中外合作经营企业	Cooperation Enterprises	8	3	84122	9781
外商独资经营企业	Enterprises with Sole Foreign Investment	275	64	9242245	2222399
外商投资股份有限公司	Share－holding Corporations Ltd. with Foreign Investment	5	1	97386	41802

主要经济指标按登记注册类型分(2015 年)
Above Designated Size by Status of Registration(2015)

(10000 yuan)

工业销售产值 Value of Industrial Products Sales	出口交货值 Export delivery value	实收资本 Total Capital Hold	国家资本 State Capital	个人资本 Personal Capital	港澳台资本 Hongkong, Macau and TaiWan Capital	外商资本 Foreign Capital	就业人员年平均人数(人) Annual Average Number of Staff and Workers (person)
88340349	9572840	16667103	1524699	6256680	18674	91273	780517
2258048	1968	126656	117721	–	–	–	5127
1239350	–	23075	23075	–	–	–	1736
1018698	1968	103581	94646	–	–	–	3391
13796	–	1456	–	589	–	–	214
40804	30	9569	–	9442	–	–	1036
4338	–	100	–	–	–	–	65
4338	–	100	–	–	–	–	65
37449955	2964363	6073703	866126	1045446	1655	13029	245655
6944325	30229	446331	349216	2000	–	–	14907
30505630	2934133	5627371	516910	1043446	1655	13029	230748
11443431	1458553	4055308	538663	1319722	15352	74081	96050
36523224	5140839	6320697	2189	3879308	1667	4164	429371
839300	114814	62502	–	42426	–	–	11217
93364	4947	9903	515	7884	–	–	1550
34154570	4751989	5873101	1674	3693991	1667	4164	404117
1435990	269089	375192	–	135008	–	–	12487
15394068	3135369	4266592	324347	326544	2487607	210441	150723
10472413	1746042	2133793	161962	139668	855904	210101	84953
77111	40473	6321	–	–	1580	–	459
3539291	1291162	1521253	–	–	1441228	300	53316
1263210	44414	523343	162386	186877	128012	40	11144
42042	13277	81883	–	–	60883	–	851
18565756	4468052	5057773	197983	67980	84099	3444660	187362
9025534	1674620	2259611	197983	65611	75636	997768	92168
85070	37486	32068	–	2181	8442	19251	1888
9355494	2710018	2706586	–	188	21	2371309	91675
97126	43509	57213	–	–	–	54038	1489

4－16 分地区规上

Added Value of Industrial Enterprises Above

单位:亿元

年 份 Year	全 市 Whole City	市 区				
		上城区 Shangcheng	下城区 Xiacheng	江干区 Jianggan	拱墅区 Gongshu	西湖区 Xihu
2000	360.97					
2001	444.91					
2002	597.01					
2003	783.51					
2004	1019.47					
2005	1126.54					
2006	1363.17					
2007	1717.65					
2008	1743.20					
2009	1792.00					
2010	2153.83					
2011	2369.00	215.48	20.83	47.25	119.11	49.03
2012	2492.00	296.64	22.05	48.00	117.08	49.07
2013	2664.13	318.89	23.33	53.33	104.34	49.62
2014	2813.51	328.06	15.16	57.60	78.34	50.45
2015	2875.05	329.70	7.13	53.79	60.64	52.30

注:2000－2010 年为主营业务收入 500 万及以上;2011－2015 年为主营业务收入 2000 万及以上。

a) Data after 2011－2015 refer to all the industrial enterprises with annual Sales income of over 20 million yuan, data in 2000－2010 refer to all the industrial enterprises with annual sales income of over 5 million yuan.

工业增加值(2000－2015 年)
Designated Size by Region (2000－2015)

(100 million yuan)

Urban District				桐庐县 Tonglu	淳安县 Chun'an	建德市 Jiande	临安市 Lin'an
高新(滨江)区 Hi－Tech (Binjiang)	萧山区 Xiaoshan	余杭区 Yuhang	富阳区 Fuyang				
	77.95	31.54	22.05	9.29	2.24	10.13	11.83
	106.28	38.50	31.69	11.98	2.99	8.86	14.71
	145.26	40.29	38.87	14.08	3.40	13.05	18.55
	199.34	69.17	52.52	18.98	5.46	16.82	25.09
	245.57	86.96	63.65	29.73	6.59	27.62	32.25
	311.61	129.16	80.22	31.60	9.29	28.54	37.84
	385.34	150.85	103.73	42.10	12.70	37.88	47.54
	401.88	195.17	136.42	57.06	17.35	50.54	62.53
	482.29	212.97	160.31	68.41	20.56	61.38	74.51
	538.91	225.60	167.30	62.17	23.48	60.03	80.02
	606.90	297.10	182.30	76.63	29.18	76.13	98.91
162.30	721.27	243.41	162.41	71.74	32.66	68.09	98.20
210.02	727.65	250.64	165.25	80.02	38.69	76.19	106.67
278.48	704.46	275.99	198.03	81.63	43.44	81.74	115.18
324.69	712.21	301.62	200.53	94.92	47.53	85.18	123.24
365.67	706.49	334.30	200.89	102.26	52.06	83.67	127.85

4－17 主要工业产品生产量(2015 年)

Output of Major Industrial Products(2015)

产品名称	Item	全市 Whole City 2015 年	全市 Whole City 为上年(%) As Compared with the Preceding Year(%)	市区 Urban District
发电量 (亿千瓦时)	Generating Capacity (100 million kwh)	189.21	92.5	131.81
#水力发电 (亿千瓦时)	of which:Hydroelectric Generation (100 million kwh)	50.60	145.5	-
垃圾发电 (亿千瓦时)	Garbage Power (100 million kwh)	4.98	99.9	4.98
罐头 (万吨)	Canned Food (10000 tons)	6.59	89.1	1.88
乳制品 (吨)	Dairy Products (ton)	142550	83.4	117544
啤酒 (千升)	Beer (1000 litres)	972319.46	100.1	656452.00
软饮料 (万吨)	Soft Drinks (10000 tons)	659.19	91.7	402.33
精制茶 (吨)	Tea (ton)	32978	85	5865
卷烟 (亿支)	Cigarettes (100 million)	602.33	105.3	602.33
方便面 (吨)	Instant Noodle (ton)	263806	92.6	263806
化学纤维 (吨)	Chemical Fiber (ton)	66963547	118.2	6668560
#合成纤维 (吨)	Synthetic Fibre (ton)	6550464	118.5	6522670
纱 (万吨)	Yarn (10000 tons)	71.62	99.6	70.95
布 (万米)	Cloth (10000 m)	424416.73	98.5	339483.40
印染布 (万米)	Printed Fabric (10000 m)	600366.74	105.1	596503.24
蚕丝及交织机织物(含蚕丝≥50%) (万米)	Silk and Woven Fabrics (Containing Greater than or Equal 50% silk) (10000 m)	2357.31	88.7	2172.89
服装 (万件)	Garment (10000 units)	37779.34	98.1	29282.39
皮革鞋靴 (万双)	Leather Footwear (10000 units)	1477.66	128.4	1477.66
家具 (万件)	Furniture (10000 units)	3572.71	96.7	3315.75
塑料制品 (吨)	Plastic Membrane (ton)	1463024	85.7	1263659
机制纸及纸板 (万吨)	Machine Made Paper and Paperboard (10000 tons)	597.12	100.9	582.09

4－17 续表1 continued 1

产品名称	Item	全市 Whole City 2015年	全市 Whole City 为上年(%) As Compared with the Preceding Year(%)	市区 Urban District
盐酸(含量31%以上)(吨)	Mariatic Acid(above 31% percent) (ton)	110286	107.9	110286
氢氧化钠(烧碱)(折100%)(吨)	Caustic Soda (ton)	186766	95.1	186766
碳酸钠(纯碱)(吨)	Soda ash (ton)	293451	108.8	293451
初级形态的塑料(塑料树脂及共聚物)(吨)	Plastics in Primary Form(Plastic Resins and Copolymers) (ton)	291316	87.3	169447
合成氨(吨)	Synthetic Ammonia (ton)	204403	117.6	185357
农用氮、磷、钾化学肥料总计(折纯)(吨)	Chemical Fertilizer (ton)	91996	107.4	85845
化学农药原药(折有效成分100%)(吨)	Chemical Pesticide (ton)	111773	93.7	14869
涂料(油漆)(吨)	Paint (ton)	250178	97.5	177526
合成洗涤剂(吨)	Synthetic Detergent (ton)	148557	100.2	114871
化学药品原药(化学原料药)(吨)	Original Drug Chemicals (ton)	9196	94.0	9196
中成药(吨)	Traditional Chinese Medicine (ton)	16000	117.2	13617
橡胶轮胎外胎(轮胎外胎)(万条)	Rubber Tires (10000 units)	4791.93	92.5	4784.68
水泥(万吨)	Cement (10000 tons)	1819.54	93.1	929.63
粗钢(万吨)	Crude Steel (10000 tons)	273.83	73.0	272.64
生铁(万吨)	Pig Iron (10000 tons)	226.33	76.9	226.33
铁合金(万吨)	Iron Alloy (10000 tons)	6.52	96.0	0.98
钢材(万吨)	Steel Products (10000 tons)	780.21	89.0	766.80
精炼铜(电解铜)(吨)	Refined Copper (ton)	237874	137.9	232053
工业锅炉(蒸发量吨)	Industry Boiler (ton)	7738	107.5	7738
金属切削机床(台)	Metal－cutting Machine Tools (unit)	43242	85.3	41468

4－17　续表2　continued 2

产品名称	Item	全市 Whole City 2015 年	为上年(%) As Compared with the Preceding Year(%)	市区 Urban District
金属成形机床(锻压设备)（台）	Metal Forming Machine(Forge Equipment) (Tai)	9058	76.7	8210
泵(液体泵)（万台）	Pump (10000 sets)	80.55	106.8	79.63
滚动轴承(轴承)（万套）	Bearings (10000 units)	13105.50	92.8	13105.50
汽车（辆）	Motor Vehicles (unit)	91081	102.7	91081
叉车（台）	Forklift (unit)	60885	83.9	8892
两轮自行车(自行车)（万辆）	Bicycles (10000 units)	262.56	70.4	261.89
交流电动机（万千瓦）	AC Motor (10000 kw)	112.23	109.9	101.28
钢绞线（吨）	Strand (ton)	52503	118.1	52469
通信及电子网络用电缆（万对千米）	Communication Cable (10000 km)	493.00	104.1	154.95
光缆(光纤通讯电缆)（万芯千米）	Electric Power Cable (10000 km)	3434.83	118.6	3413.05
家用电冰箱（万台）	Household Refrigerators (10000 units)	107.59	91.6	107.59
家用洗衣机（万台）	Household Washing Machines (10000 units)	311.76	89.6	311.76
吸排油烟机（万台）	Smoke Absorbers (10000 units)	272.40	117.6	272.40
移动通信手持机(手机)（万部）	Mobile Telephone Sets (10000 units)	540.58	101.2	540.58
电工仪器仪表（万台）	Electric Instrument and Apparatus (10000 units)	2797.77	105.5	2797.77
工业自动调节仪表与控制系统（万台）	Industrial Automatic Adjustment Meter and Control System (10000 units)	169.66	96.8	169.60
电光源(灯泡)（亿只）	Light Bulbs (100 million units)	7.17	75.6	2.52
彩色电视机（万部）	Color－Television Sets (10000 units)	6.24	62.5	6.24
微型计算机设备（万台）	Micro－computer Equipment (10000 units)	133.30	77.3	133.30

4-18 单位GDP能耗降低情况(2015年)
Increase or Decrease of Energy Consumption Per Unit of GDP(2015)

地 区	Region	单位GDP能耗(吨标准煤/万元) Energy Consumption Per Unit of GDP (tons of SCE/10000 yuan)		单位GDP电耗(千瓦时/万元) Electricity Consumption Per Unit of GDP (kwh/10000 yuan)		单位工业增加值能耗降低率 Decrease Rate of Energy Consumption Per Unit of Industriul Value - Added (±%)
		2015年	降低率 Decrease Rate (±%)	2015年	降低率 Decrease Rate (±%)	
杭州市	Hangzhou	0.43	3.9	701	8.3	1.2
#上城区	Shangcheng			253	8.2	8.5
下城区	Xiacheng			286	4.7	1.0
江干区	Jianggan			546	6.2	9.2
拱墅区	Gongshu			933	10.0	11.1
西湖区	Xihu			479	5.4	-0.2
高新(滨江)区	Hi-Tech(Binjiang)			372	3.9	17.0
杭州经济技术开发区	Hangzhou Economic and Technological Dvelopment Zone			713	2.0	5.3
萧山区	Xiaoshan	0.60	5.8	1142	6.7	-2.3
余杭区	Yuhang	0.40	6.9	719	9.3	4.0
富阳区	Fuyang	0.81	5.2	1096	10.8	-4.6
桐庐县	Tonglu	0.46	0.6	616	6.9	-4.6
淳安县	Chun'an	0.31	-1.5	573	-3.6	8.2
建德市	Jiande	0.92	-2.5	982	12.0	-5.9
临安市	Lin'an	0.45	5.3	693	11.1	4.5

4-19 工业企业主要能源
Energy Consumption of Industrial

行　业	Sector	原煤(吨) Raw Coal(Ton)	洗精煤(吨) Washing Coal(Ton)	焦炭(吨) Coke(Ton)	汽油(吨) Gasoline(Ton)	煤油(吨) Kerosene(Ton)
总　计	**Total**	**13397555**	**656718**	**1029058**	**45907**	**810**
煤炭开采和洗选业	Coal Mining and Dressing	–	–	–	–	–
黑色金属矿采选业	Ferrous Metals Mining and Dressing	–	–	–	–	–
有色金属矿采选业	Nonferrous Minerals Mining and Dressing	–	–	–	14	–
非金属矿采选业	Nonmetal Minerals Mining and Dressing	53152	–	–	5	–
农副食品加工业	Agricultural Products Processing	10523	–	–	289	–
食品制造业	Food Manufacturing	27094	–	–	994	1
酒、饮料和精制茶制造业	Wine, Beverage and Tea Manufacturing	18113	–	–	106	–
烟草制品业	Tobacco Processing	–	–	–	22	–
纺织业	Textile Processing	765705	–	3	4121	3
纺织服装、服饰业	Textile Products and Costume Industry	15365	–	468	2327	4
皮革、毛皮、羽毛及其制品和制鞋业	Leather. Furs. Downand Related and Shoes Products	9862	–	–	1187	11
木材加工和木、竹、藤、棕、草制品业	Timber Processing, Bamboo, Cane, Plam Fiber and Straw Products	118	–	–	120	–
家具制造业	Furniture Manufacturing	373	–	1052	890	12
造纸和纸制品业	Paper Making and Paper Products	379478	–	–	1187	–
印刷和记录媒介复制业	Printing	108	–	–	671	–
文教、工美、体育和娱乐用品制造业	Cultural, Educational. Industrial Arts. Sports and Entertainment Goods	755	–	96	783	–
石油加工、炼焦和核燃料加工业	Petroleum Processing, Coking and Nuclear Fuel Processing	–	–	–	58	–

消费量按行业分(2015 年)
Enterprises by Sector(2015)

柴油(吨) Diesel oil(Ton)	燃料油(吨) Fuel Oil(Ton)	液化石油气(吨) Liquefied Petroleum Gas(Ton)	天然气(万立方米) Natural Gas (10000 cu. m)	其他石油制品(吨) Other Petroleum Products(Ton)	热力(百万千焦) Heat(Million kilo - joule)	电力(万千瓦时) Electricity (10000 kwh)
148219	**26072**	**12235**	**152457**	**24154**	**89991751**	**3531255**
–	–	–	–	–	–	200
–	–	–	–	–	–	20
32	–	–	–	–	–	2491
7516	–	–	–	36	–	12583
1194	127	7	470	–	234239	13291
2503	669	145	1208	–	1121622	23310
687	101	4	815	–	1555203	50398
397	378	–	668	–	129524	7228
3863	94	143	4094	–	24098526	485067
1728	–	1	213	–	649594	25024
362	–	7	238	–	110725	13350
231	–	–	6	–	140	5166
1139	150	–	730	–	71135	11505
2131	13	–	295	–	27682729	257661
575	–	87	211	–	71397	14106
673	–	63	59	4	157419	14895
496	20	1	–	78	30079	309

4－19 续表

行业 Sector	原煤(吨) Raw Coal(Ton)	洗精煤(吨) Washing Coal(Ton)	焦炭(吨) Coke(Ton)	汽油(吨) Gasoline(Ton)	煤油(吨) Kerosene(Ton)
化学原料和化学制品制造业 Raw Chemical Materials and Chemical Products	1444808	–	4790	2647	2
医药制造业 Medical and Pharmaceutical Products	65950	–	–	585	–
化学纤维制造业 Chemical Fiber	275230	–	–	544	1
橡胶和塑料制品业 Rubber and Plastic Products	257214	–	–	2784	14
非金属矿物制品业 Nonmetal Minerals Products	2659650	–	–	1890	–
黑色金属冶炼和压延加工业 Smelting and Processing of Ferrous Metals	380180	656716	999563	798	1
有色金属冶炼和压延加工业 Smelting and Processing of Nonferrous Metals	15490	–	22279	166	–
金属制品业 Metal Products	46890	2	84	2211	7
通用设备制造业 Ordinary Machinery	27790	–	220	5669	426
专用设备制造业 Special Purpose Equipment	277	–	461	1831	4
汽车制造业 Automobile Manufacturing	2828	–	16	3742	269
铁路、船舶、航空航天和其他运输设备制造业 Railway. watercraft. Avigation spaceflight and other Equipment Manufacturing	270	–	–	339	–
电气机械和器材制造业 Electric Equipment and Machinery	4797	–	26	3542	–
计算机、通信和其他电子设备制造业 Computers. Telecommunications and Other Electronic Equipment Manufacturing	2154	–	–	2659	–
仪器仪表制造业 Instruments and Meters Manufacturing	565	–	–	1379	56
其他制造业 Other Manufacturing	270647	–	–	80	–
废弃资源综合利用业 Multiple Utilization of Waste Resouces	16025	–	–	77	–
金属制品、机械和设备修理业 Metal Products, Machinery and Equipment Repair	–	–	–	–	–
电力、热力生产和供应业 Production and Supply of Electric Power and Hot Water	6646143	–	–	1563	–
燃气生产和供应业 Production and Supply of Gas	–	–	–	281	–
水的生产和供应业 Production and Supply of Tap Water	–	–	–	346	–

continued

柴油(吨) Diesel oil(Ton)	燃料油(吨) Fuel Oil(Ton)	液化石油气(吨) Liquefied Petroleum Gas(Ton)	天然气(万立方米) Natural Gas (10000 cu. m)	其他石油制品(吨) Other Petroleum Products(Ton)	热力(百万千焦) Heat(Million kilo - joule)	电力(万千瓦时) Electricity (10000 kwh)
8953	8141	-	2065	22662	19898152	460719
1731	174	68	1701	-	690438	53828
1881	870	3	20	97	5299172	378430
2797	5684	3076	718	-	4763439	200757
79522	3878	262	6431	-	194569	232517
2202	2	742	4677	136	1470333	256522
1174	2787	81	2923	17	37052	73926
3423	2639	417	4127	6	311661	86829
8118	310	252	672	553	58992	105207
1155	-	97	344	7	181818	22946
4152	22	120	1888	529	218455	79431
376	-	369	145	-	-	6231
2535	13	5426	1415	2	226768	122200
3259	-	851	810	19	258498	104028
392	1	3	56	5	4952	17514
635	-	-	127	-	-	2932
318	-	-	-	-	57356	12255
-	-	-	-	-	-	16
1592	-	-	115297	2	407767	313504
290	-	-	33	-	-	603
186	-	8	2	-	-	64257

4－20 全市规模以上工业能源购进消费与库存(2015 年)

Purchasing,Consuming and Stocking of Energy in Industrial Enterprises Above Designated Size(2015)

能源名称		Item		购进量 Purchasing	消费量合计 Total Consumption	工业生产消费 Industry
原煤	(吨)	Raw Coal	(Ton)	13228086	13397555	13373868
洗精煤	(吨)	Washing Coal	(Ton)	605450	656718	656718
煤制品	(吨)	Coal Puoducts	(Ton)	719167	721009	720945
焦炭	(吨)	Coke	(Ton)	527048	1029058	1029046
天然气(气态)	(万立方米)	Natural Gas(Gas)	(10000 cu. m)	152284	152457	152093
液化天然气(液态)	(吨)	Liquefied Natural Gas(Liquid)	(Ton)	15905	15888	15853
汽油	(吨)	Gasoline	(Ton)	45851	45907	15769
煤油	(吨)	Kerosene	(Ton)	790	810	776
柴油	(吨)	Diesel Oil	(Ton)	147484	148219	127902
燃料油	(吨)	Fuel Oil	(Ton)	25880	26072	26017
液化石油气	(吨)	Liquefied Petroleum Gas	(Ton)	12162	12235	12030
润滑油	(吨)	Lubricating Oil	(Ton)	3681	2995	2841
溶剂油	(吨)	Solvent Oil	(Ton)	534	536	517
石油沥青	(吨)	Petroleum Asphalt	(Ton)	－	－	－
其他石油制品	(吨)	Other Petroleum Products	(Ton)	20139	24154	24154
热力	(百万千焦)	Heat	(Million kilo－joule)	72782505	89991751	89082788
电力	(万千瓦时)	Electricity	(10000 kwh)	3227751	3531255	3465540
煤矸石用于燃料	(吨)	Coal Gangue for Fuel	(Ton)	－	－	－
城市垃圾用于燃料	(吨)	Municipal Waste for Fuel	(Ton)	－	788502	788502
生物质废料用于燃料	(吨)	Biomass Waste for Fuel	(Ton)	154154	154379	154246
余热余压	(百万千焦)	Residual Heat and Pressure	(Million kilo－joule)	32525	10246801	10246801
其它工业废料用于燃料	(吨)	Other Industrial Waste for Fuel	(Ton)	71255	99228	99228
其它燃料	(吨标准煤)	Other Fuel	(Tons of SCE)	31179	46557	46555

4-21 电力消费量(2015年)

Electricity Consumption(2015)

单位:万千瓦时 (10000 kwh)

项 目	Item	2015	2014	增长% Growth %
总 计	**Total**	**6463760**	**6401917**	**0.97**
#线路损失电量	#Losses in Transmission	190625	189814	0.43
农林牧渔业	Farming, Forestry, Animal Husbandry and Fishery Conservancy	47248	49494	-4.54
工业	Industry	4070223	4200699	-3.11
#轻工业	Light Industry	1990274	2002917	-0.63
重工业	Heavy Industry	2079949	2197782	-5.36
#采矿业	#Mining and Quarrying	31828	38397	-17.11
制造业	Manufacturing Industry	3664692	3799942	-3.56
电力、燃气及水的生产和供应业	Produotion and supply of electricity, gas & water	373703	362360	3.13
建筑业	Construction	139136	130288	6.79
交通运输、仓储及邮政业	Transportation, Storage, Post & Telecommunications	117160	102555	14.24
信息传输、计算机服务和软件业	Information Transmission, Computer Services and Software	146489	124009	18.13
商业、住宿和餐饮业	Commerce, Catering and lodging	355504	330497	7.57
金融、房地产、商务及居民服务业	Finance, Real Estate Commerce and Service for the Residents	314382	272100	15.54
公共管理和社会组织	Public Management and Social Organizations	371009	353669	4.90
城乡居民生活用电	Residential Consumption	902609	838607	7.63
#城市	Cities	568580	516325	10.12
乡村	#Rural Areas	334030	322281	3.65

4－22 水资源量和总用水量(2001－2015年)

Total Water Resources and Water Consumption(2001－2015)

单位:亿立方米 (100 million Cubic Meters)

		全市 Whole City	市区 Urban District	富阳区 Fuyang	桐庐县 Tonglu	淳安县 Chan'an	建德市 Jiangde	临安市 Lin'an
2001年	水资源量 Water Resources	156.37	18.87	14.23	14.28	41.14	18.54	26.76
	用水量 Water Consumption	40.29	28.05	4.17	2.01	1.03	2.11	2.92
2002年	水资源量 Water Resources	213.00	30.21	23.54	24.30	65.46	31.59	37.90
	用水量 Water Consumption	39.92	27.51	4.35	2.01	1.05	2.18	2.82
2003年	水资源量 Water Resources	102.65	9.31	8.13	10.32	41.43	15.57	17.90
	用水量 Water Consumption	44.72	29.13	7.12	1.98	1.38	2.30	2.81
2004年	水资源量 Water Resources	85.28	12.04	9.15	10.35	27.82	11.34	14.58
	用水量 Water Consumption	48.90	32.89	7.17	2.21	1.09	2.35	3.19
2005年	水资源量 Water Resources	90.65	14.32	10.31	9.46	26.66	10.36	19.54
	用水量 Water Consumption	49.58	32.95	7.16	2.25	1.24	2.38	3.61
2006年	水资源量 Water Resources	109.80	15.14	10.36	11.70	38.42	13.41	20.75
	用水量 Water Consumption	48.73	31.39	7.13	2.39	1.42	2.68	3.72
2007年	水资源量 Water Resources	104.13	20.28	11.76	10.12	29.88	11.72	20.36
	用水量 Water Consumption	49.56	32.57	6.45	2.53	1.53	3.09	3.39
2008年	水资源量 Water Resources	154.38	24.58	14.20	14.95	49.22	18.52	32.92
	用水量 Water Consumption	56.70	39.57	6.49	2.90	1.32	2.69	3.70
2009年	水资源量 Water Resources	141.50	23.38	16.33	16.67	37.46	15.63	32.03
	用水量 Water Consumption	54.28	39.24	5.18	2.52	1.46	2.81	3.07
2010年	水资源量 Water Resources	190.40	29.58	17.92	19.03	63.61	30.36	29.91
	用水量 Water Consumption	54.95	39.00	4.80	2.79	1.61	2.88	3.87
2011年	水资源量 Water Resources	136.70	20.21	13.43	15.81	41.00	19.11	27.13
	用水量 Water Consumption	57.71	40.40	5.83	2.98	1.37	2.92	4.21
2012年	水资源量 Water Resources	221.26	36.20	23.57	24.89	66.73	31.08	38.83
	用水量 Water Consumption	56.45	39.69	5.75	2.67	1.40	2.84	4.10
2013年	水资源量 Water Resources	141.15	28.82	15.33	15.63	35.29	19.21	26.87
	用水量 Water Consumption	57.77	41.07	6.22	2.53	1.42	2.74	3.79
2014年	水资源量 Water Resources	163.00	34.87	14.39	18.37	58.11	24.30	27.36
	用水量 Water Consumption	37.14	27.04	4.27	2.57	1.40	2.76	3.37
2015年	水资源量 Water Resources	239.06	61.09	23.93	26.68	73.79	33.17	44.33
	用水量 Water Consumption	34.79	25.29	3.98	2.44	1.32	2.51	3.23

注:2002年起市区数据含萧山、余杭区,2014年起含富阳区。

a) The date of Urban district in this table include Xiaoshan District and Yuhang District since 2002, and include Fuyang District since 2014.

主要统计指标解释

工业总产值 是以货币表现的工业企业在报告期内生产的已出售或可供出售工业产品总量，它反映一定时间内工业生产的总规模和总水平，它包括：在本企业内不再进行加工，经检验、包装入库（规定不需包装的产品除外）的成品价值，对外加工费收入，自制半成品，在产品期末初差额价值。工业总产值采用“工厂法”计算，即以工业企业作为一个整体，按企业工业生产活动的最终成果来计算，企业内部不允许重复计算，不能把企业内部各个车间（分厂）生产的成果相加。

工业销售产值 是以货币表现的工业企业在一定时期内销售的本企业生产的工业产品总量。包括已销售的成品、半成品价值，对外提供的工业性作业和对本单位基本建设部门、生活福利部门等提供的产品和工业性作业及自制设备的价值。已销售的成品、半成品不论是本期生产的、还是上期生产的，只要是本期销售出去的均包括在内。对外提供的工业性作业是指企业按合同对外提供的工业性劳务。企业为本单位基本建设部门、生活福利部门等提供的产品和工业性作业及自制设备也应视同销售，这部分也作为销售统计。工业销售产值的计算范围、计算价格和计算方法与工业总产值一致，但两者计算的基础不同；工业销售产值计算的基础是产品销售总量，工业总产值计算的基础是工业产品生产总量。

工业增加值 是指工业行业在报告期内以货币表现的工业生产活动的最终成果。

固定资产原价 固定资产原值指企业在建造、购置、安装、改建、扩建、技术改造某项固定资产时所支出的全部货币总额。它一般包括买价、包装费、运杂费和安装费等。

固定资产净值 是指固定资产原价减去历年已提折旧额后的净额。

利税总额 指企业利润总额、产品销售税金及附加和应交增值税之和。

主营业务收入 指企业销售产品的销售收入和提供劳务等主要经营业务取得的收入总额。

主营业务成本 指企业销售产品和提供劳务等主要经营业务的实际成本。

主营业务税金及附加 指企业销售产品和提供工业性劳务等主要经营业务应负担的城市维护建设税、消费税、资源税和教育费附加。

主营业务利润 指企业销售产品和提供工业性劳务等主要经营业务收入和除其成本、费用、税金后的利润。

利润总额 指企业实现的利润。

应交增值税 指企业在报告期内应交纳的增值税额。

总资产 指企业拥有或控制的全部资产。包括流动资产、长期投资、固定资产、无形及递延资产、其他长期资产、递延税项等，即为企业资产负债表的资产总计项。

（1）流动资产指企业可以在一年内或者超过一年的一个生产周期内变现或耗用的资产合计。包括现金及各种存款、短期投资、应收及预付款项、存货等。

（2）固定资产指企业固定资产净值、固定资产清理、在建工程、待处理固定资产损失所占用的资金合计。

（3）无形资产指企业长期使用而没有实物形态的资产。包括专利权、非专利技术、商标权、著作权、土地使用权、商誉等。

总负债 指企业承担并需要偿还的全部债务。包括流动负债和长期负债、递延税项等，即为企业资产负债表的负债合计项。

（1）流动负债指企业在一年内或者超过一年的一个营业周期内需要偿还的债务合计，其中包括短期借款、应付及预收款项、应付工资、应交税金和应交利润等。

（2）长期负债指企业在一年以上或者超过一年的一个生产周期以上需要偿还的债务合计，其中包括长期借款、应付债务、长期应付款项等。

所有者权益 指企业投资人对企业净资产的所有权。企业净资产等于企业全部资产减去全部负债后的余额。其中包括投资者对企业的最初投入，以及资本公积金、盈余公积金和未分配利润，对股份制企业即为股东权益。

Explanatory Notes on Main Statistical Indicators

Gross Industrial Output Value is the total volume of industrial products sold or available for sale in value terms which reflects the total achievements and overall scale of industrial production during a given period. It includes the value of the finished products, which are not to be further processed in the enterprises and have been inspected, packed and put in storage, the value of industrial services rendered to other units, and the changes in the value of the semi – finished products and products in process between the beginning and closing of the period. The gross industrial output value is calculated with "factory method". No double calculations are to be made within the same enterprise. However, double counting does occur among different enterprises.

Industrial Sales Output Value is the total volume of industrial products sold in value term of an industrial enterprise during a given period. It includes the value of finished products, semi – finished products, industrial operations rendered to other units, products industrial operations & self – made equipment provided to the basic construction department, welfare department, etc. of the enterprise. For finished products & semi – finished products, whether produced in this calculation period or the previous one, if they are sold in this calculation period, they should be included. Industrial operations are industrial services rendered to other units according to contracts. Products, industrial operations & self – made equipment provided to basic construction department, welfare department, etc. of the enterprise should be regarded as act of sale, and included in sales statistics.

The scope , price and method of calculation of industrial sales output value are the same as those for gross industrial output value. But the calculation bases are different: the base for sales output value is the total volume of products sold; the base for gross industrial output value is total volume of production of industrial products.

Value – added of Industry refers to the final results of industrial production of the industrial trade in money terms during the reference period.

Original Value of Fixed Assets refers to the original value of all assets owned by industrial enterprises, calculated at the cost paid at the time of purchase, installation, reconstruction, expansion, and technical innovation and transformation of the said assets, which includes expenses on purchase, package, transportation, and installation, etc.

Net Value of Fixed Assets is obtained by deducting depreciation over years from the original value of fixed assets.

Total Pre – tax Profits refers to the sum of sales tax and extra charges adding total profits.

Sales Revenue of Industrial Products refers to the revenue from the sales of products by industrial enterprises and the revenue from services provided and etc.

Sales Cost of Industrial Products refers to the actual cost of products of industrial enterprises and industrial services provided, etc.

Tax and Extra Charges on Sales of Products refer to the tax on city maintenance and construction, consumption tax, resources tax and extra charges for education, which should be borne by the enterprises in selling products and providing industrial services.

Sales Profit of Products refers to the profit gained by the enterprises by deducting cost, charges and taxes from the business income of the enterprises obtained in selling products and providing industrial services.

Total Profits refer to the profits gained by the enterprises.

Value – added Tax Payable refers to the amount of the value added tax which should be paid by the enterprises in the reporting period.

Total Assets refer to all assets which are owned or controlled by enterprises, including circulating assets, long term investment, fixed assets, intangible assets and deferred assets, other long term assets, and deferred taxes, etc. The summation of above items is equal to total assets shown in the balance sheets of the enterprises.

(1) Circulating assets (working capital) refer to assets which can be cashed in or spent or consumed in an operating cycle of one year or over one year, including cash, all kinds of deposits, short term investment, receivables, advance payment, stock, etc.

(2) Fixed assets refer to the net value of fixed assets, clearance of fixed assets, project under construction, fixed assets losses in suspense. These are corporations' fund holdings.

(3) Intangible assets refer to assets without material form used by enterprises over a lone time, such as patents, non – patent technologies, trade marks, copyright, land use right, business reputation, etc.

Total Liabilities refer to the debts that enterprises are responsible for repayment, including liquid liabilities, long – term liabilities and deferred taxes, etc. Total liabilities correspond to the summation item of liabilities shown in the balance sheets of the enterprises.

(1) Liquid liabilities (also called quick liabilities or immediate liabilities) refer to enterprises' total debt payable within an operating cycle of one year or over one year, including short term loans, payables and advance payments, wages payable, taxes payable and profit payable, etc.

(2) Long term liabilities refers to total debt payable within an operating cycle of one year or over one year, including long – term loans, payable liabilities, long – term payables, etc.

Creditors' Equity refers to investors' ownership of net assets of the enterprise. It is equal to the total assets of the enterprise minus its total liabilities, including the primary input from investors, capital accumulation fund, surplus accumulation fund and undistributed profit. It is the shareholder's equity in share – holding companies.

五、建筑业

CONSTRUCTION

5 建筑业 Construction

主要统计指标
Major Statistical Indicators

建筑业总产值	Gross Output Value of Construction	4097.57	亿元	(100 million yuan)
为上年	As Compared with the Preceding Year	103.2	%	(%)
房屋建筑施工面积	Floor Space of Buildings Under Construction	28123	万平方米	(10, 000 sq.m)
为上年	As Compared with the Preceding Year	95.1	%	(%)
房屋建筑竣工面积	Floor Space of Buildings Completed	10137	万平方米	(10, 000 sq.m)
为上年	As Compared with the Preceding Year	106.5	%	(%)

5－01 建筑业总产值(2015 年)
Gross Output Value of Construction(2015)

单位:万元 (10000 yuan)

地 区	Region	建筑企业单位数(个) Number of Construction Enterprises (unit)	建筑业总产值 Gross Output Value of Construction	建筑工程产值 Output Value of Construction Projects	安装工程产值 Output value of Installation Projects	其他产值 Other Output Values
全 市	**Total**	**1480**	**40975734**	**36080625**	**3942809**	**951857**
市 区	Urban District	1281	38962343	34301644	3780889	879367
#上城区	Shangcheng	89	2714382	1732071	949279	32590
下城区	Xiacheng	72	1139225	918025	209523	11677
江干区	Jianggan	109	2504768	2154005	320974	29790
拱墅区	Gongshu	158	3354852	2695302	611260	48290
西湖区	Xihu	161	9001811	8256677	542142	202992
高新(滨江)区	Hi－Tech (Binjiang)	56	4086598	3945593	67248	73757
萧山区	Xiaoshan	305	11943107	10772570	780665	389873
余杭区	Yuhang	177	2114385	1938331	169109	6945
富阳区	Fuyang	130	1475705	1290060	118987	66658
桐庐县	Tonglu	51	576495	523856	28211	24427
淳安县	Chun′an	54	316355	271324	32419	12612
建德市	Jiande	38	293250	246553	35078	11619
临安市	Lin′an	56	827291	737247	66212	23832

5-02 建筑总专包

Financial Indicators on Construction Enterprises of

单位:万元

指标名称	Item	二、年末资产 Asset and Liabilities 流动资产合计 Circulating Funds	固定资产合计 Fixed Assets	资产合计 Total Assets
总 计	**Total**	**23867659**	**2829483**	**29818931**
#特、一、二级企业	of Which: Special Grade, First Grade, Second Grade	21515868	2425929	26787660
#国有及国有控股企业	of Which: State - owned and State Holding Enterprises	5214099	428829	6377027
一、按登记注册类型分组	**Grouped by Registration Status**			
内资企业	Domestic Funded	23638599	2796299	29542456
国有企业	State - owned	256376	40506	316099
集体企业	Collective - owned	32095	4236	37450
股份合作企业	Share - holding Cooperative Enterprises	-	-	-
联营企业	Joint Venture	-	-	-
有限责任公司	Limited Liability Corporations	12951736	1467294	15980036
股份有限公司	Share - holding Corporations Ltd.	1742008	228365	2303187
私营企业	Private Enterprises	8656384	1055899	10905685
其他企业	Other Enterprises	-	-	-
港、澳、台商投资企业	Funded from Hong Kong, Macao and Taiwan	197711	30521	240928
外商投资企业	Foreign Funded	31349	2663	35546
二、按国民经济行业分组	**Grouped by Sector**			
房屋建筑业	Housing Construction	13633991	1505784	17043291
土木工程建筑业	Civil Engineering Construction	7553064	1004648	9482305
建筑安装业	Installation of Lines, Pipelines and Equipment	1124039	148303	1448539
建筑装饰和其他建筑业	Fitting、Decoration of Building and Others Construction	1556566	170749	1844796

企业财务指标(2015年)

General Contractors and Specialist Contractors(2015)

(10000 yuan)

负债 at Year - end				
流动负债合计 Liquid Liabilities	负债合计 Total Liabilities	所有者权益合计 Owners´Equity	#实收资本 of Which: Paid - in Capitals	#国家资本 of Which: State Capital
17964478	**19365824**	**10453107**	**5799067**	**452274**
16557247	17880044	8907616	4538340	440613
4628979	5177500	1199527	704721	440103
17765367	19144851	10397605	5769929	452274
202224	219927	96172	57239	55736
12680	26736	10714	5814	2550
-	-	-	-	-
-	-	-	-	-
10335278	11386108	4593928	2075354	383199
1351604	1419819	883367	341956	10789
5863581	6092261	4813424	3289566	-
-	-	-	-	-
175304	197208	43720	21613	-
23807	23764	11782	7526	-
10376130	11345298	5697993	2858015	113786
5574136	5929084	3553222	2216658	315624
858755	905755	542784	289723	3180
1155458	1185687	659109	434671	19684

指标名称	Item	三、损益 Expenditure, Income	
		工程结算收入 Revenue of Project Settlement Accounts	工程结算成本 Costs of Project Settlement Accounts
总　计	**Total**	**35367024**	**32085224**
#特、一、二级企业	of Which: Special Grade, First Grade, Second Grade	32606839	29712957
#国有及国有控股企业	of Which: State - owned and State Holding Enterprises	7329859	6747668
一、按登记注册类型分组	**Grouped by Registration Status**		
内资企业	Domestic Funded	35184831	31923422
国有企业	State - owned	384950	350585
集体企业	Collective - owned	34283	24772
股份合作企业	Share - holding Cooperative Enterprises	-	-
联营企业	Joint Venture	-	-
有限责任公司	Limited Liability Corporations	19320932	17618272
股份有限公司	Share - holding Corporations Ltd.	2950937	2653090
私营企业	Private Enterprises	12493729	11276702
其他企业	Other Enterprises	-	-
港、澳、台商投资企业	Funded from Hong Kong, Macao and Taiwan	135931	119381
外商投资企业	Foreign Funded	46262	42423
二、按国民经济行业分组	**Grouped by Sector**		
房屋建筑业	Housing Construction	21571822	19814106
土木工程建筑业	Civil Engineering Construction	9717586	8646706
建筑安装业	Installation of Lines, Pipelines and Equipment	1713732	1509343
建筑装饰和其他建筑业	Fitting、Decoration of Building and Others Construction	2363884	2115071

continued (10000 yuan)

及分配 and Distribution					
工程结算税金及附加 Taxes and Extra Charges Project Settlement Accounts	销售费用 Sales Expenses	管理费用 Management Expenditure	财务费用 Financial Expenditure	利润总额 Total Profits	应交所得税 Income Taxes Payable
1009535	**100115**	**965161**	**301313**	**895484**	**212567**
924460	79059	791923	280853	798598	186733
175346	8598	223077	32082	168868	42580
1006951	98360	956510	294722	894322	212086
7774	463	17670	581	9990	2892
721	467	2092	-559	1194	307
-	-	-	-	-	-
-	-	-	-	-	-
536564	37420	461708	139824	503012	115356
76457	13396	84049	34134	91902	15427
385437	46615	390990	120742	288224	78104
-	-	-	-	-	-
1288	1664	6926	6306	727	275
1296	91	1726	285	435	207
610860	49331	388051	200232	468194	103547
282610	31312	389438	69603	327932	82639
46887	8762	93914	10003	45409	11626
69177	10710	93758	21474	53949	14755

5－03　建筑业企业生产情况（2010－2015 年）

Statistics on Production of Construction Enterprises（2010－2015）

指标名称	Item	2010	2011	2012	2013	2014	2015
一、建筑业合同情况	**Contract of Construction**						
签订的合同额（万元）	Total Value of Contracts（10000 yuan）	46427916	55290611	59279520	66234009	69933228	70729328
上年结转合同额（万元）	Value from Contracts Signed in 2014（10000 yuan）	17396267	22189586	25205183	26548398	28874679	31220942
本年新签合同额（万元）	Value from New Contracts Signed in 2015（10000 yuan）	29031649	33101025	34074337	39685611	41058549	39509226
二、承包工程完成情况	**Completion of Contracted Projects**						
直接从建设单位承揽工程完成的产值（万元）	Complete Output Value of Projects Contacted Directly from Investors（10000 yuan）	26259274	29993008	32845834	37176277	39364500	40695653
自行完成施工产值（万元）	Own－completed Output Value（10000 yuan）	25689110	29339695	31586124	35973925	38129851	39318980
分包出去工程的产值（万元）	Output Value of Out－sourced Projects（10000 yuan）	570163	653313	1259710	1202352	1234649	1377814
从建设单位以外承揽工程完成的产值（万元）	Completed Output Value of Projects Contacted from Non－investors（10000 yuan）	949202	985280	1489749	1580779	1584025	1657315
建筑业总产值（万元）	Gross Output Value（10000 yuan）	26638312	30324975	33075873	37554704	39713876	40975734
#装饰装修产值（万元）	of Which：Output Value of Fitting and Decoration of Buildings（10000 yuan）	2177414	2556382	2821922	3216682	3469325	3486860
#在外省完成的产值（万元）	of Which：Completed Output Value outside of Zhejiang Province（10000 yuan）	8882553	10267000	11179195	12048961	12425411	12018157
按构成分	by Structure						
建筑工程产值（万元）	Output Value of Construction Projects（10000 yuan）	23307310	26308977	28976550	33244948	34894095	36080625
安装工程产值（万元）	Output value of Installation Projects（10000 yuan）	2557314	2801907	3092140	3270944	3735431	3942809
其他产值（万元）	Other Output Values（10000 yuan）	773688	1214091	1007183	1038812	1084350	951857
竣工产值（万元）	Output Value of Buildings Completed（10000 yuan）	16373795	16286512	17563992	21021307	21665909	25994238
房屋建筑施工面积（万平方米）	Floor Space of Buildings Under Construction（10000 sq. m）	22650	26104	26363	29538	29581	28124
#本年新开工面积（万平方米）	of Which：Beginning Projects in this Year（10000 sq. m）	11064	12024	10541	11964	11156	9596
#实行投标承包面积（万平方米）	of Which：Floor Space of Biding System（10000 sq. m）	19792	23649	22684	24705	26927	23653
#本年新开工（万平方米）	of Which：Beginning Projects in this Year（10000 sq. m）	9706	11256	9547	10686	10431	-
房屋建筑竣工面积（万平方米）	Floor space of Buildings Completed（10000 sq. m）	8220	8556	8388	9613	9514	10137
三、年末自有施工机械设备	**Machinery and Equipment Owned（year－end）**						
年末自有施工机械设备净值（万元）	Net Value of Machinery and Equipment Owned（10000 yuan）	798573	825813	799293	832466	796789	837565
年末自有施工机械设备总台数（台）	Number of Machinery and Equipment Owned（set）	205574	204139	178639	185792	175738	173850
年末自有施工机械设备总功率（千瓦）	Total Power of Machinery and Equipment Owned（1000 kw）	3261216	3611172	3355223	3460437	4076303	3279495
四、就业人员情况	**Number of Employed Persons**						
计算劳动生产率的平均人数（人）	Average Employed Persons Overall Labor Productivity（person）	1149924		1203387	1259282	1293740	1310577
年末就业人员数（人）	Employed Persons（year－end）（person）	1117287		1002886	1274082	-	1268020

5－04 全市具有资质等级建筑业企业主要生产经营指标(2008－2015年)

Major Economic Indicators of Construction Enterprises Having Class(2008－2015)

单位:万元 (10000 yuan)

指标名称 Item	2008	2009	2010	2011	2012	2013	2014	2015
企业个数(个) Nomber of Enterprises (unit)	1174	1230	1331	1373	1430	1515	1476	1480
亏损企业个数(个) Loss Making Enterprises (unit)	135	151	124	200	216	252	224	236
建筑业总产值 Gross Output Value of Construction	18004524	21101673	26638312	30324975	33073420	37554704	39713876	40975734
竣工产值 Output Value of Buildings Completed	10976179	12919145	16373795	16286512	17557004	21021307	21665909	25994238
房屋建筑施工面积(万平方米) Floor Space of Buildings Under Construction (10,000 sq. m)	16059	19434	22650	26104	26420	29538	29581	28124
房屋建筑竣工面积(万平方米) Floor Space of Buildings Completed (10,000 sq. m)	5800	6610	8220	8556	8404	9613	9514	10137
固定资产原价 Orginal Value of Fixed Assets	1600152	1832287	2511522	2846687	2967321	3293095	3393624	3488088
实收资本合计 Total Capital Hold	2165141	2674474	3472567	3888171	4394124	5019389	5493120	5799067
流动资产合计 Circulating Funds	8419776	10148822	13758468	16267419	17809148	19959672	22168981	23867659
其中:存货 Stock	2198429	2351537	3155492	3758947	4034742	4934518	5900549	6360774
在建工程 Projects wnder Construction	121280	146641	222328	198636	235510	320533	313490	211195
固定资产合计 Fixed Assets	1265516	1392917	1896442	2199708	2233648	2371260	2826312	2829483
年末负债合计 Total Liabilities at Year－end	7183968	8420381	11760309	13868500	14970479	17591701	18186469	19365824
流动负债合计 Circulating Funds	6968771	8161089	11294749	13311213	17809148	16473990	16894050	17964478
所有者权益合计 Crediors´Equity	3496229	4427256	5689839	6634943	7381024	8559878	9656533	10453107
营业收入 Revenue of Business	16091050	19336784	24281416	27251719	29552959	33709184	34704862	35568492
营业成本 Operating Costs	14479116	17454560	21768815	24719576	27047034	30614028	31501139	32365477
营业税金及附加 Main Sales Tax and Extra Charges	552973	646066	757611	842437	880051	996370	1029405	1020437
管理费用 Management Expenditure	418438	475413	651233	720238	853136	905194	918904	965161
财务费用 Financial Expenditure	106926	110874	178931	256538	295135	318198	330680	301313
营业利润 Management Profits	361076	478513	683851	723488	759792	850362	888932	883320
利润总额 Total Profits	395459	509497	676599	731358	791175	883887	913117	895484

主要统计指标解释

建筑业总产值　建筑业总产值是以货币表现的建筑业企业在一定时期内生产的建筑业产品和服务的总和。建筑业总产值包括建筑工程产值、安装工程产值和其他产值三部分内容。

房屋建筑施工面积　指报告期内施过工的全部房屋建筑面积,它包括本期新开工的面积、上期跨入本期继续施工的房屋面积、上期停缓建在本期恢复施工的房屋面积、本期竣工的房屋面积以及本期施工后又停缓建的房屋面积。

房屋建筑竣工面积　指在报告期内房屋建筑按照设计要求已全部完工,达到了使用条件,经检查验收鉴定合格的房屋建筑面积。

工程结算收入(主营业务收入)　指本企业承包工程实现的工程价款结算收入以及向发包单位收取的除工程价款以外按规定列作营业收入的各种款项,如临时设施费、劳动保险费、施工机构调迁费等以及向发包单位收取的各种索赔款。

工程结算成本(主营业务成本)　指在报告期内与发包单位办理工程价款结算的已完工程实际成本。

Explanatory Notes on Main Statistical Indicators

Gross Output Value of Construction refers to total of construction products and services, expressed in money terms, produced or rendered by construction and installation enterprises during a given period of time. It includes: output value of construction projects, output value of installation projects and other output values.

Floor Space of Buildings Under Construction refers to floor space of buildings under construction during the reference period, including the floor space of buildings for which construction has newly started; buildings for which construction has started earlier and is continuing during the reference period; and buildings for which construction has been suspended earlier but has restarted during the reference period; buildings completed during the reference period; and buildings under construction but construction has subsequently been during the reference period.

Floor Space of Buildings Completed refers to the floor space of buildings that are completed in the reference period in accordance with the requirements of the design, up to the standard for being put into use, and having been checked and accepted by departments concerned as qualified ones.

Income from Settlement of Projects refers to the income received by the construction enterprise from the contracted project through settlement procedures, and other charges to the contractor as operational costs in addition to the value of the project, such as temporary facility fee, labor insurance premium, moving cost of construction equipment, as well as various types of claims to the contractor.

Project Settlement Costs refers to the contracting process works price of the actual settlement costs of projects have been completed during the reporting period.

六、交通运输邮电

TRANSPORTATION, POST AND TELECOMMUNICATIONS

6 交通运输、邮电
Transportation, Post and Telecommunications

主要统计指标
Major Statistical Indicators

客运量	Passenger Traffic	23942	万人次	(10, 000 person-times)
为上年	As Compared with the Preceding Year	99.5	%	(%)
货运量	Freight Traffic	29384	万吨	(10, 000 tons)
为上年	As Compared with the Preceding Year	100.2	%	(%)
邮电业务收入	Business Income of Post & Telecommunication Service	333.35	亿元	(100 million yuan)
为上年	As Compared with the Preceding Year	115.8	%	(%)
年末固定电话用户数	Number of Local Telephone Subscribers(year-end)	293.44	万户	(10, 000 subscribers)
为上年	As Compared with the Preceding Year	94.3	%	(%)
年末移动电话用户数	Number of Mobile Telephone Subscribers(year-end)	1726.76	万户	(10, 000 subscribers)
为上年	As Compared with the Preceding Year	110.6	%	(%)
年末宽带业务户数	Broadband Subscribers of Internet(year-end)	294.96	万户	(10, 000 subscribers)
为上年	As Compared with the Preceding Year	105.8	%	(%)

6-01 全市客运量(1978-2015年)
Total Passenger Traffic (1978-2015)

单位:万人次 (10,000 person-times)

年 份 Year	合 计 Total	铁 路 Railways	公 路 Highways	水 路 Waterways	民 航 Civil Aviation
1978	2878	485	-	-	3
1979	3122	560	1829	729	4
1980	3905	672	2358	870	5
1981	4484	769	2857	850	8
1982	5263	813	3377	1064	9
1983	5451	878	3530	1035	8
1984	6056	983	3912	1151	10
1985	6724	1004	4595	1111	14
1986	6765	1034	4768	941	22
1987	6905	1127	4852	896	30
1988	6593	1237	4445	877	34
1989	7493	1182	5488	801	22
1990	8119	1056	6350	691	22
1991	10701	1062	8876	710	53
1992	13358	1083	11538	670	67
1993	13070	1139	11403	454	74
1994	13373	1230	11669	390	84
1995	16620	1242	14921	339	118
1996	16714	1112	15184	273	145
1997	17034	1040	15623	260	111
1998	17395	1120	15925	235	115
1999	17882	1168	16369	235	110
2000	18607	1202	17102	179	124
2001	20342	1342	18707	148	145
2002	21089	1574	19213	108	194
2003	21348	1534	19510	89	215
2004	22833	1908	20372	237	316
2005	24124	2011	21431	304	378
2006	25810	2124	22961	267	458
2007	28026	2255	24836	306	629
2008	29084	2498	25630	277	679
2009	30116	2494	26454	372	796
2010	33772	2741	29671	456	904
2011	34778	2962	30305	595	916
2012	35819	3112	31126	592	989
2013	36409	3717	30994	547	1151
2014	24070	4689	17431	616	1334
2015	23942	5282	16591	597	1472

注:1990年以前为交通系统数,1990年起为全社会数(后同)。2014年起运输量统计方法调整。

a) The data in the table only included transportation department before 1990, while extended to the whole society after 1990 (the same below). The statistical method has been adjusted since 2014.

6－02　全市货运量(1978－2015年)
Total Freight Traffic (1978－2015)

单位:万吨　　(10000 tons)

年份 Year	合计 Total	铁路 Railways	公路 Highways	水路 Waterways	民航 Civil Aviation
1978	1706	418	633	655	
1979	1983	440	771	772	
1980	2070	444	762	864	
1981	1972	449	886	637	
1982	2261	485	795	981	
1983	2299	488	838	973	
1984	2385	510	888	987	
1985	2488	524	890	1074	
1986	2558	551	874	1133	
1987	2515	574	899	1041	1
1988	2416	555	823	1037	1
1989	7377	539	5095	1743	
1990	6522	449	4479	1594	
1991	7017	451	4891	1675	
1992	8434	534	6063	1836	1
1993	9082	580	6353	2148	1
1994	8962	491	6563	1907	1
1995	10347	482	7021	2842	2
1996	10962	445	7735	2780	2
1997	11015	406	7932	2676	1
1998	11329	418	8196	2713	2
1999	11684	403	8037	3241	3
2000	11459	417	7865	3173	4
2001	12443	452	8588	3398	5
2002	14347	446	10391	3504	6
2003	16815	438	12118	4253	6
2004	18895	480	13117	5289	9
2005	19909	525	13539	5833	12
2006	20924	569	14588	5754	13
2007	22569	573	16484	5500	12
2008	22550	483	16822	5232	13
2009	22372	427	16536	5396	13
2010	25915	379	19148	6371	17
2011	28831	331	21755	6727	18
2012	30089	322	23243	6503	20
2013	30734	284	23884	6545	22
2014	29335	312	23202	5797	24
2015	29384	307	23800	5251	25

6－03 客货运输量(2010－2015 年)
Total Passenger and Freight Traffic(2010－2015)

项 目 Item	2010	2011	2012	2013	2014	2015
一、客运量合计(万人次) Passenger Traffic(10000 person－times)	**33772**	**34778**	**35819**	**36409**	**24070**	**23942**
铁路客运量 Passenger Railways	2741	2962	3112	3717	4689	5282
民航客运量 Passenger Civil Aviation	904	916	989	1151	1334	1472
公路客运量 Passenger Highways	29671	30305	31126	30994	17431	16591
水路客运量 Passenger Waterways	456	595	592	547	616	597
二、旅客周转量合计(万人公里) Total Passenger－kilometers(10000 passenger－km)	**1422280**	**1529548**	**1598527**	**1573289**	**1151642**	**1085769**
公路旅客周转量 Passenger－kilometers Highways	1416057	1522055	1590435	1566046	1143750	1078054
水路旅客周转量 Passenger－kilometers Waterways	6223	7492.57	8092	7243	7892	7715
三、货运量合计(万吨) Total Freight Traffic(10000 tons)	**25915**	**28831**	**30089**	**30734**	**29335**	**29384**
铁路货运量 Freight Railways	379	331	322	284	312	307
民航货运量 Freight Civil Aviation	17	18	20	22	24	25
公路货运量 Freight Highways	19148	21755	23243	23884	23202	23800
水路货运量 Freight Waterways	6371	6727	6503	6545	5797	5251
四、货运周转量合计(万吨公里) Total Freight Ton－kilometers(10000 ton－km)	**3733634**	**4178684**	**4563560**	**4724588**	**4550550**	**4629814**
公路货物周转量 Freight Ton－kilometers Highways	2153961	2451057	2643428	2719204	2760873	3003728
水路货物周转量 Freight Ton－kilometers Waterways	1579673	1727627	1920132	2005384	1789677	1626086

6-04 分地区交通
Traffic and Transport

项 目		Item		全市 Whole City	市区 Urban District
铁路旅客运量	(万人)	Passenger Railways	(10,000 Persons)	5282	5282
铁路货物运量	(万吨)	Freight Railways	(10,000 tons)	307	168
公路客运量	(万人)	Passenger Highways	(10,000 Persons)	16591	12605
公路货运量	(万吨)	Freight Highway	(10,000 tons)	23800	21726
民用航空客运量	(万人)	Passenger Civil Aviation	(10,000 Persons)	1472	1472
民用航空货运量	(万吨)	Freight Civil Aviation	(10,000 tons)	25	25
水路客运量	(万人)	Passenger Waterways	(10,000 Persons)	597	306
水路货运量	(万吨)	Freight Waterways	(10,000 tons)	5251	4826
年末民用汽车拥有量	(辆)	Possession of Civil Vehicles(year-end)	(Unit)	2244767	2021550
#私人汽车拥有量	(辆)	in which:Possession of Private Vehicles	(Unit)	1849148	1657796

运输情况(2015 年)
Situation by Region(2015)

萧山区 Xiaoshan	余杭区 Yuhang	富阳区 Fuyang	桐庐县 Tonglu	淳安县 Chun'an	建德市 Jiande	临安市 Lin'an
–	70	–	–	–	–	–
38	88	–	–	55	84	–
568	377	1640	1011	808	1228	939
5700	1291	704	824	159	596	495
1472	–	–	–	–	–	–
25	–	–	–	–	–	–
22	–	4	24	224	13	29
1649	1665	569	176	53	69	128
381781	291084	112916	58775	26166	44327	93949
321074	251110	97658	49201	22907	37311	81933

6－05 全市运输线路长度(2010－2015年)
Length of Transportation Routes(2010－2015)

单位:公里 (km)

项目	Item	2010	2011	2012	2013	2014	2015
公路通车里程 (公里)	Length of Highways (km)	15266	15415	15747	15900	16024	16210
高速公路 (公里)	Expressway (km)	502	503	550	550	582	615
一级公路 (公里)	First Class Highways (km)	692	747	768	791	803	836
二级公路 (公里)	Second Class Highways (km)	1524	1520	1542	1526	1570	1616
内河通航里程 (公里)	Length of Navigable Inland Waterways (km)	2006	2006	2006	2006	2006	2006
民用航空航线 (条)	Number of Civil Aviation Routes (line)	160	159	144	185	222	235
国内航线 (条)	Domestic Routes (line)	122	123	117	156	186	196
国际航线 (条)	International Routes (line)	30	29	20	22	28	32
地区航线 (条)	Regional Routes (line)	8	7	7	7	8	7

6－06 民用机动车辆年末拥有量(2010－2015年末)

Total Number of Motor Vehicles End of the Year(End of 2010－2015)

单位:辆 (unit)

项 目	Item	2010	2011	2012	2013	2014	2015
全市合计	**Total**	**1832496**	**2078150**	**2267027**	**2542976**	**2696340**	**2733537**
一、汽车	Vehicles	1243087	1495503	1761001	2045618	2184000	2244767
1. 载客汽车	Passenger Vehicles	1076983	1313307	1570099	1860794	1992112	2056143
其中:大型	Large	14427	15458	16118	17078	17485	18657
中型	Medium	19214	18620	18096	17849	14411	10797
小型	Small	1009298	1244142	1499444	1794017	1936836	2002730
微型	Mini	34044	35087	36441	31850	23380	23959
其中:轿车	Car	–	–	–	1678453	1799442	1773864
2. 载货汽车	Trucks	155546	171039	179399	173227	180475	177674
其中:重型	Heavy	22867	27989	31154	35917	39998	41999
中型	Medium	27672	27534	25242	17530	14444	8851
轻型	Light	103807	114592	122316	119205	125508	126321
微型	Mini	1200	924	687	575	525	503
3. 其他汽车	Vehicles	10558	11157	11503	11597	11413	10950
其中:三轮汽车	Vehicles	–	–	–	385	182	179
低速货车	Low Speed Trucks	–	–	–	384	416	549
二、摩托车	Motorcycles	584440	576907	500080	190884	505360	481230
1. 普通	Genera	520932	515411	470779	466625	481027	463722
2. 轻便	Light	63508	61496	29301	24259	24333	17508
三、挂车	Trailer	–	–	–	6433	6939	7464
四、其他类型	Other	–	–	–	41	41	76

6－07　邮政、电信主要指标（2010－2015年）

Main Indicators of Post and Telecommunications（2010－2015）

项　目　Item	2010	2011	2012	2013	2014	2015
邮政业务总收入（万元） Total Business Income of Postal Service（10,000 yuan）	20037	1573563	533059	702664	1176704	1596884
#快递业务收入（万元） Business Income of Express Mail Service（10,000 yuan）	–	–	427356	563459	1022279	1437542
电信业务收入（万元） Total Business Income of Telecommunications Services（10,000 yuan）	–	–	1597344	1752286	1700825	1736600
函件（万件） Number of Letters（10,000 pcs）	113	21144	21226	20133	17412	13256
包裹（万件） Number of Parcels（10,000 pcs）	311	84	129	133	113	81
快递（万份） Pieces of Express Mail Service（10,000 copies）	–	–	25536	46852	84563	125707
#国际及港澳台快递（万份） Pieces of Express to overseas and HongKong,macao,Taiwan（10,000 copies）	–	–	525	738	1731	2046
纪特邮票（万枚） Stamps for Collettion（10,000 pcs）	1563.79	2309.30	1744.06	1412.39	1150.66	1230.91
年末固定电话用户数（万户） Number of Local Telephone Subscribers(year－end)（10,000 subscribers）	1061.80	353.76	346.22	334.87	311.14	293.44
年末移动电话用户数（万户） Number of Subscribers of Mobile Telephone(year－end)（10,000 subscribers）	218.41	1218.11	1438.67	1546.83	1561.71	1726.76
年末宽带业务户数（万户） Number of Wide Band Subscribers（10,000 subscribers）	217.89	241.14	275.91	338.63	278.78	294.96

注：邮政业务总收入含规模以上快递企业。

a) The total business income of postal services included the express enterprises above designated sice.

主要统计指标解释

货(客)运量 指在一定时期内,各种运输工具实际运送的货物(旅客)数量。是反映运输业为国民经济和人民生活服务的数量指标,也是制定和检查运输生产计划、研究运输发展规模和速度的重要指标。货运按吨计算,客运按人计算。货物不论运输距离长短、货物类别,均按实际重量统计。旅客不论行程远近或票价多少,均按一人一次作为客运量统计;半价票、小孩票也按一人统计。

货物(旅客)周转量 指在一定时期内,由各种运输工具运送的货物(旅客)数量与其相应运输距离的乘积之总和。是反映运输业生产总成果的重要指标,也是编制和检查运输生产计划,计算运输效率、劳动生产率以及核算运输单位成本的主要基础资料。通常以吨公里和人公里为计算单位。计算货物周转量通常按发出站与到达站之间的最短距离,也就是计费距离计算。

移动电话用户 指在邮电部门登记,通过移动电话交换机进入移动电话网,占有移动电话号码的电话用户。用户数量以实际办理登记手续进入邮电部门移动电话网的户数进行计算,一部或一台移动电话统计为一户。

Explanatory Notes on Main Statistical Indicators

Freight(passenger) Traffic refers to the volume of freight (passenger) transported with various means. Freight transport is calculated in tons and passenger traffic is calculated in the number of persons. Despite the type of freight and traveling distance, the freight transport is calculated in the actual weight of the goods: and despite the traveling distance and ticket price, the passenger traffic is calculated by the principle that one person can be counted only once in one travel. The passenger who travel with a half – price ticket or a child ticket is also calculated as one person. The freight (passenger) traffic provides a quantitative measure to show how the transport industry serves the national economy and people, and is also an important indicator for plan the transport industry and for studying the development scale and speed of the transport industry.

Freight Ton – kilometers(Passenger – kilometers) refers to the sum of the products of the volume of transported cargo (passengers) multiplying by the transport distance, usually using ton – kilometer and passenger – kilometer as units for measurement . Normally, the shortest distance between the departure station and the terminal station (i. e. , the payable distance) is the basis to calculate the freight ton – kilometers. This is an important indicator to show the total results of the transport industry, to prepare and examine the transport plan and to measure the efficiency, the labour productivity and the unit cost of transport.

Mobile Telephone Subscribers refer to the persons who own mobile telephone number connected with the mobile telephone communication network and registered by post and telecommunications organization. The number of subscribers is calculated only when the subscribers who have gone through all the register formalities and entered into the mobile telephone network. One mobile telephone is treated as a subscriber.

七、固定资产投资

INVESTMENT IN FIXED ASSETS

7

固定资产投资
Investment in Fixed Assets

主要统计指标
Major Statistical Indicators

固定资产投资额	Investment in Fixed Assets	5556.32	亿元	(100 million yuan)
为上年	As Compared with the Preceding Year	112.2	%	(%)
# 第一产业	Primary Industry	31.47	亿元	(100 million yuan)
为上年	As Compared with the Preceding Year	165.0	%	(%)
# 第二产业	Secondary Industry	931.78	亿元	(100 million yuan)
为上年	As Compared with the Preceding Year	101.8	%	(%)
# 第三产业	Tertiary Industry	4593.07	亿元	(100 million yuan)
为上年	As Compared with the Preceding Year	114.3	%	(%)
房地产企业营业收入	Operating Revenue of Real Estate Enterprise	1945.23	亿元	(100 million yuan)
为上年	As Compared with the Preceding Year	99.4	%	(%)
房地产企业单位数	Number of Enterprises for Real Estate Developement	1586	个	(unit)
为上年	As Compared with the Preceding Year	103.8	%	(%)

7-01 全市固定资产投资总额(1978-2015年)
Investment in Fixed Assets (1978-2015)

单位:万元 (10000 yuan)

年份 Year	固定资产投资 Investment in Fixed Assets	房地产开发投资 Investment in Real Estate Development	项目投资 Projects Investment	基础设施投资 Infrastructural Investment	工业投资 Industrial Investment	民间投资 Nongovernment Investment
1978	23941					
1979	34407					
1980	45752					
1981	51538					
1982	66123					
1983	68306					
1984	93244					
1985	141889					
1986	182398					
1987	200516					
1988	205967					
1989	202131					
1990	229214	20409				
1991	255696	25247				
1992	384136	41886				
1993	825382	218006				
1994	1059437	320532				
1995	1566280	527985				
1996	1819333	572749				
1997	2139012	572686				
1998	2681740	666244				
1999	3233609	848441				
2000	3766473	1015347				
2001	4634929	1409132				
2002	5623366	1982517				
2003	8952090	2588452	6363638	2907234	3194960	4192567
2004	11081993	3285409	7796584	3254648	4357950	5761350
2005	12777972	4105706	8672266	3715525	4438723	6723758
2006	13734482	4426534	9307948	3871462	4640261	7551249
2007	15837775	5187904	10649871	4056241	5271141	8215570
2008	18822936	6154060	12668876	5410313	5693385	9450542
2009	21951706	7046752	14904954	6018416	6091653	11127373
2010	26518839	9561970	16956869	6452236	6855587	13680327
2011	31000218	13027234	17972984	6437025	7474806	17507040
2012	37227544	15973611	21253933	7785196	8518653	20595909
2013	42638732	18532841	24105891	8524663	9104614	22560292
2014	49527010	23010823	26516187	10055306	9133973	28499239
2015	55563183	24720743	30842440	13551793	9300133	29247853

注:2011年起固定资产投资口径由计划总投资500万元以上项目投资及房地产开发投资构成。

a) Since 2011, the date of investment in fixed Assets was composed by investment projects of which each is over 5 million yuan and investment in real estate.

7－02 市区固定资产投资总额(1990－2015 年)

Investment in Fixed Assets of Urban District (1990－2015)

单位:万元 (10000 yuan)

年份 Year	固定资产投资 Investment in Fixed Assets	房地产开发投资 Investment in Real Estate Development	项目投资 Projects Investment	基础设施投资 Infrastructural Investment	工业投资 Industrial Investment	民间投资 Nongovernment Investment
1990		12750				
1991		16509				
1992		29784				
1993		115116				
1994		189357				
1995		375816				
1996		439245				
1997		445316				
1998		538499				
1999		636705				
2000		737950				
2001		1255605				
2002		1724128				
2003	7409538	2176433	5233105	2535843	2424383	3316886
2004	8963515	3088508	6153009	2624214	3299235	5238005
2005	10358519	3485810	6872709	3071506	3247399	5802542
2006	10944075	3653393	7290682	3150192	3289532	5559199
2007	12630099	4298687	8331412	3396807	3617512	6218211
2008	15184281	5269947	9914334	4726734	3676567	7076219
2009	17797778	6261562	11536216	5070500	3821313	8632900
2010	21437496	8486495	12951001	5438685	4293707	10332997
2011	25202394	11409566	13792828	5451654	4801419	13302115
2012	30160782	13749412	16411370	6495070	5554286	15669790
2013	34029665	15978470	18051195	6728552	5787728	16759259
2014	42572154	21128840	21443314	8010162	7100359	24282102
2015	47507571	22981761	24525810	10960519	6835700	24593063

注:2001 年起市区数据含萧山、余杭区,2014 年起含富阳区。

a) The data of urban district in the table have included Xiaoshan District and Yuhang District since 2001, and included Fuyang District since 2014.

7-03 三次产业固定资产投资(1978-2015年)

Investment in Fixed Assets Grouped by Three Industries (1978-2015)

单位:万元 (10000 yuan)

年份 Year	绝对数(万元) Absolute Figure(10000 yuan)				比重(以投资总额为100) Proportion(%)		
	合计 Total	第一产业 Primary Industry	第二产业 Secondary Industry	第三产业 Tertiary Industry	第一产业 Primary Industry	第二产业 Secondary Industry	第三产业 Tertiary Industry
1978	23941	2174	14455	7312	9.1	60.4	30.5
1979	34407	2454	19927	12026	7.1	57.9	35.0
1980	45752	1608	26211	17933	3.5	57.3	39.2
1981	51538	850	29176	21512	1.6	56.6	41.8
1982	66123	1352	37648	27123	2.0	57.0	41.0
1983	68306	1297	37823	29186	1.9	55.4	42.7
1984	93244	2831	46619	43794	3.0	50.0	47.0
1985	141889	3207	71608	67074	2.3	50.5	47.2
1986	182398	2265	94394	85739	1.2	51.8	47.0
1987	200516	2994	106600	90922	1.5	53.2	45.3
1988	205967	4746	118736	82485	2.3	57.6	40.1
1989	202131	3038	117651	81442	1.5	58.2	40.3
1990	229214	2181	126263	100770	1.0	55.1	43.9
1991	255696	3204	132303	120189	1.3	51.7	47.0
1992	384136	4424	206659	173053	1.2	53.8	45.0
1993	825382	5650	346416	473316	0.7	42.0	57.3
1994	1059437	3905	354672	700860	0.4	33.5	66.1
1995	1566280	5821	534687	1025772	0.4	34.1	65.5
1996	1819333	3100	640273	1175960	0.2	35.2	64.6
1997	2139012	1712	595966	1541334	-	27.9	72.1
1998	2681740	4053	706948	1970739	0.2	26.4	73.4
1999	3233609	23546	764309	2445754	0.7	23.6	75.7
2000	3766473	774	844334	2921365	0.2	22.4	77.4
2001	4634929	595	953494	3680840	-	20.6	79.4
2002	5623366	6514	1104212	4512640	0.1	19.6	80.3
2003	8952090	10489	3208885	5732716	0.1	35.9	64.0
2004	11081993	15992	4369015	6696986	0.1	39.4	60.5
2005	12777972	13982	4451936	8312054	0.1	34.8	65.1
2006	13734482	17892	4651420	9065170	0.1	33.9	66.0
2007	15837775	23278	5286340	10528157	0.1	33.4	66.5
2008	18822936	30810	5705736	13086390	0.2	30.3	69.5
2009	21951706	31335	6115482	15804889	0.1	27.9	72.0
2010	26518839	41959	6875840	19601040	0.2	25.9	73.9
2011	31000218	76931	7486832	23436455	0.2	24.2	75.6
2012	37227544	42668	8531598	28653278	0.1	22.9	77.0
2013	42638732	84018	9125316	33429398	0.2	21.4	78.4
2014	49527010	190748	9152477	40183785	0.4	18.5	81.1
2015	55563183	314688	9317825	45930670	0.6	16.8	82.6

7-04 全市固定资产投资房屋建筑面积及造价(1978-2015年)
Floor Space of Buildings and Their Cost (1978-2015)

年份 Year	施工面积(万平方米) Floor Space of Buildings Under Construction (10000sq. m)	住宅 Residential Buildings	竣工面积(万平方米) Floor Space of Buildings Completed (10000 sq. m)	住宅 Residential Buildings	竣工房屋价值(万元) Value of Buildings Completed (10000 yuan)	住宅 Residential Buildings	每平方米造价(元) Cost Per Square (yuan)	住宅 Residential Buildings
1978			101.95	39.58	8869	2810	87	71
1979			150.26	68.01	13223	4965	88	73
1980	456.54		202.58	104.44	19448	8564	96	82
1981	507.94		232.25	120.35	26709	12396	115	103
1982	554.89	258.09	281.63	148.66	34095	16470	121	111
1983	531.79	244.36	247.07	125.86	33938	15494	137	123
1984	620.71	293.21	267.85	138.71	42740	18398	160	133
1985	741.47	333.72	327.75	157.85	56561	22825	173	145
1986	674.58	278.19	338.19	160.19	50561	27338	238	170
1987	544.64	149.07	254.73	73.16	68801	14944	270	204
1988	526.70	156.92	230.21	75.44	68407	17820	297	236
1989	420.81	116.12	202.15	64.15	69750	18200	345	284
1990	472.59	209.50	236.44	112.77	93557	34266	396	304
1991	459.00	205.41	226.84	92.72	93158	28599	411	308
1992	604.85	301.21	262.11	114.97	116169	39834	452	350
1993	958.91	533.01	380.29	199.96	224251	105107	589	525
1994	1069.68	613.62	460.20	274.19	375211	212705	815	776
1995	1320.68	737.79	524.58	319.41	491705	274314	937	859
1996	1399.70	758.00	582.70	354.50	688569	370485	1182	1045
1997	1363.80	660.70	642.10	338.00	871361	449235	1357	1329
1998	1456.02	743.59	515.16	271.91	709730	390624	1378	1437
1999	1681.71	956.15	709.10	411.44	1119141	641717	1578	1560
2000	1721.58	949.32	744.42	419.80	1207767	709044	1622	1689
2001	2318.95	1251.92	830.05	402.46	1310380	679449	1579	1688
2002	2713.02	1586.28	890.05	492.95	1623662	956643	1820	1941
2003	4392.79	2083.58	1618.01	651.58	2732763	1353422	1689	2077
2004	5731.48	2909.03	1865.83	717.46	2791115	1313596	1496	1831
2005	6671.39	3628.34	1856.34	801.34	3265491	1865538	1759	2328
2006	7260.08	3747.60	1737.51	706.13	2900836	1580689	1670	2239
2007	7942.07	4040.54	1849.24	858.99	3750264	2329184	2028	2712
2008	9471.42	4160.27	2057.86	846.34	4113211	2171525	1999	2566
2009	10308.45	4441.84	2009.90	700.63	3626421	1684092	1804	2404
2010	12971.81	5534.10	2695.90	902.57	5274936	2285285	1957	2532
2011	15982.64	6442.52	3108.57	991.72	6209320	2498468	1997	2519
2012	17329.23	6938.29	2952.06	1048.95	6015778	2485123	2038	2369
2013	19226.78	7392.23	3666.67	1308.83	7744168	3530744	2112	2698
2014	20877.58	7757.60	4274.87	1350.19	9613177	3951202	2249	2926
2015	21686.34	8163.82	4877.76	1600.80	-	-	-	-

注:2015年竣工房屋价值相关指标取消。

a) Since 2015, the indicators related to floor space of buildings completed have been cancelled.

7－05 市区固定资产投资房屋建筑面积及造价(1978－2015年)

Urban District Floor Space of Buildings and Their Cost (1978－2015)

年 份 Year	施工面积(万平方米) Floor Space of Buildings Under Construction (10000 sq. m)	住 宅 Residential Buildings	竣工面积(万平方米) Floor Space of Buildings Completed (10000sq. m)	住 宅 Residential Buildings	竣工房屋价值(万元) Value of Buildings Completed (10000 yuan)	住 宅 Residential Buildings	每平方米造价(元) Cost Per Square (yuan)	住 宅 Residential Buildings
1978			71.56	29.06	6941	2237	97	77
1979			109.23	53.37	10267	4056	94	76
1980			137.11	76.73	14396	6752	105	88
1981			163.36	90.12	20093	9643	123	107
1982	378.88	172.11	189.92	100.07	25200	11980	133	120
1983	376.32	169.17	157.14	81.68	24029	11045	153	135
1984	465.27	221.72	191.13	104.55	33863	14658	177	140
1985	532.66	258.19	219.79	114.26	40344	17489	184	153
1986	465.75	203.22	219.33	116.70	58619	21149	267	181
1987	336.85	86.05	150.59	41.72	46530	9513	309	228
1988	315.80	90.98	117.71	37.63	38501	10117	330	269
1989	253.41	56.39	99.86	28.89	38680	9087	387	315
1990	301.82	128.50	137.88	62.47	60551	20361	439	326
1991	265.61	118.99	114.19	42.31	53819	12892	471	305
1992	329.16	190.55	115.59	57.36	55758	19706	483	344
1993	500.08	266.80	175.22	104.83	101528	53540	579	511
1994	618.91	352.16	212.06	123.74	182730	102924	862	832
1995	821.03	463.98	244.94	152.10	250073	139666	1021	918
1996	969.10	538.50	350.10	229.00	437239	274244	1249	1196
1997	1017.30	485.20	442.00	232.70	675762	357624	1529	1537
1998	1055.24	541.41	321.17	184.18	516400	317402	1608	1723
1999	1204.30	656.07	489.23	294.85	908844	533675	1858	1810
2000	1176.29	617.80	497.64	269.94	916212	528385	1841	1957
2001	2053.02	1085.30	698.29	325.64	1193818	615802	1710	1891
2002	2330.97	1335.78	744.48	404.35	1483862	869969	1993	2152
2003	3637.82	1699.61	1325.48	516.33	2395039	1174735	1807	2275
2004	4740.42	2453.87	1389.30	528.26	2257386	1068708	1625	2023
2005	5533.58	3039.08	1478.07	661.56	2804402	1626514	1897	2459
2006	5898.15	3114.45	1327.37	580.22	2365342	1357671	1782	2340
2007	6496.01	3357.18	1355.43	674.97	3063585	1992874	2260	2953
2008	7812.71	3466.88	1537.69	668.13	3372465	1827426	2193	2735
2009	8558.17	3807.67	1398.49	537.39	2725150	1321357	1949	2459
2010	10738.49	4759.75	1983.33	732.55	4255543	1927150	2146	2631
2011	13259.13	5451.45	2091.12	797.96	4736356	2122126	2265	2659
2012	14385.57	5680.08	2169.11	889.73	4966296	2207085	2290	2481
2013	15693.30	5910.71	2637.83	986.35	6074353	2822878	2303	2862
2014	18219.47	6591.75	3516.92	1132.80	8406996	3536426	2390	3122
2015	18872.19	6972.04	3868.26	1269.66	－	－	－	－

注:2015年竣工房屋价值相关指标取消。

a) Since 2015, the indicators related to floor space of buildings completed have been cancelled.

7－06 分地区

Investment in Fixed Assets

单位:万元

年　份 Year	全　市 Total	市　区 Urban District			
		合　计 Total	萧山区 Xiaoshan	余杭区 Yuhang	富阳区 Fuyang
2003	8952090	7409538	1835889	1162453	563603
2004	11081993	8963515	2246807	1478151	767880
2005	12777972	10338519	2161067	1718028	424962
2006	13734482	10944075	2424763	1758656	1017368
2007	15837775	12630099	2745133	1929019	1155871
2008	18822936	15184281	3184947	2317510	1334619
2009	21951706	17797778	3769557	2823192	1534401
2010	26518839	21437496	4515095	3480147	1796500
2011	31000218	25202394	5190805	4134743	1913712
2012	37227544	30160782	6169275	5121242	2343812
2013	42638732	34029665	7307304	6312261	2868320
2014	49527010	42572154	8508518	7861506	3500717
2015	55563183	47507571	9631238	9200016	4037889

固定资产投资(主要年份)
by Region(Main Years)

(10000 yuan)

桐庐县 Tonglu	淳安县 Chun'an	建德市 Jiande	临安市 Lin'an
250100	135275	246594	346980
352987	218730	299212	479669
275543	316779	896329	525840
470450	324444	377875	600270
542615	403119	432576	673495
653234	475340	509484	665978
738391	542037	575374	763725
1001737	668168	658530	956408
1158682	794383	796301	1134746
1412038	969471	961590	1379851
1725986	1193796	1176467	1644498
2096371	1450503	1432850	1975132
2472662	1512184	1758713	2312053

7－07 分地区固定
Investment in Fixed Assets

单位：万元

指 标	Item	全 市 Total	市 区 Urban District 合 计 Total
固定资产投资额	**Investment in Fixed Assets**	**55563183**	**47507571**
#民间投资	#Private Investment	29247853	24593063
#工业投资	Industrial Investment	9300133	6835700
#基础设施投资	Infrastructural Investment	13551793	10960519
一、按投资、房地产分	**Grouped by Sector**		
投资项目完成额	Investment Projects	30842440	24525810
房地产开发完成额	Real Estate	24720743	22981761
二、按登记注册类型分	**Grouped by Status of Registration**		
内资	Domestic－funded	49055060	41600744
国有	State－owned	10995285	9265830
集体	Collective－owned	967037	664836
股份合作	Cooperative	107286	98803
国有联营企业	State Joint Ownership	8353	8353
国有与集体联营	Joint State－collective Ownership	5049	3372
其他联营	Other Joint	5023	－
国有独资公司	State－owned Corporations	4167151	3388970
其他有限责任公司	Other Limited Liability Corporations	20225799	18700433
股份有限公司	Share－holding Corporations Ltd.	1171228	949844
私营	Private	11000303	8291669
其他	Other	402546	228634
港、澳、台商投资	Investment from Hong Kong, Macao and Taiwan	4815875	4481347
外商投资	Foreign Investment	1664726	1422259
个体经营	Individual	27522	3221

资产投资（2015 年）
by Region（2015）

（10000 yuan）

萧山区 Xiaoshan	余杭区 Yuhang	富阳区 Fuyang	桐庐县 Tonglu	淳安县 Chun'an	建德市 Jiande	临安市 Lin'an
9631238	**9200016**	**4037889**	**2472662**	**1512184**	**1758713**	**2312053**
4586735	5703727	2122413	1581078	815732	989973	1268007
2387369	1396691	1510742	916768	256620	707650	583395
2154691	1279107	1398877	781479	428513	662057	719225
6330165	4535515	3067719	2139897	1070175	1517551	1589007
3301073	4664501	970170	332765	442009	241162	723046
8317488	7837542	3633543	2283549	1376817	1644724	2149226
2017514	736295	387761	508739	274456	385943	560317
153373	186510	75138	226619	13745	61837	–
2104	13038	21209	2277	2494	–	3712
–	–	–	–	–	–	–
–	2680	692	1677	–	–	–
–	–	–	5023	–	–	–
784882	1402023	919031	190561	184926	155633	247061
2423550	3139478	1089060	214479	357811	492030	461046
113573	60148	114997	40284	31105	45285	104710
2795768	2291317	954006	1090290	434974	471086	712284
26724	6053	71649	3600	77306	32910	60096
749696	1068317	384259	46883	104475	47602	135568
560833	294157	20087	136267	28042	58148	20010
3221	–	–	5963	2850	8239	7249

指　　标	Item	全　市 Total	市　区 Urban District 合　计 Total
三、按行业分	**Grouped by Sector**		
农林牧渔业	Agricultare, Forestry, Animal Husbandry and Fishery	314688	59133
采矿业	Mining	91080	19392
制造业	Manufacturing	7592673	5548335
电力、热力、燃气及水的生产和供应业	Production and Supply of Electric Power, Heat Power, Gas and Tap Water	1616380	1267973
建筑业	Construction	17692	16990
批发和零售业	Wholesale & Retail Trades	883127	787176
交通运输、仓储和邮政业	Transportation, Storage and Post	3892605	3298938
住宿和餐饮业	Hotels and Catering Services	529480	297062
信息传输、软件和信息技术服务业	Information Transmission, Softuare and Information Technology	1062799	932781
金融业	Financial Intertnediation	401377	393676
房地产业	Real Estate	29475224	27093446
租赁和商务服务业	Leasing and Business Services	1154492	1151796
科学研究和技术服务业	Scientific Research and Technical Service	261189	141356
水利、环境和公共设施管理业	Management of Water Conservancy, Environment and Public Facilities	5899889	4629287
居民服务、修理和其他服务业	Residentid Service, Repairs and Other Service	26480	7658
教育	Education	1234331	1016537
卫生和社会工作	Health Care and Social Welfare	335064	242978
文化、体育和娱乐业	Culture, Sports and Entertainment	522255	413365
公共管理、社会保障和社会组织	Public Management, Social Security and Social Organizations	252358	189692

continued (10000 yuan)

萧山区 Xiaoshan	余杭区 Yuhang	富阳区 Fuyang	桐庐县 Tonglu	淳安县 Chun'an	建德市 Jiande	临安市 Lin'an
41893	1066	7878	93096	53548	41790	67121
–	–	19392	2720	10702	43651	14615
2243982	1241863	1281950	816065	222223	533635	472415
143387	154828	209400	97983	23695	130364	96365
–	1932	–	702	–	–	–
36514	213719	32931	34432	16597	26842	18080
709879	220173	183074	138442	117546	165387	172292
38639	110657	5748	101018	102160	15006	14234
71036	376260	51012	1500	128518	–	–
2104	3861	11827	3694	–	–	4007
4735277	5719889	1133199	615094	477234	415108	874342
274612	132358	621	2696	–	–	–
–	49745	–	–	20591	271	98971
1044282	614582	735552	436421	207174	321210	305797
5650	250	1155	–	12101	6721	–
95957	233212	195833	32065	37929	14112	133688
42700	55783	35570	17040	24457	37726	12863
114800	30882	77628	63774	39703	2685	2728
30526	38956	55119	15920	18006	4205	24535

7-08 分地区工业
Investment in Industrial

单位:万元

指　　标	Item	全　　市 Total	市　区 Urban District 合 计 Total
总计	**Total**	**9300133**	**6835700**
#技术改造投资	**Investment in Technique Innovation**	**6306023**	**4684386**
一、按登记注册类型分	**Grouped by Status of Registration**		
内资	Domestic - funded	7453494	5289817
国有	State - owned	1108730	986937
集体	Collective - owned	30463	13675
股份合作	Cooperative	375	375
国有联营企业	State Joint Ownership	5191	5191
国有与集体联营	Joint State - collective Ownership	1677	-
国有独资公司	State - funded Corporations	368457	306573
其他有限责任公司	Other Limited Liability Corporations	1449457	1106163
股份有限公司	Share - holding Corporations Ltd.	460164	295812
私营	Private	4002036	2572010
其他	Other	26944	3081
港、澳、台商投资	Investment from Hong Kong, Macao and Taiwan	798697	727382
外商投资	Foreign Investment	1034814	818501
个体经营	Individual	13128	-
二、按行业分	**Grouped by Sector**		
采矿业	Mining	91080	19392
制造业	Manufacturing	7592673	5548335
#农副食品加工业	Processing of Food from Agricultural Products Processing	145390	77967
食品制造业	Food Manufacturing	210137	174758
酒、饮料和精制茶制造业	Wine, Beverage and Tea Manufacturing	124100	34433
烟草制品业	Tobacco Processing	80255	80255
纺织业	Textile Processing	354286	302183
纺织服装和服饰业	Textile Products and Costume Industry	176372	106667

投资(2015 年)
Sector by Region(2015)

(10000 yuan)

萧山区 Xiaoshan	余杭区 Yuhang	富阳区 Fuyang	桐庐县 Tonglu	淳安县 Chun'an	建德市 Jiande	临安市 Lin'an
2387369	**1396691**	**1510742**	**916768**	**256620**	**707650**	**583395**
1262468	**1035384**	**1187687**	**485187**	**163940**	**493974**	**478536**
1691352	910517	1442641	747978	238118	621924	555657
93865	13180	8433	46674	10555	34105	30459
3404	6450	–	8322	1775	6691	–
–	375	–	–	–	–	–
–	–	–	–	–	–	–
–	–	–	1677	–	–	–
52506	46869	143057	10864	8517	6243	36260
385772	136301	416759	48143	26077	220967	48107
113573	19071	113259	35741	27737	42443	58431
1041645	688271	758639	596557	141505	309564	382400
587	–	2494	–	21952	1911	–
224643	352649	48014	36287	–	22332	12696
471374	133525	20087	127158	17452	58148	13555
–	–	–	5345	1050	5246	1487
–	–	19392	2720	10702	43651	14615
2243982	1241863	1281950	816065	222223	533635	472415
55194	22773	–	25313	6654	16043	19413
125831	18578	3637	11290	11232	5883	6974
7078	11535	4995	8526	32763	48378	–
–	8720	–	–	–	–	–
218302	75680	4139	16401	21086	7630	6986
39181	11666	44554	66361	–	1252	2092

指　　标	Item	全　市 Total	市区 Urban District 合计 Total
皮革、毛皮、羽毛(绒)及其制造业	Leather, Furs, Down and Related Products	22049	19883
木材加工及木、竹、藤、棕、草制品业	Timber Processing, Bamboo, Cane, Palm Fiber and Straw Products	23242	7834
家具制造业	Furniture Manufacturing	50970	34388
造纸及纸制品业	Paper Making and Paper Products	326108	258161
印刷业和记录媒介的复制业	Printing and Reproduction of Recording media	92796	41337
文教体育用品制造业	Cultural, Educational and Sports Goods	110118	30513
石油加工、炼焦及核燃料加工业	Petroleum and Nuclear Fuel Processing	2217	–
化学原料及化学制品制造业	Raw Chemical Material and Chemical Products	359662	237722
医药制造业	Medical and Pharmaceutical Products	389585	323917
化学纤维制造业	Chemical Fiber	220576	218125
橡胶和塑料制造业	Rubber and Plastic Products	319035	199422
非金属矿制品业	Nonmetal Mineral Products	544610	312885
黑色金属冶炼和压延加工业	Smelting and Pressing of Ferrous Metals	97893	79978
有色金属冶炼和压延加工业	Smelting and Pressing of Nonferrous Metal	163286	151460
金属制品业	Metal Products	368837	244950
通用设备制造业	General Purpose Machinery	611802	462965
专业设备制造业	Special Purpose Machinery	255913	200285
汽车制造业	Automobile Manufacturing	883290	808719
铁路、船舶、航空航天等制造业	Railway, Watercraft, Avigation Spaceflight and other Equipment Manufacturing	56655	49542
电气机械及器材制造业	Electric Equipment and Machinery	731205	497576
计算机、通信和其他电子设备制造业	Computers, Telecommunications and other Electronic Equipment Manufacturing	617007	440704
仪器仪表制造业	Instruments and Meters Manufacturing	131468	112648
其他制造业	Other Manufacturing	71992	26525
废弃资源综合利用业	Multiple Utilization of Waste Resouces	51817	12533
金属制品、机械和设备修理业	Metal Products, Machinery and Equipment Repair	–	–
电力、热力、燃气及水的生产和供应业	Production and Supply of Electric Power, Heat Power, Gas and Tap Water	1616380	1267973

continued (10000 yuan)

萧山区 Xiaoshan	余杭区 Yuhang	富阳区 Fuyang	桐庐县 Tonglu	淳安县 Chun'an	建德市 Jiande	临安市 Lin'an
6625	12307	–	1618	–	548	–
6344	590	900	840	10761	2188	1619
24907	5257	3683	7647	2236	6699	–
17281	24037	214373	5405	706	2114	59722
12782	12536	7500	47641	2390	1428	–
6275	21754	2134	72520	–	5168	1917
–	–	–	2217	–	–	–
166350	21021	29154	10568	7615	68556	35201
45377	67459	165823	39158	4360	396	21754
193899	–	23263	–	–	2451	–
61700	31009	77772	18661	2002	90039	8911
252128	10644	43631	39473	37265	138323	16664
11710	12314	55549	–	–	17915	–
41307	32884	74601	8244	–	2704	878
95233	42314	83583	42323	2250	30636	48678
124581	232031	60288	50662	1802	31549	64824
57605	61426	39764	39224	7725	6771	1908
484080	232868	83791	41618	2703	–	30250
32089	5414	12039	–	–	7113	–
84723	172987	130104	66143	31943	22509	113034
56671	50280	75254	136726	7789	9174	22614
16729	33663	16370	–	18820	–	–
–	3278	19354	31715	2706	5546	5500
–	6838	5695	25771	7415	2622	3476
–	–	–	–	–	–	–
143387	154828	209400	97983	23695	130364	96365

7-09 分地区房地产开发
Investment in Real Estate

指标	Item	全市 Total	市区 Urban District 合计 Total
房地产开发投资额 （万元）	**Investment in Real Estate Development (10000 yuan)**	**24720743**	**22981761**
住宅 （万元）	Residential Buildings (10000 yuan)	14416811	13185809
办公楼 （万元）	Office Buildings (10000 yuan)	2880799	2847162
商业营业用房 （万元）	Buildings for Business Use (10000 yuan)	3244278	3016271
其他 （万元）	Others (10000 yuan)	4178855	3932519
房屋建筑面积	**Floor space of Buildings**		
施工面积 （万平方米）	Under Construction (10000 sq. m)	11142.68	9720.37
#住宅 （万平方米）	#Residential Buildings (10000 sq. m)	5925.55	4920.91
新开工面积 （万平方米）	Started This Year (10000 sq. m)	2029.33	1747.27
#住宅 （万平方米）	#Residential Buildings (10000 sq. m)	998.79	807.54
竣工面积 （万平方米）	Construction Completed (10000 sq. m)	1665.23	1367.80
#住宅 （万平方米）	#Residential Buildings (10000 sq. m)	1070.27	856.21
商品房销售情况	**Selling of Commercialized Buildings**		
销售金额 （万元）	Total Sales of Buildings (10000 yuan)	21367755	20171205
#住宅 （万元）	#Residential Buildings (10000 yuan)	19051380	17972025
现房销售额 （万元）	Sales of Completed Buildings (10000 yuan)	3813347	3451016
#住宅 （万元）	#Residential Buildings (10000 yuan)	3180720	2860317
期房销售金额 （万元）	Sales of Future Buildings (10000 yuan)	17554408	16720189
#住宅 （万元）	#Residential Buildings (10000 yuan)	15870660	15111708
销售面积 （万平方米）	Floor Space of Buildings Sold (10000 sq. m)	1481.45	1319.66
#住宅 （万平方米）	#Residential Buildings (10000 sq. m)	1291.64	1142.02
现房销售面积 （万平方米）	Floor Space of Completed Buildings Sold (10000 sq. m)	309.53	252.61
#住宅 （万平方米）	#Residential Buildings (10000 sq. m)	255.01	205.10
期房销售面积 （万平方米）	Floor Space of Futures Buildings Sold (10000 sq. m)	1171.92	1067.05
#住宅 （万平方米）	#Residential Buildings (10000 sq. m)	1036.63	936.93

投资(2015 年)

Development by Region(2015)

			桐庐县 Tonglu	淳安县 Chun'an	建德市 Jiande	临安市 Lin'an
萧山区 Xiaoshan	余杭区 Yuhang	富阳区 Fuyang				
3301073	**4664501**	**970170**	**332765**	**442009**	**241162**	**723046**
2186971	2973660	657101	234212	271012	161057	564721
361048	403942	13623	12346	3775	7016	10500
239138	484037	120585	66731	80784	17901	62591
513916	802862	178861	19476	86438	55188	85234
1656.81	3065.62	415.72	379.32	322.55	240.90	479.54
829.04	1913.86	263.10	265.67	210.55	173.95	354.47
321.13	673.78	68.70	47.06	94.23	53.15	87.62
154.46	323.15	40.11	33.31	51.05	38.10	68.80
118.44	403.72	76.90	64.54	54.21	41.00	137.68
73.76	295.09	37.35	44.20	40.20	30.97	98.69
3160029	4180808	705013	296989	212378	263696	423487
2882298	3859771	656996	273775	199792	208162	397626
516825	537052	122119	79078	87364	30294	165595
458181	487040	112146	66033	81125	25333	147912
2643204	3643756	582894	217911	125014	233402	257892
2424117	3372731	544850	207742	118667	182829	249714
236.88	426.34	59.28	43.88	29.32	31.90	56.69
211.12	388.01	55.79	39.93	27.64	29.08	52.97
41.77	61.15	8.94	13.60	13.29	6.49	23.53
34.89	54.01	8.14	10.70	12.38	5.86	20.97
195.11	365.20	50.34	30.28	16.03	25.40	33.16
176.23	333.99	47.64	29.23	15.25	23.22	32.00

7 - 10 房屋建筑面积及造价(2015 年)
Floor Space of Buildings and Their Cost(2015)

指 标	Item	施工面积(万平方米) Floor Space of Buildings Under Construction (10000 sq. m)	竣工面积(万平方米) Floor Space of Buildings Completed (10000 sq. m)	竣工房屋的价值(万元) Value of Buildings Completed (10000 yuan)	每平方米造价(元) Cost Per Square Meter (yuan)
全 市	**Total**				
房屋建筑面积合计	**Floor Space of Buildings**	**21686.34**	**4877.76**	**-**	**-**
#住宅	#Residential Buildings	8163.82	1600.80	-	-
房地产开发	Real Estate Development	11142.68	1665.23	6605373	3967
#住宅	#Residential Buildings	5925.55	1070.27	4455053	4163
市 区	**Urban District**				
房屋建筑面积合计	**Floor Space of Buildings**	**18872.19**	**3868.26**	**-**	**-**
#住宅	#Residential Buildings	6972.04	1269.66	-	-
房地产开发	Real Estate Development	9720.37	1367.80	5892562	4308
#住宅	#Residential Buildings	4920.91	856.21	3943631	4606
#萧 山 区	**Xiaoshan**				
房屋建筑面积合计	**Total Floor Space of Buildings**	**3734.96**	**734.42**	**-**	**-**
#住宅	#Residential Buildings	1430.88	214.32	-	-
房地产开发	Real Estate Development	1656.81	118.44	316890	2675
#住宅	#Residential Buildings	829.04	73.76	174569	2367
余 杭 区	**Yuhang**				
房屋建筑面积合计	**Total Floor Space of Buildings**	**5752.75**	**1021.91**	**-**	**-**
#住宅	#Residential Buildings	2297.79	324.00	-	-
房地产开发	Real Estate Development	3065.62	403.72	1240730	3073
#住宅	#Residential Buildings	1913.86	295.09	916551	3106

7－10 续表 continued

指 标	Item	施工面积（万平方米）Floor Space of Buildings Under Construction (10000 sq. m)	竣工面积（万平方米）Floor Space of Buildings Completed (10000 sq. m)	竣工房屋的价值(万元) Value of Buildings Completed (10000 yuan)	每平方米造价(元) Cost Per Square Meter (yuan)
富阳区	**Fuyang**				
房屋建筑面积合计	**Total Floor Space of Buildings**	**1245.70**	**489.72**	**－**	**－**
#住宅	#Residential Buildings	393.32	105.47	－	－
房地产开发	Real Estate Development	415.72	76.90	300382	3906
#住宅	#Residential Buildings	263.10	37.35	130017	3481
桐庐县	**Tonglu**				
房屋建筑面积合计	**Total Floor Space of Buildings**	**748.81**	**307.37**	**－**	**－**
#住宅	#Residential Buildings	343.90	93.82	－	－
房地产开发	Real Estate Development	379.32	64.54	162348	2515
#住宅	#Residential Buildings	265.67	44.20	111663	2526
淳安县	**Chun'an**				
房屋建筑面积合计	**Total Floor Space of Buildings**	**623.30**	**185.71**	**－**	**－**
#住宅	#Residential Buildings	224.55	49.92	－	－
房地产开发	Real Estate Development	322.55	54.21	129633	2391
#住宅	#Residential Buildings	210.55	40.20	95551	2377
建德市	**Jiande**				
房屋建筑面积合计	**Total Floor Space of Buildings**	**615.89**	**237.65**	**－**	**－**
#住宅	#Residential Buildings	253.74	84.02	－	－
房地产开发	Real Estate Development	240.90	41.00	92239	2250
#住宅	#Residential Buildings	173.95	30.97	65945	2129
临安市	**Lin'an**				
房屋建筑面积合计	**Total Floor Space of Buildings**	**826.16**	**278.77**	**－**	**－**
#住宅	#Residential Buildings	369.59	103.38	－	－
房地产开发	Real Estate Development	479.54	137.68	328591	2387
#住宅	#Residential Buildings	354.47	98.69	238263	2414

7－11 分注册类型和资质等级

Financial Statistics of Enterprises for Real Estate Development

单位：万元

项　　目	Item	法人企业数(个) Number of Enterprises (unit)	年末 Asset and		
			流动资产合计 Circulating Funds	应收账款 Account Receivable	固定资产合计 Fixed Assets
总计	**Total**	**1586**	**119192638**	**1851814**	**1688922**
一、按登记注册类型分组	**Grouped by Registration Status**				
内资企业	Domestic Funded	1455	96351881	1434424	1562079
国有企业	State－owned	9	944431	6946	3874
集体企业	Collective－owned	－	－	－	－
股份合作企业	Share－holding Cooperative Enterprises	－	－	－	－
联营企业	Joint Venture	2	114565	12572	683
有限责任公司	Limited Liability Corporations	926	73384911	985571	1026338
股份有限公司	Share－holding Corporations Ltd.	19	2309770	245874	186332
私营企业	Private Enterprises	498	19592611	183461	344821
其他企业	Other Enterprises	1	5593	－	31
港澳台商投资企业	Funded from Hong Kong, Macao and Taiwan	98	15781905	336052	85167
外商投资企业	Foreign Funded	33	7058851	81338	41676
二、按企业资质等级分	**Grouped by Quali Fication Grade**				
一级	Grade Ⅰ	49	11239859	276968	140434
二级	Grade Ⅱ	132	9603723	87656	302173
三级	Grade Ⅲ	222	9541756	178615	535671
四级	Grade Ⅳ	70	1679732	54678	28926
暂定	Tentatine	772	64616648	746204	410511
其他	Others	341	22510920	507693	271207

房地产开发企业财务状况(2015 年)

Grouped by Registration Status and Qualification Grade(2015)

(10000 yuan)

资产负债 Liabilities at Year－end						所有者权益合计 Creditors′ Equity	
固定资产原价 Orginal Value of Fixed Assets	累计折旧 Accumulated Depreciation	#本年折旧 Depreciation This Year	在建工程 Projects wnder Construction	资产合计 Total Assets	负债合计 Total Liabilities		实收资本 Capital Hold
1769810	**543773**	**81710**	**1873191**	**139088505**	**104060360**	**35028146**	**25995037**
1613078	496255	73679	1181417	113003239	89584768	23418471	16502070
6008	2505	224	2479	970886	834260	136626	63715
－	－	－	－	－	－	－	－
－	－	－	－	－	－	－	－
1944	1261	160	－	145703	124039	21663	2800
1107942	321127	46816	1078230	86065691	68725705	17339987	12462687
89472	32516	4601	3191	3775868	1681450	2094418	699812
407666	138830	21869	97517	22039246	18219266	3819980	3267156
47	16	9	－	5846	48	5798	5900
112026	27119	5907	648809	16975133	8014124	8961009	8188005
44706	20400	2124	42965	9110133	6461468	2648666	1304963
225748	93714	10933	5501	18168202	12769109	5399093	1565353
309421	108690	13791	92439	13334774	9941591	3393183	1593710
565708	134904	20703	262542	12050771	8614050	3436722	1728617
50927	23151	3876	370713	2271620	1881631	389989	182005
347031	115375	19681	407446	68805576	52849048	15956528	14990618
270975	67938	12727	734551	24457563	18004932	6452631	5934735

单位:万元

7－11 续表

项　　目	Item	营业收入 Revenue of Business	#主营业务收入 Main Revenue of Business	营业成本 Operating Costs	#主营业务成本 Main Cost of Business
总计	**Total**	**19452315**	**19249502**	**15274718**	**15137744**
一、按登记注册类型分组	**Grouped by Registration Status**				
内资企业	Domestic Funded	16452612	16252099	13068417	12940946
国有企业	State－owned	90453	88464	87047	68577
集体企业	Collective－owned	–	–	–	–
股份合作企业	Share－holding Cooperative Enterprises	–	–	–	–
联营企业	Joint Venture	187011	186841	97237	97237
有限责任公司	Limited Liability Corporations	12989208	12811559	10389942	10287788
股份有限公司	Share－holding Corporations Ltd.	233644	226249	122526	120626
私营企业	Private Enterprises	2952295	2938985	2371666	2366717
其他企业	Other Enterprises	–	–	–	–
港澳台商投资企业	Funded from Hong Kong，Macao and Taiwan	2344754	2343490	1830482	1821585
外商投资企业	Foreign Funded	654949	653913	375819	375214
二、按企业资质等级分	**Grouped by Quali Fication Grade**				
一级	Grade Ⅰ	1034123	956451	632443	624832
二级	Grade Ⅱ	1634849	1620309	1203890	1181404
三级	Grade Ⅲ	2376801	2361249	1655602	1645243
四级	Grade Ⅳ	118134	115074	85938	84866
暂定	Tentatine	12148014	12084890	10057922	9998514
其他	Others	2140392	2111529	1638923	1602886

continued (10000 yuan)

营业税金及附加 Main Sales Tax and Extra Charges	销售费用 Cost of Sales	管理费用 Administration Cost	财务费用 Financil Cost	#利息支出 Interest Expenditure	营业利润 Management Profits	利润总额 Total Profits	应交所得税 Income Tax	就业人员年平均人数(人) Annual Average Number of Employed Persons(Person)
1602221	**749086**	**709250**	**556168**	**534991**	**1142883**	**1207423**	**339455**	**33270**
1334877	609549	592317	558084	520724	586964	651203	245421	29210
5212	655	2571	-142	1	-8120	-12377	63	264
-	-	-	-	-	-	-	-	
-	-	-	-	-	-	-	-	
43836	34748	5567	1468	1686	4185	4042	83	61
1023331	430860	421261	444165	430864	426914	498520	182489	19781
27884	11840	18669	22038	29315	148336	145493	20252	877
234614	131446	144233	90555	58859	15664	15541	42534	8220
-	-	15	-	-	-15	-15	-	7
196059	96208	61899	15426	5507	182090	181391	57488	2827
71284	43330	55034	-17341	8761	373829	374829	36546	1233
88195	36568	100372	104582	169138	661050	678403	41181	2916
134711	47705	93793	86646	81423	70932	81738	35747	3626
235660	96202	106484	103821	82610	214858	220213	63786	4469
9409	4055	11507	2078	2113	5688	5947	2713	877
969804	460938	300802	189861	142167	60206	94396	159637	15909
164441	103619	96292	69181	57540	130148	126726	36391	5473

主要统计指标解释

固定资产投资完成额 固定资产投资完成额是以货币表现的建造和购置固定资产的工作量以及与此有关的费用的总称。它是反映固定资产投资规模、速度、比例关系和使用方向的综合性指标。

房地产开发投资 包括各种经济类型的房地产开发公司、商品房建设公司及其他房地产开发单位统一开发的包括统代建、拆迁还建的住宅、厂房、仓库、饭店、宾馆、度假村、写字楼、办公楼等房屋建筑物和配套的服务设施、土地开发工程，如道路、给水、排水、供电、供热、通讯、平整场地等基础设施工程的投资。不包括单纯的土地交易活动。

施工和竣工房屋建筑面积 房屋建筑面积是从房屋外墙线算起的各层平面面积的总和，包括房屋结构(如柱、墙)占用的面积和地下室面积。多层建筑按各自然层面积总和计算，包括房屋内的楼隔层，突出墙面的眺望间、门斗、有柱雨罩的面积。不包括突出墙面结构的构件、艺术装饰等所占的面积，如台阶等。凹阳台、挑阳台按其水平投影面积一半计算建筑面积。

房屋新开工面积 指在报告期内新开工建设的房屋面积。不包括上期跨入报告期继续施工的房屋面积和上期停缓建而在本期恢复施工的房屋面积。房屋的开工应以房屋正式开始破土刨槽(地基处理或打永久桩)的日期为准。

商品房销售面积 指报告期内出售商品房屋的合同总面积(即双方签署的正式买卖合同中所确定的建筑面积)。由现房销售建筑面积和期房销售建筑面积两部分组成。

(1)现房销售面积：是指在报告期内正式签订买卖合同、已经竣工达到入住条件的商品房屋建筑面积。包括以一次性付款方式和分期付款方式销售的现房建筑面积。

(2)期房销售面积：是指在报告期内正式签订买卖合同、正在建设尚未竣工交付使用的商品房屋建筑面积。包括以一次性付款方式和分期付款方式销售的商品房屋建筑面积。期房销售建筑面积竣工后不再转为现房销售建筑面积。

新增固定资产 指通过投资活动所形成的新的固定资产价值。包括已经建成投入生产或交付使用的工程价值和达到固定资产标准的设备、工具、器具的价值及有关应摊入的费用。它是以价值形式表示的固定资产投资成果的综合性指标，可以综合反映不同时期、不同部门、不同地区的固定资产投资成果。

Explanatory Notes on Main Statistical Indicators

Total Investment in Fixed Assets refer to the volume of activities in construction and purchases of fixed assets in monetary terms and other relative expenses. It is a comprehensive indicator which shows the size, pace, proportional relations and use orientation of investment in fixed assets.

Investment in Real Estate Development include the investment by the real estate development companies, commercial buildings construction companies and other real estate development units of various types of ownership in the construction of house buildings, such as residential buildings, factory buildings, warehouses, hotels, guesthouses, holiday supply, water drainage, power supply, heating, telecommunications, land leveling and other projects of infrastructure, it excludes the activities in simple land transaction.

Floor space of Building Under Construction and Completed refer to total floor space in each story of buildings calculate from the outside line of building walls, including the space occupied by construction like pillars or walls and basements. The floor space of multi – story building includes the total floor space of each story, including area occupied by separating walls, watching rooms, door – ways, and pillars, but excluding protruding wall structures, artistic decoration, etc. (for example, flight of steps). The space of balcony is counted by half of the projection area.

Beginning to Construction Floor Space of Building refer to the area space which constructed in report period, not including the floor whose construction lasted to report period and which stopped in the last period to continue construction in the report period. And the beginning of construction of floor space should base on the date of breaking the earth(disposal the basement or piling).

Selling of the Commercial Building refer to the total area that sold by contract(which reflected in the contract), which include completed and future buildings.

(1) Floor Space of Completed Building: refer to the area which formal contract has been signed and which has been completed and reached the condition of living, including payment in one time and installment payment.

(2) Floor Space of Future Building: refer to the area which signed by formal contract and under constructing, including payment in one time and installment payment. Which can not be turned into completed building's sale when they completed.

Newly Increased Fixed Assets refer to the newly increased value of fixed assets through investment, including the value of projects completed and put into production, the value of equipment, tools, and vessels considered as fixed assets, as well as the relevant expenses as investment in fixed assets. This is a comprehensive indicator of investment in fixed assets, reflecting the achievements of investment in fixed assets in different periods, different sectors, and different regions.

八、国内贸易

DOMESTIC TRADE

8

国内贸易
Domestic Trade

主要统计指标
Major Statistical Indicators

社会消费品零售总额	Total Retail Sales of Consumer Goods	4697.23	亿元	(100 million yuan)
为上年	As Compared with the Preceding Year	111.8	%	(%)
批发和零售贸易业	Wholesale and Retail Trades	4239.34	亿元	(100 million yuan)
为上年	As Compared with the Preceding Year	112.3	%	(%)
住宿和餐饮业	Hotels and Catering Services	457.89	亿元	(100 million yuan)
为上年	As Compared with the Preceding Year	107.4	%	(%)

8－01　社会消费品零售总额(1978－2015 年)

Total Retail Sale of Consumer Goods(1978－2015)

单位:万元　　　　(10,000 yuan)

年　份 Year	全　市 Total	市　区 Urban District	县(市)合计 All Counties
1978	119509	73653	45856
1979	150462	93342	57120
1980	205381	128440	76941
1981	236188	148152	88036
1982	251068	154582	96486
1983	273664	169508	104156
1984	343722	215901	127821
1985	478117	308901	169216
1986	557963	360479	197484
1987	657838	426745	231093
1988	866373	557374	308999
1989	927019	600816	326203
1990	981713	650278	331435
1991	1155476	777559	377917
1992	1408525	928586	479939
1993	1901509	1300037	601472
1994	2616477	1733572	882905
1995	2993250	1930140	1063110
1996	3478156	2310619	1167537
1997	3815537	2537537	1278000
1998	4178013	2794171	1383842
1999	4574924	3053983	1520941
2000	5146789	3436536	1710253
2001	5790138	4993078	797060
2002	6606548	5701707	904841
2003	7425760	6401970	1023790
2004	8554476	7385662	1168814
2005	9784275	8440559	1343716
2006	11191900	9630210	1561690
2007	13082930	11247539	1835391
2008	15775872	13542665	2233207
2009	18378198	15793645	2584553
2010	22250034	19141417	3108616
2011	26902226	23152666	3749561
2012	31651929	27196536	4455393
2013	38648394	33483819	5164575
2014	42014577	37855211	4159366
2015	46972280	42300676	4671604

注:1)市区数据 2001 年起包括萧山区和余杭区,2014 年起包括富阳区。

2)根据国家统一规定,2013 年经济普查后对 2009－2013 年度数据作了相应调整。

3)从 2013 年开始,零售总额口径从“在地口径”调整为“法人口径”。

a) Data of urban district include Xiaoshan and Yuhang district since 2001,and include Fuyang district since 2014.

b) According to the standards by NBS,the data of 2009－2013 are adjusted by the resuct of economic census.

c) The donotation of retail sale has been adjusted to "legal" from" regional".

8－02 分地区社会

Total Retail Sale of Consumer Goods

单位:万元

年 份 Year	全 市 Whole City		市 区 Urban District	
	合 计 Total	为上年(%) As Compared with the Preceding Year(%)	合 计 Total	萧山区 Xiaoshan
1978	119509	112.5	73653	12985
1979	150462	125.9	93342	16270
1980	205381	136.5	128440	22292
1981	236188	115.0	148152	25297
1982	251068	106.3	154582	29007
1983	273664	109.0	169508	32136
1984	343722	125.6	215901	41210
1985	478117	139.1	308901	51879
1986	557963	116.7	360479	61421
1987	657838	117.9	426745	73159
1988	866373	131.7	557374	101227
1989	927019	107.0	600816	103419
1990	981713	105.9	650278	111757
1991	1155476	117.7	777559	123753
1992	1408525	121.9	928586	153254
1993	1901509	135.0	1300037	195472
1994	2616477	137.6	1733572	299072
1995	2993250	114.4	1930140	339447
1996	3478156	116.2	2310619	390364
1997	3815537	109.7	2537537	431742
1998	4178013	109.5	2794171	470599
1999	4574924	109.5	3053983	520482
2000	5146789	112.5	3436536	602198
2001	5790138	113.6	4993078	690721
2002	6606548	114.1	5701707	795711
2003	7425760	112.4	6401970	929390
2004	8554476	115.2	7385662	1069728
2005	9784275	114.4	8440559	1234568
2006	11191900	114.4	9630210	1462157
2007	13082930	116.9	11247539	1721511
2008	15775872	120.6	13542665	2059811
2009	18378198	116.5	15793645	2425882
2010	22250034	121.1	19141417	2955860
2011	26902226	120.9	23152666	3578930
2012	31651929	117.7	27196536	4270442
2013	38648394	115.1	33483819	4871438
2014	42014577	108.7	37855211	5156481
2015	46972280	111.8	42300676	5739163

消费品零售总额(1978 - 2015 年)
by Region(1978 - 2015)

(10000 yuan)

余杭区 Yuhang	富阳区 Fuyang	桐庐县 Tonglu	淳安县 Chun'an	建德市 Jiande	临安市 Lin'an
11472	5209	3536	3507	4390	4757
14439	6435	4283	4274	5300	6119
19917	8661	5501	5225	7119	8226
22172	10226	6456	6201	7970	9714
23435	11016	7101	6663	8562	10702
23496	12307	7694	7168	9380	11975
29292	14972	9235	8331	10770	14011
39798	21013	11826	11081	14687	18932
47499	23400	13217	12525	15832	23590
53005	27939	17394	14449	18076	27071
64653	42601	24390	18944	23545	33639
74044	48836	23029	19014	23138	34723
69360	45364	23141	18764	23820	39229
84399	52807	26350	20950	25107	44551
110075	74865	34110	23983	30770	52882
149128	76162	44909	28038	40237	67526
212955	101829	69025	34179	54562	111283
255972	127592	93736	42143	70570	133650
266467	146348	104234	51794	77620	130710
294446	163324	114032	58994	83837	131625
321241	171654	123154	67136	93169	136889
352723	185730	135223	74293	103417	149073
397166	198917	148745	81054	115062	167111
446812	223782	166892	90133	128754	187499
508919	254887	188087	101581	144849	215437
584748	289297	209153	114990	163244	247106
674799	331534	237598	130974	185772	282936
778848	382960	272394	149456	212138	326768
906960	450365	317484	173272	247425	373144
1064956	526750	371057	201769	288873	446942
1302135	643169	451356	244069	350854	543759
1534222	745144	522835	282629	406299	627647
1849231	895185	624511	338317	499388	751216
2248637	1081323	752559	409590	602059	904030
2616486	1285095	896018	488301	714702	1071278
3077344	1504100	1030908	563508	823344	1242715
3494348	1707917	1173697	640460	934093	1411117
3912097	1980415	1323402	721510	1044830	1581862

8-03 社会消费品

Total Retail Sale of

单位:万元

地 区	Region	合 计 Total
全 市	**Total**	**46972280**
市 区	Urban District	42300676
#上城区	Shangcheng	3418056
下城区	Xiacheng	9162747
江干区	Jianggan	3887534
拱墅区	Gongshu	4617536
西湖区	Xihu	5139067
高新(滨江)区	Hi-Tech(Binjiang)	1066796
萧山区	Xiaoshan	5739163
余杭区	Yuhang	3912097
富阳区	Fuyang	1980415
桐庐县	Tonglu	1323402
淳安县	Chun'an	721510
建德市	Jiande	1044830
临安市	Lin'an	1581862

零售总额(2015 年)
Consumer Goods(2015)

(10000 yuan)

按经营地分 By Location		按行业分 By Sector	
城镇 Urban Areas	乡村 Rural Areas	批发和零售贸易业 Wholesale and Retail Trades	住宿和餐饮业 Hotels and Catering Services
44577597	**2394683**	**42393376**	**4578904**
41678334	622342	38457943	3842733
3418056	–	2986635	431421
9162747	–	8494866	667881
3887534	–	3534349	353185
4617536	–	4365353	252183
5139067	–	4667171	471897
1066796	–	968120	98676
5739163	–	5027289	711874
3912097	–	3559952	352145
1358073	622342	1781289	199126
821670	501731	1133239	190163
435875	285635	570413	151098
728323	316507	854898	189932
913395	668468	1376885	204978

8－04 按登记注册类型分限额以上批发零售贸易企业商品销售总额(2015 年)

Sales of Wholesale and Retail Trades Above Designated Size by Status of Registration(2015)

单位:万元 (10000 yuan)

项　目	Item	法人企业(个) Number of Enterprises (unit)	销售总额 Total Sales	批发额 Wholesale	零售额 Retail
总　计	**Total**	**3980**	**153774093**	**122393564**	**31380530**
1.内资企业	**Domestic－funded Enterprises**	**3860**	**146909440**	**119515159**	**27394281**
国有企业	State－owned Enterprises	25	5619779	5569921	49859
集体企业	Collective－owned Enterprises	7	63575	17075	46500
股份合作企业	Cooperative Enterprises	3	2996	－	2996
联营企业	Joint Ownership Enterprises	5	48284	－	48284
国有联营企业	State Joint Ownership Enterprises	－	－	－	－
集体联营企业	Collective Joint Ownership Enterprises	－	－	－	－
国有与集体联营企业	Joint State－collective Enterprises	5	48284	－	48284
其他联营企业	Other Joint Ownership Enterprises	－	－	－	－
有限责任公司	Limited Liability Corporations	1153	72516743	59482965	13033778
国有独资公司	State－funded Corporations	45	4780479	4198040	582439
其他有限责任公司	Other Limited Liability Corporations	1108	67736264	55284925	12451339
股份有限公司	Share－holding Corporations Ltd.	103	27584964	18725490	8859474
私营企业	Private Enterprises	2510	40787345	35507424	5279921
私营独资企业	Private－funded Enterprises	32	256738	125234	131503
私营合伙企业	Private Partnership Enterprises	1	779	－	779
私营有限责任公司	Private Limited Liability Corporations	2439	39399884	34356100	5043784
私营股份有限公司	Private Share－holding Corporations Ltd.	38	1129945	1026091	103855
其他企业	Other Enterprises	54	285753	212283	73470
2.港、澳、台商投资企业	**Enterprises With Investment from Hong Kong, Macao and Taiwan**	**57**	**3782687**	**1973412**	**1809275**
合资经营企业(港或澳、台资)	Joint－venture Enterprises(With Funds from Hong Kong, Macao and Taiwan)	18	2010068	1123137	886931
合作经营企业(港或澳、台资)	Coorperative Enterprises (With Funds from Hong Kong, Macao and Taiwan)	1	57953	－	57953
港、澳、台商独资经营企业	Enterprises With Sole Investment from Hong Kong, Macao and Taiwan	37	1708895	850275	858621
港、澳、台商投资股份有限公司	Share－holding Corporations Ltd. With Investment from Hong Kong, Macao and Taiwan	1	5771	－	5771
其他港澳台投资企业	Other Enterprises With Investment from Hong Kong, Macao and Taiwan	－	－	－	－
3.外商投资企业	**Enterprises With Foreign Investment**	**63**	**3081966**	**904994**	**2176973**
中外合资经营企业	Joint－venture Enterprises	15	1363959	629638	734321
中外合作经营企业	Cooperation Enterprises	1	8138	－	8138
外资企业	Enterprises With Sole Foreign Investment	45	1638146	203632	1434514
外商投资股份有限公司	Share－holding Corporations Ltd. With Foreign Investment	－	－	－	－
其他外商投资企业	Other Enterprises With Foreign Investment	2	71724	71724	－

8－05 按国民经济行业分限额以上批发零售贸易企业商品销售总额(2015 年)

Sales of Wholesale and Retail Trades Above Designated Size by Sector(2015)

单位:万元 (10000 yuan)

项 目	Item	法人企业(个) Number of Enterprises (unit)	销售总额 Total Sales	批发额 Wholesale	零售额 Retail
总 计	**Total**	**3980**	**153774093**	**122393564**	**31380530**
一、批发业	**Wholesale**	**2786**	**129030122**	**120097254**	**8932869**
农、林、牧产品批发	Wholesale of Farm, Forestry and Animal Husbandry Products	45	801641	793763	7878
食品、饮料及烟草制品批发	Wholesale of Food, Beverages and Tobaccos	191	10001742	9799265	202477
纺织、服装及家庭用品批发	Wholesale of Textile Products, Garments and Household Articles	636	15660832	15237647	423185
文化、体育用品及器材批发	Wholesale of Cultural and Sports Goods	115	4198785	4008762	190023
医药及医疗器材批发	Wholesale of Medicines and Medical Appliances	147	7855206	5063610	2791596
矿产品、建材及化工产品批发	Wholesale of Mineral Products, Building and Chemical Materials	1159	76818238	71776726	5041512
机械设备、五金产品及电子产品批发	Wholesale of Machinery, Hardware and Electronic Products	436	12952811	12706995	245815
#汽车、摩托车及零配件批发	Wholesale of Automobiles, Motorcycle and Parts	92	5712078	5608152	103926
贸易经纪与代理	Trade Agenly	4	24165	24073	93
其他批发业	Other	53	716703	686413	30290
二、零售业	**Retail Trade**	**1194**	**24743971**	**2296310**	**22447661**
综合零售	Comprehensive Retail Trade	124	5993958	616194	5377764
食品、饮料及烟草制品专门零售	Specialism Retail of Food, Beverages and Tobaccos	105	348663	44657	304005
纺织、服装及日用品专门零售	Specialism Retail of Textile Products, Garments, Shoes and Caps	78	1120895	147644	973250
文化、体育用品及器材专门零售	Specialism Retail of Cultural and Sports Goods	55	607499	80165	527334
医药及医疗器材专门零售	Specialism Retail of Medicines and Medical Appliances	79	908812	89326	819486
汽车、摩托车、燃料及零配件专门零售	Specialism Retail of Automobiles, Motorcycle, Fuels and Parts	459	11370903	782982	10587921
#汽车零售	Specialism Retail of Automobiles	292	8189979	699748	7490231
家用电器及电子产品专门零售	Specialism Retail of Household Electric Applianes, and Electronic Products	103	1756656	315119	1441538
五金、家具及室内装饰材料专门零售	Specialism Retail of Hardware and Upholstery Materials	46	277906	37053	240853
货摊、无店铺及其他零售业	Stall, Non－shop and Other Retails	145	2358680	183171	2175509

8－06 按登记注册类型分限额以上

Main Financial Indicators of Enterprises Above Designated Size in

单位：万元

项　目	Item	法人企业数(个) Number of Enterprises (unit)	年末资产负债 Assets and Liabilities 流动资产合计 Circulating Funds	存　货 Inventory	固定资产原价 Orginal Value of Fixed Assets
批发零售贸易业企业合计	**Total**	**3980**	**55455636**	**8132892**	**5863745**
1. 内资企业	**Domestic－funded Enterprises**	**3860**	**52617284**	**7792118**	**5291623**
国有企业	State－owned Enterprises	25	2374213	244582	1150505
集体企业	Collective－owned Enterprises	7	6416	1256	4371
股份合作企业	Cooperative Enterprises	3	9216	302	2477
联营企业	Joint Ownership Enterprises	5	2185	228	1459
国有联营企业	State Joint Ownership Enterprises	－	－	－	－
集体联营企业	Collective Joint Enterprises	－	－	－	－
国有与集体联营企业	Joint State－collective Enterprises	5	2185	228	1459
其他联营企业	Other Joint Ownership Enterprises	－	－	－	－
有限责任公司	Limited Liability Corporations	1153	25079454	4292369	1741213
国有独资公司	State－funded Corporations	45	1972955	644991	176250
其他有限责任公司	Other Limited Liability Corporations	1108	23106499	3647379	1564964
股份有限公司	Share－holding Corporations Ltd.	103	6753692	1037125	1232934
私营企业	Private Enterprises	2510	18280147	2200299	1147964
私营独资企业	Private－funded Enterprises	32	74040	16150	10998
私营合伙企业	Private Partnership Enterprises	1	345	160	22
私营有限责任公司	Private Limited Liability Corporations	2439	17606663	2124285	1104236
私营股份有限公司	Private Share－holding Corporations Ltd.	38	599099	59704	32707
其他企业	Other Enterprises	54	111961	15957	10700
2. 港、澳、台商投资企业	**Enterprises With Investment from Hong Kong, Macao and Taiwan**	**57**	**1105459**	**145388**	**202988**
合资经营企业(港或澳、台资)	Joint－venture Enterprises (With Funds from Hong Kong, Macao and Taiwan)	18	396254	46369	109926
合作经营企业(港或澳、台资)	Coorperative Enterprises (With Funds from Hong Kong, Macao and Taiwan)	1	19259	408	13340
港、澳、台商独资经营企业	Enterprises With Sole Investment from Hong Kong, Macao and Taiwan	37	688903	98184	78025
港、澳、台商投资股份有限公司	Share－holding Corporations Ltd. With Investment from Hong Kong, Macao and Taiwan	1	1044	427	1697
其他港澳台投资企业	Other Enterprises With Investment from Hong Kong, Macao and Taiwan	－	－	－	－
3. 外商投资企业	**Enterprises With Foreign Investment**	**63**	**1732893**	**195387**	**369134**
中外合资经营企业	Joint－venture Enterprises	15	310190	63924	163501
中外合作经营企业	Cooperation Enterprises	1	6448	922	7399
外资企业	Enterprises With Sole Foreign Investment	45	1410072	129010	198068
外商投资股份有限公司	Share－holding Corporations Ltd. With Foreign Investment	－	－	－	－
其他外商投资企业	Other Enterprises With Foreign Investment	2	6184	1530	167

批发零售贸易企业财务状况(2015 年)

Wholesale and Retail Trades by Status of Registration(2015)

(10000 yuan)

				所有者权益合计 Creditors' Equity
累计折旧 Accumulated Depreciation	本年折旧 Depreciation	资产总计 Total Assets	负债合计 Total Liabilities	
2539007	**296924**	**75060874**	**55267957**	**19792917**
2342860	**267036**	**70949777**	**52637676**	**18312101**
758718	34879	3985801	2012379	1973422
1787	182	13153	8010	5143
669	52	14712	13191	1521
641	76	3007	688	2319
–	–	–	–	–
–	–	–	–	–
641	76	3007	688	2319
–	–	–	–	–
615657	90305	32950181	25389341	7560840
58068	5759	3213845	1744640	1469206
557589	84546	29736336	23644701	6091634
498895	62881	10564760	6577471	3987289
464141	78181	23290200	18543804	4746395
2763	641	94975	69269	25706
5	5	439	439	–
449543	75149	22160319	17712471	4447847
11831	2386	1034467	761625	272842
2353	482	127963	92790	35173
80112	**11202**	**1888488**	**1049879**	**838610**
45715	7753	628442	392966	235476
9047	-858	31572	6005	25567
24389	4181	1226648	649498	577150
961	126	1827	1410	417
–	–	–	–	–
116035	**18686**	**2222609**	**1580403**	**642206**
42166	5362	535085	436486	98599
4560	295	12632	3132	9500
69196	13013	1668497	1136791	531707
–	–	–	–	–
113	15	6395	3994	2401

单位:万元　　　　8－06　续表

项　　目	Item	营业收入 Revenue of Business	主营业务收入 Main Revenue of Business	主营业务成本 Main Cost of Business	主营业务税金及附加 Main Sales Tax and Extra Charges
批发零售贸易业企业合计	**Total**	**135564990**	**134289284**	**126986441**	**373143**
1. 内资企业	**Domestic－funded Enterprises**	**129767199**	**128597558**	**121988282**	**347427**
国有企业	State－owned Enterprises	5342096	5313173	4841176	168826
集体企业	Collective－owned Enterprises	55606	55600	51036	92
股份合作企业	Cooperative Enterprises	3106	2598	2175	6
联营企业	Joint Ownership Enterprises	41268	41267	36611	103
国有联营企业	State Joint Ownership Enterprises	－	－	－	－
集体联营企业	Collective Joint Enterprises	－	－	－	－
国有与集体联营企业	Joint State－collective Enterprises	41268	41267	36611	103
其他联营企业	Other Joint Ownership Enterprises	－	－	－	－
有限责任公司	Limited Liability Corporations	64522164	63895547	61033779	88812
国有独资公司	State－funded Corporations	4229344	4214482	4063940	4437
其他有限责任公司	Other Limited Liability Corporations	60292820	59681065	56969839	84375
股份有限公司	Share－holding Corporations Ltd.	23036637	22700620	21375007	29984
私营企业	Private Enterprises	36498258	36320690	34422824	58723
私营独资企业	Private－funded Enterprises	222542	221813	205813	314
私营合伙企业	Private Partnership Enterprises	764	764	652	2
私营有限责任公司	Private Limited Liability Corpora tions	35270564	35098061	33271684	57201
私营股份有限公司	Private Share－holding Corporations Ltd.	1004388	1000052	944676	1207
其他企业	Other Enterprises	268065	268064	225676	883
2. 港、澳、台商投资企业	**Enterprises With Investment from Hong Kong, Macao and Taiwan**	**3059578**	**3028626**	**2656539**	**12428**
合资经营企业(港或澳、台资)	Joint－venture Enterprises (With Funds from Hong Kong, Macao and Taiwan)	1583687	1567935	1393615	5349
合作经营企业(港或澳、台资)	Coorperative Enterprises (With Funds from Hong Kong, Macao and Taiwan)	42616	42616	34158	219
港、澳、台商独资经营企业	Enterprises With Sole Investment from Hong Kong, Macao and Taiwan	1427504	1412305	1224840	6836
港、澳、台商投资股份有限公司	Share－holding Corporations Ltd. With Investment from Hong Kong, Macao and Taiwan	5771	5771	3927	24
其他港澳台投资企业	Other Enterprises With Investment from Hong Kong, Macao and Taiwan	－	－	－	－
3. 外商投资企业	**Enterprises With Foreign Investment**	**2738213**	**2663100**	**2341619**	**13288**
中外合资经营企业	Joint－venture Enterprises	1207139	1166338	1092982	2840
中外合作经营企业	Cooperation Enterprises	8395	6955	5663	29
外资企业	Enterprises With Sole Foreign Investment	1460955	1428082	1181747	10384
外商投资股份有限公司	Share－holding Corporations Ltd. With Foreign Investment	－	－	－	－
其他外商投资企业	Other Enterprises With Foreign Investment	61725	61725	61227	35

continued (10000 yuan)

销售费用 Cost of Sales	管理费用 Administration Cost	财务费用 Financil Cost	营业利润 Management Profits	利润总额 Total Profits	应交所得税 Income Tax	从业人员平均人数(人) Average Number of Employees (person)
3968509	**2059907**	**617503**	**1710793**	**1861308**	**480570**	**275124**
3495168	**1866704**	**607917**	**1606341**	**1765433**	**442237**	**250984**
41167	113567	-5118	189774	195599	64727	11551
1142	841	-4	2500	2496	628	152
64	659	-1	203	189	47	56
1191	195	-25	3191	3195	761	98
-	-	-	-	-	-	-
-	-	-	-	-	-	-
1191	195	-25	3191	3195	761	98
-	-	-	-	-	-	-
1653509	717577	316728	673302	737723	187281	102395
62683	51327	14062	85442	120456	10561	3655
1590826	666250	302667	587860	617267	176720	98740
786673	324298	36959	519692	564430	108749	49483
996256	704578	259072	196723	240786	77091	85853
11576	6555	345	-2296	-2216	212	1629
18	57	21	14	14	1	15
952729	681278	240479	170543	213525	74023	82327
31932	16688	18227	28462	29462	2855	1882
15166	4990	305	20955	21015	2954	1396
269815	**82957**	**4014**	**45511**	**32640**	**16318**	**10550**
141995	34808	-4250	17377	15593	12185	3304
2390	5772	84	-7	-5555	-1378	309
125362	40643	8164	28140	22604	5512	6877
69	1734	17	-	-3	-	60
-	-	-	-	-	-	-
203527	**110246**	**5572**	**58941**	**63234**	**22015**	**13590**
71731	23327	10505	-7502	-5177	1855	4935
1580	21	-	947	942	83	54
130021	86622	-4942	65603	67646	19958	8568
-	-	-	-	-	-	-
195	277	9	-108	-177	119	33

8－07 按国民经济行业分限额以上
Main Financial Indicators of Enterprises Above Designated

单位:万元

项　　目	Item	法人企业数(个) Number of Enterprises (unit)	年末资产负债 Assets and Liabilities 流动资产合计 Circulating Funds	存　货 Inventory	固定资产原价 Orginal Value of Fixed Assets
总　　计	**Total**	**3980**	**55455636**	**8132892**	**5863745**
一、批发业	**Wholesale**	**2786**	**46781768**	**6262289**	**3962911**
农、林、牧产品批发	Wholesale of Farm, Forestry and Animal Husbandry Products	45	321145	63694	41188
食品、饮料及烟草制品批发	Wholesale of Food, Beverages and Tobaccos	191	4596151	611378	409511
纺织、服装及家庭用品批发	Wholesale of Textile Products, Garments and Household Articles	636	7225899	1235337	404179
文化、体育用品及器材批发	Wholesale of Cultural and Sports Goods	115	1424006	480052	90565
医药及医疗器材批发	Wholesale of Medicines and Medical Appliances	147	2839676	667515	147966
矿产品、建材及化工产品批发	Wholesale of Mineral Products, Building and Chemical Materials	1159	25367553	2533921	2590716
机械设备、五金产品及电子产品批发	Wholesale of Machinery, Hardware and Electronic Products	436	4619947	612678	264868
#汽车、摩托车及零配件批发	Wholesale of Automobiles, Motorcycle and Parts	92	1414643	132102	87095
其他批发业	Other	53	378172	54022	13723
二、零售业	**Retail Trade**	**1194**	**8673868**	**1870603**	**1900835**
综合零售	Comprehensive Retail Trade	124	2814940	251628	720283
食品、饮料及烟草制品专门零售	Specialism Retail of Food, Beverages and Tobaccos	105	164304	31974	30978
纺织、服装及日用品专门零售	Specialism Retail of Textile Products, Garments, Shoes and Caps	78	645852	302097	260943
文化、体育用品及器材专门零售	Specialism Retail of Cultural and Sports Goods	55	332916	122696	91372
医药及医疗器材专门零售	Specialism Retail of Medicines and Medical Appliances	79	347429	88879	35774
汽车、摩托车、燃料及零配件专门零售	Specialism Retail of Automobiles, Motorcycle, Fuels and Parts	459	2972502	672700	511524
#汽车零售	Specialism Retail of Automobiles	292	2829326	645436	420483
家用电器及电子产品专门零售	Specialism Retail of Household Electric Applianes, and Electronic Products	103	648764	162625	78231
五金、家具及室内装饰材料专门零售	Specialism Retail of Hardware and Upholstery Materials	46	144206	22817	104193
货摊、无店铺及其他零售业	Stall, Non－shop and Other Retails	145	602958	215188	67538

批发零售贸易企业财务状况(2015 年)
Size in Wholesale and Retail Trades by Sector(2015)

(10000 yuan)

累计折旧 Accumulated Depreciation	本年折旧 Depreciation	资产总计 Total Assets	负债合计 Total Liabilities	所有者权益合计 Creditors´ Equity
2539007	**296924**	**75060874**	**55267957**	**19792917**
1878538	**191123**	**63007089**	**46235134**	**16771955**
12717	1941	404190	341692	62499
154402	19999	5837015	3460443	2376572
176714	23669	8788241	7044506	1743735
39487	4247	1785051	1241559	543492
65350	11555	3556205	2559786	996419
1307353	109974	36305660	26804407	9501252
118073	19182	5875213	4383488	1491725
34543	7623	1832243	1500906	331337
4284	521	446260	392655	53604
660469	**105802**	**12053785**	**9032824**	**3020962**
309340	36873	4075029	2789388	1285641
10439	2067	227762	157428	70334
42245	8233	1014702	901035	113667
29684	3513	422567	308346	114222
14344	2857	523506	342131	181375
182903	39070	3919299	3139367	779932
146287	33732	3622548	2986815	635733
25720	5207	890743	673692	217051
21967	3258	293579	215923	77656
23827	4725	686597	505513	181085

项 目	Item	营业收入 Revenue of Business	主营业务收入 Main Revenue of Business	主营业务成本 Main Cost of Business	主营业务税金及附加 Main Sales Tax and Extra Charges
总 计	**Total**	**135564990**	**134289284**	**126986441**	**373143**
一、批发业	**Wholesale**	**115470532**	**114570041**	**109586391**	**294661**
农、林、牧产品批发业	Wholesale of Farm , Forestry and Animal Husbandry Products	734819	733860	703536	702
食品、饮料、烟草制品批发	Wholesale of Food, Beverages and Tobaccos	9237925	9047227	7785630	179270
纺织、服装及家庭用品批发	Wholesale of Textile Products, Garments and Household Articles	14425196	14332692	13345331	19773
文化、体育用品及器材批发	Wholesale of Cultural and Sports Goods	3790274	3777872	3606213	6178
医药及医疗器材批发	Wholesale of Medicines and Medical Appliances	6835669	6801245	6322310	9097
矿产品、建材及化工产品批发	Wholesale of Mineral Products, Building and Chemical Materials	68134562	67594680	66206151	62015
机械设备、五金产品及电子产品批发	Wholesale of Machinery, Hardware and Electronic Products	11630149	11602791	10964271	14507
#汽车、摩托车及零配件批发	Wholesale of Automobiles, Motorcycle and Parts	4964936	4960708	4769769	5005
其他批发业	Other	658519	656260	631736	3099
二、零售业	**Retail Trade**	**20094458**	**19719243**	**17400050**	**78482**
综合零售	Comprehensive Retail Trade	4971714	4733897	3977151	37981
食品、饮料及烟草制品专门零售	Specialism Retail of Food, Beverages and Tobaccos	314072	311466	249157	1600
纺织、服装及日用品专门零售	Specialism Retail of Textile Products, Garments, Shoes and Caps	985316	966606	665998	6149
文化、体育用品及器材专门零售	Specialism Retail of Cultural and Sports Goods	560078	555929	488893	3777
医药及医疗器材专门零售	Specialism Retail of Medicines and Medical Appliances	814723	807694	678694	2804
汽车、摩托车、燃料及零配件专门零售	Specialism Retail of Automobiles, Motorcycle, Fuels and Parts	8539865	8457785	7939756	15413
#汽车零售	Specialism Retail of Automobiles	7265822	7190460	6770795	13583
家用电器及电子产品专门零售	Specialism Retail of Household Electric Applianes, and Electronic Products	1584131	1570422	1423777	4224
五金、家具及室内装饰材料专门零售	Specialism Retail of Hardware and Upholstery Materials	246575	241460	195762	1660
货摊、无店铺及其他零售业	Stall, Non － shop and Other Retails	2077983	2073985	1780863	4874

continued (10000 yuan)

销售费用 Cost of Sales	管理费用 Administration Cost	财务费用 Financil Cost	营业利润 Management Profits	利润总额 Total Profits	应交所得税 Income Tax	从业人员平均人数(人) Average Number of Employees (person)
3968509	**2059907**	**617503**	**1710793**	**1861308**	**480570**	**275124**
2495139	**1418602**	**507494**	**1382443**	**1512818**	**378629**	**156984**
13321	13892	8497	-4788	-1133	601	1334
632050	189040	145	520419	535761	109822	30696
506692	295805	91408	206583	216132	54635	35890
61917	43920	12486	69436	70607	9930	4593
205163	124719	41954	142935	143650	30160	12191
703186	568087	325039	328542	422598	135221	53613
369063	176684	10728	122580	125899	36129	17864
197131	33935	-8866	-2744	-553	3818	4153
3029	6104	17127	-4270	-1684	1894	716
1473370	**641306**	**110009**	**328349**	**348489**	**101941**	**118140**
579955	188572	-21017	176435	182115	50701	40804
40094	15178	2356	3548	4775	1267	4652
176283	72868	27184	23206	33685	6010	11415
34771	22837	3633	4896	5651	778	3981
68369	36920	5147	31150	32020	6201	7718
256475	187170	75449	51010	50585	24043	26260
205125	173144	72972	20646	20234	16947	21883
98233	41420	8581	6410	8204	2762	9904
24118	17071	4211	1121	-734	471	4264
195072	59270	4466	30574	32190	9709	9142

8－08 分地区限额以上

The Situation of Wholesale

单位:万元

地　区	Region	企业法人数（个）Number of Enterprises (unit)	商品销售总额 Total Sales of Commodities	主营业务收入 Main Revenue of Business	主营业务成本 Main Cost of Business	主营业务税金及附加 Main Sales Tax and Extra Charges
全　市	**Total**	**3980**	**153774093**	**134289284**	**126986441**	**373143**
市　区	Urban District	3572	150497238	131326329	124255608	362661
#上城区	Shangcheng	377	28331104	25040820	23358608	195150
下城区	Xiacheng	468	33303088	29179595	27920495	50962
江干区	Jianggan	371	16423022	14519926	13811756	14975
拱墅区	Gongshu	399	14661704	13301906	12799369	23208
西湖区	Xihu	313	13143705	10171159	9287792	17625
高新（滨江）区	Hi－Tech(Binjiang)	215	12873252	11365714	10895068	12482
萧山区	Xiaoshan	671	16210700	14265807	13529878	21482
余杭区	Yuhang	494	8678675	7450349	7042831	12472
富阳区	Fuyang	200	3624568	3199792	3071352	7657
桐庐县	Tonglu	141	1100411	981864	908196	2775
淳安县	Chun'an	64	658068	555999	486974	1098
建德市	Jiande	57	331373	317995	283496	767
临安市	Lin'an	146	1187003	1107098	1052167	5842

批发零售业主要指标(2015 年)

and Retail Trades by Region(2015)

(10000 yuan)

销售费用 Cost of Sales	管理费用 Administration Cost	财务费用 Financil Cost	利润总额 Total Profits	本年应交增值税 Value Added Tax Payable	从业人员平均人数(人) Average Number of Employees (person)
3968509	**2059907**	**617503**	**1861308**	**1085889**	**275124**
3856982	2003791	592614	1775349	1045200	261648
607541	363682	51717	594866	260700	46719
643999	379016	96133	498766	169797	36482
399761	212985	73510	111451	70065	28257
311833	217832	92819	-41654	103689	36445
701074	211306	36379	98398	128390	36689
279373	148901	56807	162727	61275	13185
462030	185460	78291	150143	85997	26861
190144	182945	73712	65912	53392	20438
68374	52246	31393	-15686	47032	8014
25178	21521	7171	16084	22487	3613
46333	7699	1155	23203	8584	3935
14846	7809	2674	9382	4683	1811
25169	19088	13889	37290	4935	4117

8-09 按注册类型、行业分限额以上

Main Financial Indicators of Hotels and Catering Services

单位:万元

项目	Item	法人企业数(个) Number of Enterprises (unit)	年末资产负债 Assets and Liabilities		
			流动资产合计 Circulating Funds	存货 Inventory	固定资产原价 Orginal Value of Fixed Assets
总计	**Total**	**894**	**1763859**	**135349**	**2889398**
(一)按登记注册类型分组	**Grouped By Registered Type**				
1. 内资企业	**Domestic - funded Enterprises**	**861**	**1385316**	**103952**	**2375432**
国有企业	State - owned Enterprises	43	118351	3141	214865
集体企业	Collective - owned Enterprises	14	22598	923	74641
股份合作企业	Cooperative Enterprises	1	628	25	1089
联营企业	Joint Ownership Enterprises	1	4813	73	4817
有限责任公司	Limited Liability Corporations	250	614725	73677	1360241
股份有限公司	Share - holding Corporations Ltd.	9	61643	1865	100089
私营企业	Private Enterprises	542	561129	24216	616866
其他企业	Other Enterprises	1	1430	32	2825
2. 港、澳、台商投资企业	**Enterprises With Investment from Hong Kong, Macao and Taiwan**	**18**	**208680**	**18553**	**267239**
3. 外商投资企业	**Enterprises With Foreign Investment**	**15**	**169863**	**12844**	**246727**
(二)按国民经济行业分组	**Grouped By Sector**				
1. 住宿业	**Lodging**	**417**	**1298043**	**96785**	**2202940**
旅游饭店	Restaurants for Junketing	253	1168486	93433	1993562
一般旅馆	General Hotel	164	129556	3352	209378
2. 餐饮	**Catering Services**	**477**	**465816**	**38564**	**686458**
正餐服务	Dinner Services	433	384649	24560	571694
快餐服务	Short Order Services	19	59251	12806	104874
饮料及冷饮服务	Beverages and Services	14	4085	494	1795
其他餐饮业	Others Catering Services	11	17831	703	8096

住宿业和餐饮业财务状况(2015 年)
Enterprises Above Designated Size by Status of Registration and Sector(2015)

(10000 yuan)

累计折旧 Accumulated Depreciation	本年折旧 Depreciation	资产总计 Total Assets	负债合计 Total Liabilities	所有者权益合计 Creditors´ Equity
1182602	**153825**	**4491531**	**3083971**	**1407560**
929828	**117463**	**3679339**	**2414550**	**1264789**
113298	9999	255751	78433	177318
40970	2582	72211	58974	13238
974	26	743	337	406
3440	161	6193	1033	5160
482182	65775	1954011	1263256	690755
48595	2775	209744	64508	145236
240370	36145	1176404	947638	228766
1	1	4283	371	3912
151703	**9372**	**356784**	**247254**	**109530**
101071	**26990**	**455408**	**422167**	**33241**
960471	**107269**	**3254608**	**2150493**	**1104115**
884225	93733	2887060	1893466	993593
76246	13536	367548	257026	110522
222131	**46556**	**1236923**	**933479**	**303444**
161106	26116	1021331	769984	251347
55281	19787	186655	153462	33193
1473	131	4879	2858	2021
4271	522	24058	7175	16883

单位:万元　　　　8－09　续表

项　　目	Item	营业收入 Revenue of Business	主营业务收入 Main Revenue of Business	主营业务税金及附加 Business Tax and Extra Charges
总　　计	**Total**	**2399787**	**2367364**	**128345**
(一)按登记注册类型分组	**Grouped By Registered Type**			
1. 内资企业	**Domestic－funded Enterprises**	**1687759**	**1666068**	**90461**
国有企业	State－owned Enterprises	122878	120811	6405
集体企业	Collective－owned Enterprises	21180	21062	1227
股份合作企业	Cooperative Enterprises	2090	2090	117
联营企业	Joint Ownership Enterprises	4459	4459	249
有限责任公司	Limited Liability Corporations	646045	633655	35209
股份有限公司	Share－holding Corporations Ltd.	91900	91594	4357
私营企业	Private Enterprises	798725	791915	42853
其他企业	Other Enterprises	483	483	44
2. 港、澳、台商投资企业	**Enterprises With Investment from Hong Kong, Macao and Taiwan**	**151711**	**147016**	**7984**
3. 外商投资企业	**Enterprises With Foreign Investment**	**560317**	**554281**	**29901**
(二)按国民经济行业分组	**Grouped By Sector**			
1. 住宿业	**Lodging**	**1034940**	**1015036**	**57073**
旅游饭店	Restaurants for Junketing	855294	839195	46839
一般旅馆	General Hotel	179646	175841	10233
2. 餐饮	**Catering Services**	**1364847**	**1352328**	**71273**
正餐服务	Dinner Services	765065	757237	39912
快餐服务	Short Order Services	544901	542426	28992
饮料及冷饮服务	Beverages and Services	11469	11174	618
其他餐饮业	Others Catering Services	43412	41491	1751

continued (10000 yuan)

销售费用 Cost of Sales	管理费用 Administration Cost	财务费用 Financil Cost	营业利润 Management Profits	利润总额 Total Profits	应交所得税 Income Taxes Payable	从业人员平均人数(人) Average Number of Employees (person)
785259	**533332**	**84155**	**-7377**	**7130**	**22820**	**100961**
557579	**433469**	**63549**	**-53721**	**-37199**	**8905**	**71610**
44014	42384	-335	-2807	-2852	1166	5459
8767	6385	332	-859	-881	70	1013
950	528	9	95	93	36	15
1602	1541	-99	395	413	105	153
216633	212395	33359	-46325	-35383	2698	27233
34735	15324	972	16557	17516	713	4116
250617	153935	29329	-19823	-16387	4117	33531
261	976	-18	-955	283	1	90
48307	**34018**	**15713**	**9310**	**8626**	**1370**	**5224**
179373	**65845**	**4893**	**37034**	**35703**	**12545**	**24127**
358445	**369067**	**62195**	**-53971**	**-43118**	**5426**	**41213**
298676	307076	55997	-49019	-39890	4868	33921
59769	61990	6198	-4952	-3228	557	7292
426814	**164265**	**21960**	**46594**	**50248**	**17394**	**59748**
236593	110739	18412	1271	6827	3841	32749
177500	46915	3326	43110	41061	12945	24125
3353	2398	19	392	444	83	425
9368	4214	203	1821	1917	526	2449

8-10 按登记注册类型和国民经济行业分限额以上住宿业和餐饮业经营情况(2015年)

Management Conditions of Hotels and Catering Services Enterprises Above Designated Size by Status of Registration and Sector(2015)

单位:万元　　　　(10000 yuan)

项　　目	Item	法人企业(个) Number of Enterprises (unit)	营业额 Revenue of Business	客房收入 Revenue of Guest Rooms	餐饮收入 Revenue of Catering Services	商品销售收入 Revenue of Goods Sales
一、按登记注册类型分	**Grouped By Registered Type**					
总　计	**Total**	**894**	**2379594**	**585077**	**1644322**	**15808**
1. 内资企业	**Domestic - funded Enterprises**	**861**	**1678117**	**518062**	**1027264**	**15559**
国有企业	State - owned Enterprises	43	121360	54402	52200	689
集体企业	Collective - owned Enterprises	14	21005	14490	3419	129
股份合作企业	Cooperative Enterprises	1	2090	1297	586	32
联营企业	Joint Ownership Enterprises	1	4459	2373	1515	-
国有联营企业	State Joint Ownership Enterprises	-	-	-	-	-
集体联营企业	Collective Joint Enterprises	-	-	-	-	-
国有与集体联营企业	Joint State - collective Enterprises	1	4459	2373	1515	-
其他联营企业	Other Joint Ownership Enterprises	-	-	-	-	-
有限责任公司	Limited Liability Corporations	250	643103	253537	320085	3911
国有独资公司	State - funded Corporations	14	43300	17596	16384	288
其他有限责任公司	Other Limited Liability Corporations	236	599803	235941	303701	3623
股份有限公司	Share - holding Corporations Ltd.	9	91915	10628	75605	952
私营企业	Private Enterprises	542	793703	181135	573644	9847
私营独资企业	Private - funded Enterprises	24	14279	1765	11776	625
私营合伙企业	Private Partnership Enterprises	3	1617	-	1547	70
私营有限责任公司	Private Limited Liability Corporations	507	701329	174538	489505	9114
私营股份有限公司	Private Share - holding Corporations Ltd.	8	76478	4832	70815	38
其他企业	Other Enterprises	1	483	200	209	-

项目	Item	法人企业(个) Number of Enterprises (unit)	营业额 Revenue of Business	客房收入 Revenue of Guest Rooms	餐饮收入 Revenue of Catering Services	商品销售收入 Revenue of Goods Sales
2. 港、澳、台商投资企业	**Enterprises With Investment from Hong Kong, Macao and Taiwan**	**18**	**141874**	**42600**	**89726**	**158**
合资经营企业(港或澳、台资)	Joint－venture Enterprises (With Funds from Hong Kong, Macao and Taiwan)	9	101876	36776	56392	82
合作经营企业(港或澳、台资)	Coorperative Enterprises (With Funds from Hong Kong, Macao and Taiwan)	1	584	558	10	3
港、澳、台商独资经营企业	Enterprises With Sole Investment from Hong Kong, Macao and Taiwan	8	39413	5266	33324	73
港、澳、台商投资股份有限公司	Share－holding Corporations Ltd. With Investment from Hong Kong, Macao and Taiwan					
3. 外商投资企业	**Enterprises With Foreign Investment**	**15**	**559603**	**24414**	**527333**	**91**
中外合资经营企业	Joint－venture Enterprises	4	426646	11648	413208	－
中外合作经营企业	Cooperation Enterprises	1	4615	2881	1418	82
外资企业	Enterprises With Sole Foreign Investment	8	126948	9144	112084	4
外商投资股份有限公司	Share－holding Corporations Ltd. With Foreign Investment	2	1394	742	622	5
二、按国民经济行业分	**Grouped By Sector**					
总计	**Total**	**894**	**2379594**	**585077**	**1644322**	**15808**
1. 住宿业	**Lodging**	**417**	**1014101**	**543907**	**356196**	**4937**
旅游饭店	Restaurants for Junketing	253	836884	422598	314525	4547
一般旅馆	General Hotel	164	177216	121310	41672	390
2. 餐饮业	**Catering Services**	**477**	**1365493**	**41169**	**1288126**	**10870**
正餐服务	Dinner Services	433	763551	41169	698110	10009
快餐服务	Short Order Services	19	546641	－	537525	355
饮料及冷饮服务	Beverages and Services	14	11564	－	10822	216
其他餐饮业	Others Catering Services	11	43737	－	41669	290

8－11 分地区限额以上

The Situation of Lodging

单位:万元

地　区	Region	企业法人数(个) Number of Enterprises (unit)	营业额 Revenue of Business	客房收入 Revenue of Guest Rooms	餐饮收入 Revenue of Catering Services	主营业务收入 Main Revenue of Business
全　市	**Total**	**894**	**2379594**	**585077**	**1644322**	**2367364**
市　区	Urban District	775	2209336	511643	1559581	2198049
#上城区	Shangcheng	150	391787	114170	258507	393735
下城区	Xiacheng	101	292707	74542	202420	289620
江干区	Jianggan	81	161070	53417	88164	161559
拱墅区	Gongshu	71	118779	30796	79304	118820
西湖区	Xihu	130	688617	88005	559421	684628
高新(滨江)区	Hi－Tech(Binjiang)	33	51751	17716	32735	50809
萧山区	Xiaoshan	60	208399	40545	159906	206146
余杭区	Yuhang	49	57979	16608	34744	56923
富阳区	Fuyang	29	33459	9892	20799	32683
桐庐县	Tonglu	25	31380	13259	16642	29860
淳安县	Chun′an	46	92831	45593	40917	93308
建德市	Jiande	12	9950	1866	7495	9835
临安市	Lin′an	36	36097	12716	19687	36312

住宿餐饮业主要指标(2015 年)
and Catering by Region(2015)

(10000 yuan)

主营业务税金及附加 Business Tax and Extra Charges	销售费用 Cost of Sales	管理费用 Administration Cost	财务费用 Financil Cost	利润总额 Total Profits	从业人员平均人数(人) Average Number of Employees (person)
128345	**785259**	**533332**	**84155**	**7130**	**100961**
119476	726742	475920	70989	27172	92614
21144	136487	92564	24076	8970	14625
16158	127295	57610	7819	-7496	12124
8878	51246	46411	2005	1418	5255
6602	43147	25423	2760	-1749	4662
37270	190062	109073	8051	47240	30040
2924	12512	12928	1857	1608	2246
10618	77313	32524	16054	-6398	10955
3140	14672	19872	1914	-8390	3532
1664	8370	12144	5417	-6213	2192
1715	11565	9695	3799	-3755	1796
4790	34016	33462	6529	-11240	4044
523	3343	1976	840	-1529	652
1842	9592	12279	1998	-3518	1855

8-12 个体工商业登记注册情况(2015年末)
Statistics of Individual Owned Business(End of 2015)

项 目	Item	全市 Whole City		市区 Urban District	
		合计 Total	#城镇 Urban	合计 Total	#城镇 Urban
户数(户)	**Number of Households (household)**	**386127**	**277061**	**301802**	**231232**
农、林、牧、渔业	Farming, Forestry, Animal Husbandry and Fishery	6329	2205	4469	1693
农、林、牧、渔服务业	Service for Farming, Forestry, Animal Husbandry and Fishery	325	140	216	109
采矿业	Mining and Quarrying	51	10	20	2
开采辅助活动	Support Activity for Mining and Quarrying				
制造业	Manufacturing	19015	6634	11839	4091
金属制品、机械和设备修理业	Metal Products, Machinery and Equipment Repair	92	36	55	24
电力、热力、燃气及水的生产和供应业	Production and Supply of Electricity, Gas and Water	52	27	18	10
建筑业	Construction	1160	575	888	424
批发和零售业	Wholesale and Retail Trade & Catering Services	260181	192880	208546	164601
交通运输、仓储和邮政业	Transportation, Storage and Post	6546	3695	4917	2884
住宿和餐饮业	Lodging and Catering	43845	34088	32804	27385
信息传输、软件和信息技术服务业	Information Transmission, Computer Services and Software	717	574	520	451
金融业	Banking and Insurance				
房地产业	Real Estate	118	108	94	90
租赁和商务服务业	Renting and Business Service	5019	3654	3873	2864
科学研究和技术服务业	Scientific Research and Technical Service	1149	905	897	732
水利、环境和公共设施管理业	Water Conservancy, Environment and Public Utility	51	32	42	24
居民服务、修理和其他服务业	Service for the Residents and Other Service Sector	39514	29784	31158	24529
教育	Education	358	291	288	242
卫生和社会工作	Health Care, Sports & Social Welfare	494	349	255	190
文化、体育和娱乐业	Culture, Sports and Entertainment	1524	1247	1171	1017
其他	Others	4	3	3	3

8－12　续表1　continued 1

项　　目	Item	全　市 Whole City		市　区 Urban District	
		合　计 Total	#城　镇 Urban	合　计 Total	#城　镇 Urban
从业人员(人)	**Employed Persons(person)**	**794455**	**569194**	**599180**	**462577**
农、林、牧、渔业	Farming, Forestry, Animal Husbandry and Fishery	16981	5118	10495	3331
农、林、牧、渔服务业	Service for Farming, Forestry, Animal Husbandry and Fishery	836	351	478	241
采矿业	Mining and Quarrying	288	47	99	9
开采辅助活动	Support Activity for Mining and Quarrying				
制造业	Manufacturing	70333	21546	32977	9442
金属制品、机械和设备修理业	Metal Products, Machinery and Equipment Repair	219	79	133	53
电力、热力、燃气及水的生产和供应业	Production and Supply of Electricity, Gas and Water	101	58	22	13
建筑业	Construction	4304	1497	3097	930
批发和零售业	Wholesale and Retail Trade & Catering Services	424822	317576	336007	266496
交通运输、仓储和邮政业	Transportation, Storage and Post	10363	5884	7276	4359
住宿和餐饮业	Lodging and Catering	116177	94216	86184	73960
信息传输、软件和信息技术服务业	Information Transmission, Computer Services and Software	1406	1155	1045	924
金融业	Banking and Insurance				
房地产业	Real Estate	196	178	159	151
租赁和商务服务业	Renting and Business Service	42819	40068	39888	38009
科学研究和技术服务业	Scientific Research and Technical Service	2498	2093	1802	1555
水利、环境和公共设施管理业	Water Conservancy, Environment and Public Utility	153	74	123	45
居民服务、修理和其他服务业	Service for the Residents and Other Service Sector	96764	74012	74944	59064
教育	Education	1115	883	839	745
卫生和社会工作	Health Care, Sports & Social Welfare	1221	877	693	527
文化、体育和娱乐业	Culture, Sports and Entertainment	4907	3906	3524	3011
其他	Others	7	6	6	6

8－12 续表2 continued 2

项 目	Item	全 市 Whole City		市 区 Urban District	
		合 计 Total	#城 镇 Urban	合 计 Total	#城 镇 Urban
注册资金(万元)	**Capital Registered(10000 yuan)**	**3330334**	**2357020**	**2383398**	**1836131**
农、林、牧、渔业	Farming, Forestry, Animal Husbandry and Fishery	302269	168849	219818	144993
农、林、牧、渔服务业	Service for Farming, Forestry, Animal Husbandry and Fishery	8169	3884	5881	3473
采矿业	Mining and Quarrying	3210	606	537	101
开采辅助活动	Support Activity for Mining and Quarrying				
制造业	Manufacturing	210477	73814	99418	34823
金属制品、机械和设备修理业	Metal Products, Machinery and Equipment Repair	867	387	512	270
电力、热力、燃气及水的生产和供应业	Production and Supply of Electricity, Gas and Water	232	111	75	53
建筑业	Construction	26634	8546	21470	5986
批发和零售业	Wholesale and Retail Trade & Catering Services	1724466	1319244	1295472	1055430
交通运输、仓储和邮政业	Transportation, Storage and Post	79567	49898	59596	40781
住宿和餐饮业	Lodging and Catering	534109	408671	347958	302842
信息传输、软件和信息技术服务业	Information Transmission, Computer Services and Software	4461	3509	3075	2619
金融业	Banking and Insurance				
房地产业	Real Estate	299	241	238	192
租赁和商务服务业	Renting and Business Service	64636	39810	44480	28792
科学研究和技术服务业	Scientific Research and Technical Service	7604	6533	5450	4734
水利、环境和公共设施管理业	Water Conservancy, Environment and Public Utility	477	358	369	252
居民服务、修理和其他服务业	Service for the Residents and Other Service Sector	331709	243415	256497	189275
教育	Education	3488	2221	2117	1802
卫生和社会工作	Health Care, Sports & Social Welfare	7170	5608	3993	3355
文化、体育和娱乐业	Culture, Sports and Entertainment	29522	25583	22832	20098
其他	Others	4	3	3	3

8－13 私营企业登记注册情况（2015 年末）
Statistics of Private Owned Business（End of 2015）

项　　目	Item	全　市 Whole City		市　区 Urban District	
		合 计 Total	#城 镇 Urban	合 计 Total	#城 镇 Urban
户数(户)	**Number of Households (household)**	**334732**	**257937**	**301461**	**242213**
农、林、牧、渔业	Farming, Forestry, Animal Husbandry and Fishery	5949	2285	3705	1606
农、林、牧、渔服务业	Service for Farming, Forestry, Animal Husbandry and Fishery	868	430	679	372
采矿业	Mining and Quarrying	164	37	69	16
开采辅助活动	Support Activity for Mining and Quarrying	3	2	2	2
制造业	Manufacturing	47379	16855	36628	13847
金属制品、机械和设备修理业	Metal Products, Machinery and Equipment Repair	182	129	169	122
电力、热力、燃气及水的生产和供应业	Production and Supply of Electricity, Gas and Water	452	137	162	81
建筑业	Construction	16378	12318	14985	11514
批发和零售业	Wholesale and Retail Trade & Catering Services	120911	99631	110543	93931
交通运输、仓储和邮政业	Transportation, Storage and Post	4830	3397	4125	2976
住宿和餐饮业	Lodging and Catering	5372	4177	4690	3766
信息传输、软件和信息技术服务业	Information Transmission, Computer Services and Software	22587	20867	21834	20319
金融业	Banking and Insurance	2811	2367	2561	2216
房地产业	Real Estate	6993	5574	6149	5004
租赁和商务服务业	Renting and Business Service	49034	44603	46952	43089
科学研究和技术服务业	Scientific Research and Technical Service	28330	26239	27342	25598
水利、环境和公共设施管理业	Water Conservancy, Environment and Public Utility	858	594	662	487
居民服务、修理和其他服务业	Service for the Residents and Other Service Sector	15339	12240	14240	11538
教育	Education	1271	1155	1190	1091
卫生和社会工作	Health Care, Sports & Social Welfare	735	524	668	477
文化、体育和娱乐业	Culture, Sports and Entertainment	5318	4918	4937	4640
其他	Others	21	19	19	17

8－13 续表1 continued 1

项　目	Item	全　市 Whole City 合　计 Total	全　市 Whole City #城　镇 Urban	市　区 Urban District 合　计 Total	市　区 Urban District #城　镇 Urban
从业人员(人)	**Employed Persons(person)**	**2587449**	**1631366**	**2305783**	**1517491**
农、林、牧、渔业	Farming,Forestry,Animal Husbandry and Fishery	34770	13089	20321	8672
农、林、牧、渔服务业	Service for Farming, Forestry, Animal Husbandry and Fishery	4772	2376	3623	1960
采矿业	Mining and Quarrying	2567	570	1194	154
开采辅助活动	Support Activity for Mining and Quarrying	25	22	22	22
制造业	Manufacturing	462282	140272	319677	110064
金属制品、机械和设备修理业	Metal Products,Machinery and Equipment Repair	1133	722	1049	679
电力、热力、燃气及水的生产和供应业	Production and Supply of Electricity,Gas and Water	3416	1095	1415	625
建筑业	Construction	128118	82684	116371	75429
批发和零售业	Wholesale and Retail Trade & Catering Services	863109	549452	813487	519412
交通运输、仓储和邮政业	Transportation,Storage and Post	34828	21635	28131	16769
住宿和餐饮业	Lodging and Catering	42091	33433	36841	29709
信息传输、软件和信息技术服务业	Information Transmission, Computer Services and Software	170470	139428	165977	136010
金融业	Banking and Insurance	24008	19499	21236	17805
房地产业	Real Estate	50248	39943	44195	35362
租赁和商务服务业	Renting and Business Service	396984	297490	383363	287142
科学研究和技术服务业	Scientific Research and Technical Service	212932	171249	204085	166804
水利、环境和公共设施管理业	Water Conservancy, Environment and Public Utility	5866	3982	4679	3397
居民服务、修理和其他服务业	Service for the Residents and Other Service Sector	100396	71001	93592	66619
教育	Education	8529	7302	7924	6781
卫生和社会工作	Health Care, Sports & Social Welfare	4076	3341	3635	3024
文化、体育和娱乐业	Culture,Sports and Entertainment	42644	35793	39553	33613
其他	Others	115	108	107	100

8－13 续表2 continued 2

项 目	Item	全市 Whole City		市区 Urban District	
		合计 Total	#城镇 Urban	合计 Total	#城镇 Urban
注册资金(万元)	**Capital Registered(10000 yuan)**	**150653768**	**125728231**	**138656271**	**118347323**
农、林、牧、渔业	Farming, Forestry, Animal Husbandry and Fishery	1603505	696985	886232	421380
农、林、牧、渔服务业	Service for Farming, Forestry, Animal Husbandry and Fishery	340736	190759	237873	121350
采矿业	Mining and Quarrying	150708	61115	89780	35010
开采辅助活动	Support Activity for Mining and Quarrying	21500	21000	21000	21000
制造业	Manufacturing	17754416	7024740	14748172	5888740
金属制品、机械和设备修理业	Metal Products, Machinery and Equipment Repair	55971	45582	49788	44232
电力、热力、燃气及水的生产和供应业	Production and Supply of Electricity, Gas and Water	299522	173057	202542	137182
建筑业	Construction	9657154	7917860	8736627	7234502
批发和零售业	Wholesale and Retail Trade & Catering Services	27557521	23953869	25764246	22781123
交通运输、仓储和邮政业	Transportation, Storage and Post	1488399	1062784	1232216	891901
住宿和餐饮业	Lodging and Catering	1050998	806719	832156	707549
信息传输、软件和信息技术服务业	Information Transmission, Computer Services and Software	9314002	8331917	8871169	7962753
金融业	Banking and Insurance	7141487	6796402	6518983	6323979
房地产业	Real Estate	10417170	8867719	9452644	8132425
租赁和商务服务业	Renting and Business Service	45970024	43551445	44280183	42114697
科学研究和技术服务业	Scientific Research and Technical Service	11713480	10751510	11040114	10336780
水利、环境和公共设施管理业	Water Conservancy, Environment and Public Utility	558193	444760	438514	373907
居民服务、修理和其他服务业	Service for the Residents and Other Service Sector	4107704	3544503	3860157	3371874
教育	Education	128118	96079	101369	92076
卫生和社会工作	Health Care, Sports & Social Welfare	236243	219040	189763	188173
文化、体育和娱乐业	Culture, Sports and Entertainment	1492620	1418233	1399410	1344288
其他	Others	12504	9494	11994	8984

主要统计指标解释

社会消费品零售额 指各种经济类型的批发零售贸易业、住宿餐饮业对城乡居民和社会集团的消费品零售额总和。这个指标反映通过各种商品流通渠道向居民和社会集团供应的生活消费品来满足他们生活需要，是研究人民生活、社会消费品购买力、货币流通等问题的重要指标。社会消费品零售额包括：(1)售给城乡居民作为生活用的商品和修建房屋用的建筑材料；(2)售给机关、团体、学校、部队、企业、事业单位的职工食堂各种食品、燃料；(3)售给部队干部、战士生活用的粮食、副食品、衣着品、日用品、燃料；(4)售给来华的外国人、华侨、港澳台同胞的消费品；(5)售给社会集团的办公用品、纸张、帐册、文印用品、计算工具、书刊杂志和奖品；公共用品和纺织品、针织品；学校用的教学用具；文体用品；非专用的劳动保护用品，如工作服、套袖、围裙、手套、毛巾、肥皂等；日用百货和杂品，包括职工食堂用的餐具、炊具、设备和清洁卫生工具等；家具、设备、日用电器、电讯设备、电影器材和照相器材等；取暖用的设备和燃料、防暑、降温的饮料；非生产经营用的交通工具，如小轿车、面包车、工具车、卡车和油料；零星修理的各种零配件、材料、工具、建筑材料等；举办各种招待会、茶话会、宴会用的烟酒茶和各种食品及馈赠的礼品；从公费医疗经费中开支的中、西药品、中药材和医疗器材以及其他非生产性设备和用品。

限额以上批发零售业 指批发业年主营业务收入在2000万元及以上，零售业年主营业务收入在500万元及以上的各种经济类型商贸企业。

商品销售总额 指对本企业(单位)以外的单位和个人出售(包括对国(境)外直接出口)的商品金额。这个指标反映批发零售贸易业在国内市场上销售商品以及出口商品的总量。商品销售总额包括：(1)售给城乡居民和社会集团消费用的商品；(2)售给工业、农业、建筑业、运输邮电业、批发零售贸易业、餐饮业、服务业等作为生产、经营使用的商品；(3)售给批发零售贸易业作为转卖或加工后转卖的商品；(4)对国(境)外直接出口的商品，不包括：出售本企业(单位)自用的废旧包装用品，未通过买卖行为付出的商品，经本单位介绍，由买卖双方直接结算，本单位只收取手续费的业务，购货退出的商品以及商品损耗和损失等。

Explanatory Notes on Main Statistical Indicators

Total Retail Sales of Consumer Goods referring to the sum of retail sales of consumer goods sold by wholesale and retail, catering and lodging to urban and rural residents and social groups. This indicator is used to show the supply of consumer goods through various channels to households and institutions, and is very important for the study on people's livelihood, on the purchasing power of consumer goods and on the circulation of money. The retail sales of consumer goods include: (1) commodities sold to urban and rural residents for their daily use and building materials sold to them for the construction or repair of houses; (2) food and fuels sold to canteens of institutions, enterprises, schools and military units; (3) grains and non – staple food, clothing, daily articles and fuels sold to military personnel; (4) consumer goods sold to foreigners, overseas Chinese, and Chinese compatriots form Taiwan, Hong Kong and Macao during their stay in the mainland of China; (5) commodities sold to social groups. included under this heading are : office appliances, paper, account books, printing articles, calculaters, newspapers, magazines and prizes; public articles, textiles and knitgoods; realias for schools; cultural and sports articles; working articles for unspecial use i. e. working clothes, raglan sleeves, gloves, towels and soaps; commidities and miscellaneous goods for daily use i. e. dishwares, cookers and cleaning articles for canteens of institutions, enterprises, schools; furnishings, appliances, communications facilities , film and photograph equipments and materials; heating facilities, fuels and beverages; vehicles (exclude for business use) such as cars, microbuses, trucks and oils; parts , fittings, instruments and building materials, tobaccoes, alcohols, teas, foods for all kinds of reception meetings and banquets and prizes for presenting; Chinese and Western medicines, herbs and medical facilities expenditured by medical insurance fund and other non – production goods and equipments.

Wholesale And Retail Trade Above Designated Size wholesale trade, with year main business revenue over 20 million yuan of different status of registration; retail sale trade, with year main business revenue over 5 million yuan of different status of registration.

Total Sales of Commodities refer to selling of commodities by the establishments to other establishments and individuals (including direct export). This indictor is used to show the total value of sales of commodities at domestic markets and export. The total sales include: (1) commodities sold to urban and rural residents and social groups for their consumption; (2) commodities sold to establishments in industry, agriculture, construction, transportation, post and telecommunications, wholesale and retail trades, catering trade and public utility for their production and operation; (3) commodities sold to wholesale and retail establishment for re – selling, with or without further processing; and (4) commodities for direct export to other countries. Excluded are selling of waste packaging materials used by the establishments (units) themselves, commodities transferred without buying or selling procedures, commission income from brokerage in transactions whose settlement is directly handled by buyers and sellers, rejected commodities in the purchase, loss in commodities, etc.

Explanatory Notes on Main Statistical Indicators

[illegible]

[illegible]

[illegible]

九、对外经济旅游

FOREIGN ECONOMIC COOPERATION AND TOURISM

9 对外经济、旅游
Foreign Economic Cooperation and Tourism

主要统计指标
Major Statistical Indicators

实际利用外资金额	Foreign Investments Actually Utilized	71.13	亿美元	(USD 100 million)
为上年	As Compared with the Preceding Year	112.3	%	(%)
进出口总额	Total Imports and Exports	665.66	亿美元	(USD 100 million)
为上年	As Compared with the Preceding Year	97.9	%	(%)
# 出口总额	Total Exports	500.67	亿美元	(USD 100 million)
为上年	As Compared with the Preceding Year	101.8	%	(%)
接待境外旅游	Number of Oversea Visitor Arrivals	341.56	万人次	(10000 person-times)
为上年	As Compared with the Preceding Year	104.7	%	(%)
旅游外汇收入	Total Foreign Exchange Earnings from International Tourism	29.31	亿美元	(USD 100 million)
为上年	As Compared with the Preceding Year	107.1	%	(%)

9-01 外商直接投资情况(1978-2015年)
Foreign Direct Investment(1978-2015)

单位:万美元 (USD 10000)

年份 Year	项目个数(个) Number of Projects (unit)	协议总投资额 Total Investments of Agreements	协议利用外资金额 Contracted Foreign Investment	实际利用外资金额 Foreign Investments Actually Utilized
1978				
1979				
1980	3	153	128	
1981				
1982				
1983	2	356	100	
1984	9	6932	2697	
1985	21	6638	1731	907
1986	9	5722	2017	683
1987	10	2685	1256	1470
1988	23	6781	2734	696
1989	34	3897	1569	1860
1990	68	7817	3951	751
1991	121	11107	5551	2129
1992	583	125224	60915	9678
1993	1078	222325	121947	35713
1994	624	174406	110541	41098
1995	427	136662	90207	42659
1996	221	108150	70982	53651
1997	174	51682	27888	41187
1998	216	98219	51400	38425
1999	212	83416	56742	42025
2000	315	89781	64548	43093
2001	483	154447	103023	50324
2002	587	247888	96720	52186
2003	869	432660	200104	100850
2004	802	629727	307746	140982
2005	756	770941	400503	171274
2006	747	1080602	537986	225536
2007	574	854907	558059	280181
2008	483	862523	622788	331154
2009	554	948323	696486	401370
2010	545	1188055	770911	435627
2011	500	1291015	817108	472230
2012	510	1342616	826516	496061
2013	415	1419926	913144	527633
2014	408	1329217	723838	633460
2015	475	1649709	1038042	711253

9-02 分行业外商直接投资情况(2015年)
Foreign Direct Investment by Sector(2015)

单位:万美元　　(USD 10,000)

行 业 Sector	项目数(个) Projects (unit)	占总数 % Proportion (%)	实际利用外资金额 Foreign Investments Actually Utilized	占总数(%) Proportion (%)
合 计 Total	**475**	**100**	**711253**	**100**
第一产业 Primary Industry	**3**	**0.63**	**1005**	**0.14**
农 业 Agriculture	3	0.63	1005	0.14
第二产业 Secondary Industry	**45**	**9.47**	**190007**	**26.71**
采矿业 Mining	1	0.21	7101	1.00
制造业 Manufacturing	43	9.05	181391	25.50
电力、燃气及水的生产和供应业 Production & Supply of Electricity, Gas & Water	1	0.21	-	-
建筑业 Construction	-	-	1515	0.21
第三产业 Tertiary Industry	**427**	**89.89**	**520241**	**73.14**
交通运输、仓储、邮政业 Transportation, Storage and Post	15	3.16	10587	1.49
信息传输、计算机服务和软件业 Information Transmission, Computer Service and Software	81	17.05	94706	13.32
批发和零售贸易、餐饮业 Whole sale and Retail Tvade. Catering Services	111	23.37	50054	7.04
金融业 Banking and Insurance	16	3.37	49075	6.90
房地产业 Real Estate	14	2.95	171115	24.06
租赁及商务服务业 Renting and Business Service	101	21.26	74674	10.50
科学研究和综合技术服务业 Scientific research and Integrated Technical Service	84	17.68	62834	8.83
其他行业 Others	5	1.05	7196	1.01

9-03 分国别(地区)外商直接投资情况(2015年)

Foreign Direct Investment by Region or Territory(2015)

单位:万美元 (USD 10000)

国别(地区)	Country (territory)	历年累计 Accumulated 项目(个) Projects (unit)	总投资额 Total Investments	协议外资金额 Total Contracted Foreign Investments	2015年 In Year 2015 项目(个) Projects (unit)	总投资额 Total Investments	协议外资金额 Total Contracted Foreign Investments	实际引资 Foreign Investments Actually Utilized
合　计	**Total**	**12889**	**15351021**	**9293143**	**475**	**1649709**	**1038042**	**711253**
#香港	#Hong Kong	5611	9872552	6013569	272	1389122	780096	503873
澳门	Macao	71	71121	40453	-	-	-117	-
台湾	Taiwan	1492	389858	208297	22	1335	1543	608
日本	Japan	764	523217	238012	8	8414	4241	12546
美国	U. S. A	1640	1156326	571287	46	203118	26697	28461
新加坡	Singapore	319	499686	300926	20	77308	57196	4992
澳大利亚	Australia	184	99553	77891	6	559	13717	12943
泰国	Thailand	41	12789	3473	2	49	49	19
意大利	Italy	219	151684	67502	11	1736	1469	2501
荷兰	Netherlands	89	101730	22615	3	51	3510	11463
西班牙	Spain	70	67585	26384	3	7921	2385	-
马来西亚	Malaysia	81	41573	22817	1	26	26	39
韩国	Republic of Korea	323	104386	64030	16	9381	7106	4258
法国	France	126	72979	40664	4	2466	448	69
玻利维亚	Bolivia	12	1770	1262	-	-	-	-
加拿大	Canada	221	107967	69514	8	2606	877	1107
英国	Britain	199	190565	128257	3	323	20519	20001
奥地利	Austria	24	28800	20447	-	1889	2380	2506
波兰	Poland	4	240	147	-	-	-	-
洪都拉斯	Honduras	6	1118	563	-	-	-	-
德国	Germany	205	106774	64835	5	224	5540	10915
英属维尔京群岛	The British Virgin Islands	566	1360400	671593	14	250379	54677	20855

9－04 分地区外商直接投资情况(2015年)
Foreign Direct Investment by Region(2015)

单位:万美元 (USD 10000)

区域	Region	批准项目个数(个) Number of Projects(unit)		实际利用外资金额 Foreign Investments Actually Utilized	
		2015年 In Year 2015	历年累计 Accumulated Until the End of 2015	2015年 In Year 2015	历年累计 Accumulated Until the End of 2015
全市	**Total**	**475**	**12889**	**711253**	**5386407**
市区	Urban District	420	11496	656589	4949186
#上城	Shangcheng	36	695	24902	228770
下城	Xiacheng	28	742	31913	257513
江干	Jianggan	33	695	32529	242869
拱墅	Gongshu	32	948	39101	337761
西湖	Xihu	61	1038	79781	409270
高新(滨江)区	Hi－Tech(Binjiang)	46	1058	76615	650250
萧山	Xiaoshan	72	1649	144988	742847
余杭	Yuhang	54	1521	108620	613629
富阳	Fuyang	19	718	28212	233508
桐庐	Tonglu	25	537	18986	130340
淳安	Chun'an	5	193	3000	92946
建德	Jiande	14	249	14069	69701
临安	Lin'an	11	414	18609	144234

9-05 分地区国内招商引资情况(2014-2015年)
Domestic Investment by Region(2014-2015)

单位:亿元 (100 million yuan)

区域 Region	批准项目个数(个) Number of Projects(unit)		实际引进资金 Investments Actually Utilized	
	2015	2014	2015	2014
全市 Total	**2376**	**2187**	**1249.27**	**1054.07**
市区 Urban District	1898	1845	1100.37	927.81
#上城 Shangcheng	88	68	86.46	80.42
下城 Xiacheng	322	210	146.18	129.57
江干 Jianggan	207	147	144.39	124.32
拱墅 Gongshu	527	452	153.43	130.45
西湖 Xihu	186	423	165.36	135.76
高新(滨江)区 Hi-Tech(Binjiang)	65	62	77.91	69.67
萧山 Xiaoshan	249	157	148.35	93.3
余杭 Yuhang	121	121	101.0	71.26
富阳 Fuyang	73	72	46.69	35.52
桐庐 Tonglu	115	100	40.51	33.27
淳安 Chun'an	66	109	25.34	26.57
建德 Jiande	161	87	40.22	32.29
临安 Lin'an	136	46	42.83	34.13

注:萧山区含大江东产业集聚区,余杭含钱江开发区。

a) Date of Xianshan district includes Dajiangdong Industry Cluster District, Yuhang district includes Qianjiang Development Zone.

9－06 国家级开发区

The Construction of National－

项　目	Item	合计 Total	杭州经济技术开发区 Hangzhou Economic and Technological Development Zone
规划面积 （平方千米）	Area of planning (sq. km)	998.78	104.70
已开发面积 （平方千米）	Area of Development (sq. km)	226.18	48.48
历年累计基础设施投资额（亿元）	Accumulative Total Investments in Infrastructure (100 million yuan)	2176.35	449.49
历年累计批准进区企业（个）	Accumulative Number of Enterprises Approved (unit)	63111	12994
#三资企业 （个）	Foreign Investments Enter－prises (unit)	3045	807
历年累计协议利用外资（亿美元）	Accumulative Total Foreign Investments of Agreements (USD 100 million)	301.97	127.61
历年累计实际利用外资（亿美元）	Accumulative Total Foreign Investments Actually Used (USD 100 million)	262.22	76.14
年末实有投产企业个数（个）	Number of Enterprises in Production or Operation at the Year－end (unit)	31221	9036
#三资企业 （个）	Foreign Investments Enter－prises (unit)	1809	571
当年规模以上工业总产值（亿元）	Gross Industrial Output Value of the Year (100 million yuan)	6568.94	1798.92
当年规模以上企业主营业务收入 （亿元）	Fulfilled Profits and Tax of the Year (100 million yuan)	8974.60	2120.56
当年规模以上企业实现利润 （亿元）	Fulfilled Profits of the Enterprises above the Designated Size of the Year (100 million yuan)	573.65	145.77
当年出口创汇 （亿美元）	Foreign Exchange Earmings of Export of the Year (USD 100 million)	190.60	59.41
当年地方财政收入（亿元）	Local Financial Revenue of the Year (100 million yuan)	418.31	54.80
# 税收收入 （亿元）	Tax Revenue (unit)	338.89	50.22

建设发展情况(2015 年)
Class Development Zones(2015)

杭州高新技术开发区 Hangzhou High - tech Development Zone	杭州之江国家旅游度假区 Hangzhou Zhijiang National Tourism and Holiday Resort	萧山经济技术开发区 Xiaoshan Economic and Technological Development Zone	富阳经济技术开发区 Fuyang Economic and Technological Development Zone	余杭经济技术开发区 Yuhang Economic and Technological Development Zone	临江国家高新区 Linjiang National High - Tech Zone
12.64	156.00	96.60	126.10	75.74	427.00
12.64	13.77	24.70	24.09	32.50	70.00
282.35	280.00	184.83	407.14	487.54	85.00
23519	127	5188	7806	12694	783
502	95	652	496	261	232
–	–	76.57	27.02	32.86	37.91
66.34	18.90	39.07	18.58	23.35	19.84
2631	7	4211	5266	9674	396
502	–	199	163	299	75
1183.38	49.61	533.49	1060.99	891.30	1051.25
1308.01	6.35	1040.47	1693.78	1625.30	1180.13
200.47	2.39	52.54	62.49	54.70	55.29
50.79	–	19.92	13.45	35.60	11.43
108.46	12.81	51.55	68.26	104.10	18.33
101.50	–	51.55	49.81	68.60	17.21

9-07 省级产业集聚区建设发展情况

Development Statistics on Provincial-level Industry Cluster Districts

项目	Item	大江东产业集聚区 Dajiangdong Industry Cluster District		城西科创产业集聚区 Chengxi Technological and Creative Industry Cluster District	
		2014 年末 End of 2014	2015 年末 End of 2015	2014 年末 End of 2014	2015 年末 End of 2015
入区企业数(个)	Proposed Enterprises (unit)	752	812	3554	5413
投产企业数(个)	Operating Enterprises (unit)	115	250	481	482
已开发建设面积(平方千米)	Land Space under Construction (sq. km)	20.57	23.88	33.20	36.12
已建成投产面积(平方千米)	Land Space Completed (sq. km)	18.70	22.69	20.96	24.73
当年产业增加值(亿元)	Current year's Value-added (100 million yuan)	87.37	142.33	500.18	578.61
#工业增加值(亿元)	Value-added of Industry (100 million yuan)	70.00	116	87.00	92
#服务业增加值(亿元)	Value-added of the Tertiary Industry (100 million yuan)	2.18	3.22	392.48	486.6
当年实际引进内资(亿元)	Current Year's Amount of Domestic Investment (100 million yuan)	45.92	57.45	59.61	73.94
当年实际到位外资(亿美元)	Current Year's Amount of Foreign Investment Actually Utilized (100 million USD)	5.12	5.94	4.15	4.16
当年科技活动经费支出(亿元)	Current Year's S & T Expenditure (100 million yuan)	6.94	10.54	15.99	17.86
科技活动人员数(人)	S & T Personnel (person)	2673	3044	7193	6919
当年财政预算总收入(亿元)	Current Year's Total Financial Revenue (100 million yuan)	35.52	51.23	104.41	127.56
当年固定资产投资完成额(亿元)	Current Year's Investment in Fixed Asset's (100 million yuan)	178.61	210.73	236.28	296.26
当年工业总产值(亿元)	Current Year's Gross Industrial Output Value (100 million yuan)	411.96	629.63	475.97	475.21
当年服务业营业收入(亿元)	Current Year's Operating Revenue of the Tertiary Industry (100 million yuan)	62.26	154.32	969.70	1483.50
当年出口交货值(亿元)	Current Year's Export Delivery Value (100 million yuan)	42.13	39.77	71.10	68.23
当年利税总额(亿元)	Current Year's Total Taxes and Profits (100 million yuan)	29.57	56.11	436.96	481.47
#利润总额(亿元)	Total Profits (100 million yuan)	15.55	31.94	407.81	457.19

9-08 进出口情况(1989-2015年)
Imports and Exports (1989-2015)

单位:亿美元 (USD 100 million)

年份 Year	进出口 Exports And Imports		出口 Exports		进口 Imports	
	总值 Total Value	为上年% As Compared with the Preceding Year(%)	总值 Total Value	为上年% As Compared with the Preceding Year(%)	总值 Total Value	为上年% As Compared with the Preceding Year(%)
1989	0.84		0.50		0.34	
1990	1.45	172.6	0.99	198.0	0.46	135.3
1991	2.18	150.3	1.48	149.5	0.70	152.2
1992	3.42	156.9	2.16	146.0	1.26	180.0
1993	8.73	255.3	4.92	227.8	3.81	302.4
1994	34.96	400.5	26.11	530.7	8.85	232.3
1995	45.18	129.2	33.18	127.1	12.00	135.6
1996	43.52	96.3	31.11	93.8	12.41	103.4
1997	48.83	112.2	37.43	120.3	11.40	91.8
1998	59.73	122.3	44.16	118.0	15.57	136.6
1999	73.40	122.9	50.79	115.0	22.61	145.3
2000	104.76	142.7	69.65	137.1	35.11	155.3
2001	112.98	107.9	72.84	104.6	40.14	114.3
2002	131.07	116.0	84.81	116.4	46.26	115.3
2003	182.38	139.2	109.55	129.2	72.83	157.4
2004	244.97	134.3	151.75	138.6	93.21	128.0
2005	298.70	121.9	198.04	130.5	100.66	108.0
2006	389.09	130.3	262.28	132.4	126.81	126.0
2007	434.27	111.7	299.66	114.3	134.60	106.2
2008	480.65	110.7	336.14	112.2	144.51	107.4
2009	404.20	84.1	271.80	80.9	132.40	91.6
2010	523.55	129.5	353.37	130.0	170.18	128.6
2011	639.72	122.2	415.21	117.5	224.50	131.9
2012	616.83	96.4	412.62	99.4	204.22	91.0
2013	650.71	105.5	447.66	108.5	203.05	99.5
2014	679.98	104.5	491.66	109.8	188.32	92.8
2015	665.66	97.9	500.67	101.8	165.00	87.7

9－09 分经济类型进出口情况（2014－2015年）
Imports and Exports by Status of Registration（2014－2015）

单位：亿美元 （USD 100 million）

项　　目	Item	2015年 In Year 2015	2014年 In Year 2014	为上年(%) As Compared with year 2014（%）
全市进出口总值(海关口径)	Total Exports And Imports	665.66	679.98	97.9
一、出口总额	Exports	500.67	491.66	101.8
1.国有企业	State－owned Enterprises	76.23	80.65	94.5
2.三资企业	Foreign Investment Enterprises	124.78	138.21	90.3
（1）中外合作企业	Cooperation Enterprises	0.61	0.64	94.8
（2）中外合资企业	Joint－Venture Enterprises	59.77	65.36	91.5
（3）外商独资企业	Enterprises With Sole Foreign Investment	64.40	72.21	89.2
3.集体企业	Collective－owned Enterprises	18.49	20.40	90.6
4.私营企业	Private Enterprises	280.75	251.32	111.7
二、进口总额	Imports	165.00	188.32	87.7

9－10　分地区外贸进出口情况(2015 年)
Imports and Exports by Region(2015)

单位:万美元　　　　(USD 10000)

区　域　Region		出口总值 Exports of This Year	为上年(%) As Compared with the Preceding Year(%)	进口总值 Imports of This Year	为上年(%) As Compared with the Preceding Year(%)
全市合计	**Total**	**5006678**	**101.8**	**1649958**	**87.7**
#不含省属	#Non－provincial	4446487	104.0	1487460	87.6
#上　城	Shangcheng	117237	78.3	81650	70.5
下　城	Xiacheng	226846	111.6	91933	73.3
江　干	Jianggan	191895	100.4	19967	53.5
拱　墅	Gongshu	165834	113.3	34218	83.9
西　湖	Xihu	233970	108.4	76595	85.6
高新(滨江)区	Hi－Tech(Binjiang)	507882	108.6	140015	112.9
萧　山	Xiaoshan	916321	91.6	272718	70.8
余　杭	Yuhang	499847	89.5	37558	86.4
富　阳	Fuyang	151073	110.5	134467	91.9
桐　庐	Tonglu	140497	111.6	6830	91.1
淳　安	Chun'an	18040	87.6	2774	87.0
建　德	Jiande	94713	109.4	6252	82.1
临　安	Lin'an	175282	111.5	33868	93.3

9-11 分地区外贸进出口总值(2004-2015 年)
Imports and Exports by Region(2004-2015)

单位:万美元 (USD 10000)

年份 Year	全市 Whole City	市区 Urban District 合计 Total	#萧山区 Xiaoshan	#余杭区 Yuhang	#富阳区 Fuyang	桐庐县 Tonglu	淳安县 Chun'an	建德市 Jiande	临安市 Lin'an
2004	2449671	2364434	414374	88538	52399	32333	4461	19525	28918
2005	2986993	2892191	510950	128999	72357	30489	5211	25841	33262
2006	3890853	3769910	610201	183930	81616	38522	6797	34132	41492
2007	4342666	4181699	795487	255534	105765	48811	8319	48295	55542
2008	4806503	4545719	953377	324421	126829	71753	12478	101692	74862
2009	4041991	3821965	829827	285496	116158	60064	12039	77470	70454
2010	5235549	4946409	1135326	385736	166652	73919	17183	96651	101387
2011	6397180	6044765	1432742	484903	216575	93464	20459	105763	132729
2012	6168325	5814547	1367290	512531	224446	103153	21604	86681	142340
2013	6507102	6115754	1408929	555640	265788	119539	19692	87023	165094
2014	6799775	6355378	1384823	601220	284980	133392	23802	94202	193001
2015	6656636	6178381	1189039	537405	285540	147326	20814	100965	209150

9－12 出口企业前20位排名(2015年)
The List of Top Twenty Export Enterprises(2015)

单位:万美元 (USD 10000)

企业名称	Name of Enterprises	位次 Ranks	出口额 Export Value
浙江一达通企业服务有限公司	Zhejiang One Touch Business Service Ltd.	1	239276
杭州海康威视数字技术股份有限公司	Hangzhou Hikvision Digital Technology Co.,Ltd.	2	97059
中策橡胶集团有限公司	Zhongce Rubber Group Co. Ltd.	3	91179
东芝信息机器(杭州)有限公司	Toshiba Information Equipment (Hangzhou) Co., Ltd.	4	84179
杭州华三通信技术有限公司	H3C	5	81480
杭州巨星科技股份有限公司	Hangzhou Greatstar Industrial Co.,Ltd.	6	48587
浙江大华科技有限公司	Zhejiang Dahua Technology Co.,Ltd.	7	47632
杭州美巢进出口有限公司	Hangzhou Meichao Import & Export Co.,Ltd.	8	47361
浙江物产国际贸易有限公司	Zhejiang Materials Industry International Co.,Ltd.	9	39833
浙江正泰太阳能科技有限公司	Zhejiang Astronergy Solar Energy Technology Co.,Ltd	10	36779
杭州融易通企业服务有限公司	Hangzhou Ueasy Business Service Ltd.	11	34253
杭州意年进出口有限公司	Hangzhou Yinian Import & Export Co.,Ltd.	12	33561
杭州市轻工工艺纺织品进出口有限公司	Hangzhou Hardicrafts and Textiles Import and Export Corporation	13	32320
杭州库豆进出口有限公司	Hangzhou Icooder Import & Export Co.,Ltd.	14	28616
博世电动工具(中国)有限公司	Bosch Power Tools(China) Co.,Ltd	15	26828
西子奥的斯电梯有限公司	XiZi Otis Elevator Co.,Ltd.	16	26004
浙江恒逸石化有限公司	Zhejiang Hengyi Petrochemical Co.,Ltd.	17	23670
杭州杭丝时装进出口有限公司	Hangzhou Hangsi Fashionable Dress Export & Import Co.,Ltd.	18	22211
杭州鼎胜进出口有限公司	Hangzhou Dingsheng Import & Export Co.,Ltd.	19	22035
杭州群涵贸易有限公司	Hangzhou Qunhan Trade Co.,Ltd.	20	21739

9－13 外贸出口分国别(地区)情况(2014－2015 年)

Export of Foreign Trade by Main Countries or Regions(2014－2015)

单位:万美元 (USD 10000)

国别(地区)	Country (territory)	2015 年 In Year 2015	2014 年 In Year 2014	为上年(%) As Compared with the Preceding Year(%)
合　计	**Total**	**5006678**	**4916563**	**101.8**
#香港	#Hong Kong	98559	89263	110.4
台湾	Taiwan	54054	51843	104.3
德国	Germany	208087	237396	87.7
日本	Japan	316117	356463	88.7
美国	U.S.A	1009839	949720	106.3
新加坡	Singapore	61402	72517	84.7
澳大利亚	Australia	109283	100553	108.7
泰国	Thailand	86037	64210	134.0
意大利	Italy	108995	111263	98.0
荷兰	Netherlands	151305	165542	91.4
西班牙	Spain	84852	78633	107.9
马来西亚	Malaysia	67866	70431	96.3
韩国	Republic of Korea	123095	112995	108.9
法国	France	105441	102886	102.5
比利时	Belgium	52951	53529	98.9
加拿大	Canada	91174	86209	105.8
英国	Britain	199284	182381	109.3
印度尼西亚	Indonesia	85897	101260	84.8
丹麦	Denmark	34078	31109	109.6
俄罗斯	Russia	94893	125935	75.4
一带一路国家	One Belt and One Road Countries	1564165	1522786	102.7

9－14 旅游发展情况(1978－2015年)
Development of Tourism(1978－2015)

年份 Year	旅游总收入 (亿元) Total Tourism Revenue (100 million yuan)	国内旅游收入 (亿元) Domestic Earnings (100 million yuan)	旅游外汇收入 (亿美元) Foreign Exchange Earnings from International Tourism (USD 100 million)	旅游总人数 (万人次) Total Tourists (10000 person－times)	国内游客人数 (万人次) Domestic Tourists (10000 person－times)
1978			0.07		
1979			0.10		
1980			0.11		
1981			0.13		
1982			0.13		
1983			0.14		
1984			0.15		
1985			0.23		
1986			0.36		
1987			0.38		
1988			0.47		
1989			0.23		
1990			0.48		
1991			0.66		
1992			0.86		
1993			0.80		
1994			1.01		
1995	106.0	94.3	1.45	2148	2104
1996	136.5	122.6	1.67	2055	2009
1997	158.8	142.1	2.01	2150	2100
1998	163.4	146.0	2.10	2172	2121
1999	186.0	166.7	2.37	2266	2207
2000	214.3	190.0	2.92	2376	2305
2001	249.7	218.9	3.37	2592	2510
2002	294.4	254.8	4.77	2758	2652
2003	325.9	290.9	4.22	2862	2776
2004	410.1	361.2	5.97	3139	3016
2005	465.1	403.6	7.58	3417	3266
2006	543.7	471.2	9.09	3864	3682
2007	630.1	548.6	11.19	4320	4112
2008	707.2	617.2	12.96	4773	4552
2009	803.1	708.9	13.80	5324	5094
2010	1025.7	910.9	16.90	6581	6305
2011	1191.0	1063.8	19.60	7487	7181
2012	1392.3	1253.2	22.02	8568	8237
2013	1603.7	1469.9	21.60	9725	9409
2014	1886.3	1743.9	23.18	10933	10606
2015	2200.7	2019.7	29.31	12382	12040

9－15 境外旅游者人数(1978－2015年)
Number of International Tourists (1978－2015)

单位:人次 (person－times)

年份 Year	合计 Total	外国人 Foreigners	港澳台同胞 Compatriots from Hong Kong, Macao and Taiwan	平均逗留天数 Average days of Staying
1978	53475	728	26648	
1979	84914	44714	39131	2.59
1980	124960	61710	61382	2.70
1981	154745	87727	65014	2.71
1982	152897	89100	61314	2.49
1983	160564	97803	59625	2.18
1984	179200	105771	70915	2.12
1985	238385	156311	75063	2.18
1986	266370	170960	87092	2.38
1987	300603	183477	100078	2.38
1988	349246	149512	159745	2.08
1989	248502	66094	163589	2.08
1990	388345	86621	268131	2.09
1991	390197	136809	229690	2.00
1992	489578	183781	267256	2.03
1993	459620	199796	234640	2.06
1994	337362	201692	124346	2.10
1995	441262	249418	177236	2.06
1996	462313	273477	178845	2.07
1997	504276	288949	205267	2.20
1998	507243	261353	231609	2.20
1999	591853	324625	257978	2.09
2000	707148	400906	306242	2.15
2001	819438	447689	371749	2.41
2002	1056266	631576	424690	2.50
2003	861163	482073	379090	2.72
2004	1234063	791616	442447	2.59
2005	1513585	1020840	492745	2.63
2006	1820171	1236792	583379	2.57
2007	2085997	1453650	632347	2.67
2008	2213329	1543665	669654	2.73
2009	2304045	1572838	731207	2.87
2010	2757147	1878528	878619	2.94
2011	3063140	2108263	954877	2.96
2012	3311225	2298763	1012462	2.95
2013	3160058	2198187	961871	2.93
2014	3261337	2254866	1006471	2.93
2015	3415619	2378461	1037158	2.99

注:从1995年起为全市数。

a) Data in this table has included the tourists of whole municipality since 1995.

9－16　接待境外游客及居民出境旅游情况(2014－2015 年)

Number of International Tourists and Outbound Tourists(2014－2015)

项　　目	Item	2015 年 In Year 2015	2014 年 In Year 2014	为上年(％) As Compared with the preceding year(％)
一、接待境外游客	**International Tourists**			
全年接待人数(人次)	**Number of Foreign Tourists(person－times)**	**3415619**	**3261337**	**104.7**
#外国人	#Foreigners	2378461	2254866	105.5
港澳台同胞	Compatriots From Hong Kong, Macao and Taiwan	1037158	1006471	103.1
全年接待人天数(人天)	**Total Person－days (person－days)**	**10236003**	**9558344**	**107.1**
#外国人	#Foreigners	7428277	6803791	109.2
港澳台同胞	Compatriots From Hong Kong, Macao and Taiwan	2807726	2754553	101.9
平均逗留天数(天)	**Average Days of Staying (days)**	**2.99**	**2.93**	**102.1**
#外国人	#Foreigners	3.12	3.02	103.3
港澳台同胞	Compatriots From Hong Kong, Macao and Taiwan	2.71	2.74	98.9
旅游外汇总收入(万美元)	**Total Foreign Exchange Earnings From International Tourism (USD 10000)**	**293065**	**231811**	**107.1**
二、居民出境旅游	**Outbound Tourism**			
居民出境旅游人数(人次)	**Outbound Tourists(Person－time)**	**1507250**	**1191519**	**126.5**

注:2015 年旅游外汇总收入统计口径调整,同比增速按可比口径计算。

a) Since 2015, the date of the total foreign exchange earnings from international tourism were adjusted, the growth rate were calculated at comparable prices.

9-17 接待境外游客分国别(地区)情况(2014-2015年)

Number of International Tourists by Country or Territory(2014-2015)

单位:人次 (person-times)

国别(地区)	Country (territory)	2015年 In Year 2015	2014年 In Year 2014	为上年(%) As Compared with the Preceding Year(%)
合 计	**Total**	**3415619**	**3261337**	**104.7**
#香港	#Hong Kong	390266	378925	103.0
澳门	Macao	58740	55062	106.7
台湾	Taiwan	588152	572484	102.7
日本	Japan	210743	216557	97.3
美国	U.S.A	224628	213382	105.3
新加坡	Singapore	98497	89368	110.2
澳大利亚	Australia	45001	41759	107.8
泰国	Thailand	89702	81501	110.1
意大利	Italy	29284	27393	106.9
荷兰	Netherlands	24213	23323	103.8
西班牙	Spain	20748	20179	102.8
马来西亚	Malaysia	100186	99493	100.7
韩国	Republic of Korea	626821	586160	106.9
法国	France	57114	54409	105.0
德国	Germany	74287	73030	101.7
加拿大	Canada	44039	41235	106.8
英国	Britain	62545	58354	107.2
印度尼西亚	Indonesia	26888	27527	97.7
印度	India	29247	28329	103.2
菲律宾	Filipine	17145	11239	152.6

主要统计指标解释

利用外资　指我市政府部门，企业和其他经济组织通过对外借款，吸收外商直接投资以及用其他方式筹措的境外现汇、设备、技术等。

外商直接投资　是指外国企业和经济组织或个人（包括华侨、港澳台胞以及我国在境外注册的企业）按我国有关政策、法规，用现汇、实物、技术等在我市境内开办外商独资企业、与我市境内的企业或经济组织共同举办中外合资经营企业、合作经营企业或者合作开发资源的投资（包括外商投资收益的再投资）以及经政府有关部门批准的项目投资总额内，企业从境外借入的资金。

进出口总额　海关进出口总额指实际进出我国国境的货物总金额。包括对外贸易实际进出口货物，来料加工装配进出口货物，国家间、联合国及国际组织无偿援助物资和赠送品，华侨、港澳台同胞和外籍华人捐赠品，租赁期满归承租人所有的租赁货物，进料加工进出口货物，边境地方贸易及边境地区小额贸易进出口货物（边民互市贸易除外），中外合资经营企业、中外合作经营企业、外商独资经营企业进出口货物和公用物品，到、离岸价格在规定限额以上的进出口货样和广告品（无商业价值、无使用价值和免费提供出口的除外），从保税仓库提取在中国境内销售的进口货物，以及其他进出口货物。进出口总额以观察一个国家在对外贸易方面的总规模。我国规定出口货物按离岸价格统计，进口货物按到岸价格统计。

境外旅游者人数　指来我市参观、访问、旅行、探亲、访友、休养、考察、参加会议和从事经济、科技、文化、教育、体育、宗教等活动的外国人、华侨、港澳和台湾同胞的人数。不包括外国在我市的常驻机构，如使领馆、通讯社、企业办事处的工作人员；来我市常住的外国专家、留学生以及在岸逗留不过夜人员。

境外旅游（外汇）收入　指入境旅游的外国人、华侨、港澳台同胞在杭州旅游过程中发生的一切旅游支出，对我市来说就是境外旅游（外汇）收入。

Explanatory Notes on Main Statistical Indicators

Utilization of Foreign Capital refers to remittance, equipment and technology financed from abroad, by loans, foreign direct investment and other forms undertaken by the government units of Hangzhou, by various departments, enterprises and other economic units.

Direct Investment by Foreign Entrepreneurs refers to the investments inside China by foreign enterprises and economic organizations or individuals (including overseas Chinese, compatriots from Hong Kong, Macao and Taiwan, and Chinese enterprises registered abroad), following the relevant policies and laws of China, for the establishment of ventures exclusively with foreign own investment, Sino – foreign joint ventures and cooperative enterprises or for co – operative exploration of resources with enterprises or economic organizations in Hangzhou. It includes the re – investment of the foreign entrepreneurs with the profits gained from the investment and the funds that enterprises borrow from abroad in the total investment of projects which are approved by the relevant department of the government.

Total Imports and Exports at Customs refer to the value of commodities imported into and exported from the boundary of China. They include the actual imports and exports through foreign trade, imported and exported goods under the processing and assembling trades and materials, supplies and gifts as aid given gratis between governments and by the United Nations and other international organizations, and contributions donated by overseas Chinese, compatriots in Hong Kong, Macao and Chinese foreign citizenship, leasing commodities owned by tenant at the expiration of leasing period, the imported and exported commodities processed with imported materials, commodities trading in border areas (excluding mutual exchange goods), the imported and exported commodities and articles for public use of the Sino – foreign joint ventures, cooperative enterprises and ventures exclusively with foreign own investment. Also included are import or export of samples and advertising goods for whose CIF or FOB value are beyond the permitted ceiling (excluding goods of no trading or use value and free commodities for export), imported goods sold in China from bonded warehouses and other imported or exported goods. The indicator of the total imports and exports at customs can be used to observe the total size of external trade in a country. In accordance with the stipulation of Chinese government, imports are calculated at CIF, while exports are calculated at FOB.

Number of International Tourists refer to foreigners, overseas Chinese compatriots from Hong Kong, Macao and Taiwan coming to Hangzhou for sightseeing, visits, tours, family reunions, vacations, study tours, conferences and other activities of a business, scientific and technological, cultural, educational and religious nature. It does not include representatives and employees of resident institutions of foreign countries in China such as embassies, consulates, news agencies and offices of foreign companies and organizations, nor does it include long – term foreign experts or students residing in Hangzhou, or persons in transition without spending a night in China.

Foreign Exchange Earnings from International Tourism refer to the total expenditures of foreigners, overseas Chinese, Chinese compatriots from Hong Kong, Macao and Taiwan during their stay in the mainland of China, which are earnings of foreign exchange form international tourism from the point of vies from China.

十、财政、金融保险

FINANCE,BANKING AND INSURANCE

10 财政、金融、保险
Finance, Banking and Insurance

主要统计指标
Major Statistical Indicators

财政总收入	Total Financial Revenue	2238.75	亿元	(100 million yuan)
为上年	As Compared with the Preceding Year	111.0	%	(%)
地方一般公共预算收入	General Public Financial Budgetary Revenue of Local Government	1233.88	亿元	(100 million yuan)
为上年	As Compared with the Preceding Year	109.8	%	(%)
一般公共预算支出	General Public Financial Budgetary Expenditure	1205.48	亿元	(100 million yuan)
为上年	As Compared with the Preceding Year	115.6	%	(%)
年末金融机构各项存款余额	Balance of Deposits of Financial Institutions at Year-end	29863.83	亿元	(100 million yuan)
为上年	As Compared with the Preceding Year	113.9	%	(%)
# 住户存款余额	The Increased Amount of Household Deposits	7617.75	亿元	(100 million yuan)
为上年	As Compared with the Preceding Year	104.4	%	(%)
年末金融机构各项贷款余额	Balance of Loans of Financial Institutions at Year-end	23327.95	亿元	(100 million yuan)
为上年	As Compared with the Preceding Year	109.3	%	(%)

10－01　财政收入及支出(1978－2015 年)

Financial Revenue and Expenditure (1978－2015)

单位:万元　　　　(10000 yuan)

年　份 Year	财政总收入 Financial Revenue		地方一般公共预算收入 Public Financial Budgetary Revenue of Local Government		一般公共预算支出 Public Financial Budgetary Expenditure of Local Government	
	全　市 Total	市　区 Urban District	全　市 Total	市　区 Urban District	全　市 Total	市　区 Urban District
1978	94102	73396	–	–	16170	7779
1979	103259	81885	–	–	20334	11289
1980	118529	94015	–	–	21726	11867
1981	128564	100645	–	–	23964	13891
1982	140510	107298	–	–	24945	13687
1983	153941	116559	–	–	32765	17822
1984	172996	130757	–	–	46937	28710
1985	186472	131923	–	–	57710	35435
1986	205952	141943	–	–	73213	43959
1987	226262	152268	–	–	70717	41011
1988	246961	161208	–	–	95655	53031
1989	255003	156649	–	–	113571	61534
1990	252503	149904	–	–	118167	62587
1991	267597	158130	–	–	123134	62403
1992	286394	168341	–	–	132814	65984
1993	394946	233670	–	–	185168	90545
1994	484597	300014	197292	116733	215415	102430
1995	551262	339828	230431	135041	249050	120084
1996	635334	414557	268438	169987	302390	151016
1997	740725	485650	312797	196885	363834	197054
1998	869824	585615	368484	236269	424478	237221
1999	1026577	689394	449593	288002	563524	335243
2000	1428519	970937	691891	599910	734328	445698
2001	1884608	1612225	1042789	884738	1049330	849479
2002	2571408	2235021	1183153	1022964	1410199	1166298
2003	3297091	2861459	1503888	1290778	1635948	1340463
2004	3957516	3488744	1974523	1712813	1956282	1602303
2005	5207930	4584112	2504565	2172575	2383344	1957619
2006	6244906	5484645	3013888	2616084	2754809	2254347
2007	7884237	6929667	3916195	3421403	3357153	2747060
2008	9105489	7991043	4553531	3972842	4196674	3454599
2009	10194264	8965758	5207899	4535191	4903983	4000324
2010	12454323	10988265	6713413	5894414	6165836	4988197
2011	14889206	13009046	7851524	6822765	7475004	5971740
2012	16278879	14244888	8599875	7475989	7862800	6222930
2013	17349750	15157584	9452020	8207264	8557370	6662314
2014	19201076	17750305	10273169	9426504	9611771	8077961
2015	22387456	20738698	12338820	11360166	12054777	10235061

注:从 2001 年起市区数据包括萧山区、余杭区,2014 年起增加富阳区。

a) Data of urban district include Xiaoshan district, and Yuhang district since 2001, and include Fuyang district since 2014.

10－02 分地区财政
Local Financial

单位:万元

指标	Item	全市 Total	市区 Urban District	上城区 Shangcheng
财政总收入合计	**Total**	**22387456**	**20738698**	**1071548**
一、地方一般公共预算收入	Public Financial Budgetary Revenue of Local Government	12338820	11360166	664589
(一)税收收入	Tax Revenue	11259532	10397084	629305
1. 国内增值税25%部分	25% of Domestic Value－added Tax	1301043	1167430	39993
2. 改征增值税	Newly Changed Value－added Tax	1000427	944357	57745
3. 营业税	Business Tax	3094627	2860392	242432
4. 企业所得税40%部分	40% of Corporate Income Tax	1928567	1806722	117544
5. 个人所得税40%部分	40% of Individual Income Tax	920917	868108	72373
6. 城市维护建设税	City Construction and Maintenance Tax	792815	740857	33229
7. 房产税	Real Estate Tax	398528	363773	33738
8. 城镇土地使用税	Urban Land Use Tax	155914	118624	2490
9. 土地增值税	Land Appreciation Tax	551468	510030	19292
10. 耕地占用税	Tax on the Use of Arable Land	64426	54272	－
11. 契税	Contract Tax	761861	703962	－
12. 其他税收	Others Tax	288939	258557	10469
(二)非税收入	Non－tax Revenue	1079288	963082	35284
1. 专项收入	Special Revenue	1073893	980994	31918
#教育费附加	Revenue from Extra－Charges for Education	300857	276316	12085
地方教育附加收入	Local Education Additional Revenue	200654	184200	8034
水利建设专项收入	Special Revenue of Water Coservancy Construction	238425	219418	6267
残疾人就业保障金收入	Employment Security for The Disabled Revenue	88776	83287	5532
教育资金收入	Educational Fund Revenue	136019	123349	－
农田水利建设资金收入	Fund in The Farmland Irrigation Construction Revenue	81400	73291	－
2. 行政事业性收费收入	Income from Administrative Fees	12213	6988	－
3. 罚没收入	Penalty and Confiscatory Income	149897	128888	2609
4. 国有企业计划亏损补贴	Subsides to Loss－making of state－owned Enterprises	－197823	－188284	－
5. 国有资源(资产)有偿使用收入	Compensation for the Use of Seate－owned Assets Income	38904	33886	757
6. 其他收入	Others Revenue	2204	610	－
二、上划中央"四税"小计	Subtotal Revenue of Central Government	10048636	9378532	406959
1. 消费税	Consumption Tax	1871274	1863992	2104
2. 国内增值税75%部分	75% of Domestic Value－added Tax	3903130	3502290	119979
3. 企业所得税60%部分	60% of Corporate Income Tax	2892853	2710084	176316
4. 个人所得税60%部分	60% of Individual Income Tax	1381379	1302166	108560

总收入(2015 年)

Revenue by Region(2015)

(10000 yuan)

下城区 Xiacheng	江干区 Jianggan	拱墅区 Gongshu	西湖区 Xihu	高新(滨江)区 Hi-Tech (Binjiang)	萧山区 Xiaoshan	余杭区 Yuhang	富阳区 Fuyang	桐庐县 Tonglu	淳安县 Chun'an	建德市 Jiande	临安市 Lin'an
1374548	**1150621**	**1109955**	**1852432**	**2000262**	**2900843**	**3053119**	**915674**	**430329**	**250944**	**364699**	**602786**
856380	740355	693773	1116467	1084558	1600830	1876477	543226	269668	171420	211944	325622
808085	691463	644917	1055689	1014996	1447093	1735235	468603	239819	145971	191593	285065
69787	63551	76035	75231	117533	231561	140488	81412	31487	11646	32874	57606
80195	62362	61117	161502	176337	57071	239524	15184	30607	7632	11388	6443
264969	269510	243791	312946	173236	372769	510831	117092	61138	60892	45389	66816
126594	105786	92856	175552	218586	242603	314500	62356	26545	21340	24693	49267
72959	39839	31188	164215	156812	81351	184419	22465	17552	5657	9620	19980
44067	42824	41527	54119	79598	113850	107126	28419	10854	6441	12856	21807
35975	33586	23267	41941	35407	56858	44923	24139	9924	5997	8562	10272
2042	3987	5563	5463	4002	32612	28348	26477	12185	2630	9123	13352
37677	58689	57251	49143	39006	83256	112098	25174	13641	7746	9260	10791
–	–	–	–	–	32283	9448	7984	3187	854	5975	138
–	–	–	–	–	96233	11072	34384	16183	11618	10573	19525
73820	11329	12322	15577	14479	46646	32458	23517	6516	3518	11280	9068
48295	48892	48856	60778	69562	153737	141242	74623	29849	25449	20351	40557
44865	42476	44747	55969	66187	142412	129665	51327	22984	20643	18309	30963
16058	15910	15862	19743	28930	43608	38929	13761	6164	3628	5764	8985
10749	10734	10271	13153	19285	29212	25952	9180	4114	2476	3841	6023
9605	9373	10863	11875	9791	43877	31743	16548	5330	2858	4325	6494
8453	6459	7751	11179	8181	8001	8001	2971	1150	986	1239	2114
–	–	–	–	–	12587	13000	3954	2361	6099	580	3630
–	–	–	–	–	2402	8320	2531	1511	3904	371	2323
234	962	–	–	1074	87	–	4138	1964	723	1017	1521
2868	4980	3697	4573	2062	19300	16811	11228	4514	3342	5355	7798
–	–	–	–	–	-9935	-7000	-3000	–	-689	-4700	-4150
328	474	412	236	239	1873	1764	10930	387	80	370	4181
–	–	–	–	–	–	2	–	–	1350	–	244
518168	410266	416182	735965	915704	1300013	1176642	372448	160661	79524	152755	277164
9477	1175	2011	621	8	119398	6799	980	54	4090	2663	475
209361	190653	228105	225693	352599	694683	421464	244236	94461	34939	98622	172818
189891	158679	139284	263328	327879	363905	471750	93534	39818	32010	37040	73901
109439	59759	46782	246323	235218	122027	276629	33698	26328	8485	14430	29970

10－03 分地区公共

Local Public Financial Budgetary

单位:万元

指　　标	Item	全　市 Total	市　区 Urban District	上城区 Shangcheng
一般公共预算支出	**Public Financial Budgetary Expenditure of Local Government**	**12054777**	**10235061**	**304253**
一、一般公共服务	Expenditure for General Public Services	1011605	855121	29602
二、国防	Expenditure for National Defense	9011	7458	－
三、公共安全	Expenditure for Public Security	713498	628286	25068
四、教育	Expenditure for Education	2234425	1854997	68365
#教育费附加支出	Expenditure on Extra－Charges for Educations	288749	262910	15703
五、科学技术	Expenditure for Science and Technology	701490	635515	13240
六、文化体育与传媒	Expenditure for Culture, Sports and Media	449192	415629	5563
七、社会保障和就业	Expenditure for Social Safety Net and Employment Effort	1309862	1106800	59939
八、医疗卫生与计划生育	Expenditure for Medical and Health Care and Birth Control	766328	602695	16335
九、节能环保	Expenditure for Energy Conservation Environmental Protection	445749	350151	94
#排污费支出	Sewage Expenses	15556	14681	－
十、城乡社区	Expenditure for Urban and Rural Community	1586419	1464916	48717
十一、农林水	Expenditure for Agriculture, Forestry and Water Conservancy	880440	628966	9817
十二、交通运输	Expenditure for Trarssportation	389625	271235	43
十三、资源勘探信息等	Resources Exploration Information, etc	601637	572841	8427
十四、商业服务业等	Expenditure for Commercial Service Industry	311949	296142	8513
十五、金融支出	Expenditure for Financial Supervision	8168	7569	2521
十六、援助其他地区	Expenditure for Aiding Other Territories	54543	51769	1299
十七、国土海洋气象等	Expenditure for Land, Ocean and Meteorological Services	47292	33500	545
十八、住房保障	Expenditure on Housing Support	122825	67548	1012
十九、粮油物资储备	Expenditure for Grain and Oil Reservation and other Materials Services	15283	11454	－
二十、债务付息	Expenditure for Interest Payment of Government debt	－	－	－
二十一、其他	Other Expenditure	395436	372469	5153

预算支出(2015年)
Expenditure by Region(2015)

(10000 yuan)

下城区 Xiacheng	江干区 Jianggan	拱墅区 Gongshu	西湖区 Xihu	高新(滨江)区 Hi-Tech (Binjiang)	萧山区 Xiaoshan	余杭区 Yuhang	富阳区 Fuyang	桐庐县 Tonglu	淳安县 Chun'an	建德市 Jiande	临安市 Lin'an
331869	**424299**	**389237**	**629979**	**709676**	**1609815**	**1678036**	**689558**	**403130**	**504043**	**410936**	**501607**
29885	41617	36097	56952	24818	155283	144728	55329	28491	47308	36215	44470
302	111	42	832	-	1800	1925	195	425	349	430	349
30400	29491	30206	40762	19090	86534	78410	31931	20898	20179	18645	25490
65424	84955	84616	147279	99531	352096	318717	192603	95858	86672	83025	113873
10549	11556	17234	42372	28044	51164	37618	16027	6680	33	4134	14992
12616	25263	52611	31220	79076	87617	86918	29976	15166	9871	14605	26333
6492	5156	4043	7009	18859	26140	31436	14558	8982	6941	8367	9273
51277	56812	52325	76846	74437	157014	148372	71432	48661	45611	58883	49907
19950	24386	18090	40282	20574	92223	108822	52584	41028	46081	34197	42327
19770	3248	3461	8271	4709	139267	64622	30050	12083	25266	28640	29609
-	-	-	-	-	4484	-	6179	516	-	111	248
62498	83633	79535	93677	238750	199244	207912	27551	20257	38748	33028	29470
7588	19233	1194	25545	15407	131455	107803	105348	62484	80559	55345	53086
-	2	30	820	-	35601	32577	36726	19707	41183	17442	40058
3854	2413	2406	65357	84575	84313	142035	17440	2879	9679	1513	14725
12917	2596	16012	13283	9338	34041	168044	6115	3189	6251	2031	4336
-	247	156	372	95	100	403	-	172	13	5	409
-	2065	1150	3441	6897	8043	10469	2159	783	-	856	1135
689	668	973	2899	1288	4992	5896	3277	6226	2231	2567	2768
5636	4844	4768	6542	10113	6183	5450	9433	12322	22525	11533	8897
-	-	-	-	-	2419	98	162	1974	1483	32	340
-	-	-	-	-	-	-	-	-	-	-	-
2571	37559	1522	8590	2119	5450	13399	2689	1545	13093	3577	4752

10－04 全市分税种、支出科目财政收支情况(2010－2015 年)

Local Public Financial Budgetary Expenditure by Tax and Expenditure Account(2010－2015)

单位:万元 (10000 yuan)

指 标 Item	2010	2011	2012	2013	2014	2015
财政总收入合计 Total	**12454323**	**14889206**	**16278879**	**17349750**	**19201076**	**22387456**
一、地方一般公共预算收入 Public Financial Budgetary Revenue of Local Government	6713413	7851524	8599875	9452020	10273169	12338820
(一)税收收入 Tax Revenue	6520916	7582715	8302478	9106690	9952111	11259532
1. 国内增值税 25% 部分 25% of Domestic Value－added Tax	892292	1018017	1094696	1122297	1224336	1301043
2. 改征增值税 Newly Changed Value－added Tax				593744	837724	1000427
3. 营业税 Business Tax	2213139	2409436	2970123	2670660	2650471	3094627
4. 企业所得税 40% 部分 40% of Corporate Income Tax	992319	1308761	11448553	1518112	1723639	1928567
5. 个人所得税 40% 部分 40% of Individual Income Tax	392018	510554	498726	573227	681449	920917
6. 城市维护建设税 City Construction and Maintenance Tax	393580	549604	604523	658593	693932	792815
7. 房产税 Real Estate Tax	152443	245337	317711	323897	378171	398528
8. 城镇土地使用税 Urban Land Use Tax						155914
9. 土地增值税 Land Appreciation Tax						551468
10. 耕地占用税 Tax on the Use of Arable Land	136115	103448	102820	91622	72117	64426
11. 契税 Contract Tax	718207	722185	465946	674188	805656	761861
12. 其他税收 Others Tax	630803	715373	799380	880350	884616	288939
(二)非税收入 Non－tax Revenue	192497	268809	297397	345330	321058	1079288
1. 专项收入 Special Revenue	166645	231881	245863	267287	278423	1073893

指标 Item	2010	2011	2012	2013	2014	2015
2. 行政事业性收费收入 Income from Administrative Fees	11876	16844	19137	19738	13988	12213
3. 罚没收入 Penalty and Confiscatory Income	108275	115948	128549	148738	148190	149897
4. 国有企业计划亏损补贴 Subsides to Loss－making of state－owned Enterprises	－105338	－113682	－105032	－105699	－147887	－197823
5. 国有资源(资产)有偿使用收入 Compensation for the Use of Seate－owned Assets Income	11009	17666	8870	14314	27927	38904
6. 其他收入 Others Revenue	30	152	10	952	417	2204
二、一般公共预算支出 Public Financial Budgetary Expenditure of Local Government	6165836	7475004	7862800	8557370	9611771	12054777
1. 一般公共服务 Expenditure for General Public Services	763576	857578	893776	915881	892027	1011605
2. 教育 Expenditure for Education	1058828	1320537	1469266	1624445	1826924	2234425
3. 科学技术 Expenditure for Science and Technology	288559	350657	401878	462600	524082	701490
4. 文化体育与传媒 Expenditure for Culture, Sports and Media	153937	185042	207869	223604	242375	449192
5. 社会保障和就业 Expenditure for Social Safety Net and Employment Effort	639154	775422	871431	946033	1082564	1309862
6. 医疗卫生与计划生育 Expenditure for Medical and Health Care and Birth Control	417085	513455	559225	621518	716754	766328
7. 节能环保 Expenditure for Energy Conservation Environmental Protection	138627	141227	161518	197392	300159	445749
8. 城乡社区 Expenditure for Urban and Rural Community	982965	1231576	1042885	1064358	1143602	1586419
9. 农林水 Expenditure for Agriculture, Forestry and Water Conservancy	319655	392344	448764	506246	562286	880440
10. 交通运输 Expenditure for Trarssportation	174339	212663	253757	305919	306032	389625
11. 住房保障 Expenditure on Housing Support	31935	60192	65066	77290	93521	122825

10－05 全市金融机构存、贷款余额(1978－2015年)

Balance of Deposits and Loans of Financial Institutions (1978－2015)

单位:万元 (10000 yuan)

年份 Year \ 项目 Item	各项存款 Deposits	住户存款 Household Deposits	城镇住户存款 Urban Household Deposits	各项贷款 Loans
1978	86824	20714	17056	136759
1979	108998	28937	22640	135713
1980	180707	40447	30896	174153
1981	226949	51440	38889	236678
1982	262156	67192	50113	216040
1983	303130	86635	64736	236203
1984	388305	115766	85439	329195
1985	484999	159596	115592	580180
1986	635514	222110	153572	769841
1987	776105	302762	207505	967477
1988	839680	351943	241839	1145989
1989	1017087	501592	346318	1338984
1990	1646165	697515	479031	1803266
1991	2036334	904490	616308	2136903
1992	2652966	1144737	763309	2651983
1993	3469954	1563328	1048413	3415527
1994	5061345	2394370	1642498	4450932
1995	7079650	3423379	2448787	5672105
1996	9619291	4638458	3459439	7434243
1997	12251840	5583306	4229591	9388500
1998	14948225	6701158	5155548	11620537
1999	17886717	7425967	5760527	14937506
2000	20884723	7885579	6151084	16866431
2001	26215100	9418400	7396800	20877000
2002	33731500	11834000	9492300	27523800
2003	46527300	15899600	13079600	38187000
2004	57072000	18351700	15016100	48000400
2005	67487200	21916600	17960100	55453000
2006	78555500	25552400	20789600	66038600
2007	93109600	26348300	21154300	84306800
2008	113333500	34765900	27584600	100690500
2009	142842104	42869189	34027871	131133023
2010	170843548	49909744	39352353	150787269
2011	183965719	55474824	43464332	165737441
2012	201487672	60899841	46965391	180908011
2013	221747107	64085856	47733077	193504605
2014	244505093	67672009	49107745	213168315
2015	298638294	76177515	55659016	233279520

注:1. 1989年以前数据均为银行机构存贷款,1990年及以后年份数据为调整后金融机构存贷款。2003年起金融机构存贷款为本外币合并数据。

2. 2015年起,各项存款和各项贷款分类调整。

a) Data before 1989 belonged to banking system, data after 1990 adjusted for deposits and loans of financial institutions, data of 2003 included both RMB and foreign currency.

b) Since 2015, the classification in deposits and Loans has been adjusted.

10－06　市区金融机构存、贷款余额(1978－2015年)

Balance of Deposits and Loans of Financial Institutions of Urban District(1978－2015)

单位:万元　　(10000 yuan)

项目 Item / 年份 Year	各项存款 Deposits	住户存款 Household Deposits	城镇住户存款 Urban Household Deposits	各项贷款 Loans
1978	58372	13774	13246	101144
1979	73720	18055	17241	98792
1980	134275	24702	23282	121231
1981	172721	31358	29345	170539
1982	198350	39756	37047	142091
1983	226160	50439	46833	155297
1984	293145	66108	61934	194977
1985	359825	89114	82868	418214
1986	458142	115818	106703	557763
1987	565429	156704	142642	714313
1988	610601	180341	163466	846998
1989	737388	256238	229518	1000731
1990	1062574	354316	297390	1271779
1991	1309462	451756	397322	1469671
1992	1695011	572660	479248	1774158
1993	2263969	762234	662234	2298124
1994	3383877	1242379	1085363	3033010
1995	4851774	1853512	1639875	3907199
1996	6828786	2734904	2371657	5350499
1997	8831147	3287475	2873638	6772221
1998	10785066	3905602	3440607	8615412
1999	13051806	4336058	3835542	11462505
2000	15436286	4620235	4101716	13105849
2001	23765400	7976400	6460200	19237800
2002	30638400	10139800	8370100	25476700
2003	42522000	13834200	11693000	30297500
2004	52542100	16014700	13479900	44517600
2005	62249500	19231800	16208400	51455900
2006	72269600	22391800	18737800	61190700
2007	86197300	23124600	19132300	78456200
2008	104930100	30665200	24996500	93838100
2009	131800234	37837816	30801878	121473548
2010	156776515	43676938	35370599	138671334
2011	168052916	48263525	38996516	151756838
2012	183719227	52347969	41789531	156426086
2013	201596137	54488059	42142666	175670366
2014	222558892	57202595	43243610	191888081
2015	284321331	68516344	51360093	222078475

10－07 全市金融机构本外币

Balance of Deposits and

单位：万元

指 标	Item	全市 Total 合计 Total	全市 Total 为上年(%) As Compared with the Preceding Year(%)	市区 Urban District 小计 Subtotal
一、各项存款	**Deposits**	**298638294**	**113.9**	**284321331**
(一)境内存款	Domestic Deposits	297824649	114.0	283515939
1. 住户存款	Household Deposits	76177515	104.4	68516344
(1)活期存款	Current Deposits	30660811	111.7	27664071
(2)定期及其他存款	Term and Other Deposits	45516704	100.0	40852273
2. 非金融企业存款	Non－financial Enterprise Deposits	131207312	110.3	127200216
(1)活期存款	Current Deposits	41466315	123.5	39284534
(2)定期及其他存款	Term and Other Deposits	89740997	105.2	87915682
3. 广义政府存款	General Government Deposits	46925286	111.1	44353758
(1)财政性存款	Treasury Deposits	6038853	89.8	5821104
(2)机关团体存款	Organization Deposits	40886433	115.2	38532654
4. 非银行业金融机构存款	Non－banking Financial Institutions Deposits	43514535	160.2	43445621
(二)境外存款	Overseas Deposits	813645	84.6	805392
二、各项贷款	**Loans**	**233279520**	**109.3**	**222078475**
(一)境内贷款	Domestic Loans	231137462	109.1	219936542
1. 住户贷款	Household Loans	58594607	119.1	53749152
(1)短期贷款	Short－term Loans	18750382	105.9	16791441
(2)中长期贷款	Medium and Long term Loans	39844225	126.6	36957711
2. 非金融企业及机关团体贷款	Non－financial Enterprise and Organization Loans	172418504	106.1	166063038
(1)短期贷款	Short－term Loans	73357492	99.5	69801969
(2)中长期贷款	Medium and Long term Loans	78852523	105.4	76196464
(3)票据融资	Note Financing	13113136	179.2	12986040
(4)融资租赁	Finance lease	6635696	112.6	6635696
(5)各项垫款	Advance Money	459657	69.2	442870
3. 非银行业金融机构贷款	Non－banking Financial Institutions Loans	124351	38.6	124351
(二)境外贷款	Overseas Loans	2142058	140.2	2141933

存、贷款余额（2015 年末）
of Financial Institutions（End of 2015）

（10000 yuan）

萧山区 Xiaoshan	余杭区 Yuhang	富阳区 Fuyang	桐庐县 Tonglu	淳安县 Chun'an	建德市 Jiande	临安市 Lin'an
32732261	**19708565**	**8781794**	**3682224**	**2698565**	**3105022**	**4831151**
32630865	19690948	8779537	3679217	2697396	3103358	4828739
13209494	8952696	3807721	1989423	1352094	1967229	2352425
4374863	2874112	1471375	715222	542145	684642	1054731
8834632	6078584	2336347	1274201	809949	1282587	1297694
14621206	6961445	3867939	1212601	676035	638024	1480435
5042787	3001915	1509421	572775	428665	411995	768346
9578419	3959530	2358518	639826	247371	226029	712089
4176273	3706938	1033688	469176	665036	475518	961798
205859	848135	55661	34890	44989	36487	101382
3970413	2858803	978027	434286	620046	439031	860416
623892	69869	70189	8016	4230	22588	34080
101396	17617	2257	3007	1169	1664	2413
29098677	**13991655**	**9687139**	**3015870**	**2050287**	**2366913**	**3767974**
29096472	13990121	9687139	3015774	2050287	2366897	3767962
4980165	4189571	2618945	1391026	1007862	896347	1550220
2213177	1496242	1237858	426912	437537	331725	762767
2766989	2693329	1381087	964113	570325	564622	787453
24116307	9800550	7068194	1624748	1042425	1470550	2217742
17088672	4852006	5175462	1052795	367545	765052	1370131
5815266	4149940	1627510	545494	655527	660478	794559
1073468	769330	234690	24800	19353	33985	48958
–	–	–	–	–	–	–
138901	29275	30532	1659	–	11035	4094
–	–	–	–	–	–	–
2205	1534	–	97	–	16	12

10－08 全市金融机构人民币

Balance of RMB Deposits, RMB Loans

单位:万元

指 标	Item	全市 Total 合计 Total	全市 Total 为上年(%) As Compared with the Preceding Year(%)	市区 Urban District 小计 Subtotal
一、各项存款	**Deposits**	**290030714**	**112.8**	**275880049**
(一)境内存款	Domestic Deposits	289459907	112.9	275316729
1. 住户存款	Household Deposits	75070901	103.9	67437004
(1)活期存款	Current Deposits	30031941	110.9	27052197
(2)定期及其他存款	Term and Other Deposits	45038960	99.8	40384808
2. 非金融企业存款	Non－financial Enterprise Deposits	124372364	108.1	120503418
(1)活期存款	Current Deposits	39293642	122.7	37211863
(2)定期及其他存款	Term and Other Deposits	85078723	102.4	83291555
3. 广义政府存款	General Government Deposits	46749152	110.8	44177660
(1)财政性存款	Treasury Deposits	6038852	89.8	5821102
(2)机关团体存款	Organization Deposits	40710301	114.8	38356557
4. 非银行业金融机构存款	Non－banking Financial Institutions Deposits	43267490	160.8	43198646
(二)境外存款	Overseas Deposits	570806	71.7	563320
二、各项贷款	**Loans**	**223952892**	**109.8**	**212795217**
(一)境内贷款	Domestic Loans	223730294	109.8	212572743
1. 住户贷款	Household Loans	58584159	119.1	53738809
(1)短期贷款	Short－term Loans	18740256	105.9	16781421
(2)中长期贷款	Medium and Long term Loans	39843903	126.6	36957389
2. 非金融企业及机关团体贷款	Non－financial Enterprise and Organization Loans	165021784	106.9	158709583
(1)短期贷款	Short－term Loans	69438429	100.5	65917971
(2)中长期贷款	Medium and Long term Loans	75393801	105.5	72739917
(3)票据融资	Note Financing	13112764	179.3	12985695
(4)融资租赁	Finance lease	6635696	112.6	6635696
(5)各项垫款	Advance Money	441095	78.1	430304
3. 非银行业金融机构贷款	Non－banking Financial Institutions Loans	124351	38.6	124351
(二)境外贷款	Overseas Loans	222598	371.0	222474

存、贷款余额（2015 年末）

of Financial Institutions(End of 2015)

（10000 yuan）

萧山区 Xiaoshan	余杭区 Yuhang	富阳区 Fuyang	桐庐县 Tonglu	淳安县 Chun′an	建德市 Jiande	临安市 Lin′an
31702155	**19452675**	**8549200**	**3632635**	**2670928**	**3082722**	**4764379**
31604570	19435565	8547087	3629844	2669765	3081195	4762374
13143442	8922080	3793597	1981803	1347815	1959683	2344595
4338277	2852288	1463301	710326	539125	680704	1049591
8805166	6069792	2330297	1271478	808690	1278979	1295004
13669342	6738796	3652226	1170850	652684	623478	1421934
4644733	2887216	1436909	537784	406804	397970	739220
9024609	3851580	2215316	633066	245880	225508	682714
4174762	3704802	1031068	469176	665035	475516	961765
205859	848135	55661	34890	44989	36487	101382
3968903	2856667	975407	434286	620046	439029	860383
617023	69888	70196	8015	4230	22518	34080
97585	17109	2114	2791	1163	1527	2005
28093095	**13892058**	**9582899**	**3012490**	**2049462**	**2350684**	**3745038**
28090891	13890524	9582899	3012394	2049462	2350668	3745027
4979918	4189516	2618840	1390988	1007853	896324	1550185
2212929	1496187	1237797	426874	437528	331702	762731
2766989	2693329	1381043	964113	570325	564622	787453
23110973	9701008	6964059	1621406	1041609	1454344	2194842
16395496	4758754	5095657	1049453	366729	754843	1349433
5507784	4143747	1603736	545494	655527	660478	792384
1073468	769232	234690	24800	19353	33985	48930
–	–	–	–	–	–	–
134226	29275	29977	1659	–	5037	4094
–	–	–	–	–	–	–
2205	1534	–	97	–	16	12

10－09 住户存款余额(2015 年末)

Balance of Savings Deposits of Rural and Urban Residents(End of 2015)

单位:万元 (10000 yuan)

地区	Region	总 计 Total		城镇住户 Urban Residents		农村住户 Rural Residents	
		2015 年末 At the End of Year 2015	为上年(%) As Compared with the Preceding Year(%)	2015 年末 At the End of Year 2015	为上年(%) As Compared with the Preceding Year(%)	2015 年末 At the End of Year 2015	为上年(%) As Compared with the Preceding Year(%)
全 市	**Total**	**76177515**	**104.4**	**55659016**	**102.5**	**20518499**	**109.9**
市 区	Urban District	68516344	112.8	51360093	113.7	17156251	110.1
#萧山区	Xiaoshan	13209494	104.3	7252771	100.5	5956723	109.3
余杭区	Yuhang	8952696	104.5	4663859	98.6	4288837	111.9
富阳区	Fuyang	3807721	102.9	2079735	100.2	1727986	106.3
桐庐县	Tonglu	1989423	111.0	1084174	105.9	905249	117.8
淳安县	Chun'an	1352094	108.8	728607	107.0	623487	111.0
建德市	Jiande	1967229	106.4	1204676	103.5	762553	111.4
临安市	Lin'an	2352425	107.6	1281465	105.0	1070959	110.9

10－10 保险业务情况(2013－2015年)
Development of Insurance Business(2013－2015)

单位:万元 (10000 yuan)

指 标	Item	保险费收入 Premium			赔付金额 Indemnity Expenditure		
		2013	2014	2015	2013	2014	2015
全市总计	**Total**	**2792291**	**3204138**	**3743769**	**1023955**	**1190338**	**1396924**
为上年%	As Compared with the Preceding Year(%)	112.6	114.8	16.8	119.9	116.3	17.4
一、财产保险	Property Insurance	1268727	1410891	1569067	778746	832313	937229
企业财产险	Enterprise Property Insurance	90526	93834	90317	58570	58793	42398
家庭财产险	Family Property Insurance	5172	4516	10012	829	817	4641
机动车辆险	Transportation Equipment Insurance	969903	1075684	1153742	619381	642940	702258
工程险	Project Insurance	11551	9945	19167	2344	3965	7798
责任险	Responsibilihty Insurance	25969	31039	42734	13418	12101	15975
信用险	Export Credit Insurance	104133	111468	130809	52898	73037	101830
保证险	Guarantee Insurance	17809	24767	39963	5339	8160	13759
船舶险	Shipping Insurance	6638	5458	4326	3240	4723	4078
货运险	Cargo Insurance	18205	19005	21933	13836	10457	10172
特殊风险保险	Special Pisks Insurance	5053	6154	5455	1724	528	320
农业保险	Agriculture Insurance	12369	13722	17775	6571	5939	9312
其他险	Other	1400	15301	32834	595	10853	24688
二、人身险	Personal Insurance	1523563	1793247	2174702	245209	358025	459695
寿险	Life Insurance	1279158	1470213	1612350	181889	272796	392062
意外伤害险	Accidental Insurance	71238	86671	125954	13337	16820	23802
健康险	Health Insurance	173167	236363	436398	49983	68409	43831

主要统计指标解释

财政收入 包括:(1)各项税收。主要有增值税、营业税、土地增值税、城市维护建设税、资源税、城市土地使用税、印花税、个人所得税、企业所得税、关税和耕地占用税等。

(2)专项收入包括征收排污费、征收城市水资源费收入,教育费附加收入等。

存款 企业、机关、团体或居民根据可以收回的原则,把货币资金存入银行或其他信用机构保管并取得一定利息的一种信用活动形式。根据存款对象的不同可划分为企业存款、财政存款、机关团体存款、基本建设存款、城镇储蓄存款、农村存款等科目。它是银行信贷资金的主要来源。

贷款 银行或其他信用机构根据必须归还的原则,按一定利率,为企业、个人等提供资金的一种信用活动形式。我国银行贷款分为流动资金贷款、固定资产贷款、城乡个体工商户贷款、城乡个体工商户贷款以及农业贷款等科目。

Explanatory Notes on Main Statistical Indicators

Financial Revenue It includes the following main items: (1) various tax revenues, including value added tax, business tax, land value added tax, tax on city maintenance and construction, resources tax, tax on use of urban land, stamp tax, personal income tax, enterprise income tax and tax on occupancy of cultivated land, etc. (2) Special revenues, including revenue collected from imposing fee on sewage treatment, revenue collected from imposing fee on urban water resources, and extra – charges for education, etc.

Deposit is a form of credit by which enterprises, institutions, organizations or households can put money into banks and other credit institutions for safekeeping and interest earning under the principle of free withdrawal. According to different depositors, deposits are divided into enterprise deposits, treasury deposits, deposits of government agencies and organizations, capital construction deposits, urban savings deposits, rural deposits and other deposits. Deposits are major sources of the credit funds of banks.

Loan is a form of credit by which banks and other credit institutions provide funds at certain interest rate to enterprises and individuals in the light of the principle of unconditional repayment. Loans from Chinese banks include circulating capital loans, fixed assets loans, loans to urban and rural individuals engaged in industrial and commercial business and agricultural loans.

十一、城市建设环境保护

URBAN CONSTRUCTION AND ENVIRONMENTAL PROTECTION

11 城市建设、环境保护
Urban Construction and Environmental Protection

主要统计指标
Major Statistical Indicators

市区建成区面积	Developed Area in Urban District	506.09	平方千米	(sq.km)
市区实有道路面积	Area of Roads in Urban District at Year-end	6540	万平方米	(10, 000 sq.m)
市区用电量	Electricity Consumption of Urban District	559.54	亿千瓦时	(100 million kw/h)
# 工业用电	Industrial Electricity Consumption	345.23	亿千瓦时	(100 million kw/h)
生活用电	Electricity Consumption for Residential Use	78.27	亿千瓦时	(100 million kw/h)
市区供水能力	Water-supply Capacity of Urban District	380	万吨/日	(10, 000 tons/day)
市区供水总量	Annual Volume of Tap Water Supplied in Urban District	66760	万吨	(10, 000 tons)
市区气化率	Percentage of Population with Access to Gas in Urban District	100	%	(%)
市区公园绿地面积	Park Green Area in Urban District	7640	公顷	(hectare)
市区空气质量达标(AQI < 100)天数	The Number of Days of Air Quality Reaching(AQI<100) the Standards	242	天	(day)

11－01 市区公共交通情况(主要年份)

Urban Public Transportation in Urban Districts(Main Years)

指 标	Item	2000	2005	2010	2011	2012	2013	2014	2015
一、轨道交通	Rail Transit								
年末运营线路总长度（千米）	Length of Operating Routes (year－end) (km)	－	－	－	－	47.97	47.97	66.30	81.5
客运总量 （万人次）	Passenger Traffic (10,000 person－times)	－	－	－	－	561	9237	14521	22348
二、公共汽车	Bus								
年末运营线路条数（条）	Number of Operating Routes (year－end) (unit)	163	368	548	611	620	645	703	756
年末运营线路总长度（千米）	Length of Operating Routes (year－end) (km)	2016	4902	8594	11106	11351	11445	12032	12791
#BRT 线路长度（千米）	BRT line length (km)						122	113	128
年末运营公共汽车（辆）	Number of Public Transportation Vehicles(year－end) (unit)	1781	3997	7209	7543	7450	8249	8656	8555
#无轨电车 （辆）	Number of Operating Trolleys (unit)	223	189	65	54	51	101	115	150
客运总量 （万人次）	Passenger Traffic (10,000 person－times)	57986	70653	127967	126999	131901	132221	140928	142312
三、出租汽车	Tax								
年末实有出租汽车数（辆）	Number of Taxis (year－end) (unit)	6300	8320	9362	10905	10344	10904	11913	11963
四、公共自行车	Bicycle								
年末免费公共自行车数（万辆）	Number of free Public Bicycles (year－end) (10,000 unit)	－	－	6.06	6.50	6.80	7.80	8.11	8.68

11－02 市区城市供电、供水情况(主要年份)

Urban Electricity and Water Supply in Urban Districts(Main Years)

指标	Item	2000	2005	2010	2011	2012	2013	2014	2015
一、城市供电	**Urban Electricity Supply**								
全年用电总量（亿千瓦时）	Total Electricity Consumption (100 million kwh)	60.19	244.78	392.64	432.57	444.95	484.05	552.71	559.54
#工业（亿千瓦时）	Industrial Electricity Consumption (100 million kwh)	33.52	172.56	258.35	282.95	278.93	296.08	355.06	345.23
生活（亿千瓦时）	Electricity Consumption for Residential Use (100 million kwh)	9.86	27.98	50.74	55.49	63.62	71.52	72.56	78.27
二、城市供水（自来水）	**Urban Water Supply**								
总售水量（万吨）	Total Annual Volume of Tap Water Saled (10,000 tons)	27510	58332	45666	44335	49549	51709	56401	56478
平均日供水（万吨）	Per Capita Daily Consumption of Tap Water (10,000 tons)	92	201	147	144	159	166	165	183
供水能力（万吨/日）	Capacity of Water Supply (10,000 tons/day)	146	253	320	320	320	350	380	380
供水总量（万吨）	Total Annual Volume of Tap Water Supplied (10,000 tons)	33725	73331	53565	52660	58183	60747	66172	66760
#生产用水（万吨）	For Productive Use (10,000 tons)	8100	27327	11479	11884	12478	13005	14792	14902
生活用水（万吨）	For Residential Use (10,000 tons)	19410	35220	30978	22384	22861	23733	26894	26162
用水普及率（%）	Percentage of Population with Access to Tap Water (%)	100	100	100	100	100	100	100	100

11－03 市区市政建设情况(主要年份)

Public Utilities in Urban Districts(Main Years)

指 标	Item	2000	2005	2010	2011	2012	2013	2014	2015
一、市政建设	**Urban Infrastructure**								
建成区面积(平方公里)	Constructed Area (sq. m)	–	314.45	412.59	432.98	452.62	462.48	495.22	506.09
年末实有道路面积(万平方米)	Area of Roads (year－end) (10,000 sq. m)	1183	3175	4754	4900	5284	5426	6145	6540
年末实有道路长度(公里)	Length of Roads(year－end) (km)	1050	1782	2194	2255	2458	2479	2748	2991
年末实有桥梁数(座)	Number of Bridges(year－end) (unit)	291	991	1021	1059	1129	1165	1235	1337
排水管道长度(公里)	Length of Drainage Pipelines (km)	1431	2945	3904	4056	4280	4455	5012	5370
城市污水排放量(万立方米)	Volume of Sewage Drained (10,000 cu. m)	27010	55141	43746	44809	47330	48432	53111	56974
城市污水处理总量(万立方米)	the Total Volume of Urban Sewage Treatment (10,000 cu. m)	–	43352	41733	42781	45197	46251	50318	54137
二、城市液化气	**Urban Liquefied Petroleum Gas**								
供气总量 (万吨)	Total Volume of Liquefied Petroleum Gas Supply (10,000 tons)	7.47	15.28	11.44	11.19	11.17	11.92	9.87	12.38
#家庭用气(万吨)	Supply for Residential Use (10,000 tons)	5.08	9.51	5.77	5.93	5.90	4.70	5.08	6.08
三、人工煤气及天然气	**Coal Gas and Natural Gas**								
家庭用气总量(万立方米)	Total Volume of Coal Gas Consumed (10,000 cu. m)	4367	3225	10053	11365	13397	13869	18019	20659
家庭用气户数(万户)	Residential Households with Access to Gas (10,000 households)	14.46	25.48	62.85	72.50	81.72	91.08	111.30	130.69
四、全社会气化率 %	**Percentage of Population with Access to Gas** (%)	**95.7**	**99.17**	**100**	**100**	**100**	**100**	**100**	**100**

11－04 市区园林绿化情况（主要年份）
Urban Forestation（Main Years）

指 标	Item	2000	2005	2010	2011	2012	2013	2014	2015
一、园林绿化	**Urban Forestation**								
建城区绿化覆盖面积（公顷）	The Green Areas Coveraged in Constructed Areas (hectare)	6083	11734	16483	17336	18135	18606	20031	20464
园林绿地面积（公顷）	Total Area of Parks, Gardens and Green Areas (hectare)	6035	10774	15118	15898	16647	17071	18386	18949
#公园绿地（公顷）	Public Green Area (hectare)	976	2564	5017	5287	5635	5820	6304	7640
建城区绿化覆盖率（%）	Rate of the Green Areas Coveraged in Constructed Areas (%)	34.33	37.31	39.95	40	40.07	40.23	40.57	40.43
公园景点个数（个）	Number of Parks and Scenic Resorts (unit)	70	184	176	181	185	190	207	217
公园景点面积（公顷）	Area of Parks and Scenic Resorts (hectare)	489	997	1906	2047	2065	2094	2298	2488

11－05　环境保护情况(2015年)
Environmental Protection Situation (2015)

指标名称		Item		全　市 Whole City	市　区 Urban District
工业废水排放量	(万吨)	Industrial Wastewater Emissions	(10,000 tons)	33807	28869
工业废水中COD排放量	(吨)	COD Emissions in Industrial Wastewater	(tons)	28645	24118
工业废水中氨氮排放量	(吨)	Ammonia emissions in Industrial wastewater	(tons)	1113	961
工业二氧化硫产生量	(吨)	Industrial Sulfur Dioxide Produced	(tons)	140100	121013
工业二氧化硫排放量	(吨)	Industrial Emissions of Sulfur Dioxide	(tons)	63814	46265
工业氮氧化物排放量	(吨)	Industrial Nitrogen Oxide Emissions	(tons)	55973	38901
工业烟(粉)产生量	(吨)	Industrial Smoke (Powder) Production	(tons)	4051458	1843951
工业烟(粉)尘排放量	(吨)	Industrial Smoke, Powder and Dust Emissions	(tons)	49176	38400
一般工业固体废物综合利用率	(%)	Comprehensive Utilization Rate of General Industrial Solid Waste	(%)	88.6	-
城市污水集中处理率	(%)	Centralized Treatment Rate of Urban Sewage	(%)	94.3	-
城市生活垃圾无害化处理率	(%)	Harmless Treatment Rate of City's Living Garbage	(%)	100	100
空气质量优良天数	(天)	Air Quality Days	(days)	-	242
集中式饮用水源地水质达标率	(%)	Compliance Rate of Centralized Sources of Drinking Water	(%)	100	-
化学需氧量削减率	(%)	Chemical Oxygen Demand Reduction Rate	(%)	6.52	-
氨氮削减率	(%)	Ammonia Nitrogen Reduction Rate	(%)	4.01	-
二氧化硫削减率	(%)	Sulfur Dioxide Reduction Rate	(%)	7.65	-
氮氧化物削减率	(%)	Reduction Rate of Nitrogen Oxides	(%)	10.88	-

主要统计指标解释

自来水生产能力　指年底城建部门管理的自来水厂实际生产能力。

生活用水量　指居民日常生活与公共福利设施的用水量。包括居民、饮食店、旅馆、医院、理发店、浴池、洗衣店、游泳池、商店、学校、机关、部队等单位的用水量。

供气总量　指全年售给各类用户的全部煤气量。包括工业用量、家庭用量和其他用量。

年末实有道路长度　指除土路外，路面经过铺装宽度在3.5米以上的道路，包括高级、次高级道路和普通道路。

城市桥梁　指城市范围内，修建在河道上的桥梁和道路与道路立交、道路跨越铁路的立交桥，以及人行天桥。包括永久性桥和半永久性桥，不包括临时性桥、铁路桥、涵洞。

营运线路长度　指设置的固定营运线路的长度，包括郊区营运线路长度。不包括临时行驶的线路长度。

用水普及率　指城市用水的非农业人口数（不包括临时人口和流动人口）与城市非农业人口总数之比。计算公式为：

$$用水普及率=\frac{城市用水非农业人口数}{城市非农业人口数}\times 100\%$$

城市园林绿地面积　指城市公共绿地、专用绿地、生产绿地、防护绿地、郊区风景名胜区的全部面积。

公园绿地面积　指供游览休息的各种公园、动物园、植物园、陵园以及花园、游园和供游览休息用的林荫道绿地、广场绿地。不包括一般栽植的行道树及林荫道的面积。

Explanatory Notes on Main Statistical Indicators

Production Capacity of Tap Water refers to the actual comprehensive production capacity of the waterworks administered by the urban construction department.

Consumption of water for Residential Use refers to the water consumption of households for daily life and the water consumption of public welfare facilities, including the consumption of restaurants, hotels, hospitals, barber shops, public bathhouses, laundries, swimming pools, shops, schools, institutions, army units and other units.

Volume of Gas Supply refers to the total volume of gas Sold to users in a year, including the volume for industrial use, residential use and other uses.

Length of Roads at the Year – end refers to the length of roads with a paved surface, and with a width of more than 3 – 5 meters, including high quality, medium quality and ordinary roads.

Urban Bridges refers to bridges over river courses, great separated junctions and overpasses in urban areas. Permanent bridges and semi – permanent bridges are included. Temporary bridges, railway bridges and culverts are excluded.

Length in Operation refers to the length of the roads in fixed operation, including the suburb one, but excluding the tomporary ones.

Percentage of Urban Population with Access to Tap Water refers to the ratio of the urban non – agricultural population (excluding temporary and mobile population) with access to tap water to the tolal urban non – agricultural population. The formula is:

$$\text{Percentage of Poputalion with Access to Tap Water} = \frac{\text{Urban Non – agricultural Population with Access to Tap Water}}{\text{Urban Non – agricultural Population}} \times 100\%$$

Area of Urban Gardens and Green Areas refers to the total area of urban public green land, special green land, production green land, protection green land and suburban scenic spots.

Park Green Area refers to green area of various parks, zoos, botanical gardens, cemeteries, amusement parks, tree – flanked boulevards Greenland squares for tourism and relaxing. Areas with trees planted along – side the streets and boulevards are excluded.

十二、科技、教育
文化、卫生、体育

SCIENCE AND TECHNOLOGY,EDUCATION,
CULTURE,PUBLIC HEALTH AND SPORTS

12 科技、教育、文化、卫生、体育
Science and Technology, Education, Culture, Public Health and Sports

主 要 统 计 指 标
Major Statistical Indicators

高等学校数	Number of Regular Institution of Higher Education	39	个	(unit)
高等学校在校学生数	Number of Students in Regular Institution of Higher Education	47.56	万人	(10, 000 person)
高中在校学生数	Number of Students in Senior High Schools	11.00	万人	(10, 000 person)
初中在校学生数	Number of Students in Junior High Schools	21.13	万人	(10, 000 person)
小学在校学生数	Number of Students in Primary Schools	52.45	万人	(10, 000 person)
医疗病床数	Number of Beds in Health Institutions	6.36	万张	(10, 000 bed)
# 医院	Number of Beds in Hospitals	5.84	万张	(10, 000 bed)
卫生技术人员数	Number of Medical Technical Personnel	9.30	万人	(10, 000 person)
# 执业(助理)医师	Number of Registered (Assistant) Doctors	3.48	万人	(10, 000 person)
公共图书馆	Public Library	15	个	(unit)

12-01 全市科技活动情况(2012-2015年)

The Situation of the City's Scientific and Technological Activities(2012-2015)

指 标 Item	2012	2013	2014	2015
一、全社会科技活动 The Scientific and Technological Activities in whole Society				
研究与试验发展活动折合全时人员 (人年) Full-time Equivalent of R&D Personnel	78275	81617	90193	94323
研究与试验发展经费支出 (亿元) R&D Financial Expenditure (0.1 billion yuan)	228.00	248.73	274.00	302.19
研究与试验发展经费支出占 GDP 比重 (%) The Proportion of R&D Financial Expenditure in GDP (%)	2.92	2.96	2.98	3.01
二、规模以上工业科技活动 The Scientific and Technological Activities of Industrial Enterprises Above designated Size				
有研究与试验发展活动企业数 (个) The Number of Scientific and Technological Activities Enterprises (Unit)	1229	1453	1518	1671
研究与试验发展项目数 (项) Projeet on R&D (term)	5854	7342	7383	8265
企业有科技机构 (个) Scientific and Technological Institutions of Enterprises (Unit)	1197	1273	1346	1354
科技机构仪器和设备原价 (亿元) Original Value of Machines of Scientlfic and Technological (0.1 billion yuan)	92.75	87.06	99.61	100.73
研究与试验发展人员 (万人) R&D Personnel (10,000)	6.12	6.88	7.41	8.01
每万名从业人员中研究与试验发展活动人员数 (人) The Number of R&D Activities Personnel per 10,000 Employees (Person)	501	578	644	725
研究与试验发展经费支出 (亿元) R&D Financial Expenditure (0.1 billion yuan)	143.47	160.21	177.39	198.06
研究与试验发展经费支出占主营业务收入的比例 (%) The Proportion of R&D Financial Expenditure in Main Business Income (%)	1.15	1.33	1.42	1.66

12－02 分地区、行业含规上私营单位年末人才资源(2015 年)

Trained Personnel Resource Including Private Units above Designated Size by Region(2015)

单位:人 (person)

项 目	Item	合计 Total	非私营单位 Non－Private	#专业技术人员 Technical Personnel	非私营单位 Non－Private	#技术工人 Technical Workers	非私营单位 Non－Private
全市	**Whole City**	**2880608**	**1913628**	**935476**	**679469**	**1420780**	**859911**
市区	Urban District	2599098	1763661	843676	621438	1290852	806964
#上城区	Shangcheng	160276	132798	65360	55088	59005	48262
下城区	Xiacheng	170817	150798	80323	71770	47908	42643
江干区	Jianggan	229297	111178	63122	38115	127372	45927
拱墅区	Gongshu	239177	129814	52190	31665	156317	76888
西湖区	Xihu	395932	324090	122637	98618	209847	174112
高新(滨江)区	Hi－Tech(Binjiang)	194999	154964	112531	95146	47477	33519
萧山区	Xiaoshan	573577	366683	153929	100518	328243	208217
余杭区	Yuhang	312162	172015	98487	60266	150611	70879
富阳区	Fuyang	187139	101805	56611	34746	94286	47067
桐庐县	Tonglu	76917	31826	24128	12328	38319	10692
淳安县	Chun'an	42072	25281	16566	11909	15127	5449
建德市	Jiande	56250	33856	18316	11844	24777	13200
临安市	Lin'an	106271	59004	32790	21950	51705	23606

12－02 续表 continued

项 目	Item	合计 Total	非私营单位 Non－Private	#专业技术人员 Technical Personnel	非私营单位 Non－Private	#技术工人 Technical Workers	非私营单位 Non－Private
按国民经济行业分组	**Total**						
农、林、牧、渔业	Farming, Forestry, Animal Husbandry and Fishery	716	694	183	180	240	240
采矿业	Mining	1760	841	318	93	1065	590
制造业	Manufacturing	717965	444193	169599	113245	424829	260534
电力、热力、燃气及水生产和供应业	Production & Supply of Electricity, Heat, Gas & Water	17321	16141	3611	3369	10688	9992
建筑业	Construction	1101024	564669	233274	102966	789777	425357
批发和零售业	Wholesale & Retail Trades	117424	81698	31407	20851	36770	31463
交通运输、仓储和邮政业	Transportation, Storage and Posts	89555	73893	13612	9574	61487	54725
住宿和餐饮业	Hotels and Catering Services	27315	18448	6489	3594	8565	6636
信息传输、软件和信息技术服务业	Information Transmission, Software and Information Technology	105912	85229	79628	66524	6594	4692
金融业	Financial Intermediation	60687	60571	40512	40484	3333	3333
房地产业	Real Estate	65187	53956	20049	15165	18942	18118
租赁和商务服务业	Leasing and Business Services	64543	41543	25031	15000	16699	9854
科学研究、技术服务业	Scientific Research, Technical Services	96570	75607	72669	57076	6438	5497
水利、环境和公共设施管理业	Management of Water Conservancy, Environment and Public Facilities	22702	15728	6635	4280	10882	7534
居民服务、修理和其他服务业	Service to Honseholds, Repair and Other Services	10494	6824	2186	1444	5473	3562
教育	Education	147803	144312	121077	119024	7994	7162
卫生和社会工作	Health Care and Social Work	99463	96333	86118	83826	5570	5446
文化、体育和娱乐业	Culture, Sports and Entertainment	18248	17029	12829	12525	1542	1284
公共管理、社会保障和社会组织	Public Management, Social Security and Social Organizations	115919	115919	10249	10249	3892	3892

12－03　专利申请与授权情况(2015年)

Patent Application and Authorization(2015)

单位:件　　　　(item)

地　区	Region	专利申请合计 Patent Applications	发明 Inventions	实用新型 Utility Models	外观设计 Designs	专利授权合计 Patent Applications Granted	发明 Inventions	实用新型 Utility Models	外观设计 Designs
全市	**Whole City**	**60839**	**17777**	**29048**	**14014**	**46245**	**8296**	**24764**	**13185**
市区	Urban District	54631	16937	26647	11047	41095	7922	22782	10391
#上城区	Shangcheng	1725	447	769	521	1402	269	764	371
下城区	Xiacheng	3899	1579	1625	875	3004	853	1395	916
江干区	Jianggan	8884	3394	4026	1284	6571	1455	3491	1464
拱墅区	Gongshu	2581	474	1520	587	1913	218	1155	541
西湖区	Xihu	9885	4833	3959	1084	6623	2567	3121	934
高新(滨江)区	Hi－Tech(Binjiang)	10160	3151	4289	2720	6338	1147	3120	2071
萧山区	Xiaoshan	5311	860	3567	884	4465	709	3029	728
余杭区	Yuhang	8916	1615	4692	2606	7314	499	4013	2800
富阳区	Fuyang	3270	584	2200	486	3465	205	2694	566
桐庐县	Tonglu	2528	146	702	1680	2080	65	532	1483
淳安县	Chun'an	401	97	266	38	279	31	182	66
建德市	Jiande	1247	154	360	733	956	66	252	638
临安市	Lin'an	2032	443	1073	516	1835	212	1016	607

12-04 专利申请与授权情况(2000-2015年)
Patent Application and Authorization(2000-2015)

单位:件 (item)

年份 Year	专利申请合计 Patent Applications	发明 Inventions	实用新型 Utility Models	外观设计 Designs	专利授权合计 Patent Applications Granted	发明 Inventions	实用新型 Utility Models	外观设计 Designs
2000								
2001								
2002								
2003								
2004								
2005								
2006								
2007	13295	4592	4332	4371	7563	1320	3638	2605
2008	18549	5130	5796	7623	9831	1923	4637	3271
2009	26077	6703	9806	9568	15507	2535	5806	7166
2010	29732	7766	13108	8858	26483	3238	11888	11357
2011	40890	9717	18783	12390	29249	4511	14556	10182
2012	53785	11960	25313	16512	40651	5526	20400	14725
2013	58280	14031	25523	18726	41518	4903	23159	13456
2014	48569	14779	21711	12079	33548	5552	18147	9849
2015	60839	17777	29048	14014	46245	8296	24764	13185

12－05 文化部门机构数(2015 年末)

Number of Institutions for Culture(End of 2015)

单位:个　　　　(unit)

指　标	Item	剧场 Theaters	剧团 Opera Troupes	文化馆 Cultural Centers	文化站 Cultural Stations	图书馆 Libraries	博物馆 Museums	展览馆 Exhibition Buildings
全市	**Total**	**11**	**20**	**15**	**189**	**15**	**67**	**1**
市区	Urban District	11	18	11	118	11	59	1
#萧山区	Xiaoshan	–	1	1	27	1	9	–
余杭区	Yuhang	2	1	1	19	1	5	–
富阳区	Fuyang	–	1	1	24	1	3	–
桐庐县	Tonglu	–	–	1	14	1	2	–
淳安县	Chun'an	–	–	1	23	1	1	–
建德市	Jiande	–	1	1	16	1	4	–
临安市	Lin'an	–	–	1	18	1	1	–

12－06　全市文化事业单位数(2000－2015年)
Number of Institutions for Culture(2000－2015)

单位:个　　(unit)

年　份 Year	电影院数 Cinemas	剧场 Theaters	剧团 Opera Troupes	文化馆 Cultural Centers	文化站 Cultural Stations	图书馆 Libraries	博物馆 Museums	展览馆 Exhibition Buildings
2000	16	9	18	13	268	10	9	1
2001	16	15	18	13	226	10	11	1
2002	18	13	18	13	221	10	11	1
2003	20	11	18	13	220	10	11	1
2004	18	16	18	13	165	10	12	1
2005	22	12	19	13	204	12	12	1
2006	22	12	19	13	197	13	12	1
2007	22	12	19	13	195	14	12	1
2008	23	12	19	13	195	14	13	1
2009	22	12	20	13	198	16	35	1
2010	31	12	21	13	199	16	65	1
2011	30	11	21	15	190	15	65	1
2012	40	11	21	15	192	15	65	1
2013	48	11	21	15	189	15	65	1
2014	66	12	21	15	189	15	65	1
2015	90	11	20	15	189	15	67	1

12－07　分地区艺术表演团体演出情况(2015 年)
Basic Statistics on Performance of Art Troupes by Region(2015)

指　标	Item	艺术表演场所演出场次(场) Number of Performances in Artistic Performance Place (scene)	艺术表演场所演出收入(万元) Income of Performances in Artistic Performance Place (10000 yuan)	剧团演出场次(场) Number of Performances of Opera Troupes (scene)	农　村(场) Rural Areas (scene)	剧团演出观众人数(万人次) Number of Spectators of Opera Troupes (10000 person－times)	剧团演出收入(万元) Income of Performances of Opera Troupes (10000 yuan)
全市	**Total**	**1723**	**1052.4**	**6134**	**2872**	**591.92**	**6843.0**
为上年(%)	As Compared with the Preceding Year (%)	–	–	106	103.5	99.30	109.7
市区	Urban District	1723	1052.4	5506	2304	497.12	6711.5
#萧山区	Xiaoshan	–	–	71	49	7.20	89.3
余杭区	Yuhang	53	3.2	163	147	31.00	281.0
富阳区	Fuyang	–	–	114	66	22.80	86.4
桐庐县	Tonglu	–	–	330	300	35.00	39.9
淳安县	Chun'an	–	–	–	–	–	–
建德市	Jiande	–	–	298	268	59.80	91.6
临安市	Lin'an	–	–	–	–	–	–

12－08　市区文化事业单位数(1978－2015 年)

Cultural Institutions of Urban District (1978－2015)

单位:个　　　　(unit)

年　份 Year	电影院数 Cinemas	剧　团 Opera Troupes	剧　场 Theaters	文化馆 Cultural Centers	文化站 Cultural Stations	图书馆 Libraries	博物馆 Museums
1978	7	13	6	5	–	2	1
1979	8	14	7	5	27	2	1
1980	8	15	7	5	37	2	1
1981	8	17	7	6	40	2	1
1982	9	17	7	6	45	3	1
1983	9	15	3	6	46	3	1
1984	9	15	4	6	49	3	1
1985	8	16	9	6	47	3	2
1986	8	15	8	6	48	3	2
1987	8	15	9	6	38	3	2
1988	7	14	9	6	50	3	2
1989	7	14	9	6	48	2	2
1990	9	14	9	5	48	3	2
1991	10	14	8	5	48	3	2
1992	11	14	8	5	48	3	6
1993	10	14	9	5	42	3	6
1994	11	13	9	5	48	3	6
1995	11	13	9	5	67	3	6
1996	10	13	8	5	55	3	6
1997	10	13	8	5	52	3	6
1998	9	13	8	6	55	3	7
1999	9	13	6	6	52	3	8
2000	8	12	6	6	52	3	9
2001	49	14	11	8	89	5	11
2002	–	14	10	8	90	4	11
2003	19	14	11	13	92	4	11
2004	18	14	14	8	93	5	12
2005	16	15	10	8	94	7	12
2006	16	15	10	8	94	8	12
2007	16	15	10	8	92	9	12
2008	18	15	11	8	92	9	13
2009	15	16	11	8	95	11	34
2010	25	17	11	8	96	11	54
2011	23	17	10	10	94	10	54
2012	31	17	10	10	96	10	54
2013	31	17	11	10	94	10	54
2014	55	18	11	11	118	11	57
2015	78	18	11	11	118	11	59

注:从 2001 年起市区数据包括萧山区和余杭区,2014 年起含富阳区。

a) Data of urban district include Xiaoshan district and Yuhang district since 2001, and include Fuyang district since 2014.

12－09 幼儿园基本情况(1978－2015年)

Basic Statistics on Kindergartens(1978－2015)

单位:人 (person)

年 份 Year	园 数(个) Kindergartens(unit)	在园幼儿数 Number of Children	教职员工数 Teachers and Staff	教 师 Number of Full－time Teachers
1978	266	37597	2570	1439
1979	216	59245	3731	2201
1980	518	82182	4763	3398
1981	676	82808	5275	3691
1982	853	95733	6357	4269
1983	1034	95676	6271	4135
1984	1749	112095	7238	4900
1985	1743	115766	7360	5278
1986	1607	118792	7898	5659
1987	1678	133773	8622	6335
1988	1541	139883	9221	6608
1989	1397	132947	9595	6849
1990	1526	136277	9808	7167
1991	1422	150982	10472	7388
1992	1431	133773	9240	6487
1993	1328	171005	10779	7886
1994	1470	165860	10718	7891
1995	1493	149497	10102	7943
1996	1437	150587	10203	7625
1997	1504	146530	10480	7743
1998	1695	153035	10691	7956
1999	1787	156372	10719	8107
2000	2037	168414	11740	8770
2001	1249	174204	11447	7880
2002	1268	175891	11988	8086
2003	1285	176862	13702	9076
2004	1098	186472	14991	9544
2005	1188	188991	16161	10288
2006	1188	195552	17550	11053
2007	1071	212754	19330	12168
2008	1037	235867	21193	12917
2009	972	246336	22970	14211
2010	969	267352	25525	15203
2011	970	271128	27458	16023
2012	914	283421	29843	17811
2013	860	285406	32037	18945
2014	881	295036	35212	20088
2015	910	313385	38238	21404

12－10 小学基本情况(1978－2015年)
Basic Statistics on Primary Schools(1978－2015)

单位:人 (person)

年份 Year	学校数(个) Number of Schools (unit)	在校学生数 Enrolment	毕业生数 Graduates	教职员工数 Number of Teachers and Staff	专职教师数 Number of Full－time Teachers
1978	4959	605137	－	24103	22291
1979	4850	577811	－	25089	23220
1980	4781	560244	－	25388	22902
1981	4668	525503	－	22468	20832
1982	4528	479264	－	22213	20289
1983	4417	444301	－	20842	18945
1984	4345	427763	－	20496	18500
1985	4286	414839	－	20945	18415
1986	4250	413507	－	20796	18464
1987	4205	405856	－	21067	18751
1988	4137	426842	－	21658	19236
1989	4106	459162	－	22660	20177
1990	4077	460514	－	20542	18099
1991	3972	453055	－	20781	18369
1992	3654	450496	－	21452	19067
1993	3473	477026	－	22141	19775
1994	3352	504867	－	22751	20462
1995	3172	513988	－	23743	21380
1996	3006	525674	－	24553	22197
1997	2762	538390	－	25269	23022
1998	2395	532845	－	25718	23499
1999	1996	512874	－	26350	24120
2000	1659	485679	100405	25938	23876
2001	1354	467982	93365	25535	23179
2002	1197	456535	89752	25425	23138
2003	1044	448969	84051	25304	22955
2004	897	447971	74872	25396	23066
2005	791	458942	75337	25793	23541
2006	605	459529	79070	26040	23848
2007	437	456152	81767	26455	24251
2008	418	452143	82620	26894	24743
2009	417	445132	80441	27445	25424
2010	408	453897	76126	27881	25709
2011	409	465289	73465	27862	26395
2012	415	472613	74547	25620	27777
2013	419	483489	73682	30373	28949
2014	421	502688	73244	31490	30139
2015	443	524513	71398	32815	31280

12－11 初中基本情况(1978－2015年)

Basic Statistics on Junior Middle Schools(1978－2015)

单位:人 (person)

年 份 Year	学校数(个) Number of Schools (unit)	在校学生数 Enrolment	毕业生数 Graduates	专职教师数 Number of Full－time Teachers
1978	254	247209	－	11978
1979	363	208484	－	11020
1980	369	204073	－	10695
1981	359	194024	－	10015
1982	367	193135	－	10107
1983	370	190221	－	9948
1984	368	192971	－	9679
1985	361	196889	－	9799
1986	376	199638	－	9821
1987	385	195426	－	10264
1988	380	170079	－	10055
1989	376	151223	－	9825
1990	382	160111	－	9564
1991	387	185590	－	10020
1992	367	212022	－	10603
1993	365	203896	－	10876
1994	371	205388	－	11495
1995	373	216300	－	12058
1996	374	229466	－	12810
1997	368	227809	－	13370
1998	359	222191	－	13493
1999	339	239174	－	13723
2000	330	269484	68347	14529
2001	314	285203	75722	15685
2002	315	282951	91056	15758
2003	316	268824	98412	15836
2004	303	252291	93042	16042
2005	289	241374	90094	16205
2006	263	235527	85436	16374
2007	262	238252	76194	16591
2008	260	244464	74827	16965
2009	252	241899	77268	17317
2010	245	236014	78379	17795
2011	246	223545	78431	17652
2012	244	215701	75489	17992
2013	241	213452	71006	18260
2014	241	213936	67988	18671
2015	243	211323	69200	18909

12－12　高中基本情况(1978－2015年)

Basic Statistics on Senior High Schools(1978－2015)

单位:人　　　　(person)

年份 Year	学校数(个) Number of Schools (unit)	在校学生数 Enrolment	毕业生数 Graduates	专职教师数 Number of Full－time Teachers
1978	352	102815	－	5235
1979	182	58866	－	3471
1980	151	43661	－	3173
1981	118	34606	－	2825
1982	113	35136	－	2740
1983	111	38580	－	2740
1984	105	43167	－	2781
1985	104	47510	－	3016
1986	95	46379	－	2972
1987	92	44697	－	3006
1988	89	42196	－	2947
1989	88	39994	－	2898
1990	86	39829	－	2922
1991	82	37809	－	2896
1992	74	34620	－	2791
1993	72	32483	－	2641
1994	75	35720	－	2673
1995	72	40771	－	2880
1996	70	43692	－	3135
1997	69	47975	－	3388
1998	75	55688	－	3693
1999	82	64459	－	4172
2000	85	73049	17484	4745
2001	88	79632	22012	5262
2002	81	91635	22630	6126
2003	77	108116	25429	6879
2004	81	115303	30630	7510
2005	80	120883	34486	8041
2006	82	124177	39484	8421
2007	80	122939	39805	8542
2008	76	120294	40551	8646
2009	75	118057	41408	8751
2010	72	116983	39319	8871
2011	71	117089	38579	9061
2012	70	115652	38623	9069
2013	70	113894	37810	9125
2014	72	110478	38489	9378
2015	75	109983	37303	9630

12－13 中等专业学校基本情况(1978－2015年)

Basic Statistics on Specialized Secondary Schools(1978－2015)

单位:人 (person)

年份 Year	学校数(个) Number of Schools (unit)	在校学生数 Enrolment	毕业生数 Graduates	教职员工数 Teachers and Staff	专职教师数 Number of Full－time Teachers
1978	26	8711	–	3044	1080
1979	27	11093	–	2601	1124
1980	26	9453	–	2450	1101
1981	35	7309	–	3122	1276
1982	37	8284	–	3694	1529
1983	37	10516	–	3716	1604
1984	42	13419	–	4194	1758
1985	46	16527	–	5095	1959
1986	50	19114	–	5641	2336
1987	52	20929	–	6081	2623
1988	51	22117	–	6144	2741
1989	54	23302	–	6602	2888
1990	55	23564	–	6679	2948
1991	55	23331	–	6584	2770
1992	55	26373	–	6786	2825
1993	56	30336	–	6732	2780
1994	57	36079	–	6881	2840
1995	57	42784	–	6851	2888
1996	58	49593	–	6789	2904
1997	57	51752	–	6731	2896
1998	56	55796	–	6554	2746
1999	50	52272	–	5023	2272
2000	28	45238	15674	2950	1421
2001	26	32763	15202	2053	1051
2002	14	26255	13355	1251	566
2003	13	21735	11866	1058	457
2004	11	21262	6399	869	416
2005	10	20344	6661	893	443
2006	8	12540	5830	410	184
2007	8	8927	4849	414	194
2008	8	5514	4130	345	152
2009	8	4016	2025	233	65
2010	6	3999	1092	348	151
2011	5	4071	934	369	154
2012	5	3909	1252	376	150
2013	5	3656	1215	390	158
2014	7	3974	1077	469	226
2015	7	3968	1134	494	244

12－14 高等学校基本情况(1978－2015年)

Basic Statistics on Regular Institutions of Higher Education(1978－2015)

单位:人 (person)

年　份 Year	学校数(个) Number of Schools (unit)	招生数 Entrants	在校学生数 Enrolment	毕业生数 Graduates	教职员工数 Teachers and Staff	专职教师数 Number of Full－time Teachers
1978	9	－	13319	－	8966	3946
1979	12	－	17518	－	10182	4458
1980	13	－	23545	－	12400	5278
1981	13	－	28936	－	13090	5359
1982	13	－	25821	－	14363	6067
1983	14	－	27443	－	15267	6172
1984	16	－	31384	－	15889	6387
1985	20	－	36996	－	17507	7247
1986	22	－	40051	－	18968	7845
1987	21	－	39922	－	18965	7876
1988	21	－	40787	－	19582	8133
1989	21	－	40330	－	19680	8107
1990	21	－	39866	－	19495	8075
1991	21	－	42192	－	19489	7737
1992	19	－	43787	－	19841	7561
1993	19	－	51063	－	19787	7561
1994	19	－	59109	－	19903	7703
1995	20	－	63124	－	19883	7799
1996	20	－	66023	－	19693	7824
1997	20	－	69391	－	19540	7793
1998	17	－	76546	－	19320	7723
1999	18	－	89109	－	20136	8135
2000	32	46070	122386	17004	23791	10477
2001	33	63001	174894	22756	25805	11866
2002	34	74656	224048	27213	27307	13605
2003	35	85865	269798	41192	34508	18141
2004	36	96810	313599	53288	33325	18445
2005	36	101374	351918	63989	34816	19583
2006	36	103885	373563	80069	36929	21375
2007	36	110371	392770	90944	38843	23197
2008	36	114714	409559	97778	39762	24017
2009	36	114568	429774	96101	40420	24765
2010	37	113529	434811	101681	41582	25003
2011	38	117892	446721	104486	42222	25735
2012	38	121331	459181	107484	43216	26689
2013	38	123046	471820	108688	43992	27544
2014	38	122099	474652	110512	44710	28265
2015	39	139002	475558	125013	44825	28868

注:在校学生数包括各高校研究生。

a) Number of students include graduate students in all colleges and universities.

12－15　小学、幼儿园及特殊

Basic Statistics on Primary Schools,

单位:人

指　标	Item	全　市 Total	市　区 Urban District	萧山区 Xiaoshan
小　　学	**Primary Schools**			
学校数(所)	Number of Schools(unit)	443	309	73
班数(班)	Number of Classes(unit)	13897	11248	2382
在校学生数	Number of Students	524513	434248	94981
本年招生数	Number of New Students Enrollment	96172	80997	16861
本年毕业生数	Number of Graduates	71398	57338	13995
专职教师数	Full－time Teachers	31280	25286	5555
2016 年预计毕业生数	Number of Students Will Graduate in 2016	78246	63355	15359
幼儿园	**Kindergartens**			
园数(个)	Number of Kindergartens(unit)	910	711	171
班数(班)	Number of Classes(unit)	10702	8913	1699
在园幼儿数	Number of Children	313385	263590	50408
教师数	Full－time Teachers	21404	18217	3229
盲聋哑学校	**Schools for the Blind,Deaf and Deaf－mute**			
学校数(个)	Number of Schools(unit)	2	2	－
在校学生数	Number of Students	468	468	－
本年招生数	Number of New Students Enrollment	46	46	－
本年毕业生数	Number of Graduates	84	84	－
专职教师数	Number of Full－time Teachers	154	154	－
弱智学校	**Schools for Weaken in Intelligence**			
学校数(个)	Number of Schools(unit)	12	8	1
在校学生数	Number of Students	1114	916	255
本年招生数	Number of New Students Enrollment	159	148	65
本年毕业生数	Number of Graduates	159	143	61
专职教师数	Number of Full－time Teachers	326	281	65
工读学校	**Reformatory Schools**			
学校数(个)	Number of Schools(unit)	1	1	－
在校学生数	Number of Students	334	334	－
本年招生数	Number of New Students Enrollment	174	174	－
本年毕业生数	Number of Graduates	144	144	－
专任教师数	Number of Full－time Teachers	61	61	－

教育基本情况(2015 年)
Kindergartens and Special Education(2015)

(person)

余杭区 Yuhang	富阳区 Fuyang	桐庐县 Tonglu	淳安县 Chun'an	建德市 Jiande	临安市 Lin'an
48	44	27	38	29	40
2190	1226	643	613	584	809
87352	44988	23253	16343	20990	29679
16194	7554	3801	2554	3552	5268
11375	6839	3468	2812	3296	4484
4781	2555	1388	1580	1277	1749
13034	7300	3660	3041	3496	4694
100	88	49	36	39	75
1610	832	423	287	440	639
51810	24131	12771	7318	12181	17525
3478	1686	739	481	734	1233
–	1	–	–	–	–
–	258	–	–	–	–
–	21	–	–	–	–
–	26	–	–	–	–
–	66	–	–	–	–
1	1	1	1	1	1
89	56	53	33	30	82
8	5	1	–	2	8
–	–	–	2	1	13
24	19	11	7	6	21
–	–	–	–	–	–
–	–	–	–	–	–
–	–	–	–	–	–
–	–	–	–	–	–
–	–	–	–	–	–

12－16 普通中学、职业中学
Basic Statistics on Senior, Junior High

单位:人

指 标	Item	全 市 Total	市 区 Urban District	萧山区 Xiaoshan
高　　中	**Senior High Schools**			
学校数(所)	Number of Schools(unit)	75	55	9
在校学生数	Number of Students	109983	81932	18923
本年招生数	Number of New Students Enrollment	37642	28474	6346
本年毕业生数	Number of Graduates	37303	26969	6454
专职教师数	Full－time Teachers	9630	7268	1705
2016 年预计毕业生数	Number of Students Will Graduate in 2016	36540	26844	6325
初　　中	**Junior High Schools**			
学校数(所)	Number of Schools(unit)	243	178	38
在校学生数	Number of Students	211323	168163	38728
本年招生数	Number of New Students Enrollment	69563	55884	13281
本年毕业生数	Number of Graduates	69200	53309	12112
专职教师数	Full－time Teachers	18909	14670	3133
2016 年预计毕业生数	Number of Students Will Graduate in 2016	70329	55249	12445
职业中学	**Vocational Schools**			
学校数(所)	Number of Schools(unit)	32	23	4
在校学生数	Number of Students	62092	49853	12363
本年招生数	Number of New Students Enrollment	20632	16435	3649
本年毕业生数	Number of Graduates	22038	17462	4598
专职教师数	Full－time Teachers	4420	3515	823
2016 年预计毕业生数	Number of Students Will Graduate in 2016	21211	17108	4708
技工学校	**Technical Schools**			
学校数(所)	Number of schools(unit)	18	15	1
在校学生数	Number of Students	24722	22719	2049
专职教师数	Full－time Teachers	1709	1407	217

和技工学校基本情况(2015年)
Schools and Vacational, Technical Schools(2015)

(person)

余杭区 Yuhang	富阳区 Fuyang	桐庐县 Tonglu	淳安县 Chun'an	建德市 Jiande	临安市 Lin'an
11	6	4	5	6	5
13446	12601	5212	6403	8744	7692
4601	4093	1708	2123	2896	2441
4260	4457	2055	2454	2963	2862
1144	1049	500	534	681	647
4434	4405	1770	2193	3014	2719
32	16	13	17	17	18
31373	19535	9982	9434	10681	13063
10728	6523	3269	2844	3234	4332
9343	6427	3457	3805	4352	4277
2666	1594	936	1041	1191	1071
9999	6516	3375	3439	3960	4306
5	2	2	2	3	2
10364	7464	2865	3544	2171	3659
3565	2309	1150	1208	542	1297
3484	2950	979	1241	942	1414
721	557	200	230	135	340
3454	2639	825	1212	860	1206
1	1	–	1	1	1
194	296	–	–	1225	778
142	17	–	176	75	51

12 - 17 高等学校

Basic Statistics on Regular

单位:人

单位名称	Item	在校学生数 Enrolment	
		2015	为上年(%) As Compared with the Preceding Year(%)
全　　市	**Total**	**425384**	**101.5**
#市　　区	**Urban District**	**403415**	**101.6**
浙江大学	Zhejiang University	23897	101.12
杭州电子科技大学	Hangzhou Dianzi University	16392	98.92
浙江工业大学	Zhejiang Univesity of Technology	20548	98.01
浙江理工大学	Zhejiang Sci - Tech University	17632	100.23
浙江农林大学	Zhejiang Forestry University	14377	101.09
浙江中医药大学	Zhejiang University of Traditional Chinese Medicine	6704	108.13
杭州师范大学	Hangzhou Normal University	17499	105.62
浙江工商大学	Zhejiang Gongshang University	15066	99.48
中国美术学院	China Academy of Art	7989	95.63
中国计量学院	China Institute of Metrology	14965	102.48
浙江科技学院	Hangzhou Application Engineering and Technology College	16290	104.08
浙江广播电视大学	Zhejiang Radio & TV University	11741	101.26
浙江水利水电专科学校	Zhejiang Water Conservancy and Hydroelectricity College	8929	110.63
浙江财经学院	Zhejiang Institute of Finance and Economics	13429	99.64
浙江警察学院	Zhejiang Police College	3921	100.1
浙江传媒学院	Zhejiang Institute of Media and Communications	13884	105.65
浙江树人大学	Zhejiang Shuren University	15278	101.91
浙江大学城市学院	Zhejiang University City College	13245	100.34

注:本表不含在校研究生。

a) Data in this table does not contain post - graduate students.

基本情况(2015 年)
Institutions of Higher Education(2015)

(person)

本年招生数 Entrants	本年毕业生数 Graduates	教职员工数 Number of Teachers and Staff	
		合 计 Total	其中:专职教师 Full - time Teachers
122326	**111853**	**44825**	**28868**
116811	**106575**	**42703**	**27351**
5868	5349	8255	3562
4144	4161	1823	1449
4838	5013	3043	2076
4447	4367	1873	1405
3614	3368	1673	1114
1904	1403	1081	755
4870	3909	2248	1511
3892	3937	1794	1364
1936	2213	1001	652
3795	3296	1477	984
4077	3564	1270	948
3585	3785	265	74
3019	2001	664	478
3511	3521	1430	979
1030	525	471	228
3538	2588	1277	734
4046	3664	784	602
3280	3000	979	689

12－18 各级成人教育

Basic Statistics on

单位:人

指 标	Item	成人高等学历教育 Higher Education for Adults	成人高校 Adult Institutions of Higher Education	普通高校成人高等学历教育 Adult Higher Education in Ordinary Universities
全　市	**Total**			
学校数(所)	Number of Schools(unit)	3	3	
在校学生数	Number of Students	122880	15786	107094
本年招生数	Number of New Students Enrollment	52334	5620	46714
本年毕业生数	Number of Graduates	52673	5327	47346
教职员工数	Number of Teachers and Staff	452	452	
#专职教师	#Full－time Teachers	187	187	
市　区	**Urban District**			
学校数(所)	Number of Schools(unit)	3	3	
在校学生数	Number of Students	116685	15786	100899
本年招生数	Number of New Students Enrollment	49169	5620	43549
本年毕业生数	Number of Graduates	50280	5327	44953
教职员工数	Number of Teachers and Staff	452	452	
#专职教师	#Full－time Teachers	187	187	

基本情况(2015 年)
Various Adult Education(2015)

(person)

成人中等学历教育 Adult Secondary Education	成人中等专业 Adult Secondary Specialized	成人中学 Secondary Schools for Adults
198	6	192
235008	15994	219014
7378	7378	-
234047	7647	226400
1482	-	1482
1125	-	1125
92	6	86
121136	15994	105142
7378	7378	-
118394	7647	110747
1597	664	933
1043	342	701

12－19 医疗卫生机构数(1978－2015 年)
Number of Health Institutions(1978－2015)

单位:个 (unit)

年 份 Year	全市合计 Total	医 院 Hospitals	市区合计 Urban District	医 院 Hospitals
1978	1361	421	689	45
1979	1390	426	696	50
1980	1381	425	675	51
1981	1476	424	749	51
1982	1540	432	798	56
1983	1540	435	800	58
1984	1574	437	807	54
1985	1582	404	787	47
1986	1636	407	826	53
1987	1693	420	865	55
1988	1710	438	878	55
1989	1721	443	882	57
1990	1738	440	890	58
1991	1789	441	889	58
1992	1767	436	885	58
1993	1730	403	882	68
1994	1717	416	882	72
1995	1712	414	883	72
1996	1712	416	893	83
1997	1711	411	891	81
1998	1491	419	757	89
1999	1530	400	789	85
2000	1599	396	853	85
2001	1496	391	1072	191
2002	1817	116	1277	88
2003	1901	99	1323	73
2004	1985	114	1396	87
2005	2196	127	1604	97
2006	2570	134	1886	107
2007	2607	138	1872	104
2008	2544	141	1813	108
2009	2687	144	1887	111
2010	2819	151	1906	113
2011	2958	167	1992	122
2012	3017	198	2004	146
2013	4139	208	2233	156
2014	4198	218	2763	173
2015	4428	244	2982	198

注:市区数据从 2001 年起包括萧山区和余杭区,2014 年起含富阳区。2002 年起医院数据不包括卫生院。

a) Data of urban district include Xiaoshan district and Yuhang district since 2001, and include Fuyang district since 2014. From 2002, the figures of hospitals exclude health centers.

12－20　医疗病床数(1978－2015年)

Number of Beds in Health Institutions(1978－2015)

单位:张　　　　(bed)

年　份 Year	全　市 Total	医　院 Hospitals	市　区 Urban District	医　院 Hospitals
1978	14042	11704	6588	5789
1979	15124	12682	7335	6282
1980	16317	13478	8244	6940
1981	17408	13576	9646	7185
1982	17179	14350	9194	7580
1983	17338	14584	9411	7833
1984	17694	14691	9536	7867
1985	19637	15010	11095	7933
1986	20555	16035	11657	8448
1987	21465	16770	12203	8863
1988	23394	17954	13204	9651
1989	24111	18363	13581	9773
1990	24121	18879	13219	10041
1991	24966	19444	13968	10437
1992	25606	20243	14206	10821
1993	25653	20884	14058	10982
1994	25984	20870	14231	11045
1995	26684	21360	14731	11336
1996	28141	22217	15427	12132
1997	26616	22341	15076	12190
1998	27327	23110	15530	12766
1999	26713	22952	14988	12691
2000	27166	23303	15496	13068
2001	27063	23520	20523	17770
2002	27609	22797	21200	18667
2003	29144	22036	22641	18205
2004	31738	24444	25008	20338
2005	33251	25907	26732	21931
2006	33972	27186	27172	23184
2007	36928	29987	29884	25664
2008	38114	31416	30663	26882
2009	40226	33094	32412	28031
2010	42828	36148	34693	30639
2011	45291	39363	36633	33291
2012	49471	44019	40534	37383
2013	52056	46636	42506	39489
2014	55779	50805	48406	44639
2015	63632	58400	55540	51672

12－21 医疗卫生

Number of Health

单位:个

指　　标	Item	全　市 Total	市区 Urban District
总　　计	**Total**	**4428**	**2982**
一、医院	Number of Hospitals	244	198
1.综合医院	General Hospitals	121	103
2.中医医院	Hospitals of Chinese Medicine	29	18
3.中西医结合医院	Chinese Therapeutics with Western	6	5
4.专科医院	Specialized Hospitals	81	65
#口腔医院	Hospitals for Mouth	11	10
眼科医院	Hospitals for Eye	3	2
耳鼻喉科医院	ENT Hospitals	–	–
肿瘤医院	Tumor Hospitals	3	3
心血管病医院	Cardiovascular Hospitals	–	–
胸科医院	Chest Hospitals	–	–
血液病医院	Blood Diseases Hospitals	–	–
妇产(科)医院	Hospitals for Pregnant Woman	12	11
儿童医院	Children Hospitals	3	3
精神病医院	Mental Hospitals	6	3
传染病医院	Hospitals for Infectious Diseases	1	1
皮肤病医院	Dermatology Hospital	2	2
结核病医院	Tuberculosis Hospitals	–	–
麻疯病医院	Leprosy Hospitals	–	–
职业病医院	Occupational Disease Hospitals	–	–
骨科医院	Orthopaedics Hospitals	9	5
康复医院	Healing Hospitals	12	10
整型外科医院	Plastic Hospitals	1	1
美容医院	Beauty Hospitals	9	8
其他专科医院	Other Special Hospitals	9	6
5.护理院	Nursing Centers	7	7
二、基层医疗卫生机构	Community Medical Institutions	4081	2708
1.社区卫生服务中心(站)	Health Service Centers for Community	1278	1026
#社区卫生服务中心	Health Service Centers	133	122
社区卫生服务站	Health Service Stations	1145	904
2.卫生院	Health Service Centers	89	9
#街道卫生院	Rural Township Hospitals in Subdistrict	–	–
乡镇卫生院	Rural Township Hospitals in Country	89	9
3.村卫生室	Health Offices in Village	938	259
4.门诊部	Clinics	443	401
5.诊所、卫生所、医务室、护理站	Other Health Care Institutions	1333	1013
三、专业公共卫生机构	Professional Public Health Institutions	63	40
疾病预防控制中心	Centers for Disease Prevention and Control	15	11
专科疾病防治所(所、站)	Specialized Centers for Disease Prevention and Control(stations)	2	–
健康教育所(站、中心)	Education Center for Health(stations)	1	–
妇幼保健院(所、站)	Maternity and Child Care Centers(stations)	9	5
急救中心(站)	First－aid Centers(stations)	10	5
采供血机构	Blood Supplying Agencies	3	2
卫生监督所	Institutions of Public Health Inspection	16	12
计划生育服务机构	Family Planning Service Institutions	7	5
四、其他卫生机构	Other Health Care Institutions	40	36
疗养院	Sanatoriums	7	7
医学科学研究机构	Research Institutions of Medical Science	1	1
医学在职培训机构	Medical Training Organization for Incumbent	6	3
临床检验中心(所、站)	Clinical Laboratory Center	5	5
统计信息中心	Statistical Information Centers	2	2
其他	Other	19	18

机构数(2015 年末)

Institutions(End of 2015)

(unit)

萧山区 Xiaoshan	余杭区 Yuhang	富阳区 Fuyang	桐庐县 Tonglu	淳安县 Chun'an	建德市 Jiande	临安市 Lin'an
696	**418**	**474**	**317**	**312**	**371**	**446**
47	17	12	10	7	8	21
40	7	5	5	3	2	8
4	1	3	1	2	1	7
–	–	–	–	–	1	–
3	5	4	4	2	4	6
1	1	1	–	–	–	1
–	–	–	–	–	1	–
–	–	–	–	–	–	–
–	–	1	–	–	–	–
–	–	–	–	–	–	–
–	–	–	–	–	–	–
–	–	–	–	–	–	–
–	1	–	–	–	–	1
–	–	–	–	–	–	–
–	1	1	1	1	1	–
–	–	–	–	–	–	–
1	–	–	–	–	–	–
–	–	–	–	–	–	–
–	–	–	–	–	–	–
–	–	–	–	–	–	–
–	2	–	1	–	1	2
1	–	–	–	1	1	–
–	–	–	–	–	–	–
–	–	–	–	–	–	1
–	–	1	2	–	–	1
–	4	–	–	–	–	–
641	395	454	303	297	355	418
317	181	181	106	50	20	76
29	20	25	3	2	1	5
288	161	156	103	48	19	71
–	–	9	10	21	22	27
–	–	–	–	–	–	–
–	–	9	10	21	22	27
124	–	135	122	180	230	147
36	74	25	14	1	13	14
164	140	104	51	45	70	154
6	5	4	4	7	6	6
1	1	1	1	1	1	1
–	–	–	–	–	1	1
–	–	–	–	–	–	1
–	1	1	1	1	1	1
2	1	1	–	3	1	1
1	–	–	–	–	1	–
1	1	1	1	1	1	1
1	1	–	1	1	–	–
2	1	4	–	1	2	1
1	–	4	–	–	–	–
–	–	–	–	–	–	–
–	1	–	–	1	1	1
1	–	–	–	–	–	–
–	–	–	–	–	–	–
–	–	–	–	–	1	–

12－22 医疗病床
Number of Beds in

单位:张

指 标	Item	全 市 Total	市区 Urban District
总 计	**Total**	**63632**	**55540**
一、医院	Number of Hospitals	58400	51672
1.综合医院	General Hospitals	33749	29643
2.中医医院	Hospitals of Chinese Medicine	7374	6070
3.中西医结合医院	Chinese Therapeutics with Western	4158	3961
4.专科医院	Specialized Hospitals	12190	11069
#口腔医院	Hospitals for Mouth	189	169
眼科医院	Hospitals for Eye	160	140
耳鼻喉科医院	ENT Hospitals	–	–
肿瘤医院	Tumor Hospitals	2587	2587
心血管病医院	Cardiovascular Hospitals	–	–
胸科医院	Chest Hospitals	–	–
血液病医院	Blood Diseases Hospitals	–	–
妇产(科)医院	Hospitals for Pregnant Woman	1765	1745
儿童医院	Children Hospitals	1608	1608
精神病医院	Mental Hospitals	1916	1535
传染病医院	Hospitals for Infectious Diseases	600	600
皮肤病医院	Dermatology Hospital	90	90
结核病医院	Tuberculosis Hospitals	–	–
麻疯病医院	Leprosy Hospitals	–	–
职业病医院	Occupational Disease Hospitals	–	–
骨科医院	Orthopaedics Hospitals	866	408
康复医院	Healing Hospitals	1549	1407
整型外科医院	Plastic Hospitals	160	160
美容医院	Beauty Hospitals	183	163
其他专科医院	Other Special Hospitals	517	457
5.护理院	Nursing Centers	929	929
二、基层医疗卫生机构	Community Medical Institutions	3374	2693
1.社区卫生服务中心(站)	Health Service Centers for Community	2770	2643
#社区卫生服务中心	Health Service Centers	2750	2643
社区卫生服务站	Health Service Stations	20	–
2.卫生院	Health Service Centers	582	38
#街道卫生院	Rural Township Hospitals in Subdistrict	–	–
乡镇卫生院	Rural Township Hospitals in Country	582	38
3.村卫生室	Health Offices in Village	–	–
4.门诊部	Clinics	22	12
5.诊所、卫生所、医务室、护理站	Other Health Care Institutions	–	–
三、专业公共卫生机构	Professional Public Health Institutions	1271	588
疾病预防控制中心	Centers for Disease Prevention and Control	–	–
专科疾病防治所(所、站)	Specialized Centers for Disease Prevention and Control(stations)	400	–
健康教育所(站、中心)	Education Center for Health(stations)	–	–
妇幼保健院(所、站)	Maternity and Child Care Centers(stations)	852	588
急救中心(站)	First－aid Centers(stations)	19	–
采供血机构	Blood Supplying Agencies	–	–
卫生监督所(中心)	Institutions of Public Health Inspection	–	–
计划生育技术服务机构	Family Planning Service Institutions	–	–
四、其他卫生机构	Other Health Care Institutions	587	587
#疗养院	Sanatoriums	587	587
医学科学研究机构	Research Institutions of Medical Science	–	–
医学在职培训机构	Medical Training Organization for Incumbent	–	–
临床检验中心(所、站)	Clinical Laboratory Center	–	–
统计信息中心	Statistical Information Centers	–	–
其他	Other	–	–

数(2015 年末)
Health Institutions(End of 2015)

(bed)

萧山区 Xiaoshan	余杭区 Yuhang	富阳区 Fuyang	桐庐县 Tonglu	淳安县 Chun'an	建德市 Jiande	临安市 Lin'an
8266	**4568**	**3048**	**1648**	**1677**	**2309**	**2458**
7733	3660	2124	1392	1457	1670	2209
6483	1982	1234	1114	835	800	1357
1135	400	625	200	482	200	422
–	–	–	–	–	197	–
115	856	265	78	140	473	430
15	1	15	–	–	–	20
–	–	–	–	–	20	–
–	–	–	–	–	–	–
–	–	20	–	–	–	–
–	–	–	–	–	–	–
–	–	–	–	–	–	–
–	–	–	–	–	–	–
–	35	–	–	–	–	20
–	–	–	–	–	–	–
–	520	150	–	90	291	–
–	–	–	–	–	–	–
40	–	–	–	–	–	–
–	–	–	–	–	–	–
–	–	–	–	–	–	–
–	–	–	–	–	–	–
–	300	–	38	–	70	350
60	–	–	–	50	92	–
–	–	–	–	–	–	–
–	–	–	–	–	–	20
–	–	80	40	–	–	20
–	422	–	–	–	–	–
473	658	252	176	84	281	140
471	654	212	22	–	28	77
471	654	212	22	–	8	77
–	–	–	–	–	20	–
–	–	38	154	84	253	53
–	–	–	–	–	–	–
–	–	38	154	84	253	53
–	–	–	–	–	–	–
2	4	2	–	–	–	10
–	–	–	–	–	–	–
–	250	338	80	136	358	109
–	–	–	–	–	–	–
–	–	–	–	–	300	100
–	–	–	–	–	–	–
–	250	338	80	136	48	–
–	–	–	–	–	10	9
–	–	–	–	–	–	–
–	–	–	–	–	–	–
–	–	–	–	–	–	–
60	–	334	–	–	–	–
60	–	334	–	–	–	–
–	–	–	–	–	–	–
–	–	–	–	–	–	–
–	–	–	–	–	–	–
–	–	–	–	–	–	–
–	–	–	–	–	–	–

12－23 医院诊疗

Number of

指　标	Item	机构数(个) Number of Institutions (unit)	诊疗人次数(万人次) Total Number of Patients Treate (10000 person－times)
总　计	**Total**	**4428**	**11734.47**
一、医院	Number of Hospitals	244	6332.41
综合医院	General Hospitals	121	3974.50
中医医院	Hospitals of Chinese Medicine	29	1039.26
中西医结合医院	Chinese Therapeutics with Western	6	449.75
专科医院	Specialized Hospitals	81	866.33
#口腔医院	Hospitals for Mouth	11	119.69
眼科医院	Hospitals for Eye	3	14.44
肿瘤医院	Tumor Hospitals	3	66.06
妇产(科)医院	Hospitals for Pregnant Woman	12	189.44
儿童医院	Children Hospitals	3	285.08
精神病医院	Mental Hospitals	6	35.41
传染病医院	Hospitals for Infectious Diseases	1	50.72
皮肤病医院	Dermatology Hospital	2	20.60
骨科医院	Orthopaedics Hospitals	9	29.69
康复医院	Healing Hospitals	12	18.65
整型外科医院	Plastic Hospitals	1	5.03
美容医院	Beauty Hospitals	9	16.59
其他专科医院	Other Special Hospitals	9	14.92
护理院	Nursing Centers	7	2.56
二、基层医疗卫生机构	Community Medical Institutions	4081	5194.13
社区卫生服务中心(站)	Health Service Centers for Community	1278	3357.71
#社区卫生服务中心	Health Service Centers	133	3263.58
社区卫生服务站	Health Service Stations	1145	94.13
卫生院	Health Service Centers	89	429.58
乡镇卫生院	Rural Township Hospitals in Country	89	429.58
#乡卫生院	Township Health Centers	938	194.79
门诊部	Clinics	443	717.09
诊所、卫生所、医务室	Other Health Care Institutions	1333	488.10
三、专业公共卫生机构	Professional Public Health Institutions	63	198.23
专科疾病防治院(所、站)	Specialized Centers for Disease Prevention and Control(stations)	2	10.46
妇幼保健院(所、站)	Maternity and Child Care Centers(stations)	9	175.99
急救中心(站)	First－aid Centers(stations)	10	11.78
四、其他机构	Other Institutions	40	9.70
疗养院	Sanatoriums	7	9.70

次数和入院人数（2015年）
Hospital Patients(2015)

门、急诊人次数(万人次) Out - Patients and Emergency Patients (10000 person - times)	入院人数 (人) Hospital Admissions(person)	每百门急诊次入院人数(人) Hospital Admissions Per 100 Patient - time (person)
11462.14	**1809659**	**1.77**
6300.27	1721727	2.73
3952.24	1085300	2.75
1035.61	204503	1.97
449.75	102616	2.28
860.64	326430	3.79
119.69	801	0.07
14.37	6649	4.63
66.06	97053	14.69
185.52	81029	4.37
285.08	68301	2.40
35.39	17257	4.88
49.91	20156	4.04
20.60	2	-
29.22	15869	5.43
18.60	6327	3.40
5.03	3842	7.63
16.51	5373	3.25
14.67	3771	2.57
2.03	2878	14.16
4954.54	18516	0.05
3236.75	12207	0.04
3142.67	12056	0.04
94.08	151	0.02
419.41	5956	0.14
419.41	5956	0.14
191.77	1207	0.06
626.25	-	-
477.97	-	-
198.23	49574	2.66
10.46	1339	1.28
175.99	48235	2.74
11.78	-	-
9.10	19842	21.8
9.10	19842	21.8

12－24 卫生事业

Number of Medical

单位：人

指　　标	Item	全　　市 Total	市　　区 Urban District
总　　计	**Total**	**113762**	**99015**
一、卫生技术人员	Number of Medical Technical Personnel	93036	80799
1. 执业(助理)医师	Registered (Assistant) Doctor	34832	30316
#执业医师	Registered Doctor	32310	28473
2. 注册护士	Registered Nurse	38182	33672
3. 药剂师	Druggist	6313	5283
4. 技师人员	Checking Member	5348	4652
#检验师	Docimaster	3940	3420
5. 其他	Others	8361	6876
二、其他技术人员	Other Medical Technical Personnel	5208	4779
三、管理人员	Managerial Personnel	4705	4211
四、工勤人员	Logistics Worker	10019	8961

人员数(2015 年末)

Technical Personnel(End of 2015)

(person)

萧山区 Xiaoshan	余杭区 Yuhang	富阳区 Fuyang	桐庐县 Tonglu	淳安县 Chun'an	建德市 Jiande	临安市 Lin'an
13755	**9379**	**5676**	**4018**	**2629**	**3855**	**4245**
11313	7885	4615	3385	2164	3102	3586
4035	2910	1846	1117	834	1071	1494
3490	2564	1568	930	736	905	1266
4470	3005	1637	1188	803	1270	1249
846	557	265	291	184	261	294
517	468	224	183	128	188	197
387	336	141	143	96	142	139
1445	942	643	606	215	312	352
443	302	245	109	67	65	188
465	276	215	168	56	158	112
1398	919	472	334	168	315	241

12－25　卫生技术人员（1978－2015 年）
Number of Medical Technical Personnel（1978－2015）

单位：人　　　　（person）

年　份 Year	全　市 Total	执业（助理）医师 Number of Registered（Assistant）Doctors	注册护士 Registered Nurses	市　区 Urban District	执业（助理）医师 Number of Registered（Assistant）Doctors	注册护士 Registered Nurses
1978	19059	7375	3483	10867	4346	2510
1979	20060	7539	3536	11779	4733	2632
1980	21110	8311	3885	12376	5179	2804
1981	22737	9284	4139	13697	5946	3032
1982	23558	9883	4369	14221	6204	3193
1983	24914	10833	4562	15213	6990	3352
1984	25648	11291	4817	15807	7393	3487
1985	25593	11503	5071	15840	7644	3705
1986	26489	12623	5391	16543	8239	3940
1987	27663	12369	5805	17361	8329	4156
1988	28676	13674	6938	18022	8710	4801
1989	29791	14177	7348	18619	9146	5085
1990	30990	14483	7822	19231	9374	5397
1991	32169	14858	8153	19630	9494	5610
1992	32628	14842	8417	19690	9373	5736
1993	33172	15181	8643	19708	9499	5797
1994	33964	15465	8979	19907	9472	5940
1995	34245	16465	9531	19943	9607	6249
1996	34946	16789	9794	20695	9889	6508
1997	35423	17112	10019	20728	9902	6571
1998	35857	16022	10577	21035	9452	6788
1999	35256	16668	10587	20519	9610	6856
2000	35487	16317	11186	20344	9050	7300
2001	36643	16994	11576	28293	12968	9343
2002	37193	16092	11922	28818	12332	9653
2003	39019	16614	12460	30299	12731	10161
2004	39816	16770	13248	30886	12894	10840
2005	42353	17833	14514	33206	13802	12034
2006	45375	18831	15557	35904	14689	12986
2007	49780	20701	17455	39860	16290	14601
2008	52379	21223	18702	42015	16747	15556
2009	56270	22753	20997	45219	17996	17530
2010	61117	24345	23418	49232	19414	19481
2011	65869	25773	25231	53008	20566	20949
2012	71618	27369	28382	57971	22004	23760
2013	78340	29686	30996	63359	23886	25808
2014	85614	31977	34724	74064	27675	30528
2015	93036	34832	38182	80799	30316	33672

注：市区数据从 2001 年起包括萧山区和余杭区，2014 年起含富阳区。

a）Data of urban district include Xiaoshan and Yuhang district since 2001，and include Fuyang district since 2014.

12 - 26 体育运动情况(2013 - 2015 年)
Basic Statistics on Sports Activities(2013 - 2015)

单位:人 (person)

指 标	Item	2013 年	2014 年	2015 年
一、年末体委工作人员数	**Workers in Sports Commissions at Year - end**	**923**	**685**	**695**
#教练员	#Full - time Coaches	140	131	151
二、等级裁判员发展人数	**Number of Referees in Grades**	**417**	**520**	**266**
#女	#Female	140	157	66
一级裁判员	First Grade Referees	89	55	34
二级裁判员	Second Grade Referees	328	465	232
三级裁判员	Third Grade Referees		-	
三、等级运动员发展人数	**Number of Athletes in Grades**	**385**	**425**	**349**
#女	#Female	149	183	149
一级运动员	First Grade Athlete	47	124	64
二级运动员	Second Grade Athlete	338	301	285
三级运动员	Third Grade Athlete		-	

主要统计指标解释

文化事业机构 指从事专业文化工作和为专业文化工作服务的独立建制的单独核算的单位。不包括这些单位另外举办独立核算的其他机构和各部门的业余文化组织。

艺术表演团体 指从事戏曲、音乐、舞蹈、杂技等专业艺术表演,有独立帐户,实行单独核算的团体。不包括半工半艺、半农半艺和民间职业剧团。

普通高等学校 指按照国家规定的设置标准和审批程序批准举办,通过国家统一招生考试,招收高中毕业生为主要培养对象,实施高等教育的全日制大学、独立设置的学院和高等专科学校、短期职业大学。

成人高等学校 指按照国家有关规定审批,招收通过全国成人高教统一招生考试的具有高中毕业或同等学历的在职从业人员利用脱产、半脱产、业余或函授等多种形式对其实施高等学历教育,培养高等教育专科或本科毕业水平的专门人才,修业年限、课程设置和总学时数均按高等学历教育要求付诸实施的学校。包括广播电视大学、职工高等学校、农民高等学校、管理干部学院、教育学院、独立设置的函授学院等。

小学学龄儿童入学率 指调查范围内已入小学学习的学龄儿童占校内外学龄儿童总数(包括弱智儿童在内,但不包括盲聋哑儿童)的比重。计算公式:

$$小学学龄儿童入学率=\frac{已入学的小学学龄儿童数}{校内外小学学龄儿童总数}*100\%$$

等级运动员人数 指经考核正式批准授予等级运动员称号的人数。运动员等级分为国际级运动健将、运动健将、一级运动员、二级运动员、三级运动员、少年级运动员。

等级裁判员人数 指经考核正式批准授予等级裁判员称号的人数。裁判员等级分为国际裁判、国家级裁判、一级裁判、二级裁判、三级裁判。

卫生机构 卫生机构是指从卫生行政部门取得《医疗机构执业许可证》,或从民政、工商行政、机构编制管理部门取得法人单位登记证书,为社会提供医疗保健、疾病控制、卫生监督等服务或从事医学科研、医学教育等卫生单位和卫生社会团体。不包括卫生行政机构、香港和澳门特别行政区以及台湾所属卫生机构。

卫生技术人员 卫生技术人员包括执业(助理)医师、注册护士、药剂人员、检验和影像技师(士、员)等卫生专业人员。

执业(助理)医师、执业(中)药师和注册护士 执业(助理)医师、执业(中)药师和注册护士是指领取医师、药师执业证书和注册护士证书的人员。不包括从事管理工作的医师、药师和护士。

Explanatory Notes on Main Statistical Indicators

Cultural Institutions refer to units which have their own organizational system and independent accounting system and specialize in or serve cultural development. They exclude other establishments run by these cultural institutions and amateur cultural groups established by various departments.

Art Troupe refers to the troupe which is engaged in drama, opera, music, dance, acrobatics or other art performance, opens independent accounts with banks and has self – supporting accounting system; excluding the troupes which are engaged partly in industrial or agricultural activities, partly in art performance and the professional troupes organized by the people.

Regular Institutions of Higher Learning refer to educational establishments set up according to the government evaluation and approval procedures, enrolling graduates from senior secondary schools and providing higher education courses and training for senior professionals, They include full – time universities, colleges, high professional schools and short – term professional universities.

Institutions of Higher Learning for Adults refer to educational establishments, set up in line with relevant rules approved by the government, enrolling staff and workers with senior secondary school or equivalent education, and providing higher education courses in many forms of full – time, part – time, space – time, or correspondence for adults. Professionals thus trained receive a qualification equivalent to graduates studying regular courses at regular universities, colleges and professional colleges. Institutions of higher learning for adults include Radio and TV universities, schools of high education for staff and workers and peasants, colleges for management cadres, pedagogical colleges, independent correspondence colleges.

Enrollment Rate of Primary School – age Children refer to the proportion of school – age children enrolled at schools to the total number of school – age children both in and outside schools (including retarded children, but excluding blind, deaf and mute children). The formula is:

$$\text{Enrollment Rate of Primary School – age Children} = \frac{\text{Total primary School – age Children at Schools}}{\text{Total Primary School – age Children Both at and Outside Schools}}$$

Number of Athletes in Grades refers to the number of athletes who have been given titles through examination. The titles of athletes include international masters of sports, masters of sports, first – grade, second – grade and third – grade sportsmen and young athletes.

Number of Referees in Grades refers to the number of referees who have been given titles after examination. They are classified as international referees, national referees and referees of the first, second and third grades.

Health Institutions refers to the Institutions and Society organization that get the registered license of health and medical institution from the health adiministration department, or get the registered license of units from civil administration department, industry and business administration and organization management department, and offers medical treatment, controlling of disease, supervision of sanitation. Health institution excludes health administration department and Institutions of Hong Kong, Macao, and Taiwan.

Medical Technical Personnel include registered (Assistant) doctor, registered nurse, druggist, checking members and photo artificer.

Registered (Assistant) Doctor, Registered Druggist and Registered Nurse refers to the personnel who get the licence of doctor, druggist and nurse, the management staff excluded.

十三、人民生活物价、民政

PEOPLE’ S LIVELIHOOD,
PRICE INDICES AND CIVIL ADMINISTRATION

13 人民生活、物价、民政

People's Livelihood, Price Indices and Civil Administration

主要统计指标
Major Statistical Indicators

非私营单位就业人员工资总额	Total Wages of Employed Persons of Non-private Units	2152.40	亿元	(100 million yuan)
非私营单位就业人员平均工资	Annual Average Wages of Employed Persons of Non-private Units	76073	元	(yuan)
全体居民人均可支配收入	Per Capita Disposable Income of Urban and Rural Residents	42642	元	(yuan)
为上年	As Compared with the Preceding Year	108.7	%	(%)
城镇常住居民人均可支配收入	Per Capita Disposable Income of Permanent Urban Residents	48316	元	(yuan)
为上年	As Compared with the Preceding Year	108.3	%	(%)
农村常住居民人均可支配收入	Per Capita Disposable Income of Permanent Rural Residents	25719	元	(yuan)
为上年	As Compared with the Preceding Year	109.2	%	(%)
市区居民消费价格指数	Consume Price Index of Urban District	101.8	上年=100	(Preceding Year=100)
市区商品零售价格指数	Commodity Retail Price Index of Urban District	100.2	上年=100	(Preceding Year=100)
工业品出厂价格指数	Ex-factory Price Index of Industrial Products	96.5	上年=100	(Preceding Year=100)

13－01　居民家庭人均收入支出(2013－2015 年)
Per Capita Income and Expenditure of Households(2013－2015)

单位:元　　(yuan)

项　目 Item	全体居民 Urban and Rural Residents			城镇常住居民 Permanent Urban Residents			农村常住居民 Permanent Rural Residents		
	2015	2014	2013	2015	2014	2013	2015	2014	2013
一、可支配收入 Disposable Income	42642	39237	35763	48316	44632	40925	25719	23555	21208
工资性收入 Icome from Wages	–	–	–	28891	27638	25580	15860	14809	13029
经营净收入 Income of Staff & workers in Other－owned Units	–	–	–	4502	4365	3716	6628	6021	5611
财产净收入 Property Income	–	–	–	6851	6039	5691	982	879	818
转移净收入 Transfer Income	–	–	–	8072	6590	5938	2249	1846	1750
二、消费支出 Expenditure	30181	28492	26827	33818	32165	30659	19334	17816	16021
食品烟酒 Food alcohol and tobacco	–	–	–	9171	8688	7928	5358	5091	4530
衣着 Clothing	–	–	–	2157	2193	2108	1157	1094	923
居住 Residence	–	–	–	9111	8565	8316	4990	4539	4250
生活用品及服务 Daily necessities and services	–	–	–	1622	1683	1588	1008	933	823
交通通信 Transportation and Communication	–	–	–	5707	5364	5105	3904	3299	2930
教育文化娱乐 Education, Cultural and Recreation Service	–	–	–	3141	2990	2934	1507	1485	1296
医疗保健 Medicine and Medical Service	–	–	–	2002	1708	1762	1055	1052	958
其他用品和服务 Other Supplies and Services	–	–	–	907	974	918	355	323	311

注:2013－2015 年为城乡住户一体化改革后新口径数据。(以下相关表同)

a) The data in this table are calculated at new rage by the results of integrated survey of urban households and rural households since 2013. The same applies to the tables following.

13－02 城镇住户调查情况(1978－2015年)
Basic Conditions of Urban Households (1978－2015)

年份 Year	调查户数(户) Number of Households Surveyed (household)	平均每户人口(人) Average Household Size (person)	平均每户就业人数(人) Average Number of Employed Persons Per Household(person)	年人均可支配收入(元) Per Capita Annual Disposable Income (yuan)	年人均消费支出(元) Per Capita Annual Consumption Expenditure(yuan)	人均住房建筑面积(平方米) Per Capita Living Space in City Areas (sq. m)
1978	28	4.20	2.89	338	301	
1979	28	4.19	2.77	396	365	
1980	28	4.18	2.79	521	491	
1981	100	3.97	2.37	540	513	
1982	100	3.90	2.35	532	532	
1983	100	3.90	2.42	578	535	11.7
1984	100	3.90	2.36	729	679	12.4
1985	150	3.53	2.26	1026	908	12.9
1986	150	3.49	2.27	1169	1072	13.2
1987	150	3.42	2.25	1260	1118	14.1
1988	200	3.41	2.16	1565	1515	14.1
1989	200	3.40	2.15	1764	1615	14.1
1990	200	3.37	2.15	1985	1685	14.5
1991	200	3.40	2.20	2128	1894	14.4
1992	200	3.28	2.14	2580	2296	14.8
1993	200	3.21	2.10	3525	3183	14.9
1994	200	3.31	2.10	5249	4559	15.9
1995	200	3.20	2.05	6301	5559	15.6
1996	200	3.20	2.00	7206	6095	15.9
1997	200	3.14	1.99	7896	6766	16.5
1998	300	3.12	1.93	8465	7235	18.8
1999	300	3.11	1.92	9085	7424	19.5
2000	300	3.10	1.83	9668	7790	19.9
2001	440	2.98	1.72	10896	8968	20.7
2002	500	2.93	1.53	11778	9215	21.7
2003	500	2.92	1.51	12898	9950	22.9
2004	500	2.92	1.48	14565	11213	23.7
2005	600	2.84	1.42	16601	13438	27.6
2006	600	2.81	1.44	19027	14472	28.0
2007	600	2.72	1.45	21689	14896	28.8
2008	600	2.75	1.29	24104	16719	29.9
2009	600	2.68	1.25	26864	18595	30.8
2010	600	2.70	1.25	30035	20219	30.9
2011	600	2.71	1.32	34065	22642	33.7
2012	600	2.69	1.31	37511	22800	34.4
2013	1920	2.79	1.51	40925	30659	34.9
2014	1920	2.79	1.53	44632	32165	35.1
2015	1920	2.79	1.48	48316	33818	35.5

注:2000年及以前为主城区数据;2001－2012年为包括萧山区和余杭区在内的市区数据;2013－2015年为包括所有区、县(市)城乡住户一体化改革后新口径数据。

a) The data on the table include the main urban districts before 2000; The data include Xiaoshan district and Yuhang district in 2001－2012; The date include all districts and counties since 2013; The data in this table are calculated at new rage by the results of integrated survey of urban households and rural households sine 2013.

13－03 城镇居民家庭平均每百户耐用消费品拥有量(主要年份)

Number of Major Durable Consumer Goods Owned Per 100 Urban Households(Main Years)

项目 Item	1995	2000	2005	2010	2011	2012	2013	2014	2015
家用汽车 Family Car (辆)(unit)		0.7	12.8	22.8	31.2	34.3	40.2	45.4	48.7
摩托车 Motorcycle (辆)(unit)	1.5	3.6	11.0	4.5	4.1	4.0	6.6	6.8	5.4
电冰箱 Refrigerator (台)(unit)	103.5	101.7	100.0	102.3	102.5	102.5	88.0	92.3	92.2
洗衣机 Washing Machine (台)(unit)	93.5	96.3	94.2	96.2	96.3	96.6	82.6	86.8	86.9
热水器 Water Heater (台)(unit)	43.5	81.3	92.3	99.4	103.4	105.4	89.4	93.7	95.5
空调器 Air Conditioner (台)(unit)	43.0	104	183.3	214.6	212.0	214.7	189.6	201.5	207.3
彩色电视机 Color TV Set (台)(unit)	102.3	146.7	182.7	179.2	176.9	178.4	166.4	174.0	174.1
摄像机 Video Recorder (架)(unit)		3.3	7.5	11.1	11.6	12.4	10.0	10.5	10.5
照相机 Camera (架)(unit)	54.0	64.7	59.0	54.8	62.1	63.5	50.6	54.4	51.5
计算机 Computer (台)(unit)		23.0	74.5	99.0	109.7	112.2	103.7	110.6	110.1
#接入互联网的计算机 of which:Internet－connected computer (台)(unit)				78.7	92.3	98.6	92.5	100.2	99.8
固定电话 Telephone (部)(set)		95.0	99.8	89.6	84.7	83.6	51.6	54.2	50.7
移动电话 Mobile Phone (部)(set)		19.0	178.7	193.6	211.0	213.1	217.4	227.9	229.9
#接入互联网的移动电话 of which:Internet－connected Mobile Phone (部)(set)							125.1	140.8	155.8

注:2000年及以前为主城区数据;2001－2012年为包括萧山区和余杭区在内的市区数据;2013－2015年为包括所有区、县(市)城乡住户一体化改革后新口径数据。

a)The data on the table include the main urban districts before 2000;The data include Xiaoshan district and Yuhang district in 2001－2012;The date include all districts and counties since 2013;The data in this table are calculated at new rage by the results of integrated survey of urban households and rural households sine 2013.

13－04 全市农村住户调查情况(1978－2015 年)

Basic Conditions of Whole Municipality Rural Households(1978－2015)

年 份 Year	调查户数(户) Number of Households Surveyed (household)	平均每户人口(人) Average Number of Residents per Household (person)	平均每户就业人数(人) Average Number of Employed Persons Per Household (person)	人均可支配收入(元) Per Capita Annual Net Income of Rural Households (yuan)	人均消费支出(元) Per Capita Annual Consumption Expenditure (yuan)	人均住房建筑面积(平方米) Per Capita Floor Space (sq. m)
1978				162		
1979				204		
1980	60	4.72	2.93	250	287	23.3
1981	60	4.60	2.70	333	294	25.2
1982	60	4.43	2.73	405	328	26.3
1983	170	4.55	2.85	395	355	29.9
1984	170	4.44	2.81	510	416	31.7
1985	420	4.40	2.88	624	542	29.9
1986	620	4.39	2.88	675	601	31.3
1987	620	4.34	2.86	820	714	33.1
1988	620	4.26	2.87	996	925	35.5
1989	620	4.17	2.85	1117	1011	36.8
1990	620	4.16	2.89	1171	923	39.6
1991	620	4.03	2.81	1308	1018	38.0
1992	620	4.01	2.81	1493	1129	37.5
1993	540	3.91	2.76	1748	1276	37.1
1994	630	3.85	2.35	2267	1884	37.8
1995	630	3.87	2.30	3012	2373	40.5
1996	630	3.81	2.77	3482	2772	42.2
1997	630	3.87	2.86	3785	2762	42.0
1998	630	3.87	2.88	4006	2858	46.2
1999	630	3.80	2.80	4209	2851	48.0
2000	630	3.61	2.59	4894	3393	49.0
2001	630	3.57	2.53	5330	3909	52.0
2002	630	3.53	2.53	5708	4444	52.7
2003	670	3.48	2.53	6250	5142	54.7
2004	670	3.48	2.54	6950	5608	58.9
2005	1100	3.34	2.34	7655	6004	66.0
2006	1100	3.63	2.52	8515	6901	66.5
2007	1100	3.60	2.61	9549	7568	68.0
2008	1100	3.56	2.58	10692	8446	69.7
2009	1100	3.57	2.59	11822	9065	70.7
2010	1100	3.58	2.59	13186	10267	71.2
2011	1100	3.46	2.49	15245	12125	72.5
2012	1100	3.45	2.50	17017	13612	71.0
2013	1280	3.38	2.03	21208	16021	66.9
2014	1280	3.35	2.05	23555	17816	67.9
2015	1280	3.36	2.02	25719	19334	68.8

注:2013－2015 年为城乡住户一体化改革后新口径数据。

a) The data in this table are calculated at new rage by the results of integrated survey of urban households and rural households sine 2013; The data of income are net income before 2012.

13－05 农村居民家庭平均每百户耐用消费品拥有量(主要年份)

Number of Major Durable Consumer Goods Owned Per 100 Rural Households(Main Years)

项　　目	Item	2000	2005	2010	2011	2012	2013	2014	2015
家用汽车（辆）	Family Car (Unit)		4.0	15.7	21.6	27.5	28.8	34.3	38.2
摩托车（辆）	Motorcycle (Unit)	38.0	73.0	66.2	40.8	42.6	33.5	32.7	30.7
电冰箱（台）	Refrigerator (Unit)	46.0	72.0	98.1	93.3	101.8	93.8	99.5	103.9
洗衣机（台）	Washing Machine (Unit)	34.0	62.0	85.1	78.2	87.8	78.3	82.7	86.4
热水器（台）	Water Heater (Unit)			84.5	80.7	90.9	79.3	85.9	93.2
空调机（台）	Air Conditioner (Unit)	8.0	12.0	111.2	120.3	143.3	122.9	135.9	147.6
彩色电视机（台）	Color TV Set (Unit)	86.0	141.0	186.3	192.5	210.6	186.0	196.1	202
摄像机（架）	Video Recorder (Unit)			2.0	1.3	1.8	2.3	2.5	2.9
照相机（架）	Camera (Unit)	7.0	14.0	22.6	21.7	26.5	21.1	21.1	19.6
计算机（台）	Personal Computer (Unit)	1.0	12.0	44.2	51.3	60.4	59.3	67.3	69.6
#接入互联网的计算机（台）	of which: Internet－connected computer (Unit)				44.6	51.8	51.5	59.8	64.2
固定电话（部）	Telephone (Set)						49.6	52.7	46.4
移动电话（部）	Mobile Phone (Set)	17.0	125.0	212.9	230.4	253.1	235.5	244.6	253.8
#接入互联网的移动电话（部）	of which: Internet－connected Mobile Phone (Set)						106.0	121.2	141.7

注:2013－2015年为城乡住户一体化改革后新口径数据。

a) The data in this table are calculated at new rage by the results of integrated survey of urban households and rural households since 2013.

13－06　全市就业人员工资总额(1978－2015年)

Total Wages of Employed Persons(1978－2015)

单位:万元　　　　(10000 yuan)

年　份 Year	全市(含规上私营) Total (includes private units above designated size)	非私营单位 Non－private	市区(含规上私营) Urban District (includes private units above designated size)	非私营单位 Non－private
1978		43775		28256
1979		52127		34318
1980		67918		45574
1981		72896		48809
1982		75584		50959
1983		78336		52909
1984		102223		69135
1985		130114		87774
1986		157471		105995
1987		180077		121003
1988		230868		152859
1989		253956		167055
1990		277910		182985
1991		313906		209052
1992		377614		253653
1993		534537		359041
1994		772236		521669
1995		890488		615450
1996		973592		683244
1997		1073862		762957
1998		1112718		803264
1999		1180947		864418
2000		1267524		949872
2001		1481659		1279749
2002		1614676		1398222
2003		1867776		1617504
2004	2844691	2188159	2313930	1859164
2005	3711915	2970200	3112937	2584779
2006	4526841	3811735	3830043	3338568
2007	6233799	4954813	5256791	4317965
2008	8592198	6416424	7338932	5679543
2009	9909330	7549145	8475547	6665279
2010	12305726	9330552	10531483	8238017
2011	15012179	11222834	12934215	9954506
2012	19540005	14839012	17115217	13217453
2013	23604682	17582336	20762852	15820468
2014	26630950	19822713	24629017	18551986
2015	28884146	21523984	26718242	20179320

注:口径范围,1997年及以前为全市全部职工,1998－2012为在岗职工,2013年起为就业人员。2004年起包含规模以上私营单位。

a) Data on this table refer to wages of all employees before 1997, that refer to all staff and workers in 1998－2012, and refer to employed persons since 2013. Data on this bill includes Private units above designated size since 2004.

13-07 全市就业人员年平均工资(1978-2015年)

Average Annual Wages of Employed Persons(1978-2015)

单位:元 (yuan)

年份 Year	全市(含规上私营) Total (includes private units above designated size)	非私营单位 Non-private	市区(含规上私营) Urban District (includes private units above designated size)	非私营单位 Non-private	市区全社会在岗职工 The Fully Employed Persons in Urban Districts
1978		597		642	
1979		643		692	
1980		777		814	
1981		783		810	
1982		791		809	
1983		813		835	
1984		1036		1071	
1985		1266		1316	
1986		1469		1536	
1987		1616		1690	
1988		1986		2073	
1989		2173		2261	
1990		2382		2486	
1991		2586		2706	
1992		3071		3233	
1993		4220		4561	
1994		6118		6597	
1995		7156		7786	
1996		7966		7851	
1997		9108		10048	
1998		10555		11512	
1999		12187		13225	
2000		14257		15454	
2001		18319		18962	18205
2002		21418		22091	19749
2003		24668		25535	20113
2004	21879	28891	24204	30719	22235
2005	24685	31069	26366	32166	22645
2006	27620	32791	29397	33967	23581
2007	29864	36496	31625	37991	25489
2008	32513	40193	34107	41501	27863
2009	35638	43947	37270	45149	30480
2010	39772	48772	41303	49938	34330
2011	45775	54408	47695	55958	38837
2012	51077	56417	52610	57548	42493
2013	55124	63664	56857	64941	46831
2014	60904	69209	61924	70034	51449
2015	66322	76073	67569	77061	55908

注:口径范围,1997年及以前为全市全部职工,1998-2012为在岗职工,2013年起为就业人员。2004年起包含规模以上私营单位。
a) Data on this table refer to wages of all employees before 1997, that refer to all staff and workers in 1998-2012, and refer to employed persons since 2013. Data on this bill includes Private units above designated size since 2004.

13－08 全市含规上私营单位就业人员工资总额(2015 年)

Total Wages of Employed Persons Including Private Units Above Designated Size(2015)

单位：万元 (10000 yuan)

项 目 Item		就业人员工资总额 Total Wages of Employed Persons	非私营 Non－private	在岗职工工资总额 Total Wages of Fully Employed Staff and Workers	非私营 Non－private	其他就业人员工资总额 Total Wages of Other Employed Persons	非私营 Non－private
全市总计	**Whole city Total**	**28884146**	**21523984**	**27341885**	**20601998**	**1542261**	**921986**
市区总计	Urban District	26718242	20179320	25263113	19299899	1455129	879421
#上城区	Shangcheng	2196219	1910948	2032426	1809441	163793	101507
下城区	Xiacheng	2369418	2177574	2273750	2105543	95667	72031
江干区	Jianggan	2710584	1718325	2249134	1525772	461450	192553
拱墅区	Gongshu	1966431	1177871	1858991	1101473	107440	76398
西湖区	Xihu	4061417	3503450	3841664	3353516	219753	149934
高新(滨江)区	Hi－Tech(Binjiang)	2651741	2250403	2605388	2212224	46354	38179
萧山区	Xiaoshan	4915700	3279567	4785587	3195929	130114	83638
余杭区	Yuhang	3025929	1977927	2947257	1934938	78673	42989
富阳区	Fuyang	1220147	718426	1167546	690093	52601	28334
桐庐县	Tonglu	548670	278421	526516	268780	22154	9641
淳安县	Chun'an	359856	247928	336389	239499	23466	8430
建德市	Jiande	422796	280617	403760	272361	19036	8256
临安市	Lin'an	834583	537699	812106	521460	22477	16238

单位:万元　　13-08　续表　continued　　(10000 yuan)

项　目 Item	就业人员工资总额 Total Wages of Employed Persons	非私营 Non-private	在岗职工工资总额 Total Wages of Fully Employed Staff and Workers	非私营 Non-private	其他就业人员工资总额 Total Wages of Other Employed Persons	非私营 Non-private
按国民经济行业分组 Grouped by Sector						
农、林、牧、渔业 Farming, Forestry, Animal Husbandry & Fishery	4789	4784	4633	4628	156	156
采矿业 Mining	15610	7030	15022	6533	588	497
制造业 Manufacturing	6607413	4534026	6512971	4467760	94442	66267
电力、热力、燃气及水生产和供应业 Production & Supply of Electricity, Heat, Gas & Water	232265	223707	229773	221263	2492	2444
建筑业 Construction	7413514	3796121	6534546	3457101	878968	339020
批发和零售业 Wholesale & Retail Trades	1811964	1383182	1749359	1327955	62606	55227
交通运输、仓储和邮政业 Transportation, Storage and Post	1006177	870370	995602	863756	10575	6614
住宿和餐饮业 Hotels and Catering Services	407265	280510	387023	264440	20241	16070
信息传输、软件和信息技术服务业 Information Transmission, Software and Information Technology	1847537	1617222	1838893	1610608	8643	6614
金融业 Financial Intermediation	1734547	1732464	1606611	1604846	127936	127619
房地产业 Real Estate	821849	677540	796447	656696	25402	20844
租赁和商务服务业 Leasing and Business Services	884601	667017	838697	631212	45904	35805
科学研究、技术服务业 Scientific Research, Technical Services	1067702	885129	1022250	850113	45452	35016
水利、环境和公共设施管理业 Management of Water Conservancy, Environment and Public Facilities	261005	183735	251388	177791	9618	5944
居民服务、修理和其他服务业 Service to Honseholds, Repair and Other Services	104468	61740	99825	58965	4643	2775
教育 Education	1696494	1670734	1644137	1618850	52357	51884
卫生和社会工作 Health Care and Social Work	1292967	1267964	1199800	1177453	93167	90511
文化、体育和娱乐业 Culture, Sports and Entertainment	251773	238503	224111	211231	27663	27272
公共管理、社会保障和社会组织 Public Management, Social Security and Social Organizations	1422207	1422207	1390798	1390798	31409	31409

13－09 全市含规上私营单位就业人员平均工资(2015 年)

Average Annual Wages of Employed Persons Including Private Units Above Designated Size(2015)

单位:元 (yuan)

项目	Item	就业人员 Total employment	非私营单位 Non－private	在岗职工 Staff and Workers	非私营单位 Non－private
全市	**Total**	**66322**	**76073**	**67685**	**77816**
市区	Urban District	67569	77061	69016	78868
#上城区	Shangcheng	85465	96381	87544	98575
下城区	Xiacheng	90722	99058	93926	101734
江干区	Jianggan	67056	81953	69212	81745
拱墅区	Gongshu	59447	68974	61334	73359
西湖区	Xihu	65176	68371	67340	70748
高新(滨江)区	Hi－Tech(Binjiang)	93097	103182	94852	105566
萧山区	Xiaoshan	56685	62669	56873	62929
余杭区	Yuhang	65594	80527	66548	82264
富阳区	Fuyang	51931	60515	52846	62376
桐庐县	Tonglu	52750	65202	53301	66164
淳安县	Chun'an	57700	66708	59816	68452
建德市	Jiande	54047	63824	55351	65269
临安市	Lin'an	53406	61853	53729	62782

项目 Item	就业人员 Total employment	非私营单位 Non－private	在岗职工 Staff and Workers	非私营单位 Non－private
按国民经济行业分组 Grouped by Sector				
农、林、牧、渔业 Farming, Forestry, Animal Husbandry & Fishery	45306	46220	46707	47714
采矿业 Mining	55571	55489	55843	56370
制造业 Manufacturing	58562	65965	58485	65826
电力、热力、燃气及水生产和供应业 Production & Supply of Electricity, Heat, Gas & Water	106004	109790	107345	111277
建筑业 Construction	48306	50475	48654	51062
批发和零售业 Wholesale & Retail Trades	62941	69700	63464	70635
交通运输、仓储和邮政业 Transportation, Storage and Post	75581	79768	76551	80907
住宿和餐饮业 Hotels and Catering Services	40916	42781	43503	47099
信息传输、软件和信息技术服务业 Information Transmission, Software and Information Technology	130472	141606	131245	142241
金融业 Financial Intermediation	173668	174215	190395	190790
房地产业 Real Estate	66735	68583	67665	69454
租赁和商务服务业 Leasing and Business Services	63198	64262	64789	66474
科学研究、技术服务业 Scientific Research, Technical Services	95248	102687	97291	104986
水利、环境和公共设施管理业 Management of Water Conservancy, Environment and Public Facilities	60768	61870	61880	63237
居民服务、修理和其他服务业 Service to Honseholds, Repair and Other Services	41459	44242	41682	44731
教育 Education	91708	93261	96480	98299
卫生和社会工业 Health Care and Social Work	115014	116975	119996	122083
文化、体育和娱乐业 Culture, Sports and Entertainment	96339	103167	105528	115056
公共管理、社会保障和社会组织 Public Management, Social Security and Social Organizations	103490	103490	106809	106809

13－10 市区消费价格指数(1978－2015 年)
Consumer Price Indices in Urban District(1978－2015)

(上年＝100) (Preceding Year＝100)

年 份 Year	居民消费价格指数 General Consumer Price Index	商品零售价格指数 General Retail Price Index
1978	100.1	100.1
1979	100.4	100.9
1980	100.8	109.3
1981	102.0	102.0
1982	102.0	102.3
1983	102.1	102.3
1984	103.1	103.1
1985	117.2	117.5
1986	106.0	106.1
1987	110.5	111.3
1988	121.9	123.4
1989	117.8	118.2
1990	104.6	104.4
1991	107.5	106.9
1992	110.4	110.2
1993	121.4	117.3
1994	121.5	118.8
1995	116.5	113.3
1996	110.5	107.2
1997	106.7	102.4
1998	101.8	99.8
1999	100.4	98.2
2000	100.8	98.3
2001	99.5	95.3
2002	98.8	97.9
2003	99.5	98.1
2004	102.5	101.6
2005	101.7	100.3
2006	101.2	100.2
2007	103.5	103.1
2008	104.9	106.0
2009	98.6	98.6
2010	103.9	103.7
2011	104.8	104.4
2012	102.5	101.9
2013	102.5	101.5
2014	102.0	100.8
2015	101.8	100.2

13－11　市区居民消费价格分类指数(2014－2015年)

Consumer Price Indices by Category in Urban District(2014－2015)

(上年＝100)　　(Preceding Year＝100)

项目	Item	2015	2014
居民消费价格总指数	**Consumer Price Indices**	**101.8**	**102.0**
一、食品	**Food**	**102.8**	**102.9**
1. 粮食	Grain	100.7	101.4
2. 淀粉及制品	Starches and Tubers	107.3	102.9
3. 干豆类及豆制品	Bean and Its Products	97.5	103.2
4. 油脂	Oil and Fat	95.5	93.0
5. 肉禽及其制品	Meal Poultry and Their Products	106.7	100.8
6. 蛋	Eggs	102.9	114.0
7. 水产品	Aquatic Products	102.0	105.1
8. 菜	Vegetables	110.7	98.8
9. 调味品	Flavoring	106.5	99.9
10. 糖	Sugar	100.2	97.8
11. 茶及饮料	Tea and Beverages	100.8	102.9
12. 干鲜瓜果	Dried and Fresh Melons and Fruits	99.8	109.0
13. 糕点饼干面包	Cake、Biscuit and Bread	101.8	101.0
14. 液体乳及乳制品	Milk and Its Products	97.3	101.8
15. 在外用膳食品	Outward Dinner	101.8	104.0
16. 其他食品	Other Food	104.2	100.5
二、烟酒及用品	**Tobacco、Liquor and Articles**	**103.9**	**99.9**
1. 烟草	Tobacco	104.8	100.4
2. 酒	Liquor	101.1	98.2
三、衣着	**Clothing**	**101.1**	**101.7**
1. 服装	Garments	100.0	103.2
2. 衣着材料	Clothing Material	100.2	100.5

项　　目	Item	2015	2014
3. 鞋袜帽	Shoes, Socks and Hats	105.5	96.3
4. 衣着加工服务费	Clothing Processing Service	102.3	101.0
四、家庭设备用品及维修服务	**Household Facilities, Articles and Repair Service**	**101.4**	**102.7**
1. 耐用消费品	Durable Consumer Goods	100.6	99.4
2. 室内装饰品	Interior Decorations	99.1	101.7
3. 床上用品	Bed Articles	96.7	101.2
4. 家庭日用杂品	Daily Use Household Articles	100.4	101.1
5. 家庭服务及加工维修服务	Household and Repair Service	107.4	115.0
五、医疗保健和个人用品	**Medical Articles and Personal Articles**	**102.4**	**101.4**
1. 医疗保健	Medical Care	103.7	101.6
2. 个人用品及服务	Personel Articles and Service	97.5	100.6
六、交通和通信	**Transportation and Communication**	**96.6**	**99.4**
1. 交通	Transportation	95.4	99.3
2. 通信	Communication	99.9	99.7
七、娱乐教育文化用品及服务	**Recreation, Education and Culture Articles**	**101.0**	**101.8**
1. 文娱用耐用消费品及服务	Durable Consumer Goods and Recreation Service	100.3	95.7
2. 教育	Education	102.1	100.9
3. 文化娱乐类	Cultural and Recreational Articles	101.5	100.5
4. 旅游	Tourism and Outgoing	97.9	108.3
八、居住	**Residence**	**103.5**	**102.7**
1. 建房及装修材料	Construction and Upholstery Materials	101.7	102.1
2. 住房租金	House Renting	104.0	102.7
3. 自有住房	Private Owned Houses	102.8	103.5
4. 水、电、燃料	Water, Electricity and Fuels	107.1	100.6

13－12　市区零售价格分类指数(2014－2015年)
Retail Price Indices by Category in Urban District(2014－2015)

(上年＝100)　　(Preceding Year＝100)

项目	Item	2015	2014
商品零售价格总指数	**Retail Price Indices**	**100.2**	**100.8**
一、食品	**Food**	**103.0**	**103.1**
1.粮食	Grain	100.7	101.5
2.淀粉及制品	Starches and Tubers	107.3	102.9
3.干豆类及豆制品	Bean and Its Products	97.5	103.4
4.油脂	Oil and Fat	95.7	93.0
5.肉禽及其制品	Meal Poultry and Their Products	106.8	100.6
6.蛋	Eggs	102.9	114.0
7.水产品	Aquatic Products	101.8	104.9
8.菜	Vegetables	110.7	98.8
9.调味品	Flavoring	106.5	99.9
10.糖	Carbohydrate	99.9	97.5
11.干鲜瓜果	Dried and Fresh Melons and Fruits	99.7	110.2
12.糕点饼干面包	Cake、Biscuit and Bread	101.9	101.0
13.液体乳及乳制品	Milk and Its Products	97.3	102.6
14.在外用膳食品	Outward Dinner	101.8	104.1
15.其他食品	Other Food	104.2	100.5
二、饮料、烟酒	**Beverages,Tobacco and Liquor**	**102.8**	**100.2**
1.茶及饮料	Tea and Beverages	100.6	102.6
2.烟草	Tobacco	104.6	100.4
3.酒	Liquor	101.3	98.6
三、服装、鞋帽	**Garments,Shoes and Hats**	**101.2**	**101.7**
1.服装	Garments	100.0	103.2
2.鞋袜帽	Shoes,Socks and Hats	105.5	96.3
3.其他	Other	104.7	107.7
四、纺织品	**Textiles**	**98.0**	**101.2**
1.衣着材料	Clothing Material	100.2	100.5
2.床上用品	Bed Articles	96.5	101.7
五、家用电器及音像器材	**Household Electric Appliances,Audio and Video Equipment**	**99.9**	**98.5**
1.家庭设备	Household Equipment	100.0	99.0
2.文娱用耐用消费品	Durable Consumer Goods for Entertainment	100.1	96.7

项目	Item	2015	2014
3. 专业音像器材	Audio and Video Equipment	99.1	99.5
六、文化办公用品	**Stationery and Office Supplies**	**100.2**	**98.2**
七、日用品	**Commodities**	**100.2**	**100.0**
1. 日用百货	General Merchandise for Daily Use	99.8	100.0
2. 日用杂品	Sundries for Daily Use	100.6	100.3
3. 洗涤用品	Washing Articles	98.6	100.4
4. 其他日用品	Other Commodity	101.7	99.6
八、体育娱乐用品	**Sports and Entertainment Goods**	**99.5**	**103.4**
1. 体育用品	Sports Goods	99.1	105.9
2. 娱乐用品	Entertainment Goods	99.7	102.4
九、交通、通信用品	**Transportation and Communications Articles**	**98.8**	**98.9**
1. 交通运输机械	Transportation Vehicles	99.1	99.0
2. 通讯器材	Equipment of Communication	96.6	97.8
十、家具	**Funishings**	**101.9**	**100.1**
十一、化妆品	**Cosmetics**	**94.1**	**104.0**
十二、金银珠宝	**Jewellery**	**96.8**	**96.7**
十三、中西药品及医疗保健用品	**Chinese and Western Medicine, Health Care Articles**	**102.7**	**98.9**
1. 医疗器具及用品	Medical Instruments and Articles	99.7	100.0
2. 中药材及中成药	Chinese Medicinal Materials and Chinese Traditional Medicine	103.9	101.3
3. 西药	Western Medicine	98.2	92.0
4. 保健器具及用品	Articles for Health Care	110.5	110.7
十四、书报杂志及电子出版物	**Books, Newspapers, Magazines and Electron Publications**	**104.8**	**99.7**
1. 教材及参考书	Teaching Materials and Reference Books	98.1	99.1
2. 书报杂志	Books, Newspapers and Magazines	115.2	100.0
3. 电子音像制品	Electronic Music and Film Products	100.6	100.0
十五、燃料	**Fuels**	**90.0**	**100.4**
1. 煤炭及制品	Coal and Coal Products	102.6	104.0
2. 石油及制品	Oil and Oil Products	88.1	99.8
十六、建筑材料及五金电料	**Construction Materials and Hardware**	**98.7**	**99.7**
1. 建筑装潢材料	Construction and Upholstery Materials	98.4	99.6
2. 五金电料	Hardware and Electric Materials	99.5	100.0

13－13 工业生产者出厂价格指数(主要年份)

Producer Price Indices for Industrial Products by Category(Main Years)

(上年＝100) (Preceding Year＝100)

项目 Item	2000	2005	2010	2011	2012	2013	2014	2015
工业生产者出厂价格总指数 Total Producer Price Indices for Industrial Products	**100.3**	**103.5**	**104.9**	**104.7**	**97.2**	**98.5**	**98.6**	**96.5**
一、按轻重工业分 Grouped by Industries								
轻工业 Light Industry	**99.3**	**101.8**	**105.0**	**105.5**	**98.1**	**99.9**	**99.2**	**97.4**
以农产品为原料 Made from Agricultural Products	99.9	102.0	103.9	104.6	99.4	100.8	99.9	98.5
以非农产品为原料 Made from Non－agricultural Products	98.0	101.7	106.0	106.8	96.1	98.4	98.2	95.8
重工业 Heavy Industry	**101.1**	**105.6**	**104.7**	**104.2**	**96.5**	**97.5**	**98.2**	**95.8**
采掘 Mining & Quarrying Industry	99.5	103.0	114.0	116.6	101.3	101.0	104.2	94.9
原料 Raw Materials Industry	104.4	107.7	110.7	108.7	96.9	97.5	96.7	92.5
加工 Manufacturing Industry	98.9	104.3	102.5	102.8	96.4	97.5	98.5	96.7
二、按二大部类分 Grouped by Means of Producting and Consumer Goods								
生产资料 Means of Production	**101.9**	**104.8**	**106.2**	**105.1**	**95.5**	**97.8**	**98.0**	**95.3**
采掘 Mining	99.6	103.0	114.0	116.6	101.3	101.0	104.2	94.9
原料 Raw Materials	103.8	110.7	114.5	110.6	92.6	96.5	95.7	91.0
加工 Manufacture	100.3	101.6	103.9	103.3	96.4	98.2	98.7	96.6
生活资料 Consumer Goods	**97.5**	**101.2**	**101.0**	**103.7**	**102.6**	**100.6**	**100.6**	**100.1**
食品 Foods	96.4	101.6	100.1	104.3	101.8	101.0	101.1	100.9
衣着 Clothing	101.1	101.4	102.4	104.5	104.6	102.0	100.1	100.1
一般日用品 Articles for Daily Use	97.8	101.7	100.8	103.9	102.3	99.8	100.7	99.9
耐用消费品 Durable Consumer Goods	94.5	99.5	100.9	101.5	102.0	99.6	100.0	99.2

(上年=100) 13－13 续表 continued (Preceding Year=100)

项 目 Item	2000	2005	2010	2011	2012	2013	2014	2015
三、按工业部门分 Grouped by Industrial Sector								
冶金工业 Metallurgical Industry	104.0	104.8	108.0	107.1	93.3	95.4	96.2	93.2
电力工业 Power Industry	96.0	106.2	105.2	102.0	101.7	99.1	99.6	98.2
煤炭及炼焦工业 Coal and Coking Industry	107.9	102.1		–				
石油工业 Petroleum Industry	131.6	124.7	117.0	110.4	103.0	100.5	100.5	92.4
化学工业 Chemical Industry	101.1	106.0	111.9	109.3	93.8	97.3	95.8	92.7
机械工业 Machine Building Industry	96.7	102.9	100.8	101.3	97.6	98.1	98.9	97.6
建材材料工业 Building Materials Industry	103.0	91.7	109.3	109.8	94.0	97.3	103.0	94.0
森林工业 Timber Industry	96.9	101.4	101.6	102.0	100.7	101.0	101.3	99.9
食品工业 Food Industry	95.8	100.6	100.1	105.1	102.0	101.2	100.5	100.2
纺织工业 Textile Industry	107.3	103.4	107.5	105.1	95.5	101.1	98.9	96.3
缝纫工业 Tailoring Industry	100.5	101.5	102.2	105.6	104.6	102.6	100.5	99.8
皮革工业 Leather Industry	98.0	101.4	102.9	101.9	103.4	101.1	101.0	100.4
造纸工业 Paper Industry	102.9	100.3	104.6	102.0	96.7	96.3	99.7	98.5
文教艺术用品工业 Cultural, Educational & Handicrafts Articles	98.7	99.7	97.3	100.9	100.1	100.0	98.8	98.9
其它工业 Others	103.6	102.2	104.7	109.0	103.9	101.3	104.6	102.9

13－14　工业生产者购进价格分类指数(主要年份)
Purchasing Price Indices for Industrial Producers(Main Years)

(上年＝100)　　　(Preceding Year＝100)

项　目 Item	1999	2000	2005	2010	2011	2012	2013	2014	2015
工业生产者购进价格指数 Purchasing Price Index for Industrial Producers	**97.2**	**107.4**	**106.9**	**112.1**	**110.8**	**94.6**	**97.3**	**97.3**	**92.9**
燃料动力类 Fuel and Power	103.0	108.0	116.4	111.3	110.6	98.2	96.9	99.0	95.1
黑色金属材料类 Ferrous and Metals	96.3	102.7	105.2	108.6	107.0	88.7	95.0	92.4	85.9
1. 钢材 Rolled－steel	94.9	103.2	104.9	108.2	106.6	88.5	95.4	92.5	86.3
2. 其他 Other	98.2	101.0	105.7	113.0	113.1	91.2	90.1	90.3	80.5
有色金属材料及电线类 Non－ferrous Metals and Electric Wire	97.6	108.0	111.2	129.3	113.4	93.1	93.7	94.5	92.2
化工原料类 Chemical Raw Materials	97.6	111.0	110.1	113.3	114.3	94.2	97.0	97.7	91.7
木材及纸浆类 Wood and Paper Pulps	95.5	104.5	101.0	106.4	104.0	97.7	98.8	98.5	98.5
建筑材料及非金属类 Building Materials	98.2	100.6	102.3	108.8	116.8	99.5	99.4	105.7	96.9
农副产品类 Farm and Sideline Products	95.0	104.0	103.9	114.1	112.8	97.2	98.4	100.4	99.3
其他工业原材料及半成品类 Other Industrial Raw Materials and Semi－products	97.2	111.0	103.6	109.8	107.2	99.1	97.8	98.9	96.7
纺织原料类 Textile Raw Materials	89.4	104.7	99.9	110.4	110.5	96.3	101.9	99.9	97.1

13－15　住宅销售价格指数(2015 年)
Sales Price Indices of Houses(2015)

月份　Month	新建住宅 New Residential Building		新建商品住宅 New Residential Commodities Building		二手住宅 The Second－hand House	
	上月＝100	上年同期＝100 Preceding Year ＝100	上月＝100	上年同期＝100 Preceding Year ＝100	上月＝100	上年同期＝100 Preceding Year ＝100
全年　Annual Total		**97.6**		**97.5**		**99.1**
一月　January	99.7	89.9	99.7	89.5	99.7	94.6
二月　February	99.7	89.6	99.6	89.2	99.8	94.8
三月　March	99.6	89.2	99.5	88.8	99.9	94.8
四月　April	100.4	90.1	100.4	89.7	100.2	95.7
五月　May	100.5	91.8	100.6	91.5	100.3	96.4
六月　June	101.3	94.6	101.3	94.4	100.7	97.9
七月　July	100.8	97.7	100.9	97.6	100.6	99.5
八月　August	100.6	100.3	100.7	100.3	100.5	100.6
九月　September	100.6	102	100.6	102.1	100.4	101.7
十月　October	100.6	103	100.6	103.2	100.2	101.6
十一月　November	100.6	104.1	100.7	104.3	100.7	102.4
十二月　December	101.1	105.6	101.2	105.8	101	103.7

13－16 社会办福利院情况(2015年末)
Basic Statistics on Welfare Homes(End of 2015)

指标 Item	单位 (个) Homes (unit)	职工 (人) Staff and Workers (person)	床位数 (张) Beds (bed)	在院人数 (人) Persons Housed (person)	老人(人) Seniors(person)
全市 Total	**316**	**3957**	**61913**	**27329**	**26361**
市区 Urban District	202	3203	46372	19879	18991
#萧山区 Xiaoshan	40	523	10083	3401	3331
余杭区 Yuhang	35	405	7709	2954	2903
富阳区 Fuyang	31	187	4241	1499	1479
桐庐县 Tonglu	25	201	3343	1603	1589
淳安县 Chun'an	29	133	3452	1601	1597
建德市 Jiande	31	272	4523	2096	2061
临安市 Lin'an	29	148	4223	2150	2123

13－17 优抚对象

Number of Persons Enjoying

单位:人

指 标 Item	全 市 Total	市 区 Urban District	上城区 Shangcheng	下城区 Xiacheng	江干区 Jianggan
享受定期抚恤金人数 Number of Persons Receiving Periodical Commiseration	600	294	10	4	6
烈属 Number of Martyr Kinsfolk	312	120	5	2	1
牺牲军人家属 Number of the Sacrifice Soldiers	97	61	–	2	–
病故军人家属 Number of Kinsfolks of the Illness－died Soldiers	191	113	5	–	5
享受定期补助人数 Number of Persons Enjoying Regular Subsidies	38903	21272	310	338	600
#红军失散人员 Number of Persons be Scattered of the Red Army	–	–	–	–	–
在乡复员军人 Rural Demobilized Soldier	2329	1138	3	11	11
抗日 The War of Resistance Against Japan	23	10	3	3	–
优待优抚对象带病回乡退伍军人 Number of Rural Veterans with Illness Receiving Subsiders	2722	1404	1	2	13
优待优抚对象户数 Number of Households Receiving Subsiders	38903	21272	310	338	600
优待军属户数 Number of Households Sacrifice Soldiers	7097	4088	150	160	165

人员情况(2015 年)
Public Subsidies(2015)

(person)

拱墅区 Gongshu	西湖区 Xihu	高新(滨江)区 Hi - Tech (Binjiang)	萧山区 Xiaoshan	余杭区 Yuhang	富阳区 Fuyang	桐庐县 Tonglu	淳安县 Chun'an	建德市 Jiande	临安市 Lin'an
7	20	3	79	57	108	88	89	70	59
5	11	3	27	27	39	48	59	43	42
1	6	–	9	10	33	17	5	10	4
1	3	–	43	20	36	23	25	17	13
303	1552	159	8118	4735	5157	4801	2923	4681	5226
–	–	–	–	–	–	–	–	–	–
16	44	27	336	317	373	303	290	260	338
1	1	–	1	1	–	8	–	–	5
1	19	11	349	194	814	694	142	333	149
303	1552	159	8118	4735	5157	4801	2923	4681	5226
275	323	142	1243	838	792	1332	438	628	611

13－18　市、县级社会

Basic Statistics on Institutions and

单位:个

指　　标	Item	全　市 Total	市　区 Urban District	萧山区 Xiaoshan
合　　计	**Total**	**2812**	**2072**	**260**
按活动区域分	**Grouped by Region**			
地级社团	City－level Societies	730	730	
县级社团	County－level Societies	2082	1342	260
按性质分	**Grouped by Category**			
科技与研究	Technology and Research	294	228	37
生态环境	Ecological Envirenment	20	12	1
教育	Education	60	29	2
卫生	Health	96	70	3
社会服务	Social Services	128	102	7
文化	Culture	241	177	13
体育	Sport	298	219	23
法律	Law	5	5	1
工商业服务	Industry and Business Services	649	509	83
宗教	Religion	38	27	5
农业及农村发展	Agricure and Rural Development	195	90	10
职业及从业组织	Vocational and Business Organizations	152	103	26
国际及涉外组织	International and Foreign Organizations	－	－	－
其他	Other	636	501	49

团体机构情况(2015 年)

Organizations at County Level(2015)

(unit)

余杭区 Yuhang	富阳区 Fuyang	桐庐县 Tonglu	淳安县 Chun'an	建德市 Jiande	临安市 Lin'an
244	**224**	**195**	**122**	**223**	**200**
244	224	195	122	223	200
26	22	19	17	14	16
1	1	3	1	2	2
3	2	1	1	24	5
15	5	2	4	14	6
7	14	8	13	–	5
24	23	3	10	34	17
25	19	7	9	40	23
–	1	–	–	–	–
64	70	38	13	50	39
4	5	5	3	–	3
27	35	17	17	45	26
9	11	–	23	–	26
–	–	–	–	–	–
39	16	92	11	–	32

13－19　社会保障情况(主要年份)
Social Security(Main Years)

单位:万人　　(10000 persons)

项　目 Item	2000	2005	2010	2011	2012	2013	2014	2015
城镇登记失业人员 Number of the Registered Unemployed Persons in Urban	5.60	6.09	4.85	4.40	3.97	4.60	4.03	3.67
城镇登记失业率(%) The Registered Rate of Unemployment in Urban (%)	3.48	3.71	2.19	1.86	1.63	1.85	1.84	1.74
失业人员再就业 The Re－employed Persons of Unemployment	14.69	13.09	15.54	13.17	13.29	13.13	13.50	14.22
职工基本养老保险参保人数 Number of Persons in the Basic Pension Program in Urban	123.69	227.58	383.97	428.12	492.62	530.70	559.48	569.09
失业保险参保人数 Number of Persons in the Unemployment Insurance Program	96.66	118.36	243.98	277.53	299.78	316.36	331.83	349.42
职工基本医疗保险参保人数 Number of Persons in the Basic Medical Insurance Program	－	187.71	345.24	386.33	425.82	448.35	469.40	500.21
工伤保险参保人数 Number of Persons in the Work－injure Insurance Program	47.86	111.03	314.95	355.28	382.21	394.82	406.65	418.17
生育保险参保人数 Number of Persons in the Bear Insurance Program	63.99	96.41	228.53	254.38	277.11	292.01	309.23	324.59
城乡居民养老保险(障)人数 Number of Persons in the Urban and Rural old－age Security	－	－	106.30	112.35	112.98	106.40	103.97	99.45
城乡居民参加医疗保险人数 Number of urban and rural residents participated in medical insurance	－	350.60	408.32	392.69	378.99	373.93	370.81	370.50

13－20 分地区社会保障情况(2015 年末)

Social Security by Region(End of 2015)

单位:人 (persons)

指标 Item	职工基本养老保险参保人数 Number of Employed Persons in the Basic Pension Program	职工基本医疗保险参保人数 Number of Persons in the Basic Medical Insurance Program	工伤保险参保人数 Number of Persons in the Work－injure Insurance Program	生育保险参保人数 Number of Persons in the Bear Insurance Program	失业保险参保人数 Number of Persons in the Unemployment Insurance Program
全　市 Total	**5690943**	**5002110**	**4181749**	**3245864**	**3494229**
市　区 Urban District	5022653	4474506	3729226	2962480	3211354
#萧山区 Xiaoshan	1106048	723606	473374	464095	471625
余杭区 Yuhang	723169	610195	538256	386501	404143
富阳区 Fuyang	381956	261801	275937	168040	189454
桐庐县 Tonglu	161071	129762	123777	76340	60468
淳安县 Chun'an	95407	93489	87003	44709	45789
建德市 Jiande	178835	124011	83151	71756	75907
临安市 Lin'an	232977	180342	158592	90579	100711

主要统计指标解释

就业人员劳动报酬 指各单位在一定时期内直接支付给本单位全部就业人员的劳动报酬总额。

在岗职工工资总额 指各单位在一定时期内直接支付给本单位全部在岗职工的劳动报酬总额。

工资总额的计算原则应以直接支付给职工的全部劳动报酬为根据。各单位支付给本单位全部职工的劳动报酬,不论是计入成本的还是不计入成本的,不论是以货币形式支付还是以实物形式支付的,不论是单位自筹的资金还是上级(或政府财政部门)下拨的资金,不论是厂级单位筹集的资金还是下属车间(科室)及附属经营单位筹集的资金,均应列入工资总额计算的范围。

在岗职工平均工资 指各单位的在岗职工在一定时期内平均每人所得的工资额。它表明一定时期内在岗职工工资收入的高低程度,是反映在岗职工工资水平的主要指标。计算公式为:

$$在岗职工平均工资=\frac{报告期实际支付的全部在岗职工工资总额}{报告期全部在岗职工平均人数}$$

全社会单位 包括独立核算的机关、事业单位,非私营企业和私营企业,但不含个体工商户。

离休、退休、退职人员 指正式办理了离休、退休、退职手续,并享受相应的离休、退休、退职待遇的人员。

保险福利费用 指企业、事业、机关单位在工资以外实际支付给职工和离休、退休、退职人员个人以及用于集体的劳动保险和福利费用。

社会福利事业单位 指集中收养社会孤、老、残、幼的机构。包括由民政部门管理的社会福利院、儿童福利院、精神病人福利院和城镇集体办的福利院,以及农村集体举办的敬老院。

社会福利事业单位收养人数 包括民政部门管理和城镇及农村集体举办的社会福利事业单位中收养的老人,少年儿童,缺乏生活自理能力的残疾人员和精神病人。

商品零售价格指数 是反映城乡商品零售价格变动趋势的一种经济指数。零售物价的调整变动直接影响到城乡居民的生活支出和国家的财政收入,影响居民购买力和市场供需平衡,影响消费与积累的比例。因此,计算零售价格指数,可以从一个侧面对上述经济活动进行观察和分析。

居民消费价格指数 是反映一定时期内城乡居民所购买的生活消费品价格和服务项目价格变动趋势和程度的相对数。是综合了城市居民消费价格指数和农民消费价格指数计算取得。利用居民消费价格指数,可以观察和分析消费品的零售价格和服务价格变动对城乡居民实际生活支出的影响程度。

工业生产者出厂价格指数 是反映全部工业产品出厂价格总水平的变动趋势和程度的相对数。其中除包括工业企业售给商业、外贸、物资部门的产品外,还包括售给工业和其他部门的生产资料以及直接售给居民的生活消费品。通过工业生产价格指数能观察出厂价格变动对工业总产值的影响。

Explanatory Notes on Main Statistical Indicators

Labour Remuneration refers to total payment by various units to their employees during a certain period of time, including total wage bill of permanent workers and staff and remuneration payment to other employees.

Total Wages of Fully Employed Staff and Workers refer to the total remuneration payment to fully employed staff and workers in various units during a certain period of time. The calculation of total wages is based on the total remuneration payment to the staff and workers. Therefore, all the wages and salaries and other payments to staff and workers are included in the total wages regardless of their sources, category, and forms (in kind or cash). (Total wages of staff and workers in this yearbook include only total wages of fully employed staff and workers, excluding the living allowances distributed to those who have left their working units while keeping their labour contract/employment relation unchanged).

Average Wage of Fully Employed Staff and Workers refers to the average wage per person during a certain period of time for fully employed staff and workers in enterprises, institutions, and government agencies, which reflects the general level of wage income during a certain period of time and is calculated as follows:

$$\text{Average Wage of Fully Employed Staff and Workers} = \frac{\text{Total wages of Fully employed staff and workers in Reference Period}}{\text{Average Number of Fully employed Staff and workers in Reference period}}$$

Units of Whole Society refers to independent accounting units of government organizations and institutions, non – private and private enterprises, but excluding individual business.

Retired and Resigned Person refers to the persons who have form ally gone through the formalities for their retirement or quitting work and enjoy the corresponding treatments.

Insurance and welfare Funds refers to labour insurance and welf are funds paid by enterprises, organizations and institutions to their staff and workers as well as retired and resigned persons in addition to their wages and salaries.

Social Welfare Institutions refer to institutions taking care of old people without children, handicapped people and orphans. They include social welfare institutions run by civil affairs departments, children welfare institutions, social welfare institutions for mental patients, and collective – owned old people's home in rural areas.

Number of People Taken in by social welfare Institutions refers to the number of old people, children, totally dependent handicapped people and mental patients taken in by social welfare institutions run by civil affairs departments and those run by collective units in urban and rural areas.

Retail price Index reflects the general change in retail prices of commodities. The change and adjustment in retail prices directly affect the living expenditure of urban and rural residents, government revenue, purchasing power of residents and the equilibrium of market supply and demand, and the ratio of consumption to accumulation. Therefore, the calculation of retail price index is useful to analyze the changes of the above economic activities.

Consumer Price Index reflects the trend and degree of changes in prices of consumer goods and services purchased by urban and rural residents, and is a composite index derived from the urban consumer price index and the rural consumer price index. Consumer price index can be used to analyze the impact of consumer price change on actual expenditure for living cost of urban and rural residents.

Ex – factory price index of Industrial Products reflects the trend and degree of changes in general ex – factory prices of all industrial products, including sales of industrial products by and industrial enterprise to all units outside the enterprise, as well as sales of consumer goods to residents. It can be used to analyze the impact of ex – factory prices on gross industrial output value.

中国统计出版社最新图书简目

（仅供参考，以实际出版为准）

统计资料

中国统计年鉴　中国统计摘要　中国发展报告
中国经济普查年鉴 2013　国际统计年鉴　金砖国家联合统计手册
中国－东盟国家统计手册　中国农村统计年鉴　中国县域统计年鉴
中国城市统计年鉴　中国对外直接投资统计公报　中国地区经济监测报告
中国贸易外经统计年鉴　中国零售和餐饮连锁企业统计年鉴　中国商品交易市场统计年鉴
大中型批发零售和住宿餐饮企业统计年鉴　中国农产品价格调查年鉴　中国住户调查年鉴
中国价格统计年鉴　中国能源统计年鉴　全国农产品成本收益资料汇编
中国环境统计年鉴　中国建筑业统计年鉴　国外资源、能源和环境统计资料汇编
中国工业统计年鉴　中国城乡建设统计年鉴　中国房地产统计年鉴
中国城市建设统计年鉴　中国科技统计年鉴　中国第三产业统计年鉴
中国证券期货统计年鉴　中国劳动统计年鉴　中国高技术产业统计年鉴
工业企业科技活动资料　中国社会统计年鉴　中国人口和就业统计年鉴
中国人才资源统计报告　中国教育经费统计年鉴　中国文化及相关产业统计年鉴
文化及相关产业统计概览　中国民政统计年鉴　中国民族统计年鉴
中国残疾人事业统计年鉴　中国妇女儿童状况统计资料（英）　中国乡镇街道行政区域简册
中国基本单位统计年鉴

省级综合统计年鉴系列

北京 天津 河北 山西 内蒙古 辽宁 吉林 黑龙江 上海 江苏 浙江 安徽 福建 江西 山东 河南 湖北 湖南
广东 广西 海南 重庆 四川 贵州 云南 西藏 陕西 甘肃 青海 宁夏 新疆 新疆生产建设兵团

市（县）级综合统计年鉴系列

天津滨海新区 石家庄 唐山 邯郸 保定 沧州 邢台 廊坊 承德 衡水 秦皇岛 张家口 太原 大同 阳泉 长治 晋城 朔州
晋中 运城 忻州 临汾 呼和浩特 呼和浩特新城区 鄂尔多斯 包头 沈阳 大连 长春 延吉 四平 通化 哈尔滨 齐齐哈尔
黑龙江垦区 上海浦东新区 南京 无锡 徐州 常州 苏州 南通 连云港 淮安 盐城 扬州 镇江 泰州 宿迁 江阴 丹阳 杭州
宁波 温州 嘉兴 湖州 绍兴 金华 衢州 舟山 台州 丽水 合肥 安庆 马鞍山 福州 厦门 宁德 漳州 南昌 九江 上饶 新余
抚州 萍乡 赣州 吉安 景德镇 济南 青岛 潍坊 枣庄 日照 滕州 郑州 洛阳 平顶山 三门峡 商丘 信阳 济源 武汉 十堰
荆州 宜昌 荆门 咸宁 长沙 广州 深圳 惠州 东莞 南宁 柳州 桂林 来宾 海口 三亚 成都 贵阳 昆明 西安 安康 兰州
庆阳 银川 乌鲁木齐 兵团一师 兵团十师

调查年鉴系列

天津 山西 内蒙古 辽宁 吉林 上海　福建 江西 河南 湖北 湖南 广西　重庆 四川 云南 甘肃 宁夏 新疆

统计方法应用/实用手册

实用 SAS 统计分析教程　马克威统计分析与数据挖掘应用案例
乡镇统计人员岗位知识培训系列教材：辅助调查员岗位基础知识　乡镇统计人员岗位基础知识
县级统计人员岗位知识培训系列教材：Excel 在统计工作中的应用　简明统计分析
EXCEL 在基层统计工作中的应用　统计公文知识问答

统计通俗读物/统计科普图书

漫话诺贝尔经济学大师与数学情缘　魅力统计　漫话信息时代的统计学　统计使人更聪明
漫游数据王国　探访随机世界　新中国统计工作历史流变 1949－1999　无处不在的统计

重点图书

新编英汉汉英统计大词典　中华医学统计百科全书
挑大学选专业 2016—考研择校指南　挑大学选专业 2016—高考志愿填报指南